Praise for *Effective TypeScript*

Effective TypeScript explores the most common questions we see when working with TypeScript and provides practical, results-oriented advice. Regardless of your level of TypeScript experience, you can learn something from this book.

—*Ryan Cavanaugh, engineering lead for TypeScript at Microsoft*

Effective TypeScript's second edition is a marvelous addition to an already excellent book. It combines the great tips and tricks from the first edition with deep suggestions on TypeScript practices that have only solidified over the last few years. The knowledge here is a must-have for working with TypeScript on any project size. I particularly appreciated that many recommendations include nuance around when and why they apply. I would encourage any developer who wants to be deeply proficient at writing TypeScript to give this book two enthusiastic read-throughs and take detailed notes.

—*Josh Goldberg, open source developer and author of* Learning TypeScript

Effective TypeScript is not just a guide to one of the world's most popular programming languages. At its core, it teaches you how to think in types with applicable real-world advice. You can see Dan's experience oozing from every single page. It's daring! And will potentially change your view on programming beyond TypeScript.

—*Stefan Baumgartner, senior product architect, Dynatrace, and author of* TypeScript Cookbook

Effective TypeScript, 2nd ed., is a great companion book for engineers who are already familiar with the basics of TypeScript and are writing it day-to-day, or are considering adopting TypeScript for their codebase.

—*Boris Cherny, author of* Programming TypeScript

I've been engaged with TypeScript for over 10 years, both in teaching and professional practice. *Effective TypeScript* offers sound advice that aligns well with my experience. The book effectively highlights how understanding TypeScript's syntax is one thing, but knowing when to use its features is another. It's a helpful guide for those who are familiar with TypeScript but want to refine their use of its capabilities.

—Titian-Cornel Cernicova-Dragomir,
software engineer at Bloomberg LP

This book is packed with practical recipes and must be kept on the desk of every professional TypeScript developer. Even if you think you know TypeScript already, get this book and you won't regret it.

—Yakov Fain, Java champion

This book is not just about what TypeScript can do—it teaches why each language feature is useful, and where to apply patterns to get the greatest effect. The book focuses on practical advice that will be useful in day-to-day work, with just enough theory to give the reader a deep understanding of how everything works. I consider myself to be an advanced TypeScript user, and I learned a number of new things from this book.

—Jesse Hallett, senior software engineer, Hasura

SECOND EDITION

Effective TypeScript

83 Specific Ways to Improve Your TypeScript

Dan Vanderkam

Beijing · Boston · Farnham · Sebastopol · Tokyo

Effective TypeScript

by Dan Vanderkam

Published by O'Reilly Media, Inc., 1005 Gravenstein Highway North, Sebastopol, CA 95472.

O'Reilly books may be purchased for educational, business, or sales promotional use. Online editions are also available for most titles (*http://oreilly.com*). For more information, contact our corporate/institutional sales department: 800-998-9938 or *corporate@oreilly.com*.

Acquisitions Editor: Amanda Quinn
Development Editor: Angela Rufino
Production Editor: Clare Laylock
Copyeditor: Sonia Saruba
Proofreader: M & R Consultants Corporation

Indexer: nSight, Inc.
Interior Designer: David Futato
Cover Designer: Karen Montgomery
Illustrator: Kate Dullea

November 2019:   First Edition
May 2024:   Second Edition

Revision History for the Second Edition

2024-04-26:   First Release

See *http://oreilly.com/catalog/errata.csp?isbn=9781098155063* for release details.

978-1-098-15506-3

[LSI]

For Alex.
You're just my type.

Table of Contents

Preface to the Second Edition

It's hard to believe it's been nearly five years since the first edition of *Effective TypeScript* was published. The book and its companion website (*https://effectivetype script.com*) have both been well received and have helped countless developers improve their understanding and usage of the language.

I was surprised how quickly I began to get asked whether the book was out-of-date. It only took six months! Given the pace of change in TypeScript in the years leading up to the first edition, this was a real concern of mine. I tried to avoid printing material that would soon be out-of-date. This meant focusing more on timeless topics like language fundamentals and program design, rather than on libraries and frameworks. By and large, the material in *Effective TypeScript* has held up well.

As TypeScript developed and gained new features, it didn't invalidate the first edition as much as it created gaps in its coverage. Writing an "effective" item requires more than just knowing how a feature works. It requires experience *using* that feature: time spent learning which patterns work well and which ones don't hold up. Conditional types had only recently been added to the language in 2019, so I had little experience with them. They're covered more extensively in this edition. Template literal types have been the biggest addition to TypeScript in the past five years. They've opened whole new worlds of possibilities and are covered in Item 54.

Moreover, thanks to projects like the Type Challenges (*https://tsch.js.org*), TypeScript developers have become much more ambitious in what they do in the type system. Generics and type-level programming were covered only lightly in the first edition. Now they get an entire chapter, Chapter 6.

More than eight years after I first tried TypeScript, I continue to enjoy it and get excited every time I read the latest release notes or see an ambitious new PR from Anders Hejlsberg making the rounds. I also continue to enjoy helping other developers learn TypeScript and improve their usage of it. I hope that comes across in these pages, and I hope that reading this book helps you enjoy working in TypeScript as much as I do!

Wallkill, NY
March 2024

Who This Book Is For

The *Effective* books are intended to be the "standard second book" on their topic. You'll get the most out of *Effective TypeScript* if you have some previous practical experience working with JavaScript and TypeScript. My goal with this book is not to teach you TypeScript or JavaScript but to help you advance from a beginning or intermediate user to an expert. The items in this book do this by helping you build mental models of how TypeScript and its ecosystem work, making you aware of pitfalls and traps to avoid, and by guiding you toward using TypeScript's many capabilities in the most effective ways possible. Whereas a reference book will explain the five ways that a language lets you do X, an *Effective* book will tell you which of those five to use and why.

TypeScript has evolved rapidly over the past few years, but my hope is that it has stabilized enough that the content in this book will remain valid for years to come. This book focuses primarily on the language itself, rather than any frameworks or build tools. You won't find any examples of how to use React or Vue with TypeScript, or how to configure TypeScript to work with webpack or Vite. The advice in this book should be relevant to all TypeScript users.

Why I Wrote This Book

When I first started working at Google, I was given a copy of the third edition of *Effective C++* by Scott Meyers (Addison-Wesley Professional). It was unlike any other programming book I'd read. It made no attempt to be accessible to beginners or to be a complete guide to the language. Rather than telling you what the different features of C++ did, it told you how you should and should not use them. It did so through dozens of short, specific items motivated by concrete examples.

The effect of reading all these examples while using the language daily was unmistakable. I'd used C++ before, but for the first time I felt comfortable with it and knew how to think about the choices it presented to me. In later years I would have similar experiences reading *Effective Java* by Joshua Bloch (Addison-Wesley Professional) and *Effective JavaScript* by David Herman (Addison-Wesley Professional).

If you're already comfortable working in a few different programming languages, then diving straight into the odd corners of a new one can be an effective way to challenge your mental models and learn what makes it different. I've learned an enormous amount about TypeScript from writing this book. I hope you'll have the same experience reading it!

How This Book Is Organized

This book is a collection of "items," each of which is a short technical essay that gives you specific advice about some aspect of TypeScript. The items are grouped thematically into chapters, but feel free to jump around and read whichever ones look most interesting to you.

Each item's title conveys the key takeaway. These are the things you should remember as you're using TypeScript, so it's worth skimming the table of contents to get them in your head. If you're writing documentation, for example, and have a nagging sense that you shouldn't be writing type information, then you'll know to read Item 31: Don't Repeat Type Information in Documentation.

The text of the item expands on the advice in the title and backs it up with concrete examples and technical arguments. Almost every point made in this book is demonstrated through example code. I tend to read technical books by looking at the examples and skimming the prose, and I assume you do something similar. I hope you'll read the prose and explanations! But the main points should still come across if you skim the examples.

After reading the item, you should understand why it will help you use TypeScript more effectively. You'll also know enough to understand if it doesn't apply to your situation. Scott Meyers, the author of *Effective C++*, gives a memorable example of this. He met a team of engineers who wrote software that ran on missiles. They knew they could ignore his advice about preventing resource leaks, because their programs would always terminate when the missile hit the target and their hardware blew up. I'm not aware of any missiles with JavaScript runtimes, but the James Webb Space Telescope has one, so you never know!

Finally, each item ends with "Things to Remember." These are a few bullet points that summarize the item. If you're skimming through, you can read these to get a sense for what the item is saying and whether you'd like to read more. You should still read the item! But the summary will do in a pinch.

Conventions in TypeScript Code Samples

All code samples are TypeScript except where it's clear from the context that they are JSON, HTML, or some other language. Much of the experience of using TypeScript involves interacting with your editor, which presents some challenges in print. I've adopted a few conventions to make this work.

Most editors surface errors using squiggly underlines. To see the full error message, you hover over the underlined text. To indicate an error in a code sample, I put squiggles in a comment line under the place where the error occurs:

```
let str = 'not a number';
let num: number = str;
//  ~~~ Type 'string' is not assignable to type 'number'
```

I occasionally edit the error messages for clarity and brevity, but I never remove an error. If you copy/paste a code sample into your editor, you should get exactly the errors indicated—no more, no less.

To draw attention to the lack of an error, I use // OK:

```
let str = 'not a number';
let num: number = str as any;  // OK
```

You should be able to hover over a symbol in your editor to see what TypeScript considers its type. To indicate this in text, I use a comment with Twoslash syntax (^?):

```
let v = {str: 'hello', num: 42};
//  ^? let v: { str: string; num: number; }
```

The comment indicates what you'd see in your editor if you moused over the symbol above the caret (^). This matches the convention used on the TypeScript playground. If you copy a code sample over there and drop everything after the ^?, TypeScript will fill in the rest for you. What you see on the playground (Figure P-1) should precisely match what you see in print.

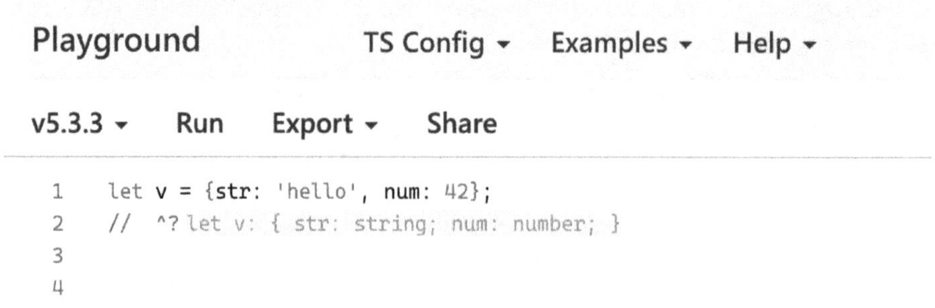

Figure P-1. Twoslash syntax on the TypeScript playground.

I will occasionally introduce no-op statements to indicate the type of a variable on a specific line of code:

```
function foo(value: string | string[]) {
  if (Array.isArray(value)) {
    value;
    // ^? (parameter) value: string[]
  } else {
    value;
    // ^? (parameter) value: string
  }
}
```

The `value;` lines are only there to demonstrate the type in each branch of the conditional. You don't need to (and shouldn't) include statements like this in your own code.

Unless otherwise noted or clear from context, code samples are intended to be checked with the `--strict` flag. While printed copies of a book don't change, TypeScript does, and it's inevitable that some of the types or errors in code samples will be different in the future. Check the Effective TypeScript repo (*https://github.com/danvk/effective-typescript*) for updated versions of the examples in this book. All samples were verified with literate-ts (*https://oreil.ly/LFR0l*) using TypeScript 5.4.

Typographical Conventions Used in This Book

The following typographical conventions are used in this book:

Italic
: Indicates new terms, URLs, email addresses, filenames, and file extensions.

`Constant width`
: Used for program listings, as well as within paragraphs to refer to program elements such as variable or function names, databases, data types, environment variables, statements, and keywords.

`Constant width bold`
: Shows commands or other text that should be typed literally by the user.

`Constant width italic`
: Shows text that should be replaced with user-supplied values or by values determined by context.

 This element signifies a tip or suggestion.

This element signifies a general note.

 This element indicates a warning or caution.

Using Code Examples

Supplemental material (code examples, exercises, etc.) is available for download at *https://github.com/danvk/effective-typescript*.

This book is here to help you get your job done. In general, if example code is offered with this book, you may use it in your programs and documentation. You do not need to contact us for permission unless you're reproducing a significant portion of the code. For example, writing a program that uses several chunks of code from this book does not require permission. Selling or distributing examples from O'Reilly books does require permission. Answering a question by citing this book and quoting example code does not require permission. Incorporating a significant amount of example code from this book into your product's documentation does require permission.

We appreciate, but generally do not require, attribution. An attribution usually includes the title, author, publisher, and ISBN. For example: "*Effective TypeScript*, 2nd ed., by Dan Vanderkam (O'Reilly). Copyright 2024 Dan Vanderkam, 978-1-492-05374-3."

If you feel your use of code examples falls outside fair use or the permission given above, feel free to contact us at *permissions@oreilly.com*.

O'Reilly Online Learning

O'REILLY® For more than 40 years, *O'Reilly Media* has provided technology and business training, knowledge, and insight to help companies succeed.

Our unique network of experts and innovators share their knowledge and expertise through books, articles, and our online learning platform. O'Reilly's online learning platform gives you on-demand access to live training courses, in-depth learning paths, interactive coding environments, and a vast collection of text and video from O'Reilly and 200+ other publishers. For more information, visit *https://oreilly.com*.

How to Contact Us

Please address comments and questions concerning this book to the publisher:

O'Reilly Media, Inc.
1005 Gravenstein Highway North
Sebastopol, CA 95472
800-889-8969 (in the United States or Canada)
707-827-7019 (international or local)
707-829-0104 (fax)
support@oreilly.com
https://www.oreilly.com/about/contact.html

We have a web page for this book, where we list errata, examples, and any additional information. You can access this page at *https://oreil.ly/effective-typescript-2e*.

For news and information about our books and courses, visit *http://www.oreilly.com*.

Find us on LinkedIn: *https://linkedin.com/company/oreilly-media*.

Watch us on YouTube: *http://youtube.com/oreillymedia*.

Acknowledgments

Despite my hopes, writing a second edition did not prove any easier or less time-consuming than the first. In the process, the book has grown from 62 items to 83. In addition to writing 22 new items (one old item was consolidated into another), I've reviewed and thoroughly revised all the original material. Some parts, such as Items 45 and 55, are near complete rewrites.

Many new items are based on material that first appeared on the *Effective TypeScript* blog (*https://effectivetypescript.com*), though all of these have seen significant revision. Chapter 6 is largely based on my personal experiences building the crosswalk (*https://oreil.ly/-XQ6A*) and crudely-typed (*https://oreil.ly/E7_gV*) libraries for Delve at Sidewalk Labs.

Here are the origins of the new items in the second edition:

- Item 28 is adapted from the blog post "Use Classes and Currying to Create New Inference Sites" (*https://oreil.ly/OAApn*).

- Item 32 arose from code reviews. I didn't know this was a rule until I saw it broken!

- Item 36 was inspired by feedback I've given on countless code reviews.

- Item 37 is based on personal experience and Evan Martin's blog post "Why Not Add an Option for That?" (*https://oreil.ly/YJWQR*). Cory House's frequent tweets on this topic gave me courage to include it in the book.

- Item 38 was inspired by the Alan Perlis quote, which I frequently cite, as well as by Scott Meyers's rule.

- Item 39 is based on my team's experience with the Jsonify adapter, which we were excited to adopt and then even more excited to ditch. The experience led to the blog post "The Trouble with Jsonify: Unify Types Instead of Modeling Small Differences" (*https://oreil.ly/zVod4*).

- Item 48 is adapted from the blog post "The Seven Sources of Unsoundness in TypeScript" (*https://oreil.ly/NiTnr*) with significant input from Ryan Cavanaugh.

- Item 50 was inspired by lots of thinking about what types really are, and a Stack Overflow answer explaining dependent types.

- Item 51 is an adaptation of the blog post "The Golden Rule of Generics" (*https://oreil.ly/yaxs8*), which is, in turn, an adaptation of advice in the TypeScript handbook.

- Item 53 was inspired by my work on crosswalk and crudely-typed, and curiosity about all those [T] wrappers I was seeing.

- Item 54 was inspired by my own explorations of template literal types after TypeScript 4.1 was released, which culminated in the blog post "TypeScript Splits the Atom!" (*https://oreil.ly/Es6Ep*).

- Item 56 is the culmination of my long-standing interest in this topic. This was kicked off by Titian Cernicova-Dragomir's answer to a Stack Overflow question about typing _.invert, followed by my own experiences in crosswalk and crudely-typed, which eventually led to the blog post "The Display of Types" (*https://oreil.ly/bue9Q*).

- Item 57 was inspired by the release notes for TypeScript 4.5, which added tail recursion.

- Item 58 was inspired by experience connecting TypeScript with databases that eventually led to my TypeScript Congress 2022 talk: "TypeScript and SQL: Six Ways to Bridge the Divide" (*https://oreil.ly/ofuph*).

- Item 59 presents a widespread trick that Jesse Hallett introduced me to while reviewing the first edition. The "pairs" variation comes from a 2021 tweet by Tom Hicks.

- Item 62 was inspired by an Artsy blog post: "Conditional Types in TypeScript" (*https://oreil.ly/r-7E0*).

- Item 63 originated with Ryan Cavanaugh's feedback on the first edition, which I eventually distilled into a blog post: "Exclusive Or and the Optional never Trick" (*https://oreil.ly/os01S*). Stefan Baumgartner's enthusiasm for this trick in the *TypeScript Cookbook* (O'Reilly) encouraged me to include it in the book.

- Item 71 was inspired by a discussion with Evan Martin on reddit and a frustrating bug that came back to `new Set("string")`. This led to the blog post "In Defense of Interface: Using Declaration Merging to Disable 'Bad Parts'" (*https://oreil.ly/iYGLY*).

- Item 74 is a topic that comes up frequently, especially if you don't have the right mental model of TypeScript.

- Item 76 was inspired by countless debugging sessions that came back to an incorrect model of your environment.

- Item 77 was inspired by personal curiosity about this topic, a few Stack Overflow questions, and a Gary Bernhardt talk.

- Item 78 was inspired by painful personal experience with TypeScript getting slow. It's based on the TypeScript wiki and the blog post "What's Typescript Compiling? Use a Treemap to Find Out" (*https://oreil.ly/QRilV*).

Thanks to my tech reviewers, Josh Goldberg, Stefan Baumgartner, Ryan Cavanaugh, Boris Cherny, and Titian Cernicova-Dragomir. Your feedback made this book immensely better. Thanks to my coworkers on the Delve experience squad (particularly Stephanie Chew, Luda Zhao, Ha Vu, and Amanda Meurer) for all the code reviews and for accommodating my boundless enthusiasm for TypeScript. Thanks to everyone at O'Reilly who helped make this book happen: Angela Rufino, Ashley Stussy, Amanda Quinn, Clare Laylock, Sonia Saruba. Thanks to Chris Mischaikow for the last-minute proofreading. Spotify's Jazzy Morning playlist, starting with Arta Porting's *Beautiful Sunrise*, provided a soundtrack for writing and editing.

Finally, thanks to Alex for all her support: through a pandemic, online and in-person weddings, a job change, and a big move, I'm glad at least one thing has stayed constant!

Preface to the First Edition (2019)

In the spring of 2016, I visited my old coworker Evan Martin at Google's San Francisco office and asked him what he was excited about. I'd asked him this same question many times over the years because the answers were wide-ranging and unpredictable but always interesting: C++ build tools, Linux audio drivers, online crosswords, emacs scripts. This time, Evan was excited about TypeScript and Visual Studio Code.

I was surprised! I'd heard of TypeScript before, but I knew only that it was created by Microsoft and that I mistakenly believed it had something to do with .NET. As a lifelong Linux user, I couldn't believe that Evan had hopped on team Microsoft.

Then Evan showed me VS Code and the TypeScript playground and I was instantly converted. Everything was so fast, and the code intelligence made it easy to build a mental model of the type system. After years of writing type annotations in JSDoc comments for the Closure Compiler, this felt like typed JavaScript that really worked. And Microsoft had built a cross-platform text editor on top of Chromium? Perhaps this was a language and toolchain worth learning.

I'd recently joined Sidewalk Labs and was writing our first JavaScript. The codebase was still small enough that Evan and I were able to convert it all to TypeScript over the next few days.

I've been hooked ever since. TypeScript is more than just a type system. It also brings a whole suite of language services which are fast and easy to use. The cumulative effect is that TypeScript doesn't just make JavaScript development safer: it also makes it more fun!

Brooklyn, NY
October 2019

Acknowledgments to the First Edition

There are many people who helped make this book possible. Thanks to Evan Martin for introducing me to TypeScript and showing me how to think about it. To Douwe Osinga for connecting me with O'Reilly and being supportive of the project. To Brett Slatkin for advice on structure and for showing me that someone I knew could write an *Effective* book. To Scott Meyers for coming up with this format and for his "Effective *Effective* Books" blog post, which provided essential guidance.

To my reviewers, Rick Battagline, Ryan Cavanaugh, Boris Cherny, Yakov Fain, Jesse Hallett, and Jason Killian. To all my coworkers at Sidewalk who learned TypeScript with me over the years. To everyone at O'Reilly who helped make this book happen: Angela Rufino, Jennifer Pollock, Deborah Baker, Nick Adams, and Jasmine Kwityn. To the TypeScript NYC crew, Jason, Orta, and Kirill, and to all the speakers. Many items were inspired by talks at the Meetup, as described in the following list:

- Item 3 was inspired by a blog post of Evan Martin's that I found particularly enlightening as I was first learning TypeScript.

- Item 7 was inspired by Anders's talk about structural typing and `keyof` relationships at TSConf 2018, and by a talk of Jesse Hallett's at the April 2019 TypeScript NYC Meetup.

- Both Basarat's guide and helpful answers by DeeV and GPicazo on Stack Overflow were essential in writing Item 9.

- Item 10 builds on similar advice in Item 4 of *Effective JavaScript*.

- I was inspired to write Item 11 by mass confusion around this topic at the August 2019 TypeScript NYC Meetup.

- Item 13 was greatly aided by several questions about `type` vs. `interface` on Stack Overflow. Jesse Hallett suggested the formulation around extensibility.

- Jacob Baskin provided encouragement and early feedback on Item 15.

- Item 18 was inspired by several code samples submitted to the r/typescript subreddit.

- Item 24 is based on my own writing on Medium and a talk I gave at the October 2018 TypeScript NYC Meetup.

- Item 29 is based on common advice in Haskell ("make illegal states unrepresentable"). The Air France 447 story is inspired by Jeff Wise's incredible 2011 article in *Popular Mechanics*.

- Item 30 is based on an issue I ran into with the Mapbox type declarations. Jason Killian suggested the phrasing in the title.

- The advice about naming in Item 41 is common, but this particular formulation was inspired by Dan North's short article in *97 Things Every Programmer Should Know* (Kevlin, Henney, O'Reilly).
- Item 64 was inspired by Jason Killian's talk at the very first TypeScript NYC Meetup in September 2017.
- Item 25 is based on the TypeScript 2.1 release notes. The term "evolving any" is not widely used outside the TypeScript compiler itself, but I find it useful to have a name for this unusual pattern.
- Item 46 was inspired by a blog post of Jesse Hallett's.
- Item 47 was greatly aided by feedback from Titian Cernicova-Dragomir in TypeScript issue #33128.
- Item 49 is based on York Yao's work on the `type-coverage` tool. I wanted something like this and it existed!
- Item 66 is based on a talk I gave at the December 2017 TypeScript NYC Meetup.
- Item 52 owes a debt of gratitude to David Sheldrick's post on the *Artsy* blog on conditional types, which greatly demystified the topic for me.
- Item 70 was inspired by a talk Steve Faulkner, aka southpolesteve, gave at the February 2019 Meetup.
- Item 55 is based on my own writing on Medium and work on the typings-checker tool, which eventually got folded into dtslint.
- Item 72 was inspired/reinforced by Kat Busch's Medium post on the various types of enums in TypeScript, as well as Boris Cherny's writings on this topic in *Programming TypeScript* (O'Reilly).
- Item 60 was inspired by my own confusion and that of my coworkers on this topic. The definitive explanation is given by Anders on TypeScript PR #12253.
- The MDN documentation was essential for writing Item 75.
- Chapter 10 is based on my own experience migrating the aging dygraphs library.

I found many of the blog posts and talks that led to this book through the excellent r/typescript subreddit. I'm particularly grateful to developers who provided code samples there which were essential for understanding common issues in beginner TypeScript. Thanks to Marius Schulz for the TypeScript Weekly newsletter. While it's only occasionally weekly, it's always an excellent source of material and a great way to keep up with TypeScript. To Anders, Daniel, Ryan, and the whole TypeScript team at Microsoft for the talks and all the feedback on issues. Most of my issues were misunderstandings, but there is nothing quite so satisfying as filing a bug and immediately seeing Anders Hejlsberg himself fix it!

Finally, thanks to Alex for being so supportive during this project and so understanding of all the working vacations, mornings, evenings, and weekends I needed to complete it.

CHAPTER 1

Getting to Know TypeScript

Before we dive into the details, this chapter helps you understand the big picture of TypeScript. What is it and how should you think about it? How does it relate to JavaScript? Are its types nullable or are they not? What's this about any? And ducks?

TypeScript is an unusual language in that it neither runs in an interpreter (as Python and Ruby do) nor compiles down to a lower-level language (as Java and C do). Instead, it compiles to another high-level language, JavaScript. It is this JavaScript that runs, not your TypeScript. So understanding TypeScript's relationship with JavaScript is essential and will help you be a more effective TypeScript developer.

TypeScript's type system also has some unusual aspects that you should be aware of. Later chapters cover the type system in much greater detail, but this one will hit a few of the most important highlights.

You should read this chapter even if you've already written lots of TypeScript. It will help you build correct mental models of what TypeScript is and how its type system works, and it may clear up some misconceptions you didn't realize you had.

Item 1: Understand the Relationship Between TypeScript and JavaScript

If you use TypeScript for long, you'll inevitably hear the phrase "TypeScript is a superset of JavaScript" or "TypeScript is a typed superset of JavaScript." But what does this mean, exactly? And what is the relationship between TypeScript and JavaScript? Since these languages are so closely linked, a strong understanding of how they relate to each other is the foundation for using TypeScript well.

A is a "superset" of B if everything in B is also in A. TypeScript is a superset of Java-Script in a syntactic sense: so long as your JavaScript program doesn't have any syntax errors then it is also a TypeScript program. It's quite likely that TypeScript's type checker will flag some issues with your code. But this is an independent problem. TypeScript will still parse your code and emit JavaScript. (This is another key part of the relationship. We'll explore this more in Item 3.)

TypeScript files use a *.ts* extension, rather than the *.js* extension of a JavaScript file.[1] This doesn't mean that TypeScript is a completely different language! Since Type-Script is a superset of JavaScript, the code in your *.js* files is already TypeScript. Renaming *main.js* to *main.ts* doesn't change that.

This is enormously helpful if you're migrating an existing JavaScript codebase to TypeScript. It means that you don't have to rewrite any of your code in another lan-guage to start using TypeScript and get the benefits it provides. This would not be true if you chose to rewrite your JavaScript in a language like Java. This gentle migra-tion path is one of the best features of TypeScript. There will be much more to say about this topic in Chapter 10.

All JavaScript programs are TypeScript programs, but the converse is not true: there are TypeScript programs that are not JavaScript programs. This is because TypeScript adds additional syntax for specifying types. (There are some other bits of syntax it adds, too, largely for historical reasons. See Item 72.)

For instance, this is a valid TypeScript program:

```
function greet(who: string) {
  console.log('Hello', who);
}
```

But when you run this through a program like node that expects JavaScript, you'll get an error:

```
function greet(who: string) {
                 ^

SyntaxError: Unexpected token :
```

The `: string` is a type annotation that is specific to TypeScript. Once you use one, you've gone beyond plain JavaScript (see Figure 1-1).

---

1 You may run across *.tsx*, *.jsx*, *.mts*, *.mjs*, and a few other extensions. These are all TypeScript and JavaScript files.

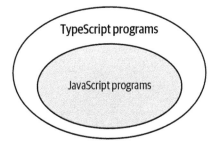

Figure 1-1. All JavaScript is TypeScript, but not all TypeScript is JavaScript.

This is not to say that TypeScript doesn't provide value for plain JavaScript programs. It does! For example, this JavaScript program:

```
let city = 'new york city';
console.log(city.toUppercase());
```

will throw an error when you run it:

```
TypeError: city.toUppercase is not a function
```

There are no type annotations in this program, but TypeScript's type checker is still able to spot the problem:

```
let city = 'new york city';
console.log(city.toUppercase());
//                 ~~~~~~~~~~~ Property 'toUppercase' does not exist on type
//                             'string'. Did you mean 'toUpperCase'?
```

You didn't have to tell TypeScript that the type of `city` was `string`: it inferred it from the initial value. Type inference is a key part of TypeScript, and Chapter 3 explores how to use it well.

One of the goals of TypeScript's type system is to detect code that will throw an exception at runtime, without having to run your code. When you hear TypeScript described as a "static" type system, it refers to this ability. The type checker cannot always spot code that will throw exceptions, but it will try.

Even if your code doesn't throw an exception, it still might not do what you intend. TypeScript tries to catch some of these issues, too. For example, this JavaScript program:

```
const states = [
  {name: 'Alabama', capital: 'Montgomery'},
  {name: 'Alaska',  capital: 'Juneau'},
  {name: 'Arizona', capital: 'Phoenix'},
  // ...
];
for (const state of states) {
  console.log(state.capitol);
}
```

will log:

```
undefined
undefined
undefined
```

Whoops! What went wrong? This program is valid JavaScript (and hence Type-Script). And it ran without throwing any errors. But it clearly didn't do what you intended. Even without adding type annotations, TypeScript's type checker is able to spot the error and offer a helpful suggestion:

```
for (const state of states) {
  console.log(state.capitol);
  //                ~~~~~~~ Property 'capitol' does not exist on type
  //                        '{ name: string; capital: string; }'.
  //                        Did you mean 'capital'?
}
```

We did, in fact, mean capital with an "a." States and countries have capital ("a") cities, whereas legislatures meet in capitol ("o") buildings.

While TypeScript can catch errors even if you don't provide type annotations, it's able to do a much more thorough job if you do. This is because type annotations tell Type-Script what your *intent* is, and this lets it spot places where your code's behavior does not match your intent. For example, what if you'd reversed the capital/capitol spelling mistake in the previous example?

```
const states = [
  {name: 'Alabama', capitol: 'Montgomery'},
  {name: 'Alaska',  capitol: 'Juneau'},
  {name: 'Arizona', capitol: 'Phoenix'},
  // ...
];
for (const state of states) {
  console.log(state.capital);
  //                ~~~~~~~ Property 'capital' does not exist on type
  //                        '{ name: string; capitol: string; }'.
  //                        Did you mean 'capitol'?
}
```

The error that was so helpful before now gets it exactly wrong! The problem is that you've spelled the same property two different ways, and TypeScript doesn't know which one is right. It can guess, but it may not always be correct. The solution is to clarify your intent by explicitly declaring the type of states:

```
interface State {
  name: string;
  capital: string;
}
const states: State[] = [
  {name: 'Alabama', capitol: 'Montgomery'},
  //                 ~~~~~~~
  {name: 'Alaska',  capitol: 'Juneau'},
  //                 ~~~~~~~
  {name: 'Arizona', capitol: 'Phoenix'},
  //                 ~~~~~~~ Object literal may only specify known properties,
  //                         but 'capitol' does not exist in type 'State'.
  //                         Did you mean to write 'capital'?
  // ...
];
for (const state of states) {
  console.log(state.capital);
}
```

Now the errors match the problem and the suggested fix is correct. By spelling out your intent, you've also helped TypeScript spot other potential problems. For instance, had you only misspelled capitol once in the array, there wouldn't have been an error before. But with the type annotation, there is:

```
const states: State[] = [
  {name: 'Alabama', capital: 'Montgomery'},
  {name: 'Alaska',  capitol: 'Juneau'},
  //                 ~~~~~~~ Did you mean to write 'capital'?
  {name: 'Arizona', capital: 'Phoenix'},
  // ...
];
```

This will become a familiar dynamic as you work with the type checker: the more information you give it, the more problems it will be able to find.

In terms of the Venn diagram, we can add in a new group of programs: TypeScript programs which pass the type checker (see Figure 1-2).

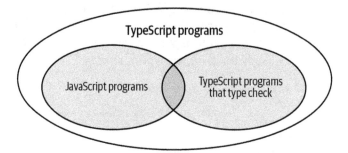

Figure 1-2. All JavaScript programs are TypeScript programs. But only some JavaScript (and TypeScript) programs pass the type checker.

If the statement that "TypeScript is a superset of JavaScript" feels wrong to you, it may be because you're thinking of this third set of programs in the diagram. In practice, this is the most relevant one to the day-to-day experience of using TypeScript. Generally when you use TypeScript, you try to keep your code passing all the type checks.

TypeScript's type system *models* the runtime behavior of JavaScript. This may result in some surprises if you're coming from a language with stricter runtime checks. For example:

```
const x = 2 + '3';  // OK
//    ^? const x: string
const y = '2' + 3;  // OK
//    ^? const y: string
```

These statements both pass the type checker, even though they are questionable and do produce runtime errors in many other languages. But this does accurately model the runtime behavior of JavaScript, where both expressions result in the string "23".

TypeScript does draw the line somewhere, though. The type checker flags issues in all of these statements, even though they do not throw exceptions at runtime:

```
const a = null + 7;  // Evaluates to 7 in JS
//         ~~~~ The value 'null' cannot be used here.
const b = [] + 12;  // Evaluates to '12' in JS
//         ~~~~~~ Operator '+' cannot be applied to types ...
alert('Hello', 'TypeScript');  // alerts "Hello"
//             ~~~~~~~~~~~~ Expected 0-1 arguments, but got 2
```

The guiding principle of TypeScript's type system is that it should model JavaScript's runtime behavior. But in all of these cases, TypeScript considers it more likely that the odd usage is the result of an error than the developer's intent, so it goes beyond simply modeling the runtime behavior. We saw another example of this in the capital/capitol example, where the program didn't throw (it logged undefined) but the type checker still flagged an error.

How does TypeScript decide when to model JavaScript's runtime behavior and when to go beyond it? Ultimately this is a matter of taste. By adopting TypeScript you're trusting the judgment of the team that builds it. If you enjoy adding null and 7 or [] and 12, or calling functions with superfluous arguments, then TypeScript might not be for you!

If your program type checks, could it still throw an error at runtime? The answer is "yes." Here's an example:

```
const names = ['Alice', 'Bob'];
console.log(names[2].toUpperCase());
```

When you run this, it throws:

```
TypeError: Cannot read properties of undefined (reading 'toUpperCase')
```

TypeScript assumed the array access would be within bounds, but it was not. The result was an exception.

Uncaught errors also frequently come up when you use the any type, which we'll discuss in Item 5 and in more detail in Chapter 5.

The root cause of these exceptions is that TypeScript's understanding of a value's type (its static type) and its actual type at runtime have diverged. A type system that can guarantee the accuracy of its static types is said to be *sound*. TypeScript's type system is very much not sound, nor was it ever intended to be. Item 48 explores more ways that unsoundness can arise.

If soundness is important to you, you may want to look at other languages like Reason, PureScript, or Dart. While these do offer more guarantees of runtime safety, this comes at a cost: it takes more work to convince their type checkers that your code is correct, and none of these are a superset of JavaScript, so migration will be more complicated.

Things to Remember

- TypeScript is a superset of JavaScript: all JavaScript programs are syntactically valid TypeScript programs, but not all TypeScript programs are valid JavaScript programs.
- TypeScript adds a static type system that models JavaScript's runtime behavior and tries to spot code that will throw exceptions at runtime.
- It is possible for code to pass the type checker but still throw at runtime.
- TypeScript disallows some legal but questionable JavaScript constructs such as calling functions with the wrong number of arguments.
- Type annotations tell TypeScript your intent and help it distinguish correct and incorrect code.

Item 2: Know Which TypeScript Options You're Using

Does this code pass the type checker?

```
function add(a, b) {
  return a + b;
}
add(10, null);
```

Without knowing which options you're using, it's impossible to say! The TypeScript compiler has an enormous set of these, over a hundred at the time of this writing.

They can be set via the command line:

```
$ tsc --noImplicitAny program.ts
```

or via a configuration file, *tsconfig.json*:

```
{
  "compilerOptions": {
    "noImplicitAny": true
  }
}
```

You should prefer the configuration file. It ensures that your coworkers and tools all know exactly how you plan to use TypeScript. You can create one by running `tsc --init`.

Many of TypeScript's configuration settings control where it looks for source files and what sort of output it generates. But a few control core aspects of the language itself. These are high-level design choices that most languages do not leave to their users. TypeScript can feel like a very different language depending on how it is configured. To use it effectively, you should understand the most important of these settings: `noImplicitAny` and `strictNullChecks`.

noImplicitAny

`noImplicitAny` controls what TypeScript does when it can't determine the type of a variable. This code is valid when `noImplicitAny` is off:

```
function add(a, b) {
  return a + b;
}
```

If you mouse over the `add` symbol in your editor, it will reveal what TypeScript has inferred about the type of that function:

```
function add(a: any, b: any): any
```

The any types effectively disable the type checker for code involving these parameters. any is a useful tool, but it should be used with caution. For much more on any, see Item 5 and Chapter 5.

These are called *implicit anys* because you never wrote the word "any" but still wound up with dangerous any types. This becomes an error if you set the noImplicitAny option:

```
function add(a, b) {
  //         ~     Parameter 'a' implicitly has an 'any' type
  //             ~ Parameter 'b' implicitly has an 'any' type
  return a + b;
}
```

These errors can be fixed by explicitly writing type declarations, either : any or a more specific type:

```
function add(a: number, b: number) {
  return a + b;
}
```

TypeScript is the most helpful when it has type information, so you should be sure to set noImplicitAny whenever possible. Once you grow accustomed to all variables having types, TypeScript without noImplicitAny feels almost like a different language.

For new projects, you should start with noImplicitAny on, so that you write the types as you write your code. This will help TypeScript spot problems, improve the readability of your code, and enhance your development experience (see Item 6).

Leaving noImplicitAny off is only appropriate if you're transitioning a project from JavaScript to TypeScript (see Chapter 10). Even then, this should only be a temporary state and you should turn it on as soon as possible. TypeScript without noImplicitAny is surprisingly loose. Item 83 explores how this can lead to trouble.

strictNullChecks

strictNullChecks controls whether null and undefined are permissible values in every type.

This code is valid when strictNullChecks is off:

```
const x: number = null;  // OK, null is a valid number
```

but triggers an error when you turn strictNullChecks on:

```
const x: number = null;
//    ~ Type 'null' is not assignable to type 'number'
```

A similar error would have occurred had you used undefined instead of null.

If you mean to allow `null`, you can fix the error by making your intent explicit:

```
const x: number | null = null;
```

If you do not wish to permit `null`, you'll need to track down where it came from and add either a check or an assertion:

```
const statusEl = document.getElementById('status');
statusEl.textContent = 'Ready';
// ~~~~ 'statusEl' is possibly 'null'.

if (statusEl) {
  statusEl.textContent = 'Ready';  // OK, null has been excluded
}
statusEl!.textContent = 'Ready';  // OK, we've asserted that el is non-null
```

Using an `if` statement in this way is known as "narrowing" or "refining" a type, and this pattern is explored in Item 22. The "`!`" on the last line is called a "non-null assertion." Type assertions have their place in TypeScript, but they can also lead to runtime exceptions. Item 9 will explain when you should and should not use a type assertion.

`strictNullChecks` is tremendously helpful for catching errors involving `null` and `undefined` values, but it does increase the difficulty of using the language. If you're starting a new project and you've used TypeScript before, set `strictNullChecks`. But if you're new to the language or migrating a JavaScript codebase, you may elect to leave it off. You should certainly set `noImplicitAny` before you set `strictNullChecks`.

If you choose to work without `strictNullChecks`, keep an eye out for the dreaded "undefined is not an object" runtime error. Every one of these is a reminder that you should consider enabling stricter checking. Changing this setting will only get harder as your project grows, so try not to wait too long before enabling it. Most TypeScript code uses `strictNullChecks`, and this is eventually where you want to be.

Other Options

There are many other settings that affect language semantics (e.g., `noImplicitThis` and `strictFunctionTypes`), but these are minor compared to `noImplicitAny` and `strictNullChecks`. To enable all of these checks, turn on the `strict` setting. TypeScript is able to catch the most errors with `strict`, so this should be your goal.

If you create a project using `tsc --init`, you'll be in `strict` mode by default.

There are also a few "stricter than strict" options available. You can opt into these to make TypeScript even more aggressive about finding errors in your code. One of these options is `noUncheckedIndexedAccess`, which helps to catch errors around object and array access. For example, this code has no type errors under `--strict` but throws an exception at runtime:

```
const tenses = ['past', 'present', 'future'];
tenses[3].toUpperCase();
```

With noUncheckedIndexedAccess set, this is an error:

```
const tenses = ['past', 'present', 'future'];
tenses[3].toUpperCase();
//     ~~~~~~ Object is possibly 'undefined'.
```

This is not a free lunch, however. Many valid accesses will also be flagged as possibly undefined:

```
tenses[0].toUpperCase();
//     ~~~~~~ Object is possibly 'undefined'.
```

Some TypeScript projects use this setting, while others don't. You should at least be aware that it exists. There will be more to say about this setting in Item 48.

Know which options you're using! If a coworker shares a TypeScript example and you're unable to reproduce their errors, make sure your compiler options are the same.

Things to Remember

- The TypeScript compiler includes several settings that affect core aspects of the language.
- Configure TypeScript using *tsconfig.json* rather than command-line options.
- Turn on noImplicitAny unless you are transitioning a JavaScript project to TypeScript.
- Use strictNullChecks to prevent "undefined is not an object"-style runtime errors.
- Aim to enable strict to get the most thorough checking that TypeScript can offer.

Item 3: Understand That Code Generation Is Independent of Types

At a high level, tsc (the TypeScript compiler) does two things:

- It converts next-generation TypeScript/JavaScript to an older version of JavaScript that works in browsers or other runtimes ("transpiling").
- It checks your code for type errors.

What's surprising is that these two behaviors are entirely independent of one another. Put another way, the types in your code cannot affect the JavaScript that TypeScript emits. Since it's this JavaScript that gets executed, this means that your types can't affect the way your code runs.

This has some surprising implications and should inform your expectations about what TypeScript can and cannot do for you.

You Cannot Check TypeScript Types at Runtime

You may be tempted to write code like this:

```typescript
interface Square {
  width: number;
}
interface Rectangle extends Square {
  height: number;
}
type Shape = Square | Rectangle;

function calculateArea(shape: Shape) {
  if (shape instanceof Rectangle) {
    //                ~~~~~~~~~ 'Rectangle' only refers to a type,
    //                          but is being used as a value here
    return shape.height * shape.width;
    //            ~~~~~~ Property 'height' does not exist on type 'Shape'
  } else {
    return shape.width * shape.width;
  }
}
```

The `instanceof` check happens at runtime, but `Rectangle` is a type and so it cannot affect the runtime behavior of the code. TypeScript types are "erasable": part of compilation to JavaScript is simply removing all the `interfaces`, `types`, and type annotations from your code. This is easiest to see if you look at the JavaScript that this sample compiles down to:

```javascript
function calculateArea(shape) {
  if (shape instanceof Rectangle) {
    return shape.height * shape.width;
  } else {
    return shape.width * shape.width;
  }
}
```

There's no mention of `Rectangle` before the `instanceof` check here, hence the problem.[2] To ascertain the type of shape you're dealing with, you'll need some way to

---

2 The best way to build an intuition for this is by using the TypeScript playground (*https://oreil.ly/R0_D5*), which shows your TypeScript and the resulting JavaScript side by side.

reconstruct its type at runtime, i.e., some way that makes sense in the generated Java-Script, not just in the original TypeScript.

There are several ways to do this. One is to check for the presence of a `height` property:

```
function calculateArea(shape: Shape) {
  if ('height' in shape) {
    return shape.width * shape.height;
    //      ^? (parameter) shape: Rectangle
  } else {
    return shape.width * shape.width;
  }
}
```

This works because the property check only involves values available at runtime, but still allows the type checker to refine shape's type to `Rectangle`.

Another way would be to introduce a "tag" to explicitly store the type in a way that's available at runtime:

```
interface Square {
  kind: 'square';
  width: number;
}
interface Rectangle {
  kind: 'rectangle';
  height: number;
  width: number;
}
type Shape = Square | Rectangle;

function calculateArea(shape: Shape) {
  if (shape.kind === 'rectangle') {
    return shape.width * shape.height;
    //      ^? (parameter) shape: Rectangle
  } else {
    return shape.width * shape.width;
    //      ^? (parameter) shape: Square
  }
}
```

Here the `kind` property acts as the "tag," and we say that the `Shape` type is a "tagged union." It's also sometimes called a "discriminated union," in which case `kind` is the "discriminant." The terms are interchangeable. Because they make it so easy to recover type information at runtime, tagged/discriminated unions are ubiquitous in TypeScript.

Some constructs introduce both a type (which is not available at runtime) and a value (which is). The `class` keyword is one of these. Making `Square` and `Rectangle` classes would be another way to fix the error:

```
class Square {
  width: number;
  constructor(width: number) {
    this.width = width;
  }
}
class Rectangle extends Square {
  height: number;
  constructor(width: number, height: number) {
    super(width);
    this.height = height;
  }
}
type Shape = Square | Rectangle;

function calculateArea(shape: Shape) {
  if (shape instanceof Rectangle) {
    return shape.width * shape.height;
    //      ^? (parameter) shape: Rectangle
  } else {
    return shape.width * shape.width;
    //      ^? (parameter) shape: Square
  }
}
```

This works because `class Rectangle` introduces both a type *and* a value, whereas `interface` only introduced a type.

The Rectangle in `type Shape = Square | Rectangle` refers to the *type*, but the Rectangle in `shape instanceof Rectangle` refers to the *value*, in this case the constructor function. This distinction is important to understand but can be quite subtle. Item 8 shows you how to tell which is which.

Code with Type Errors Can Produce Output

Because code output is independent of type checking, it follows that code with type errors can produce output!

```
$ cat test.ts
let x = 'hello';
x = 1234;
$ tsc test.ts
test.ts:2:1 - error TS2322: Type '1234' is not assignable to type 'string'

2 x = 1234;
  ~

$ cat test.js
var x = 'hello';
x = 1234;
```

This can be quite surprising if you're coming from a language like C or Java where type checking and output go hand in hand. You can think of all TypeScript errors as being similar to warnings in those languages: it's likely that they indicate a problem and are worth investigating, but they won't stop the build.

Compiling and Type Checking

This is likely the source of some sloppy language that is common around TypeScript. You'll often hear people say that their TypeScript "doesn't compile" as a way of saying that it has errors. But this isn't technically correct! Only the code generation is "compiling." So long as your TypeScript is valid JavaScript (and often even if it isn't), the TypeScript compiler will produce output. At the risk of sounding pedantic, it's better to say that your code has errors, or that it "doesn't type check."

Code emission in the presence of errors is helpful in practice. If you're building a web application, you may know that there are problems with a particular part of it. But because TypeScript will still generate code in the presence of errors, you can test the other parts of your application before you fix them.

You should aim for zero errors when you commit code, lest you fall into the trap of having to remember what is an expected or unexpected error. If you want to disable output on errors, you can use the `noEmitOnError` option in *tsconfig.json*, or the equivalent in your build tool.

Type Operations Cannot Affect Runtime Values

Suppose you have a value that could be a string or a number and you'd like to normalize it so that it's always a number. Here's a misguided attempt that the type checker accepts:

```
function asNumber(val: number | string): number {
  return val as number;
}
```

Looking at the generated JavaScript makes it clear what this function really does:

```
function asNumber(val) {
  return val;
}
```

There is no conversion going on whatsoever. The `as number` is a type operation, so it cannot affect the runtime behavior of your code. To normalize the value you'll need to check its runtime type and do the conversion using JavaScript constructs:

```
function asNumber(val: number | string): number {
  return Number(val);
}
```

"as number" is a *type assertion*, sometimes inaccurately called a "cast." For more on when it's appropriate to use type assertions, see Item 9.

Runtime Types May Not Be the Same as Declared Types

Could this function ever hit the final `console.log`?

```
function setLightSwitch(value: boolean) {
  switch (value) {
    case true:
      turnLightOn();
      break;
    case false:
      turnLightOff();
      break;
    default:
      console.log(`I'm afraid I can't do that.`);
  }
}
```

TypeScript usually flags dead code, but it does not complain about this, even with the `strict` option. How could you hit this branch?

The key is to remember that `boolean` is the *declared* type. Because it is a TypeScript type, it goes away at runtime. In JavaScript code, a user might inadvertently call `setLightSwitch` with a value like `"ON"`.

There are ways to trigger this code path in pure TypeScript, too. Perhaps the function is called with a value that comes from a network call:

```
interface LightApiResponse {
  lightSwitchValue: boolean;
}
async function setLight() {
  const response = await fetch('/light');
  const result: LightApiResponse = await response.json();
  setLightSwitch(result.lightSwitchValue);
}
```

You've declared that the result of the `/light` request is `LightApiResponse`, but nothing enforces this. If you misunderstood the API and `lightSwitchValue` is really a `string`, then a string will be passed to `setLightSwitch` at runtime. Or perhaps the API changed after you deployed.

TypeScript can get quite confusing when your runtime types don't match the declared types, and you should avoid these so-called "unsound" types whenever you can. But be aware that it's possible for a value to have a runtime type other than the one you've declared. For more on soundness, see Item 48.

You Cannot Overload a Function Based on TypeScript Types

Languages like C++ allow you to define multiple versions of a function that differ only in the types of their parameters. This is called "function overloading." Because the runtime behavior of your code is independent of its TypeScript types, this construct isn't possible in TypeScript:

```
function add(a: number, b: number) { return a + b; }
//          ~~~ Duplicate function implementation
function add(a: string, b: string) { return a + b; }
//          ~~~ Duplicate function implementation
```

TypeScript *does* provide a facility for overloading functions, but it operates entirely at the type level. You can provide multiple type signatures for a function, but only a single implementation:

```
function add(a: number, b: number): number;
function add(a: string, b: string): string;

function add(a: any, b: any) {
  return a + b;
}

const three = add(1, 2);
//     ^? const three: number
const twelve = add('1', '2');
//     ^? const twelve: string
```

The first two signatures of add only provide type information. When TypeScript produces JavaScript output, they are removed, and only the implementation remains. The any parameters in the implementation aren't great. We'll explore how to handle those in Item 52, which also covers some subtleties to be aware of with TypeScript function overloads.

TypeScript Types Have No Effect on Runtime Performance

Because types and type operations are erased when you generate JavaScript, they cannot have an effect on runtime performance. TypeScript's static types are truly zero cost. The next time someone offers runtime overhead as a reason to not use TypeScript, you'll know exactly how well they've tested this claim!

There are two caveats to this:

- While there is no *runtime* overhead, the TypeScript compiler will introduce *build time* overhead. The TypeScript team takes compiler performance seriously and compilation is usually quite fast, especially for incremental builds. If the overhead becomes significant, your build tool may have a "transpile only" option to skip the type checking. There will be more to say about compiler performance in Item 78.

- The code that TypeScript emits to support older runtimes *may* incur a performance overhead versus native implementations. For example, if you use generator functions and target ES5, which predates generators, then `tsc` will emit some helper code to make things work. This will incur some overhead versus a native implementation of generators. This is the case for any JavaScript "transpiler," not just TypeScript. Regardless, this has to do with the emit target and language levels and is still independent of the *types*.

Things to Remember

- Code generation is independent of the type system. This means that TypeScript types cannot affect the runtime behavior of your code.
- It is possible for a program with type errors to produce code ("compile").
- TypeScript types are not available at runtime. To query a type at runtime, you need some way to reconstruct it. Tagged unions and property checking are common ways to do this.
- Some constructs, such as `class`, introduce both a TypeScript type and a value that is available at runtime.
- Because they are erased as part of compilation, TypeScript types cannot affect the runtime performance of your code.

Item 4: Get Comfortable with Structural Typing

JavaScript encourages "duck typing": if you pass a function a value with all the right properties, it won't care how you made the value. It will just use it. (This term refers to the saying, "If it walks like a duck and talks like a duck, then it probably is a duck.")

TypeScript models this behavior using what's known as a structural type system. This can sometimes lead to surprising results because the type checker's understanding of a type may be broader than what you had in mind. Having a good grasp of structural typing will help you make sense of errors and non-errors and help you write more robust code.

Say you're working on a physics library and have a 2D vector type:

```
interface Vector2D {
  x: number;
  y: number;
}
```

You write a function to calculate its length:

```
function calculateLength(v: Vector2D) {
  return Math.sqrt(v.x ** 2 + v.y ** 2);
}
```

Now you introduce the notion of a named vector:

```
interface NamedVector {
  name: string;
  x: number;
  y: number;
}
```

The `calculateLength` function will work with `NamedVector`s because they have `x` and `y` properties that are `number`s. TypeScript is smart enough to figure this out:

```
const v: NamedVector = { x: 3, y: 4, name: 'Pythagoras' };
calculateLength(v);  // OK, result is 5
```

What's interesting is that you never declared the relationship between `Vector2D` and `NamedVector`. And you didn't have to write an alternative implementation of `calculateLength` for `NamedVector`s. TypeScript's type system is modeling JavaScript's runtime behavior (Item 1). It allowed `calculateLength` to be called with a `NamedVector` because its *structure* was compatible with `Vector2D`. This is where the term "structural typing" comes from.

But this can also lead to trouble. Say you add a 3D vector type:

```
interface Vector3D {
  x: number;
  y: number;
  z: number;
}
```

and write a function to normalize them (make their length 1):

```
function normalize(v: Vector3D) {
  const length = calculateLength(v);
  return {
    x: v.x / length,
    y: v.y / length,
    z: v.z / length,
  };
}
```

If you call this function, you're likely to get a vector with a length greater than 1:

```
> normalize({x: 3, y: 4, z: 5})
{ x: 0.6, y: 0.8, z: 1 }
```

This vector has a length of around 1.4, not 1. So what went wrong, and why didn't TypeScript catch the error?

The bug is that `calculateLength` operates on 2D vectors, but `normalize` operates on 3D vectors. So the `z` component is ignored in the normalization.

What's perhaps more surprising is that the type checker does not catch this issue. Why are you allowed to call `calculateLength` with a 3D vector, despite its type declaration saying that it takes 2D vectors?

What worked so well with named vectors has backfired here. Calling `calculate Length` with an {x, y, z} object doesn't throw an error. So the type checker doesn't complain either, and this behavior has led to a bug.

(If you want this to be an error, you have some options. Item 63 presents a trick to specifically prohibit the z property, and Item 64 shows how you can use "brands" to prevent this sort of structural typing altogether.)

As you write functions, it's easy to imagine that they will be called with arguments having the properties you've declared *and no others*. This is known as a "closed," "sealed," or "precise" type, and it cannot be expressed in TypeScript's type system. Like it or not, your types are "open."

This can sometimes lead to surprises:

```
function calculateLengthL1(v: Vector3D) {
  let length = 0;
  for (const axis of Object.keys(v)) {
    const coord = v[axis];
    //              ~~~~~~~ Element implicitly has an 'any' type because ...
    //                      'string' can't be used to index type 'Vector3D'
    length += Math.abs(coord);
  }
  return length;
}
```

Why is this an error? Since `axis` is one of the keys of v, which is a `Vector3D`, it should be either "x", "y", or "z". And according to the declaration of `Vector3D`, these are all numbers, so shouldn't the type of `coord` be `number`?

Is this error a false positive? No! TypeScript is correct to complain. The logic in the previous paragraph assumes that `Vector3D` is sealed and does not have other properties. But it could:

```
const vec3D = {x: 3, y: 4, z: 1, address: '123 Broadway'};
calculateLengthL1(vec3D);  // OK, returns NaN
```

Since v could conceivably have any properties, the type of `axis` is `string`. TypeScript has no reason to believe that `v[axis]` is a number because, as you just saw, it might not be. (The `vec3D` variable here avoids excess property checking, which is the subject of Item 11.)

Iterating over objects can be tricky to type correctly. We'll return to this topic in Item 60, but in this case an implementation without loops would be better:

```
function calculateLengthL1(v: Vector3D) {
  return Math.abs(v.x) + Math.abs(v.y) + Math.abs(v.z);
}
```

Structural typing can also lead to surprises with classes, which are compared structurally for assignability:

```
class SmallNumContainer {
  num: number;
  constructor(num: number) {
    if (num < 0 || num >= 10) {
      throw new Error(`You gave me ${num} but I want something 0-9.`)
    }
    this.num = num;
  }
}

const a = new SmallNumContainer(5);
const b: SmallNumContainer = { num: 2024 };  // OK!
```

Why is b assignable to SmallNumContainer? It has a num property that's a number. So the structures match. This might lead to trouble if you write a function that assumes the validation logic in SmallNumContainer's constructor has run. This is less likely to happen by chance for classes with more properties and methods, but it is quite different than languages like C++ or Java, where declaring a parameter of type SmallNumContainer guarantees that it will be either SmallNumContainer or a subclass of it, and hence that the validation logic in the constructor will have run.

Structural typing is beneficial when you're writing tests. Say you have a function that runs a query on a database and processes the results:

```
interface Author {
  first: string;
  last: string;
}
function getAuthors(database: PostgresDB): Author[] {
  const authorRows = database.runQuery(`SELECT first, last FROM authors`);
  return authorRows.map(row => ({first: row[0], last: row[1]}));
}
```

To test this, you could create a mock PostgresDB. But a simpler approach is to use structural typing and define a narrower interface:

```
interface DB {
  runQuery: (sql: string) => any[];
}
function getAuthors(database: DB): Author[] {
  const authorRows = database.runQuery(`SELECT first, last FROM authors`);
  return authorRows.map(row => ({first: row[0], last: row[1]}));
}
```

You can still pass `getAuthors` a `PostgresDB` in production since it has a `runQuery` method. Because of structural typing, the `PostgresDB` doesn't need to say that it implements `DB`. TypeScript will figure out that it does.

When you write your tests, you can pass in a simpler object instead:

```
test('getAuthors', () => {
  const authors = getAuthors({
    runQuery(sql: string) {
      return [['Toni', 'Morrison'], ['Maya', 'Angelou']];
    }
  });
  expect(authors).toEqual([
    {first: 'Toni', last: 'Morrison'},
    {first: 'Maya', last: 'Angelou'}
  ]);
});
```

TypeScript will verify that our test `DB` conforms to the interface. And your tests don't need to know anything about your production database: no mocking libraries necessary! By introducing an abstraction (`DB`), we've freed our logic (and tests) from the details of a specific implementation (`PostgresDB`).

Another advantage of structural typing is that it can cleanly sever dependencies between libraries. For more on this, see Item 70.

Things to Remember

- Understand that JavaScript is duck typed and TypeScript uses structural typing to model this: values assignable to your interfaces might have properties beyond those explicitly listed in your type declarations. Types are not "sealed."

- Be aware that classes also follow structural typing rules. You may not have an instance of the class you expect!

- Use structural typing to facilitate unit testing.

Item 5: Limit Use of the any Type

TypeScript's type system is *gradual* and *optional*: *gradual* because you can add types to your code bit by bit (with `noImplicitAny`), and *optional* because you can disable the type checker whenever you like. The key to these features is the any type:

```
let ageInYears: number;
ageInYears = '12';
//  ~~~~~~ Type 'string' is not assignable to type 'number'.
ageInYears = '12' as any;  // OK
```

The type checker is right to complain here, but you can silence it by typing as any. As you start using TypeScript, it's tempting to use any types and type assertions (as any) when you don't understand an error, think the type checker is incorrect, or just don't want to take the time to write out type declarations.

In some cases this may be OK, but be aware that using any eliminates many of the advantages of using TypeScript. You should at least understand its dangers before you use it.

There's No Type Safety with any Types

In the preceding example, the type declaration says that ageInYears is a number. But any lets you assign a string to it. The type checker will believe that it's a number (that's what you said, after all), and the chaos will go uncaught:

```
ageInYears += 1;  // OK; at runtime, ageInYears is now "121"
```

any Lets You Break Contracts

When you write a function, you are specifying a contract: if the caller gives you a certain type of input, you'll produce a certain type of output. But with an any type, you can break these contracts:

```
function calculateAge(birthDate: Date): number {
  // ...
}

let birthDate: any = '1990-01-19';
calculateAge(birthDate);  // OK
```

The birth date parameter should be a Date, not a string. The any type has let you break the contract of calculateAge. This can be particularly problematic because JavaScript is often willing to implicitly convert between types. A string will sometimes work where a number is expected, only to break in other circumstances.

There Are No Language Services for any Types

When a variable has a non-any type, the TypeScript language services are able to provide intelligent autocomplete and contextual documentation (as shown in Figure 1-3).

```
let person = { first: 'George', last: 'Washington' };
person.
```
```
    ● first
    ● last
```

Figure 1-3. The TypeScript Language Service is able to provide contextual autocomplete for symbols with types.

But for symbols with an any type, you're on your own (Figure 1-4).

```
let person: any = { first: 'George', last: 'Washington' };
person.
```

Figure 1-4. There is no autocomplete for properties on symbols with any types.

Renaming is another such service. If you have a Person type and functions to format a person's name:

```
interface Person {
  first: string;
  last: string;
}

const formatName = (p: Person) => `${p.first} ${p.last}`;
const formatNameAny = (p: any) => `${p.first} ${p.last}`;
```

then you can select first in your editor, choose "Rename Symbol," and change it to firstName (see Figures 1-5 and 1-6).

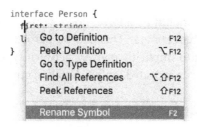

```
interface Person {
  first: string;
  l
}
```

Go to Definition	F12
Peek Definition	⌥F12
Go to Type Definition	
Find All References	⌥⇧F12
Peek References	⇧F12
Rename Symbol	F2

Figure 1-5. Renaming a symbol in VS Code.

```
interface Person {
  first: string;
    firstName
}
```

Figure 1-6. Choosing the new name.

This changes the formatName function but not the any version:

```
interface Person {
  firstName: string;
  last: string;
}
const formatName = (p: Person) => `${p.firstName} ${p.last}`;
const formatNameAny = (p: any) => `${p.first} ${p.last}`;
```

One of TypeScript's tag lines is "JavaScript that scales." A key part of "scales" is the language services, which are an essential part of the TypeScript experience (see Item 6). Losing them will lead to a loss in productivity, not just for you but for everyone else working with your code.

any Types Mask Bugs When You Refactor Code

Suppose you're building a web application in which users can select some sort of item. One of your components might have an onSelectItem callback. Writing a type for an item seems like a hassle, so you just use any as a stand-in:

```
interface ComponentProps {
  onSelectItem: (item: any) => void;
}
```

Here's code that manages that component:

```
function renderSelector(props: ComponentProps) { /* ... */ }

let selectedId: number = 0;
function handleSelectItem(item: any) {
  selectedId = item.id;
}

renderSelector({onSelectItem: handleSelectItem});
```

Later you rework the selector in a way that makes it harder to pass the whole item object through to onSelectItem. But that's no big deal since you just need the ID. You change the signature in ComponentProps:

```
interface ComponentProps {
  onSelectItem: (id: number) => void;
}
```

You update the component and everything passes the type checker. Victory!

... or is it? handleSelectItem takes an any parameter, so it's just as happy with an item as it is with an ID. It produces a runtime exception, despite passing the type checker. Had you used a more specific type, this would have been caught by the type checker.

any Hides Your Type Design

The type definition for complex objects, like your application state, can get quite long. Rather than writing out types for the dozens of properties in your app's state, you may be tempted to just use an any type and be done with it.

This is problematic for all the reasons listed in this item. But it's also problematic because it hides the design of your state. As Chapter 4 explains, good type design is essential for writing clean, correct, and understandable code. With an any type, your type design is implicit. This makes it hard to know whether the design is a good one, or even what the design is at all. If you ask a coworker to review a change, they'll have to reconstruct whether and how you changed the application state. Better to write it out for everyone to see.

any Undermines Confidence in the Type System

Every time you make a mistake and the type checker catches it, it boosts your confidence in the type system. But when you see a type error at runtime that TypeScript didn't catch, that confidence takes a hit. If you're introducing TypeScript on a larger team, this might make your coworkers question whether TypeScript is worth the effort. any types are often the source of these uncaught errors.

TypeScript aims to make your life easier, but TypeScript with lots of any types can be harder to work with than untyped JavaScript because you have to fix type errors *and* still keep track of the real types in your head. When your types match reality, it frees you from the burden of having to keep type information in your head. TypeScript will keep track of it for you.

For the times when you must use any, there are better and worse ways to do it. For much more on how to limit the downsides of any, see Chapter 5.

Things to Remember

- TypeScript's any type allows you to disable most forms of type checking for a symbol.
- The any type eliminates type safety, lets you break contracts, harms developer experience, makes refactoring error prone, hides your type design, and undermines confidence in the type system.
- Avoid using any when you can!

CHAPTER 2

TypeScript's Type System

TypeScript can generate JavaScript (Item 3), but the type system is the main event. This is why you're using the language!

This chapter walks you through the nuts and bolts of TypeScript's type system: how to think about it, how to use it, choices you'll need to make, and features you should avoid. TypeScript's type system is surprisingly powerful and able to express things you might not expect a type system to be able to. The items in this chapter will give you a solid foundation to build upon as you write TypeScript and read the rest of this book.

Item 6: Use Your Editor to Interrogate and Explore the Type System

When you install TypeScript, you get two executables:

- `tsc`, the TypeScript compiler
- `tsserver`, the TypeScript standalone server

You're much more likely to run the TypeScript compiler directly, but the server is every bit as important because it provides *language services*. These include autocomplete, inspection, navigation, and refactoring. You typically use these services through your editor. If yours isn't configured to provide them, then you're missing out! Services like autocomplete are one of the things that make TypeScript such a joy to use. But beyond convenience, your editor is the best place to build and test your knowledge of the type system. This will help you build an intuition for when TypeScript is able to infer types, which is key to writing compact, idiomatic code (see Item 18).

The details will vary from editor to editor, but you can generally hover over a symbol to see what TypeScript considers its type (see Figure 2-1).

```
let num: number
let num = 10;
```

Figure 2-1. An editor (VS Code) showing that the inferred type of the num *symbol is* number.

You didn't write number here, but TypeScript was able to figure it out based on the value 10.

You can also inspect functions, as shown in Figure 2-2.

```
function add(a: number, b: number): number
function add(a: number, b: number) {
    return a + b;
}
```

Figure 2-2. Using an editor to reveal the inferred return type for a function.

The noteworthy bit of information is the inferred value for the return type, number. If this does not match your expectation, you should add a type declaration and track down the discrepancy (see Item 9).

Seeing what TypeScript thinks a variable's type is at any given point is essential for building an intuition around widening (Item 20) and narrowing (Item 22). Watching the type of a variable change in the branch of a conditional is a tremendous way to build confidence in the type system (see Figure 2-3).

```
function logMessage(message: string | null) {
    if (message) {

        (parameter) message: string
        message
    }
}
```

Figure 2-3. The type of message is string | null *outside the branch, but* string *inside.*

You can inspect individual properties in a larger object to see what TypeScript has inferred about them (see Figure 2-4).

```
const foo = {
    (property) x: number[]
    x: [1, 2],
    bar: {
        name: 'Fred'
    }
};
```

Figure 2-4. Inspecting how TypeScript has inferred types in an object.

If your intention was for x to be a tuple type ([number, number]), then a type annotation will be required.

To see inferred generic types in the middle of a chain of operations, inspect the method name (as shown in Figure 2-5).

```
function restOfPath(path: string) {
```

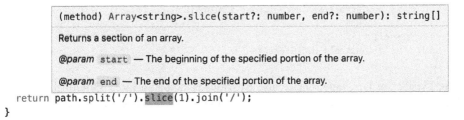

```
    return path.split('/').slice(1).join('/');
}
```

Figure 2-5. Revealing inferred generic types in a chain of method calls.

The Array<string> indicates that TypeScript understands that split produced an array of strings. While there was little ambiguity in this case, this information can prove essential in writing and debugging long chains of function calls. TypeScript has also brought up some helpful documentation for the slice method. Item 68 will explain how this works.

Seeing type errors in your editor can also be a great way to learn the nuances of the type system. For example, this function tries to get an HTMLElement by its ID, or return a default one. TypeScript flags two errors:

```
function getElement(elOrId: string | HTMLElement | null): HTMLElement {
  if (typeof elOrId === 'object') {
    return elOrId;
    // ~~~ Type 'HTMLElement | null' is not assignable to type 'HTMLElement'
  } else if (elOrId === null) {
    return document.body;
  }
  elOrId
```

```
// ^? (parameter) elOrId: string
return document.getElementById(elOrId);
// ~~~ Type 'HTMLElement | null' is not assignable to type 'HTMLElement'
}
```

The intent in the first branch of the if statement was to filter down to just the objects, namely, the HTMLElements. But oddly enough, in JavaScript typeof null is "object", so elOrId could still be null in that branch. You can fix this by putting the null check first. The second error is because document.getElementById can return null, so you need to handle that case as well, perhaps by throwing an exception:

```
function getElement(elOrId: string|HTMLElement|null): HTMLElement {
  if (elOrId === null) {
    return document.body;
  } else if (typeof elOrId === 'object') {
    return elOrId;
    //     ^? (parameter) elOrId: HTMLElement
  }
  const el = document.getElementById(elOrId);
  //                                 ^? (parameter) elOrId: string
  if (!el) {
    throw new Error(`No such element ${elOrId}`);
  }
  return el;
  //     ^? const el: HTMLElement
}
```

The TypeScript language service also provides refactoring tools. One of the simplest but most useful of these is renaming a symbol. This is more complicated than find and replace because the same name might refer to different variables in different places. In this code, for example, there are three distinct variables all named i:

```
let i = 0;
for (let i = 0; i < 10; i++) {
  console.log(i);
  {
    let i = 12;
    console.log(i);
  }
}
console.log(i);
```

In VS Code, if you click an i in the for loop and hit F2, a text box will pop up that lets you put in a new name (Figure 2-6).

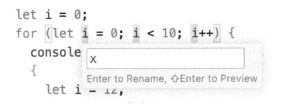

```
let i = 0;
for (let i = 0; i < 10; i++) {
    console
    {
        let i = 12;
```

x

Enter to Rename, ⇧Enter to Preview

Figure 2-6. Renaming a symbol in your editor.

When you apply the refactor, only the references to the i that you renamed will change:

```
let i = 0;
for (let x = 0; x < 10; x++) {
  console.log(x);
  {
    let i = 12;
    console.log(i);
  }
}
console.log(i);
```

If you rename a symbol that's imported from another module, those imports will also update. There are many other useful refactors available, such as renaming or moving a file (which updates all imports) and moving a symbol into a new file. You should familiarize yourself with these because they can significantly increase your productivity while working with large TypeScript projects.

Language services can also help you navigate through both your own code as well as external libraries and type declarations. Suppose you see a call to the global fetch function in code and want to learn more about it. Your editor should provide a "Go to Definition" option. In mine it looks like Figure 2-7.

```
const response = fetch('http://example.com');
```

Go to Definition	F12
Go to Type Definition	
Go to Implementations	⌘F12
Go to References	⇧F12
Go to Source Definition	
Peek	>

Figure 2-7. The TypeScript language service provides a "Go to Definition" feature that should be available in your editor.

Selecting this option takes you into *lib.dom.d.ts*, the type declarations that TypeScript includes for the DOM:

```
declare function fetch(
    input: RequestInfo | URL, init?: RequestInit
): Promise<Response>;
```

You can see that `fetch` returns a `Promise` and takes two arguments. Clicking through on `RequestInfo` brings you here:

```
type RequestInfo = Request | string;
```

from which you can go to `Request`:

```
interface Request extends Body {
  // ...
}
declare var Request: {
  prototype: Request;
  new(input: RequestInfo | URL, init?: RequestInit | undefined): Request;
};
```

Here you can see that the `Request` type and value are being modeled separately (see Item 8). You've seen `RequestInfo` already. Clicking through on `RequestInit` shows all the options you can use in constructing a `Request`:

```
interface RequestInit {
  body?: BodyInit | null;
  cache?: RequestCache;
  credentials?: RequestCredentials;
  headers?: HeadersInit;
  // ...
}
```

There are many more types you could follow here, but you get the idea. Type declarations can be challenging to read at first, but they're an excellent way to see what can be done with TypeScript, how the library you're using is modeled, and how you might debug errors. For much more on type declarations, see Chapter 8.

Things to Remember

- Take advantage of the TypeScript language services by using an editor that supports them.

- Use your editor to build an intuition for how the type system works and how TypeScript infers types.

- Familiarize yourself with TypeScript's refactoring tools, e.g., renaming symbols and files.

- Know how to jump into type declaration files to see how they model behavior.

Item 7: Think of Types as Sets of Values

At runtime, every variable has a single value chosen from JavaScript's universe of values. There are many possible values, including:

- `42`
- `null`
- `undefined`
- `'Canada'`
- `{animal: 'Whale', weight_lbs: 40_000}`
- `/regex/`
- `new HTMLButtonElement`
- `(x, y) => x + y`

But before your code runs, when TypeScript is checking it for errors, a variable just has a *type*. This is best thought of as a *set of possible values*. This set is known as the *domain* of the type. For instance, you can think of the `number` type as the set of all number values. `42` and `-37.25` are in it, but `'Canada'` is not. Depending on `strict NullChecks`, `null` and `undefined` may or may not be part of the set.

 You won't often see the term "domain" in TypeScript documentation or literature, or even elsewhere in this book. Types are spoken of interchangeably with their sets of values. But in this item, it will be helpful to have a term to refer specifically to the set of values for a type, as opposed to the type itself.

The smallest set is the empty set, which contains no values. It corresponds to the `never` type in TypeScript. Because its domain is empty, no values are assignable to a variable with a `never` type:

```
const x: never = 12;
//    ~ Type 'number' is not assignable to type 'never'.
```

Because it sits at the bottom of the type hierarchy, `never` is sometimes called a "bottom type."

The next smallest sets are those that contain single values. These correspond to literal types in TypeScript. (In other languages these are sometimes called "unit types.")

```
type A = 'A';
type B = 'B';
type Twelve = 12;
```

To form types with two or three values, you can union literal types:

```
type AB = 'A' | 'B';
type AB12 = 'A' | 'B' | 12;
```

The domain of a union type is the union of the domains of its constituent types, as shown in Figure 2-8. This is what the "union" in "union type" refers to.

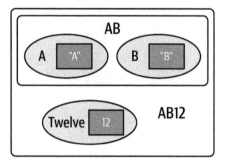

Figure 2-8. Values and types as sets of values. The boxes are values ("A", "B", 12) and the rounded shapes are types (A, B, AB, AB12, Twelve), which include a set of values. One type is assignable to another if it's entirely contained within it.

The word "assignable" appears in many TypeScript errors. In the context of sets of values, it means either "member of" (for a relationship between a value and a type) or "subset of" (for a relationship between two types):

```
const a: AB = 'A';  // OK, value 'A' is a member of the set {'A', 'B'}
const c: AB = 'C';
//      ~ Type '"C"' is not assignable to type 'AB'
```

The type "C" is a literal type. Its domain consists of the single value "C". This is not a subset of the domain of AB (which consists of the values "A" and "B"), so this is an error. At the end of the day, much of what the type checker is doing is testing whether one set is a subset of another:

```
// OK, {"A", "B"} is a subset of {"A", "B"}:
const ab: AB = Math.random() < 0.5 ? 'A' : 'B';
const ab12: AB12 = ab;  // OK, {"A", "B"} is a subset of {"A", "B", 12}

declare let twelve: AB12;
const back: AB = twelve;
//    ~~~~ Type 'AB12' is not assignable to type 'AB'
//         Type '12' is not assignable to type 'AB'
```

The sets for these types are straightforward to reason about because they are finite. You can compare the elements one by one. But most types that you work with in practice have infinite domains. Reasoning about these can be harder. You can think of them as either being built by listing out their elements:

```
type Int = 1 | 2 | 3 | 4 | 5 // | ...
```

or by describing their members:

```
interface Identified {
  id: string;
}
```

Think of this interface as a description of the values in the domain of its type. Is the value an object? Does it have an `id` property whose value is assignable to `string`? Then it's an `Identified`.

That's *all* it says. As Item 4 explained, TypeScript's structural typing rules mean that the value could have other properties, too. It could even be callable! This fact can sometimes be obscured by excess property checking (see Item 11).

Thinking of types as sets of values helps you reason about operations on them. For example:

```
interface Person {
  name: string;
}
interface Lifespan {
  birth: Date;
  death?: Date;
}
type PersonSpan = Person & Lifespan;
```

The & operator computes the intersection of two types. What sorts of values belong to the `PersonSpan` type? On first glance, the `Person` and `Lifespan` interfaces have no properties in common, so you might expect it to be the empty set (i.e., the `never` type). But type operations apply to the sets of values (the domain of the type), not to the properties in the interface. And remember that values with additional properties still belong to a type. So a value that has the properties of *both* `Person` *and* `Lifespan` will belong to the intersection type:

```
const ps: PersonSpan = {
  name: 'Alan Turing',
  birth: new Date('1912/06/23'),
  death: new Date('1954/06/07'),
};  // OK
```

Of course, a value could have more than those three properties and still belong to the type! The general rule is that the values in an intersection type contain the union of properties in each of its constituents.

The intuition about intersecting properties is correct, but for the *union* of two interfaces, rather than their intersection:

```
type K = keyof (Person | Lifespan);
//    ^? type K = never
```

There are no keys that TypeScript can be certain will be present on a value in the union type, so keyof for the union must be the empty set (never). Or, more formally:

```
// Disclaimer: these are relationships, not TypeScript code!
keyof (A&B) = (keyof A) | (keyof B)
keyof (A|B) = (keyof A) & (keyof B)
```

If you can build an intuition for why these equations hold, you'll have come a long way toward understanding TypeScript's type system!

A more idiomatic way to write the PersonSpan type would be with extends:

```
interface Person {
  name: string;
}
interface PersonSpan extends Person {
  birth: Date;
  death?: Date;
}
```

Thinking of types as sets of values, what does extends mean? Just like "assignable to," you can read it as "subset of." Every value in PersonSpan must have a name property that is a string. And every value must also have a birth property, so it's a proper subset.

While extends is typically used to add fields to an interface, anything matching a subset of the values of the base type will do. This lets you model more nuanced type relationships:

```
interface NullyStudent {
  name: string;
  ageYears: number | null;
}
interface Student extends NullyStudent {
  ageYears: number;
}
```

Not every language would let you change the type of ageYears like this, but so long as it's assignable to the type in the base type (NullyStudent), TypeScript allows it. This makes sense when you think about the domains of these two interfaces. If you try to expand the type of ageYears instead, you'll get an error:

```
interface StringyStudent extends NullyStudent {
  //        ~~~~~~~~~~~~~~
  // Interface 'StringyStudent' incorrectly extends interface 'NullyStudent'.
  ageYears: number | string;
}
```

You might hear the term "subtype." This is another way of saying that one type's domain is a subset of the other's. Thinking in terms of one-, two-, and three-dimensional vectors:

```
interface Vector1D { x: number; }
interface Vector2D extends Vector1D { y: number; }
interface Vector3D extends Vector2D { z: number; }
```

You'd say that a Vector3D is a subtype of Vector2D, which is a subtype of Vector1D (in the context of classes, you'd say "subclass"). This relationship is usually drawn as a hierarchy, but thinking in terms of sets of values, a Venn diagram is more appropriate (see Figure 2-9).

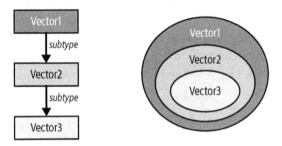

Figure 2-9. Two ways of thinking of type relationships: as a hierarchy or as overlapping sets.

With the Venn diagram, it's clear that the subset/subtype/assignability relationships are unchanged if you rewrite the interfaces without extends:

```
interface Vector1D { x: number; }
interface Vector2D { x: number; y: number; }
interface Vector3D { x: number; y: number; z: number; }
```

The sets haven't changed, so neither has the Venn diagram.

While both interpretations are workable for object types, the set interpretation becomes much more intuitive when you start thinking about literal types and union types.

The extends keyword can also appear as a constraint in a generic type, and it also means "subset of" in this context (Item 15):

```
function getKey<K extends string>(val: any, key: K) {
  // ...
}
```

What does it mean to extend string? If you're used to thinking in terms of object inheritance, it's hard to interpret. You could define a subclass of the object wrapper type String (Item 10), but that seems inadvisable.

Thinking in terms of sets, on the other hand, it stands to reason that any type whose domain is a subset of `string` will do. This includes string literal types, unions of string literal types, template literal types (Item 54), and `string` itself:

```
getKey({}, 'x');  // OK, 'x' extends string
getKey({}, Math.random() < 0.5 ? 'a' : 'b');  // OK, 'a'|'b' extends string
getKey({}, document.title);  // OK, string extends string
getKey({}, 12);
//          ~~ Type 'number' is not assignable to parameter of type 'string'
```

"extends" has turned into "assignable" in the last error, but this shouldn't trip us up since we know to read both as "subset of."

The set interpretation also makes more sense when you have types whose relationship isn't strictly hierarchical. What's the relationship between `string|number` and `string|Date`, for instance? Their intersection is non-empty (it's `string`), but neither is a subtype of the other. The relationship between their domains is clear, even though these types don't fit into a strict hierarchy (see Figure 2-10).

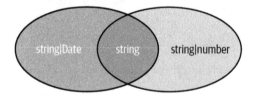

Figure 2-10. Union types may not fit into a hierarchy but can be thought of in terms of sets of values.

Thinking of types as sets can also clarify the relationships between arrays and tuples. For example:

```
const list = [1, 2];
//    ^? const list: number[]
const tuple: [number, number] = list;
//    ~~~~ Type 'number[]' is not assignable to type '[number, number]'
//         Target requires 2 element(s) but source may have fewer
```

Are there lists of numbers that are not pairs of numbers? Sure! The empty list and the list `[1]` are examples. It therefore makes sense that `number[]` is not assignable to `[number, number]` since it's not a subset of it. (The reverse assignment does work.)

Is a triple assignable to a pair? Thinking in terms of structural typing, you might expect it to be. A pair has 0 and 1 keys, so mightn't it have others, too, like 2?

```
const triple: [number, number, number] = [1, 2, 3];
const double: [number, number] = triple;
//    ~~~~~~ '[number, number, number]' is not assignable to '[number, number]'
//           Source has 3 element(s) but target allows only 2.
```

The answer is "no," and for an interesting reason. Rather than modeling a pair of numbers as {0: number, 1: number}, TypeScript models it as {0: number, 1: number, length: 2}. This makes sense—you can check the length of a tuple—and it precludes this assignment. And that's probably for the best!

TypeScript is constantly testing for assignability which, as you've seen many times now, is a subset/subtype relationship. Interestingly, TypeScript rarely checks for type *equality*. This makes it challenging to write tests for types, which is the subject of Item 55.

If types are best thought of as sets of values, that means that two types with the same sets of values are the same. And indeed this is true (with one caveat, explained below). Unless two types are semantically different and just happen to have the same domain, there's no reason to define the same type twice.

At the extreme opposite end of the spectrum from never (the empty type) is unknown. The domain of this type is all values in JavaScript. Every type is assignable to unknown. Since it sits on top of the type hierarchy, it's called a "top type." Item 46 explains how to use the unknown type in your own code.

Finally, it's worth noting that not all sets of values correspond to TypeScript types. There is no TypeScript type for all the integers, or for all the objects that have x and y properties but no others. You can sometimes subtract types using Exclude, but only when it would result in a proper TypeScript type:

```
type T = Exclude<string|Date, string|number>;
//   ^? type T = Date
type NonZeroNums = Exclude<number, 0>;
//   ^? type NonZeroNums = number
```

Table 2-1 summarizes the correspondence between TypeScript terms and terms from set theory.

Table 2-1. TypeScript terms and set terms

TypeScript term	Set term
never	∅ (empty set)
Literal type	Single element set
Value assignable to T	Value ∈ T (member of)
T1 assignable to T2	T1 ⊆ T2 (subset of)
T1 extends T2	T1 ⊆ T2 (subset of)
T1 | T2	T1 ∪ T2 (union)
T1 & T2	T1 ∩ T2 (intersection)
unknown	Universal set

There's an important caveat to this interpretation: it works best when you think of values as immutable. For example, what's the difference between these two types?

```
interface Lockbox {
  code: number;
}
interface ReadonlyLockbox {
  readonly code: number;
}
```

The domain of these two types is precisely the same, but they're observably different:

```
const box: Lockbox = { code: 4216 };
const robox: ReadonlyLockbox = { code: 3625 };
box.code = 1234;   // ok
robox.code = 1234;
//     ~~~~ Cannot assign to 'code' because it is a read-only property.
```

For this reason, you'll sometimes hear a variation on this item's title: "types are sets of values *and the things you can do with them*." Item 14 has more to say about readonly but, as a general rule, the type checker is more effective when you work with immutable values.

Things to Remember

- Think of types as sets of values (the type's *domain*). These sets can either be finite (e.g., boolean or literal types) or infinite (e.g., number or string).
- TypeScript types form intersecting sets (a Venn diagram) rather than a strict hierarchy. Two types can overlap without either being a subtype of the other.
- Remember that an object can still belong to a type even if it has additional properties that were not mentioned in the type declaration.
- Type operations apply to a set's domain. The domain of A | B is the union of the domains of A and B.
- Think of "extends," "assignable to," and "subtype of" as synonyms for "subset of."

Item 8: Know How to Tell Whether a Symbol Is in the Type Space or Value Space

A symbol in TypeScript exists in one of two spaces:

- Type space
- Value space

This can get confusing because the same name can refer to different things depending on which space it's in:

```
interface Cylinder {
  radius: number;
  height: number;
}

const Cylinder = (radius: number, height: number) => ({radius, height});
```

`interface Cylinder` introduces a symbol in type space. `const Cylinder` introduces a symbol with the same name in value space. They have nothing to do with one another. Depending on the context, when you write `Cylinder`, you'll either be referring to the type or the value. Sometimes this can lead to errors:

```
function calculateVolume(shape: unknown) {
  if (shape instanceof Cylinder) {
    shape.radius
    //     ~~~~~ Property 'radius' does not exist on type '{}'
  }
}
```

What's going on here? You probably intended the `instanceof` to check whether the shape was of the `Cylinder` type. But `instanceof` is JavaScript's runtime operator, and it operates on values. So `instanceof Cylinder` refers to the function, not the type.

It's not always obvious at first glance whether a symbol is in type space or value space. You have to tell from the context in which the symbol occurs. This can get especially confusing because many type-space constructs look exactly the same as value-space constructs.

Literal types, for example:

```
type T1 = 'string literal';
const v1 = 'string literal';
type T2 = 123;
const v2 = 123;
```

The symbols after a `type` or `interface` are in type space, while those introduced in a `const` or `let` declaration are values.

One of the best ways to build an intuition for the two spaces is through the Type-Script playground (*https://oreil.ly/R0_D5*), which shows you the generated JavaScript for your TypeScript source. Types are erased during compilation (Item 3), so if a symbol disappears then it was in type space (see Figure 2-11).

Playground   TS Config ▾   Examples ▾   Help ▾   Settings

v5.3.3 ▾   Run   Export ▾   Share   →┃   .JS .D.TS Errors Logs Plugins

```
1   type T1 = 'string literal';
2   const v1 = 'string literal';
3   type T2 = 123;
4   const v2 = 123;
```

```
const v1 = 'string literal';
const v2 = 123;
```

Figure 2-11. The TypeScript playground showing generated JavaScript. The symbols on the first two lines go away, so they were in type space.

Statements in TypeScript can alternate between type space and value space. The symbols after a type declaration (:) or an assertion (as) are in type space, while everything after an = in an assignment is in value space. For example:

```
interface Person {
  first: string;
  last: string;
}
const jane: Person = { first: 'Jane', last: 'Jacobs' };
//    ───          ──────────────────────────────── Values
//          ────── Type
```

Function statements, in particular, can alternate repeatedly between the spaces:

```
function email(to: Person, subject: string, body: string): Response {
//    ───  ──      ──────          ────                Values
//             ──────        ──────       ──────   ──────── Types
//  ...
}
```

The class and enum constructs introduce both a type and a value. Returning to the first example, for instance, Cylinder could have been a class:

```
class Cylinder {
  radius: number;
  height: number;
  constructor(radius: number, height: number) {
    this.radius = radius;
    this.height = height;
  }
}

function calculateVolume(shape: unknown) {
  if (shape instanceof Cylinder) {
    shape
    // ^? (parameter) shape: Cylinder
```

```
        shape.radius
    //      ^? (property) Cylinder.radius: number
    }
}
```

The TypeScript type introduced by a class is based on its shape (its properties and methods), while the value is the constructor.

There are many operators and keywords that mean different things in a type or value context. `typeof`, for instance:

```
type T1 = typeof jane;
//   ^? type T1 = Person
type T2 = typeof email;
//   ^? type T2 = (to: Person, subject: string, body: string) => Response

const v1 = typeof jane;  // Value is "object"
const v2 = typeof email;  // Value is "function"
```

In a type context, `typeof` takes a value and returns its TypeScript type. You can use these as part of a larger type expression, or use a `type` statement to give them a name.

In a value context, `typeof` is JavaScript's runtime `typeof` operator. It returns a string containing the runtime type of the symbol. This is *not* the same as the TypeScript type! JavaScript's runtime type system is much simpler than TypeScript's static type system. In contrast to the infinite variety of TypeScript types, JavaScript's `typeof` operator only has eight possible return values: `"string"`, `"number"`, `"boolean"`, `"undefined"`, `"object"`, `"function"`, `"symbol"`, and `"bigint"`.

The `[]` property accessor also has an identical-looking equivalent in type space. But be aware that while `obj['field']` and `obj.field` are equivalent in value space, they are not in type space. You must use the former to get the type of another type's property:

```
const first: Person['first'] = jane['first'];  // Or jane.first
//           ────                              ──────────── Values
//                    ──── ────                              Types
```

`Person['first']` is a *type* here since it appears in a type context (after a `:`). You can put any type in the index slot, including union types or primitive types:

```
type PersonEl = Person['first' | 'last'];
//   ^? type PersonEl = string
type Tuple = [string, number, Date];
type TupleEl = Tuple[number];
//   ^? type TupleEl = string | number | Date
```

See Item 15 for more on type operations and how to map between types.

There are many other constructs that have different meanings in the two spaces:

- `this` in value space is JavaScript's `this` keyword (Item 69). As a type, `this` is the TypeScript type of `this`, aka "polymorphic this." It's helpful for implementing method chains with subclasses.

- In value space, & and | are bitwise AND and OR. In type space they are the intersection and union operators.

- In value space, `const` introduces a new variable, but in type space, `as const` changes the inferred type of a literal or literal expression (Item 20).

- In value space, `extends` defines a subclass (`class A extends B`), but in type space it defines a subtype (`interface A extends B`) or a constraint on a generic type (`Generic<T extends number>`).

- In value space, "in" is used in `for` loops (`for (key in object)`), while in type space it's used in mapped types (Item 15).

- In value space, ! is JavaScript's logical not operator (`!x`), but in type space it's a non-null type assertion (`x!`; see Item 9).

If TypeScript doesn't seem to understand your code at all, it may be because of confusion around type and value space. For example, say you change the `email` function from earlier to take its arguments in a single object parameter (Item 38 explains why this is a good idea):

```
function email(options: {to: Person, subject: string, body: string}) {
  // ...
}
```

In JavaScript you can use destructuring assignment to create local variables for each property in the object:

```
function email({to, subject, body}) {
  // ...
}
```

If you try to do the same in TypeScript, you get some confusing errors:

```
function email({
  to: Person,
  //  ~~~~~~ Binding element 'Person' implicitly has an 'any' type
  subject: string,
  //       ~~~~~~ Binding element 'string' implicitly has an 'any' type
  body: string
  //    ~~~~~~ Binding element 'string' implicitly has an 'any' type
}) { /* ... */ }
```

The problem is that `Person` and `string` are being interpreted in a value context. You're trying to create a variable named `Person` and two variables named `string`. Instead, you should separate the types and values:

```
function email(
  {to, subject, body}: {to: Person, subject: string, body: string}
) {
  // ...
}
```

This is significantly more verbose, but in practice you may have a named type for the parameters or be able to infer them from context (Item 24).

While the similar constructs in type and value space can be confusing at first, they're eventually useful as a mnemonic once you get the hang of it.

Things to Remember

- Know how to tell whether you're in type space or value space while reading a TypeScript expression. Use the TypeScript playground to build an intuition for this.

- Every value has a static type, but this is only accessible in type space. Type space constructs such as `type` and `interface` are erased and are not accessible in value space.

- Some constructs, such as `class` or `enum`, introduce both a type and a value.

- `typeof`, `this`, and many other operators and keywords have different meanings in type space and value space.

Item 9: Prefer Type Annotations to Type Assertions

TypeScript seems to have two ways of assigning a value to a variable and giving it a type:

```
interface Person { name: string };

const alice: Person = { name: 'Alice' };
//    ^? const alice: Person
const bob = { name: 'Bob' } as Person;
//    ^? const bob: Person
```

While these achieve similar ends, they are actually quite different! The first (`alice: Person`) adds a *type annotation* to the variable and ensures that the value conforms to the type. The latter (`as Person`) performs a *type assertion*. This tells TypeScript that, despite the type it inferred, you know better and would like the type to be `Person`.

In general, you should prefer type annotations to type assertions. Here's why:

```
const alice: Person = {};
//    ~~~~~ Property 'name' is missing in type '{}' but required in type 'Person'
const bob = {} as Person;  // No error
```

The type annotation verifies that the value conforms to the interface. Since it does not, TypeScript flags an error. The type assertion silences this error by telling the type checker that, for whatever reason, you know better than it does.

The same thing happens if you specify an additional property:

```
const alice: Person = {
  name: 'Alice',
  occupation: 'TypeScript developer'
// ~~~~~~~~~~ Object literal may only specify known properties,
//            and 'occupation' does not exist in type 'Person'
};
const bob = {
  name: 'Bob',
  occupation: 'JavaScript developer'
} as Person;  // No error
```

While undeclared properties are valid from a structural typing perspective (Item 4), they are often mistakes. TypeScript has an additional tool known as *excess property checking* that flags extra properties in objects with declared types, but it doesn't apply if you use an assertion. Item 11 will have much more to say about excess property checking.

Because they provide additional safety checks, you should use type annotations unless you have a specific reason to use a type assertion.

 You may also see code that looks like const bob = <Person>{}. This was the original syntax for assertions and is equivalent to {} as Person. It is less common now because <Person> is interpreted as a start tag in *.tsx* files (TypeScript + React).

It can be tricky to use a type annotation with arrow functions. What if you wanted to use the named Person interface in this code?

```
const people = ['alice', 'bob', 'jan'].map(name => ({name}));
// { name: string; }[]... but we want Person[]
```

It's tempting to use a type assertion here, and it seems to solve the problem:

```
const people = ['alice', 'bob', 'jan'].map(
  name => ({name} as Person)
); // Type is Person[]
```

But this suffers from all the same issues as a more direct use of type assertions. For example:

```
const people = ['alice', 'bob', 'jan'].map(name => ({} as Person));
// No error
```

So how do you use a type annotation in this context instead? The most straightforward way is to declare a variable in the arrow function:

```
const people = ['alice', 'bob', 'jan'].map(name => {
  const person: Person = {name};
  return person
}); // Type is Person[]
```

But this introduces considerable noise compared to the original code. A more concise way is to annotate the return type of the arrow function:

```
const people = ['alice', 'bob', 'jan'].map(
  (name): Person => ({name})
); // Type is Person[]
```

This performs all the same checks on the value as the previous version. The parentheses are significant here! (name): Person allows the type of name to be inferred and specifies that the return type should be Person. But (name: Person) would specify that the type of name is Person while allowing the return type to be inferred, which would produce an error. See Item 24 for more about how type inference works with function parameters.

In this case you could have also written the final desired type and let TypeScript check the validity of the assignment:

```
const people: Person[] = ['alice', 'bob', 'jan'].map(name => ({name})); // OK
```

But in the context of a longer chain of function calls, it may be necessary or desirable to have the named type in place earlier. And it will help flag errors close to where they occur.

So when *should* you use a type assertion? Type assertions make the most sense when you truly do know more about a type than TypeScript does, typically from context that isn't available to the type checker. If you're working in a browser, for instance, you may know the type of a DOM element more precisely than TypeScript does:

```
document.querySelector('#myButton')?.addEventListener('click', e => {
  e.currentTarget
  // ^? (property) Event.currentTarget: EventTarget | null
  // currentTarget is #myButton is a button element
  const button = e.currentTarget as HTMLButtonElement;
  //    ^? const button: HTMLButtonElement
});
```

Because TypeScript doesn't have access to the DOM of your page, it has no way of knowing that #myButton is a button element. And it doesn't know that the current Target of the event should be that same button. Since you have information that TypeScript does not, a type assertion makes sense here. For more on DOM types, see Item 75.

When you use a type assertion, it's a good idea to include an explanation of why it's valid in a comment. This provides the missing information for human readers and will help them evaluate whether the assertion is still justified.

What if a variable's type includes null but you know from context that this isn't possible? You can use a type assertion to remove null from a type:

```
const elNull = document.getElementById('foo');
//    ^? const elNull: HTMLElement | null
const el = document.getElementById('foo') as HTMLElement;
//    ^? const el: HTMLElement
```

This sort of type assertion is so common that it gets a special syntax and is known as a *non-null assertion*:

```
const el = document.getElementById('foo')!;
//    ^? const el: HTMLElement
```

Used as a prefix, ! is JavaScript's logical not operator. But as a suffix, ! is interpreted as a type assertion that the value is non-null. This is an improvement over as because it allows the non-null part of the type to pass through unaltered.

Still, you should treat ! with as much caution as any other assertion: it is erased during compilation, so you should only use it if you have information that the type checker lacks and can ensure that the value is non-null. If you can't, you should use a conditional to check for the null case.

If you're accessing a property or method on an object that might be null, it can be convenient to use the "optional chaining" operator, ?.:

```
document.getElementById('foo')?.addEventListener('click', () => {
  alert('Hi there!');
});
```

This has some superficial resemblance to !. but it's quite different. a?.b is a Java-Script construct that checks if the object is null (or undefined) at runtime before continuing to evaluate the expression. a!.b is a type-level construct that compiles to just a.b. If the object is null at runtime, it will throw an exception. a?.b is safer than a!.b, but don't go too crazy with it. If it's essential for your application to add an event listener, then you probably want to know if it fails!

Type assertions have their limits: they don't let you convert between arbitrary types. The general rule is that you can use a type assertion to convert between A and B if they are "comparable" to one another. Using the set terminology from Item 7, this means that A and B must have a non-empty intersection. In particular, subtypes are allowed. `HTMLElement` is a subtype of `HTMLElement | null`, so this type assertion is OK. (The intersection of these types is `HTMLElement`.) `HTMLButtonElement` is a subtype of `EventTarget`, so that is OK, too. And `Person` is a subtype of `{}`, so that assertion is also fine.

But you can't convert between a `Person` and an `HTMLElement` since their intersection is empty (i.e., the `never` type):

```
interface Person { name: string; }
const body = document.body;
const el = body as Person;
//         ~~~~~~~~~~~~~~~
// Conversion of type 'HTMLElement' to type 'Person' may be a mistake because
// neither type sufficiently overlaps with the other. If this was intentional,
// convert the expression to 'unknown' first.
```

The error suggests an escape hatch, namely, using the unknown type (Item 46). Every type is a subtype of unknown, so assertions involving unknown are always OK. This lets you convert between arbitrary types, but at least you're being explicit that you're doing something suspicious!

```
const el = document.body as unknown as Person;  // OK
```

Not every type assertion uses the keyword `as`. Item 22 explains "user-defined type guards" (`is`), which allow you to associate some logic with a type assertion to check whether it's valid. It's also possible to use generic type inference to assert a type, but this is a bad idea since it's easy to convince yourself that TypeScript is checking your types when it's really not. This pattern ("return-only generics") is explored in Item 51.

Type assertions are sometimes called "casts." This terminology is misleading, however, and is best avoided. In languages like C, a cast can change a value at runtime (say from an `int` to a `float`). Type assertions cannot do this. They are type-level constructs that are erased at runtime. They don't change a value. Rather, they "assert" something that is already true about it.

Finally, there's `as const`. While this looks like a type assertion, it's more properly called a "const context." While `as T` should make you suspicious, `as const` makes types more precise and is completely safe. Item 24 shows how you can use const contexts to improve type inference.

Things to Remember

- Prefer type annotations (`: Type`) to type assertions (`as Type`).
- Know how to annotate the return type of an arrow function.

- Use type assertions and non-null assertions only when you know something about types that TypeScript does not.

- When you use a type assertion, include a comment explaining why it's valid.

Item 10: Avoid Object Wrapper Types (String, Number, Boolean, Symbol, BigInt)

In addition to objects, JavaScript has seven types of primitive values: strings, numbers, booleans, `null`, `undefined`, symbol, and bigint. The first five have been around since the beginning. The symbol primitive was added in ES2015, and bigint joined the family with ES2020.

Primitives are distinguished from objects by being immutable and not having methods. You might object that strings *do* have methods:

```
> 'primitive'.charAt(3)
'm'
```

But things are not quite as they seem. There's actually something surprising and subtle going on here. While a string *primitive* does not have methods, JavaScript also defines a `String` *object* type that does. JavaScript freely converts between these types. When you access a method like `charAt` on a string primitive, JavaScript wraps it in a `String` object, calls the method, and then throws the object away.

You can observe this if you monkey-patch `String.prototype` (Item 47):

```
// Don't do this!
const originalCharAt = String.prototype.charAt;
String.prototype.charAt = function(pos) {
  console.log(this, typeof this, pos);
  return originalCharAt.call(this, pos);
};
console.log('primitive'.charAt(3));
```

This produces the following output:

```
[String: 'primitive'] object 3
m
```

The `this` value in the method is a `String` object wrapper, not a string primitive. You can instantiate a `String` object directly and it will sometimes behave like a string primitive. But not always. For example, a `String` object is only ever equal to itself:

```
> "hello" === new String("hello")
false
> new String("hello") === new String("hello")
false
```

The implicit conversion to object wrapper types explains an odd phenomenon in JavaScript—if you assign a property to a primitive, it disappears:

```
> x = "hello"
'hello'
> x.language = 'English'
'English'
> x.language
undefined
```

Now you know the explanation: x is converted to a String instance, the language property is set on that, and then the object (with its language property) is thrown away.

There are object wrapper types for the other primitives as well: Number for numbers, Boolean for booleans, Symbol for symbols, and BigInt for bigints (there are no object wrappers for null and undefined).

These wrapper types exist as a convenience to provide methods on the primitive values and to provide static methods (e.g., String.fromCharCode). But there's usually no reason to instantiate them directly.

TypeScript models this distinction by having distinct types for the primitives and their object wrappers:

- string and String
- number and Number
- boolean and Boolean
- symbol and Symbol
- bigint and BigInt

It's easy to inadvertently type String (especially if you're coming from Java or C#), and it even seems to work, at least initially:

```
function getStringLen(foo: String) {
  return foo.length;
}

getStringLen("hello");  // OK
getStringLen(new String("hello"));  // OK
```

But things go awry when you try to pass a String object to a method that expects a string:

```
function isGreeting(phrase: String) {
  return ['hello', 'good day'].includes(phrase);
  //                                    ~~~~~~
  // Argument of type 'String' is not assignable to parameter of type 'string'.
```

```
  // 'string' is a primitive, but 'String' is a wrapper object.
  // Prefer using 'string' when possible.
}
```

So `string` is assignable to `String`, but `String` is not assignable to `string`. Confusing? Follow the advice in the error message and stick with `string`. All the type declarations that ship with TypeScript use it, as do the typings for almost all other libraries.

Another way you can wind up with wrapper objects is if you provide an **explicit type** annotation with a capital letter:

```
const s: String = "primitive";
const n: Number = 12;
const b: Boolean = true;
```

This only changes the TypeScript types and, as Item 3 explained, this can't affect the runtime values. They are still primitives, not objects. But TypeScript permits these declarations because the primitive types are assignable to the object wrappers. These annotations are both misleading and redundant (Item 18). Better to stick with the primitive types.

As a final note, it's fine to call `BigInt` and `Symbol` without `new`, since these create primitives:

```
> typeof BigInt(1234)
'bigint'
> typeof Symbol('sym')
'symbol'
```

These are the `BigInt` and `Symbol` *values*, not the TypeScript types (Item 8). Calling them results in values of type `bigint` and `symbol`. You can construct a `bigint` directly by putting an "n" at the end of a numeric literal: 123n.

If you use `typescript-eslint` in your project, the `ban-types` rule prohibits the use of object wrapper types. This is enabled with the `@typescript-eslint/recommended` configuration.

Things to Remember

- Avoid TypeScript object wrapper types. Use the primitive types instead: `string` instead of `String`, `number` instead of `Number`, `boolean` instead of `Boolean`, `symbol` instead of `Symbol`, and `bigint` instead of `BigInt`.

- Understand how object wrapper types are used to provide methods on primitive values. Avoid instantiating them or using them directly, with the exception of `Symbol` and `BigInt`.

Item 11: Distinguish Excess Property Checking from Type Checking

When you assign an object literal to a variable with a declared type, TypeScript makes sure it has the properties of that type *and no others*:

```
interface Room {
  numDoors: number;
  ceilingHeightFt: number;
}
const r: Room = {
  numDoors: 1,
  ceilingHeightFt: 10,
  elephant: 'present',
// ~~~~~~~ Object literal may only specify known properties,
//         and 'elephant' does not exist in type 'Room'
};
```

While it is odd that there's an `elephant` property, this error doesn't make much sense from a structural typing point of view (Item 4). That constant *is* assignable to the Room type, which you can see by introducing an intermediate variable:

```
const obj = {
  numDoors: 1,
  ceilingHeightFt: 10,
  elephant: 'present',
};
const r: Room = obj;  // OK
```

The type of `obj` is inferred as { `numDoors: number; ceilingHeightFt: number;` `elephant: string` }. This type includes a subset of the values in the Room type because it only permits `string` elephants, whereas Room would permit any type of elephant. Hence it is assignable to Room, and the code passes the type checker. (If the term "subset" is unfamiliar, head over to Item 7 for a refresher.)

So what's different about these two examples? In the first you've triggered a process known as "excess property checking," which helps catch an important class of errors that the structural type system would otherwise miss. But this process has its limits, and conflating it with regular assignability checks can make it harder to build an intuition for structural typing. Recognizing excess property checking as a distinct process will help you build a clearer mental model of TypeScript's type system.

As Item 1 explained, TypeScript goes beyond trying to flag code that will throw exceptions at runtime. It also tries to find code that doesn't do what you intend. Here's an example of the latter:

```
interface Options {
  title: string;
  darkMode?: boolean;
```

```
  }
  function createWindow(options: Options) {
    if (options.darkMode) {
      setDarkMode();
    }
    // ...
  }
  createWindow({
    title: 'Spider Solitaire',
    darkmode: true
  // ~~~~~~ Object literal may only specify known properties,
  //        but 'darkmode' does not exist in type 'Options'.
  //        Did you mean to write 'darkMode'?
  });
```

This code doesn't throw any sort of error at runtime. But it's also unlikely to do what you intended for the exact reason that TypeScript says: it should be darkMode (capital M), not darkmode.

A purely structural type checker wouldn't be able to spot this sort of error because the Options type is incredibly broad: it includes all objects with a title property that's a string and *any other properties*, so long as those don't include a darkMode property set to something other than true or false.

It's easy to forget how expansive TypeScript types can be. Here are a few more values that are assignable to Options:

```
  const o1: Options = document;  // OK
  const o2: Options = new HTMLAnchorElement();  // OK
```

Both document and instances of HTMLAnchorElement have title properties that are strings, so these assignments are allowed. Options is a broad type indeed!

Excess property checking tries to rein this in without compromising the fundamentally structural nature of the type system. It does this by disallowing unknown properties on object literals when they're used in a context with a declared type. (It's sometimes called "strict object literal checking" for this reason, or "freshness" because it applies to freshly created objects.)

This context could be an assignment to a variable with a declared type, a function argument, or the return value of a function with a declared return type. Neither document nor new HTMLAnchorElement is an object literal, so they did not trigger excess property checking. But the {title, darkmode} object is, so it does:

```
  const o: Options = { darkmode: true, title: 'Ski Free' };
                  // ~~~~~~~~~ 'darkmode' does not exist in type 'Options'...
```

This explains why using an intermediate variable without a type annotation makes the error go away:

```
const intermediate = { darkmode: true, title: 'Ski Free' };
const o: Options = intermediate;  // OK
```

While the righthand side of the first line is an object literal, the righthand side of the second line (`intermediate`) is not, so excess property checking does not apply, and the error goes away.

Excess property checking does not happen when you use a type assertion:

```
const o = { darkmode: true, title: 'MS Hearts' } as Options;  // OK
```

This is a good reason to prefer type annotations to assertions (Item 9).

If you don't want this sort of check, you can tell TypeScript to expect additional properties using an index signature:

```
interface Options {
  darkMode?: boolean;
  [otherOptions: string]: unknown;
}
const o: Options = { darkmode: true };  // OK
```

Item 16 discusses when this is and is not an appropriate way to model your data.

A related check happens for so-called "weak" types, which have *only* optional properties:

```
interface LineChartOptions {
  logscale?: boolean;
  invertedYAxis?: boolean;
  areaChart?: boolean;
}
function setOptions(options: LineChartOptions) { /* ... */ }

const opts = { logScale: true };
setOptions(opts);
//          ~~~~ Type '{ logScale: boolean; }' has no properties in common
//               with type 'LineChartOptions'
```

From a structural point of view, the `LineChartOptions` type should include almost all objects. For "weak" types like this, TypeScript adds another check to make sure that the value type and declared type have at least one property in common. Much like excess property checking, this is effective at catching typos and isn't strictly structural. But unlike excess property checking, it happens during all assignability checks involving weak types. Factoring out an intermediate variable doesn't bypass this check.

 In TypeScript, "weak type" is a technical term that specifically refers to interfaces with only optional properties. It has nothing to do with the merits of your type, and the opposite of a "weak type" is not a "strong type," a term that has no specific meaning in TypeScript or programming languages in general.

Excess property checking is an effective way of catching typos and other mistakes in property names that would otherwise be allowed by the structural typing system. It's particularly useful with types like Options that contain optional fields. But it is also very limited in scope: it only applies to object literals. Recognize this limitation, and distinguish between excess property checking and ordinary assignability checking. This will help you build a mental model of both.

For a concrete example of how excess property checking can catch bugs and open up new design possibilities, see Item 61.

Things to Remember

- When you assign an object literal to a variable with a known type or pass it as an argument to a function, it undergoes excess property checking.
- Excess property checking is an effective way to find errors, but it is distinct from the usual structural assignability checks done by the TypeScript type checker. Conflating these processes will make it harder for you to build a mental model of assignability. TypeScript types are not "closed" (Item 4).
- Be aware of the limits of excess property checking: introducing an intermediate variable will remove these checks.
- A "weak type" is an object type with only optional properties. For these types, assignability checks require at least one matching property.

Item 12: Apply Types to Entire Function Expressions When Possible

JavaScript (and TypeScript) distinguishes between a function *statement* and a function *expression*:

```
function rollDice1(sides: number): number { /* ... */ }  // Statement
const rollDice2 = function(sides: number): number { /* ... */ };  // Expression
const rollDice3 = (sides: number): number => { /* ... */ };  // Also expression
```

An advantage of function expressions in TypeScript is that you can apply a type declaration to the entire function at once, rather than specifying the types of the parameters and return type individually:

```
type DiceRollFn = (sides: number) => number;
const rollDice: DiceRollFn = sides => { /* ... */ };
```

If you mouse over sides in your editor, you'll see that TypeScript knows its type is number. The function type doesn't provide much value in such a short example, but the technique does open up a number of possibilities.

One is reducing repetition. If you wanted to write several functions for doing arithmetic on numbers, for instance, you could write them like this:

```
function add(a: number, b: number) { return a + b; }
function sub(a: number, b: number) { return a - b; }
function mul(a: number, b: number) { return a * b; }
function div(a: number, b: number) { return a / b; }
```

or consolidate the repeated function signatures with a single function type:

```
type BinaryFn = (a: number, b: number) => number;
const add: BinaryFn = (a, b) => a + b;
const sub: BinaryFn = (a, b) => a - b;
const mul: BinaryFn = (a, b) => a * b;
const div: BinaryFn = (a, b) => a / b;
```

This has fewer type annotations than before, and they're separated away from the function implementations. This makes the logic more apparent. You've also gained a check that the return type of all the function expressions is number.

Libraries often provide types for common function signatures. For example, the React typings provide a MouseEventHandler type that you can apply to an entire function rather than specifying MouseEvent as a type for the function's parameter. If you're a library author, consider providing type declarations for common callbacks.

Another situation in which you should apply a type to a function expression is to match the signature of some other function. In a web browser, for example, the fetch function issues an HTTP request:

```
const response = fetch('/quote?by=Mark+Twain');
//    ^? const response: Promise<Response>
```

You extract data from the response via response.json() or response.text():

```
async function getQuote() {
  const response = await fetch('/quote?by=Mark+Twain');
  const quote = await response.json();
  return quote;
}
// {
//   "quote": "If you tell the truth, you don't have to remember anything.",
//   "source": "notebook",
//   "date": "1894"
// }
```

(See Item 27 for more on Promises and async/await.)

There's a bug here: if the request for /quote fails, the response body is likely to contain an explanation like "404 Not Found." This isn't JSON, so response.json() will return a rejected Promise with a message about invalid JSON. This obscures the real error, which was a 404.

It's easy to forget that an error response with fetch does not result in a rejected Promise. Let's write a checkedFetch function to do the status check for us. The type declarations for fetch in *lib.dom.d.ts* look like this:

```
declare function fetch(
  input: RequestInfo, init?: RequestInit,
): Promise<Response>;
```

So you can write checkedFetch like this:

```
async function checkedFetch(input: RequestInfo, init?: RequestInit) {
  const response = await fetch(input, init);
  if (!response.ok) {
    // An exception becomes a rejected Promise in an async function.
    throw new Error(`Request failed: ${response.status}`);
  }
  return response;
}
```

This works, but it can be written more concisely:

```
const checkedFetch: typeof fetch = async (input, init) => {
  const response = await fetch(input, init);
  if (!response.ok) {
    throw new Error(`Request failed: ${response.status}`);
  }
  return response;
}
```

We've changed from a function statement to a function expression and applied a type (typeof fetch) to the entire function. This allows TypeScript to infer the types of the input and init parameters.

The type annotation also guarantees that the return type of checkedFetch will be the same as that of fetch. Had you written return instead of throw, for example, Type-Script would have caught the mistake:

```
const checkedFetch: typeof fetch = async (input, init) => {
  //    ~~~~~~~~~~~~
  //    'Promise<Response | HTTPError>' is not assignable to 'Promise<Response>'
  //       Type 'Response | HTTPError' is not assignable to type 'Response'
  const response = await fetch(input, init);
  if (!response.ok) {
    return new Error('Request failed: ' + response.status);
  }
  return response;
}
```

The same mistake in the first example would likely have led to an error, but in the code that called checkedFetch, rather than in the implementation. In addition to being more concise, typing this entire function expression instead of its parameters has given you better safety.

What if you want to match the parameter types of another function but change the return type? This is possible using a rest parameter and the built-in `Parameters` utility type:

```
async function fetchANumber(
    ...args: Parameters<typeof fetch>
): Promise<number> {
  const response = await checkedFetch(...args);
  const num = Number(await response.text());
  if (isNaN(num)) {
    throw new Error(`Response was not a number.`);
  }
  return num;
}
```

If you inspect `fetchANumber` in your editor, you'll see that `args` doesn't appear at all. It's replaced by the parameter names for `fetch`, which is exactly what you want:

```
fetchANumber
// ^? function fetchANumber(
//       input: RequestInfo | URL, init?: RequestInit | undefined
//     ): Promise<number>
```

The syntax here is a bit more cumbersome than applying a type to an entire function. Use your judgment on whether it would be better to just write out the parameter types. Item 62 will discuss rest parameters in the context of generic types.

While you may or may not be aware of it, you benefit from this technique whenever you pass a callback to another function. When you use the `map` or `filter` method of an `Array`, for example, TypeScript is able to infer a type for the callback parameter, and it applies that type to your function expression. For more on how context is used in type inference, see Item 24.

When you're writing a function that has the same type signature as another one, or writing many functions with the same type signature, consider whether you can apply a type declaration to entire functions, rather than repeating types of parameters and return values. The words "many" and "repeating" are important here. Don't take this to extremes! You don't need to factor out a type for every function. For the common case of a single, standalone function with a distinct type signature, an old-fashioned function statement is just fine. Use function types when there are many functions with the same or related type signatures.

Things to Remember

- Consider applying type annotations to entire function expressions, rather than to their parameters and return type.
- If you're writing the same type signature repeatedly, factor out a function type or look for an existing one.

- If you're a library author, provide types for common callbacks.

- Use `typeof fn` to match the signature of another function, or `Parameters` and a rest parameter if you need to change the return type.

Item 13: Know the Differences Between type and interface

If you want to define a named type in TypeScript, you have two options. You can use a type alias, as shown here:

```
type TState = {
  name: string;
  capital: string;
};
```

or define an `interface`:

```
interface IState {
  name: string;
  capital: string;
}
```

(You could also use a `class`, but that is a JavaScript runtime concept that also introduces a value. See Item 8.)

Which should you use, `type` or `interface`? The line between these two options has become increasingly blurred over the years, to the point that in most situations you can use either. You should be aware of the distinctions that remain between `type` and `interface` and be consistent about which you use in which situation. But you should also know how to write the same types using both, so that you'll be comfortable reading TypeScript that uses either.

For new code where you need to pick a style, the general rule of thumb is to use `interface` where possible, using `type` either where it's required (e.g., union types) or has a cleaner syntax (e.g., function types). We'll get to the arguments for this toward the end of this item, but for now let's explore the similarities and differences between these two constructs.

 The examples in this item prefix type names with I or T solely to indicate how they were defined. You should not do this in your code! Prefixing interface types with I is common in C#, and this convention made some inroads in the early days of TypeScript. But it is considered bad style today because it's unnecessary, adds little value, and is not consistently followed in the standard libraries.

First, the similarities: the two State types are nearly indistinguishable from one another. If you define an IState or a TState value with an extra property, the errors you get from excess property checking (Item 11) are character-by-character identical:

```
const wyoming: TState = {
  name: 'Wyoming',
  capital: 'Cheyenne',
  population: 578_000
// ~~~~~~~ Object literal may only specify known properties,
//         and 'population' does not exist in type 'TState'
};
```

You can use an index signature with both interface and type:

```
type TDict = { [key: string]: string };
interface IDict {
  [key: string]: string;
}
```

You can also define function types with either:

```
type TFn = (x: number) => string;
interface IFn {
  (x: number): string;
}
type TFnAlt = {
  (x: number): string;
};

const toStrT: TFn = x => '' + x;  // OK
const toStrI: IFn = x => '' + x;  // OK
const toStrTAlt: TFnAlt = x => '' + x;  // OK
```

The first type alias form (TFn) looks more natural and is more concise for function types. This is the preferred form and is the one you're most likely to encounter in type declarations. The latter two forms reflect the fact that functions in JavaScript are callable objects. They are sometimes useful with overloaded function signatures (Item 52).

Both type aliases and interfaces can be generic:

```
type TBox<T> = {
  value: T;
};
interface IBox<T> {
  value: T;
}
```

An `interface` can extend a `type` (with some caveats, explained momentarily), and a `type` can extend an `interface`:

```
interface IStateWithPop extends TState {
  population: number;
}
type TStateWithPop = IState & { population: number; };
```

Again, these types are identical. The caveat is that an `interface` can only extend object types that could have been defined with `interface` (even if you happened to define them with `type`). You can't extend a union type, for example. If you want to do that, you'll need to use `type` and &.

A `class` can implement either an `interface` or a simple type:

```
class StateT implements TState {
  name: string = '';
  capital: string = '';
}
class StateI implements IState {
  name: string = '';
  capital: string = '';
}
```

Finally, both `type` and `interface` can be recursive (Item 57).

Those are the similarities. What about the differences? You've seen one already—there are union `types` but no union `interfaces`:

```
type AorB = 'a' | 'b';
```

An `interface` can extend some `types`, but not this one. Extending union types can sometimes be useful. If you have separate types for `Input` and `Output` variables and a mapping from name to variable:

```
type Input = { /* ... */ };
type Output = { /* ... */ };
interface VariableMap {
  [name: string]: Input | Output;
}
```

then you might want a type that attaches the name to the variable. This would be:

```
type NamedVariable = (Input | Output) & { name: string };
```

This type cannot be expressed with `interface`. A `type` is, in general, more capable than an `interface`. It can be a union, and it can also take advantage of fancy type-level features like mapped types (Item 15) and conditional types (Item 52).

`interface` and `extends` give a bit more error checking than `type` and `&`:

```
interface Person {
  name: string;
  age: string;
}

type TPerson = Person & { age: number; };  // no error, unusable type

interface IPerson extends Person {
  //         ~~~~~~ Interface 'IPerson' incorrectly extends interface 'Person'.
  //                Types of property 'age' are incompatible.
  //                  Type 'number' is not assignable to type 'string'.
  age: number;
}
```

It's fine to change the type of a property in a subtype, so long it's compatible with the base type (see Item 7). Generally you want more safety checks, so this is a good reason to use `extends` with `interfaces`.

Type aliases are the natural way to express tuple and array types:

```
type Pair = [a: number, b: number];
type StringList = string[];
type NamedNums = [string, ...number[]];
```

An `interface` does have some abilities that a `type` doesn't, however. One of these is that an `interface` can be *augmented*. Going back to the `State` example, you could have added a `population` field in another way:

```
interface IState {
  name: string;
  capital: string;
}
interface IState {
  population: number;
}
const wyoming: IState = {
  name: 'Wyoming',
  capital: 'Cheyenne',
  population: 578_000
}; // OK
```

This is known as "declaration merging," and it's quite surprising if you've never seen it before. This is primarily used with type declaration files (Chapter 8), and if you're writing one, you should follow the norms and use `interface` to support it. The idea is that there may be gaps in your type declarations that users need to fill, and this is how they do it. (Item 71 walks you through this process.)

To understand why this unusual feature is useful, it's instructive to look at how Type-Script itself uses declaration merging to model the different versions of JavaScript's standard library. The Array interface, for example, is defined in *lib.es5.d.ts*:

```
// lib.es5.d.ts
interface Array<T> {
  /** Gets or sets the length of the array. */
  length: number;
  // ...
  [n: number]: T;
}
```

If you set target to ES5 in your *tsconfig.json* (Item 2), then this is all you get. This definition includes all the properties and methods that were available on arrays when ES5 was published in 2009. But if you target ES2015, TypeScript will also include *lib.es2015.core.d.ts*. This includes another declaration of the Array interface:

```
// lib.es2015.core.d.ts
interface Array<T> {
  /** Returns the index of the first element in the array where predicate... */
  findIndex(
    predicate: (value: T, index: number, obj: T[]) => unknown,
    thisArg?: any
  ): number;

  // ... also find, fill, copyWithin
}
```

This declaration includes just the four new Array methods that were added in ES2015: find, findIndex, fill, and copyWithin. They get added to the ES5 Array interface via declaration merging. The net effect is that you get a single Array type with exactly the right methods for the version of JavaScript that you're targeting.

As the name implies, declaration merging makes the most sense in declaration files. It *can* happen in user code, but only if the two interfaces are defined in the same module (i.e., the same *.ts* file). This prevents accidental collisions with global interfaces with generic-sounding names like Location and FormData.

Another difference is that TypeScript will always try to refer to an interface by its name, whereas it takes more liberties replacing a type alias with its underlying definition. You'll sometimes see this in error messages and type display (Item 56) but it can also affect concrete outputs such as *.d.ts* files, which TypeScript will emit if you set declaration: true in your *tsconfig.json*.

For example, consider this function which returns an object statically typed using a type alias with a limited scope:

```
export function getHummer() {
  type Hummingbird = { name: string; weightGrams: number; };
  const ruby: Hummingbird = { name: 'Ruby-throated', weightGrams: 3.4 };
```

```
    return ruby;
  };

const rubyThroat = getHummer();
//     ^? const rubyThroat: Hummingbird
```

It's interesting that TypeScript reports the type here using an out-of-scope type name (Hummingbird). Even more interesting is what happens when you generate a *.d.ts* file for this code:

```
// get-hummer.d.ts
export declare function getHummer(): {
  name: string;
  weightGrams: number;
};
```

Since there's no function body in which to define the type alias (this is a type declaration file), TypeScript has elected to inline the type alias. The name is gone and only the structure remains. Because the type system is structural (Item 4) this has no effect on the values assignable to the type. But it does affect the display, and it affects the generated *.d.ts* file. In some cases, this inlining behavior can cause duplication of types extreme enough to affect compiler performance (Item 78).

Here's what happens if you use an interface instead:

```
export function getHummer() {
  //          ~~~~~~~~~
  // Return type of exported function has or is using private name 'Hummingbird'.
  interface Hummingbird { name: string; weightGrams: number; };
  const bee: Hummingbird = { name: 'Bee Hummingbird', weightGrams: 2.3 };
  return bee;
};
```

Because Hummingbird is an interface, TypeScript wants to refer to it by name. But the name isn't available in the type declaration file, hence the error.[1] While the inlining behavior may initially seem preferable here, it can lead to massive types and, as Item 67 explains, it's generally better to export your types anyway. The better solution here is to keep the interface and make it a top-level export.

Returning to the question at the start of the item, should you use type or interface? For complex types, you have no choice: you need to use a type alias. And for function types, tuple types, and array types, the type syntax is more concise and natural than the interface syntax. But what about simpler object types that can be represented either way?

---

1 If you don't see this error, make sure to set declaration: true set in your *tsconfig.json*.

If you're working in a codebase with an established style, stick with that. You probably won't go too wrong.

For a new project without an established style, prefer interface. Your type name will appear more consistently in error messages and type display, and you'll get more checks that you extend other interfaces correctly. Here's what the official TypeScript handbook has to say:

> For the most part, you can choose based on personal preference, and TypeScript will tell you if it needs something to be the other kind of declaration. If you would like a heuristic, use interface until you need to use features from type.

In other words, use interface when you can and type when you must, or when it's more ergonomic. But don't sweat it too much either way.

You can enforce consistent use of type or interface using typescript-eslint's consistent-type-definitions rule, which is part of the stylistic preset (it prefers interface by default).

Things to Remember

- Understand the differences and similarities between type and interface.
- Know how to write the same types using either syntax.
- Be aware of declaration merging for interface and type inlining for type.
- For projects without an established style, prefer interface to type for object types.

Item 14: Use readonly to Avoid Errors Associated with Mutation

Here's some code to print the triangular numbers (1, 1 + 2 = 3, 1 + 2 + 3 = 6, etc.):

```
function printTriangles(n: number) {
  const nums = [];
  for (let i = 0; i < n; i++) {
    nums.push(i);
    console.log(arraySum(nums));
  }
}
```

(We'll get to the definition of arraySum shortly.)

This code appears straightforward, if inefficient, but here's what happens when you run it:

```
> printTriangles(5);
0
1
2
3
4
```

Whoops! Those aren't the numbers we were expecting. What went wrong? Let's take a look at my implementation of arraySum:

```
function arraySum(arr: number[]) {
  let sum = 0, num;
  while ((num = arr.pop()) !== undefined) {
    sum += num;
  }
  return sum;
}
```

This function does calculate the sum of the numbers in the array. But it also has the side effect of emptying the array! TypeScript is fine with this, because JavaScript arrays are mutable. The problem is that printTriangles made an assumption about arraySum, namely that it doesn't modify nums.

Mutation is the root cause of many hard-to-find bugs. Mutable is the default in JavaScript, but TypeScript's readonly modifier can help you catch and prevent surprise mutations. Because it can prevent such a pernicious set of bugs, it's worth learning how to use this feature in your own code.

JavaScript primitives are already immutable. There are no methods on string, number, or boolean that will mutate these values. (You may reassign a variable declared with let to another primitive, but you are not changing the primitive value itself.)

As you saw with the destructive arraySum function, arrays (and objects) very much *are* mutable. This is where TypeScript's readonly modifier comes in.

Placed on a property in an object type, readonly prevents assignments to that property:

```
interface PartlyMutableName {
  readonly first: string;
  last: string;
}

const jackie: PartlyMutableName = { first: 'Jacqueline', last: 'Kennedy' };
jackie.last = 'Onassis';  // OK
jackie.first = 'Jacky';
//      ~~~~~ Cannot assign to 'first' because it is a read-only property.
```

Typically, you'll want to prevent assignments to *all* properties on an object. TypeScript provides a generic utility type, Readonly<T>, that does just that:

```
interface FullyMutableName {
  first: string;
  last: string;
}
type FullyImmutableName = Readonly<FullyMutableName>;
//   ^? type FullyImmutableName = {
//         readonly first: string;
//         readonly last: string;
//      }
```

(Focus on the readonlys: the change from interface to type isn't important here.)

If a function takes an object as a parameter and doesn't modify it, it's a good idea to wrap that type in Readonly to advertise this to callers and enforce it in the implementation.

There are two important caveats to know about with the readonly property modifier and Readonly<T>. The first is that they are shallow. Just like a const declaration, a readonly property cannot be reassigned but it can be mutated:

```
interface Outer {
  inner: {
    x: number;
  }
}
const obj: Readonly<Outer> = { inner: { x: 0 }};
obj.inner = { x: 1 };
//  ~~~~ Cannot assign to 'inner' because it is a read-only property
obj.inner.x = 1;  // OK
```

You can create a type alias and then inspect it in your editor to see exactly what's happening:

```
type T = Readonly<Outer>;
//   ^? type T = {
//         readonly inner: {
//            x: number;
//         };
//      }
```

The important thing to note is that there's a readonly modifier on inner but not on x. There is no built-in support for deep readonly types, but it is possible to write a generic type to produce them. Getting this right is tricky, so I recommend using a library rather than rolling your own. The DeepReadonly generic in ts-essentials is one implementation.

The second caveat about Readonly is that it only affects properties. If you apply it to a type with methods that mutate the underlying object, it won't remove them:

```
const date: Readonly<Date> = new Date();
date.setFullYear(2037);  // OK, but mutates date!
```

If you want both a mutable and immutable version of a class, you'll generally need to separate them yourself. A great example of this in the standard library is the Array and ReadonlyArray interfaces. Here's what Array<T> looks like (in *lib.es5.d.ts*):

```
interface Array<T> {
  length: number;
  // (non-mutating methods)
  toString(): string;
  join(separator?: string): string;
  // ...
  // (mutating methods)
  pop(): T | undefined;
  shift(): T | undefined;
  // ...
  [n: number]: T;
}
```

And here's the corresponding immutable version, ReadonlyArray<T>:

```
interface ReadonlyArray<T> {
  readonly length: number;
  // (non-mutating methods)
  toString(): string;
  join(separator?: string): string;
  // ...
  readonly [n: number]: T;
}
```

The key differences are that the mutating methods (such as pop and shift) aren't defined on ReadonlyArray, and the two properties, length and the index type ([n: number]: T), have readonly modifiers. This prevents resizing the array and assigning to elements in the array. (number as an index type isn't something you should use in your own code; see Item 17.)

Since both Array<T> and ReadonlyArray<T> are so common, they get a special syntax: T[] and readonly T[]. Because T[] is strictly more capable than readonly T[], it follows that T[] is a subtype of readonly T[]. (It's easy to get this backwards—remember Item 7!)

So you can assign a mutable array to a readonly array, but not vice versa:

```
const a: number[] = [1, 2, 3];
const b: readonly number[] = a;
const c: number[] = b;
//     ~ Type 'readonly number[]' is 'readonly' and cannot be
//       assigned to the mutable type 'number[]'
```

This makes sense: the readonly modifier wouldn't be much use if you could get rid of it without even a type assertion.

Now we have the tools we need to improve the `printTriangles` and `arraySum` functions. If `printTriangles` wants to prevent `arraySum` from mutating the `nums` array, it can pass it a `readonly` view:

```
function printTriangles(n: number) {
  const nums = [];
  for (let i = 0; i < n; i++) {
    nums.push(i);
    console.log(arraySum(nums as readonly number[]));
    //                    ~~~~~~~~~~~~~~~~~~~~~~~~~~
    // The type 'readonly number[]' is 'readonly' and cannot be
    // assigned to the mutable type 'number[]'.
  }
}
```

We can't declare that `nums` is `readonly number[]` since *we* still need to mutate it. We just want to make sure that `arraySum` doesn't. Since it's declared to take a mutable array, we get a type error.

You can fix this by making it take a `readonly` array instead. Now we get a type error in `arraySum`:

```
function arraySum(arr: readonly number[]) {
  let sum = 0, num;
  while ((num = arr.pop()) !== undefined) {
    //               ~~~ 'pop' does not exist on type 'readonly number[]'
    sum += num;
  }
  return sum;
}
```

This error message makes sense in light of the `Array` and `ReadonlyArray` interfaces that we saw earlier. pop exists on `Array` but not `ReadonlyArray`.

We can fix the type error in `arraySum` by not mutating the array:

```
function arraySum(arr: readonly number[]) {
  let sum = 0;
  for (const num of arr) {
    sum += num;
  }
  return sum;
}
```

Now `printTriangles` does what you expect:

```
> printTriangles(5)
0
1
3
6
10
```

When you give a parameter a read-only type (either `readonly` for an array or `Readonly` for an object type), a few things happen:

- TypeScript checks that the parameter isn't mutated in the function body.
- You advertise to callers that your function doesn't mutate the parameter.
- Callers may pass your function a `readonly` array or `Readonly` object.

If your function does not mutate its parameters, then you should declare them `readonly`. There's relatively little downside: users will be able to call them with a broader set of types (Item 30), and inadvertent mutations will be caught.

(Note that you can still *reassign* `readonly` parameters. They're like variables declared with `let` rather than `const`. Reassignment isn't visible to the function's caller, whereas mutation is.)

One problem is that you may need to call functions that haven't marked their parameters `readonly`. If these functions don't mutate their parameters and are in your control, make them `readonly`! `readonly` tends to be contagious: once you mark one function with `readonly`, you'll also need to mark many of the functions that it calls. This is a good thing since it leads to clearer contracts and better type safety. But if you're calling a function in another library, you may not be able to change its type declarations. In this case, you'll have to either resort to a type assertion (`param as number[]`) or patch the type declarations (Item 71).

There is often an assumption in JavaScript (and TypeScript) that functions don't mutate their parameters unless explicitly noted. But as we'll see time and again in this book (particularly Items 31 and 33), these sorts of implicit understandings can lead to trouble with type checking. Better to make them explicit, both for human readers and for `tsc`.

Things to Remember

- If your function does not modify its parameters, declare them `readonly` (arrays) or `Readonly` (object types). This makes the function's contract clearer and prevents inadvertent mutations in its implementation.
- Understand that `readonly` and `Readonly` are shallow, and that `Readonly` only affects properties, not methods.
- Use `readonly` to prevent errors with mutation and to find the places in your code where mutations occur.
- Understand the difference between `const` and `readonly`: the former prevents reassignment, the latter prevents mutation.

Item 15: Use Type Operations and Generic Types to Avoid Repeating Yourself

This script prints the dimensions, surface areas, and volumes of a few cylinders:

```
console.log(
  'Cylinder r=1 × h=1',
  'Surface area:', 6.283185 * 1 * 1 + 6.283185 * 1 * 1,
  'Volume:', 3.14159 * 1 * 1 * 1
);
console.log(
  'Cylinder r=1 × h=2',
  'Surface area:', 6.283185 * 1 * 1 + 6.283185 * 2 * 1,
  'Volume:', 3.14159 * 1 * 2 * 1
);
console.log(
  'Cylinder r=2 × h=1',
  'Surface area:', 6.283185 * 2 * 1 + 6.283185 * 2 * 1,
  'Volume:', 3.14159 * 2 * 2 * 1
);
```

Is this code uncomfortable to look at? It should be. It's extremely repetitive, as though the same line was copied and pasted, then modified. It repeats both values and constants. This has allowed an error to creep in (did you spot it?).

Much better would be to factor out some functions, a constant, and a loop:

```
type CylinderFn = (r: number, h: number) => number;
const surfaceArea: CylinderFn = (r, h) => 2 * Math.PI * r * (r + h);
const volume: CylinderFn = (r, h) => Math.PI * r * r * h;

for (const [r, h] of [[1, 1], [1, 2], [2, 1]]) {
  console.log(
    `Cylinder r=${r} × h=${h}`,
    `Surface area: ${surfaceArea(r, h)}`,
    `Volume: ${volume(r, h)}`);
}
```

With the formulas written out clearly, the bug is gone (the last example had an r*h for the surface area instead of an r*r). This is the DRY principle: don't repeat yourself. It's the closest thing to universal advice that you'll find in software development. Yet developers who assiduously avoid repetition in code may not think twice about it in types:

```
interface Person {
  firstName: string;
  lastName: string;
}

interface PersonWithBirthDate {
  firstName: string;
```

```
  lastName: string;
  birth: Date;
}
```

Duplication in types has many of the same problems as duplication in code. What if you decide to add an optional `middleName` field to `Person`? Now `Person` and `Person WithBirthDate` have diverged.

One reason that duplication is more common in types is that the mechanisms for factoring out shared patterns are less familiar than they are with code: what's the type system equivalent of factoring out a helper function? By learning how to map between types, you can bring the benefits of DRY to your type definitions.

The simplest way to reduce repetition is by naming your types. Rather than writing a distance function this way:

```
function distance(a: {x: number, y: number}, b: {x: number, y: number}) {
  return Math.sqrt((a.x - b.x) ** 2 + (a.y - b.y) ** 2);
}
```

create a name for the type and use it:

```
interface Point2D {
  x: number;
  y: number;
}
function distance(a: Point2D, b: Point2D) { /* ... */ }
```

This is the type system equivalent of factoring out a constant instead of writing it repeatedly. Duplicated types aren't always so easy to spot. Sometimes they can be obscured by syntax.

If several functions share the same type signature, for instance:

```
function get(url: string, opts: Options): Promise<Response> { /* ... */ }
function post(url: string, opts: Options): Promise<Response> { /* ... */ }
```

then you can follow the advice of Item 12 and factor out a named type for this signature:

```
type HTTPFunction = (url: string, opts: Options) => Promise<Response>;
const get: HTTPFunction = (url, opts) => { /* ... */ };
const post: HTTPFunction = (url, opts) => { /* ... */ };
```

The `CylinderFn` type from the beginning of this item is another example of this.

What about the `Person` / `PersonWithBirthDate` example? You can eliminate the repetition by making one interface extend the other:

```
interface Person {
  firstName: string;
  lastName: string;
}
```

```
interface PersonWithBirthDate extends Person {
  birth: Date;
}
```

Now you only need to write the additional fields. If the two interfaces share a subset of their fields, then you can factor out a base interface with just these common fields. For example, rather than defining independent types for birds and mammals:

```
interface Bird {
  wingspanCm: number;
  weightGrams: number;
  color: string;
  isNocturnal: boolean;
}
interface Mammal {
  weightGrams: number;
  color: string;
  isNocturnal: boolean;
  eatsGardenPlants: boolean;
}
```

you might factor out a `Vertebrate` class with some of the shared properties:

```
interface Vertebrate {
  weightGrams: number;
  color: string;
  isNocturnal: boolean;
}
interface Bird extends Vertebrate {
  wingspanCm: number;
}
interface Mammal extends Vertebrate {
  eatsGardenPlants: boolean;
}
```

Now if you change the base properties or add TSDoc comments to them (Item 68), the changes will be reflected in both `Bird` and `Mammal`. Continuing the analogy with code duplication, this is akin to writing `PI` and `2*PI` instead of `3.141593` and `6.283185`.

You can also use the intersection operator (&) to extend an existing type, though this is somewhat less common:

```
type PersonWithBirthDate = Person & { birth: Date };
```

This technique is most useful when you want to add some additional properties to a union type (which you cannot `extend`). For more on this, see Item 13.

You can also go the other direction. What if you have a type, `State`, which represents the state of an entire application, and another, `TopNavState`, which represents just a part?

```
interface State {
  userId: string;
  pageTitle: string;
  recentFiles: string[];
  pageContents: string;
}
interface TopNavState {
  userId: string;
  pageTitle: string;
  recentFiles: string[];
  // omits pageContents
}
```

Rather than building up State by extending TopNavState, you'd like to define TopNav State as a subset of the fields in State. This way you can keep a single interface defining the state for the entire app.

You can remove duplication in the types of the properties by indexing into State:

```
interface TopNavState {
  userId: State['userId'];
  pageTitle: State['pageTitle'];
  recentFiles: State['recentFiles'];
};
```

While it's longer, this *is* progress: a change in the type of pageTitle in State will get reflected in TopNavState. But it's still repetitive. You can do better with a *mapped type*:

```
type TopNavState = {
  [K in 'userId' | 'pageTitle' | 'recentFiles']: State[K]
};
```

Mousing over TopNavState shows that this definition is, in fact, exactly the same as the previous one (see Figure 2-12).

```
type TopNavState = {
    userId: string;
    pageTitle: string;
    recentFiles: string[];
}
type TopNavState = {
  [k in 'userId' | 'pageTitle' | 'recentFiles']: State[k]
}
```

Figure 2-12. Showing the expanded version of a mapped type in your text editor. This is the same as the initial definition, but with less duplication.

Mapped types are the type system equivalent of looping over the fields in an array. This particular pattern is so common that it's part of the standard library, where it's called Pick:

```
type Pick<T, K> = { [k in K]: T[k] };
```

(This definition isn't *quite* complete. We'll revisit it in Item 50.) You use it like this:

```
type TopNavState = Pick<State, 'userId' | 'pageTitle' | 'recentFiles'>;
```

Pick is an example of a *generic type*. Continuing the analogy to removing code duplication, using Pick is the equivalent of calling a function. Pick takes two types, T and K, and returns a third, much as a function might take two values and return a third. Chapter 6 is all about programming at the type level, and Item 50 explores the idea of generic types as "functions on types."

Another form of duplication can arise with tagged unions. What if you want a type for just the tag?

```
interface SaveAction {
  type: 'save';
  // ...
}
interface LoadAction {
  type: 'load';
  // ...
}
type Action = SaveAction | LoadAction;
type ActionType = 'save' | 'load';  // Repeated types!
```

You can define ActionType without repeating yourself by indexing into the Action union:

```
type ActionType = Action['type'];
//    ^? type ActionType = "save" | "load"
```

As you add more types to the Action union, ActionType will incorporate them automatically. This type is distinct from what you'd get using Pick, which would give you an interface with a type property:

```
type ActionRecord = Pick<Action, 'type'>;
//    ^? type ActionRecord = { type: "save" | "load"; }
```

If you're defining a class that can be initialized and later updated, the type for the parameter to the update method might optionally include most of the same parameters as the constructor:

```
interface Options {
  width: number;
  height: number;
  color: string;
  label: string;
}
interface OptionsUpdate {
  width?: number;
  height?: number;
  color?: string;
```

```
    label?: string;
  }
  class UIWidget {
    constructor(init: Options) { /* ... */ }
    update(options: OptionsUpdate) { /* ... */ }
  }
```

You can construct `OptionsUpdate` from `Options` using a mapped type and keyof:

```
type OptionsUpdate = {[k in keyof Options]?: Options[k]};
```

keyof takes a type and gives you a union of the types of its keys:

```
type OptionsKeys = keyof Options;
//    ^? type OptionsKeys = keyof Options
//       (equivalent to "width" | "height" | "color" | "label")
```

The mapped type ([k in keyof Options]) iterates over these and looks up the corresponding value type in Options. The ? makes each property optional. This pattern is also very common and is included in the standard library as Partial:

```
class UIWidget {
  constructor(init: Options) { /* ... */ }
  update(options: Partial<Options>) { /* ... */ }
}
```

Mapped types have a few other tricks up their sleeve. You can include an as clause in them to rename the keys. There are many uses for this, but one is to invert the keys and values in a mapping:

```
interface ShortToLong {
  q: 'search';
  n: 'numberOfResults';
}
type LongToShort = { [k in keyof ShortToLong as ShortToLong[k]]: k };
//    ^? type LongToShort = { search: "q"; numberOfResults: "n"; }
```

This works particularly well with *template literal types*, which let you manipulate string literal types at the type level. These are the subject of Item 54.

If the index clause in your mapped type is of the form K in keyof T or a few variants on it, then TypeScript treats it as a "homomorphic" mapped type. This means that modifiers (like readonly and ? for optional) and documentation are transferred over to the new type:

```
interface Customer {
  /** How the customer would like to be addressed. */
  title?: string;
  /** Complete name as entered in the system. */
  readonly name: string;
}

type PickTitle = Pick<Customer, 'title'>;
```

```
//    ^? type PickTitle = { title?: string; }
type PickName = Pick<Customer, 'name'>;
//    ^? type PickName = { readonly name: string; }
type ManualName = { [K in 'name']: Customer[K]; };
//    ^? type ManualName = { name: string; }
```

In this case, `Pick` is a homomorphic mapped type and preserves the optional and readonly modifiers. The `ManualName` mapped type does not use a `keyof` expression, so it is not homomorphic and it does not transfer modifiers. If you define a value using one of the homomorphic types, you'll see that the documentation has been transferred over as well (Figure 2-13).

```
const title: PickTitle = {

    ┌──────────────────────────────────────────┐
    │ (property) title?: string | undefined    │
    ├──────────────────────────────────────────┤
    │ How the customer would like to be addressed. │
    └──────────────────────────────────────────┘
    title: 'Brigadier General'
};
```

Figure 2-13. The TSDoc documentation has been copied over to the homomorphic mapped type.

Another curious behavior of homomorphic mapped types is that they allow primitive (nonobject) types to pass through unmodified:

```
type PartialNumber = Partial<number>;
//    ^? type PartialNumber = number
```

This looks a bit odd, but it can be convenient when you're building generic types of your own, as we'll see in Item 56.

As you define mapped types, think about whether they are homomorphic and whether you would like them to be.

You may also find yourself wanting to define a type that matches the shape of a *value*:

```
const INIT_OPTIONS = {
  width: 640,
  height: 480,
  color: '#00FF00',
  label: 'VGA',
};
interface Options {
  width: number;
  height: number;
  color: string;
  label: string;
}
```

You can do so with `typeof`:

```
type Options = typeof INIT_OPTIONS;
```

This intentionally looks like JavaScript's runtime `typeof` operator, but it operates at the level of TypeScript types and is much more precise. For more on `typeof`, see Item 8. Be careful about deriving types from values, however. It's typically better to define types first and declare that values are assignable to them. This makes your types more explicit and less subject to the vagaries of widening (Item 20).

The canonical use case for `typeof` is if you have a single value that you'd like to be the source of truth for a type (perhaps it's some kind of schema or API specification). By making the value the source of truth, you avoid duplication in defining the type.

Similarly, you may want to create a named type for the inferred return value of a function or method:

```
function getUserInfo(userId: string) {
  // ...
  return {
    userId,
    name,
    age,
    height,
    weight,
    favoriteColor,
  };
}
// Return type inferred as { userId: string; name: string; age: number, ... }
```

Doing this directly requires conditional types (see Item 52). But, as we've seen before, the standard library defines generic types for common patterns like this one. In this case the `ReturnType` generic does exactly what you want:

```
type UserInfo = ReturnType<typeof getUserInfo>;
```

Note that `ReturnType` operates on `typeof getUserInfo`, the function's *type*, rather than `getUserInfo`, the function's *value*. As with `typeof`, use this technique judiciously. Don't get mixed up about your source of truth.

As you factor out repetition in your types, don't go overboard. Just because two type declarations share the same characters in source code doesn't necessarily mean they're the same thing. For example, these two types share some common properties:

```
interface Product {
  id: number;
  name: string;
  priceDollars: number;
}
interface Customer {
  id: number;
```

```
  name: string;
  address: string;
}
```

But this wouldn't be a wise refactor:

```
// Don't do this!
interface NamedAndIdentified {
  id: number;
  name: string;
}
interface Product extends NamedAndIdentified {
  priceDollars: number;
}
interface Customer extends NamedAndIdentified {
  address: string;
}
```

This is because while the `id` and `name` properties happen to have the same name and type, they're not referring to the same thing. In the future you might change one `id` to be a `string` but not the other. Or you might split the customer `name` into `firstName` and `lastName`, which wouldn't make sense for a product. In this case, factoring out the common base interface is a premature abstraction which may make it harder for the two types to evolve independently in the future.

A good rule of thumb is that if it's hard to name a type (or a function), then it may not be a useful abstraction. In this case, `NamedAndIdentified` just describes the structure of the type, not what it *is*. The `Vertebrate` type from before, on the other hand, is meaningful on its own. Remember, "duplication is far cheaper than the wrong abstraction."[2]

Repetition and copy/paste coding are just as bad in type space as they are in value space. The constructs you use to avoid repetition in type space may be less familiar than those used for program logic, but they are worth the effort to learn. Don't repeat yourself!

Things to Remember

- The DRY (don't repeat yourself) principle applies to types as much as it applies to logic.
- Name types rather than repeating them. Use `extends` to avoid repeating fields in interfaces.

---

2 Sandi Metz, "All the Little Things" (*https://oreil.ly/XRdLA*), RailsConf 2014.

- Build an understanding of the tools provided by TypeScript to map between types. These include `keyof`, `typeof`, indexing, and mapped types.

- Generic types are the equivalent of functions for types. Use them to map between types instead of repeating type-level operations.

- Familiarize yourself with generic types defined in the standard library, such as `Pick`, `Partial`, and `ReturnType`.

- Avoid over-application of DRY: make sure the properties and types you're sharing are really the same thing.

Item 16: Prefer More Precise Alternatives to Index Signatures

One of the best features of JavaScript is its convenient syntax for creating objects:

```
const rocket = {
  name: 'Falcon 9',
  variant: 'Block 5',
  thrust: '7,607 kN',
};
```

Objects in JavaScript map string (or symbol) keys to values of any type. TypeScript lets you represent flexible mappings like this by specifying an *index signature* on the type:

```
type Rocket = {[property: string]: string};
const rocket: Rocket = {
  name: 'Falcon 9',
  variant: 'v1.0',
  thrust: '4,940 kN',
}; // OK
```

The `[property: string]: string` is the index signature. It specifies three things:

A name for the keys
  This is purely for documentation; it is not used by the type checker in any way.

A type for the key
  This needs to be a subtype of `string | number | symbol` (aka `PropertyKey`). Typically it's `string` or a subtype of `string` such as a union of string literals. `number` indexes are best avoided, as you'll see in Item 17. `symbol` is rare in application code.

A type for the values
  This can be anything.

While this code does type check, it has a few downsides:

- It allows any keys, including incorrect ones. Had you written Name instead of name, it would have still been a valid Rocket type.

- It doesn't require any specific keys to be present. {} is also a valid Rocket.

- It cannot have distinct types for different keys. For example, we might want thrust to be a number rather than a string.

- TypeScript's language services can't help you with types like this. As you're typing name:, there's no autocomplete because the key could be anything.

In short, index signatures are not very precise. There are almost always better alternatives to them. In this case, Rocket could be an interface:

```
interface Rocket {
  name: string;
  variant: string;
  thrust_kN: number;
}
const falconHeavy: Rocket = {
  name: 'Falcon Heavy',
  variant: 'v1',
  thrust_kN: 15200,
};
```

Now thrust_kN is a number and TypeScript will check for the presence of all required fields. All the great language services that TypeScript provides are available: autocomplete, jump to definition, and rename.

What should you use index signatures for? Historically, they were the best way to model truly dynamic data. This might come from a CSV file, for instance, where you have a header row and want to represent data rows as objects mapping column names to values:

```
function parseCSV(input: string): {[columnName: string]: string}[] {
  const lines = input.split('\n');
  const [headerLine, ...rows] = lines;
  const headers = headerLine.split(',');
  return rows.map(rowStr => {
    const row: {[columnName: string]: string} = {};
    rowStr.split(',').forEach((cell, i) => {
      row[headers[i]] = cell;
    });
    return row;
  });
}
```

There's no way to know in advance what the column names are in such a general setting, so there's no way to get a more precise type. If the user of parseCSV knows more about what the columns are in a particular context, they could use an assertion to get more specific:

```
interface ProductRow {
  productId: string;
  name: string;
  price: string;
}

declare let csvData: string;
const products = parseCSV(csvData) as unknown[] as ProductRow[];
```

Of course, there's no guarantee that the columns at runtime will actually match your expectation. You can guard against this possibility by changing the value type to string|undefined or by setting the noUncheckedIndexedAccess compiler option (see Item 48).

But a better way to model dynamic data is by using a Map type, also known as an associative array. Here's how you might implement parseCSV using a Map:

```
function parseCSVMap(input: string): Map<string, string>[] {
  const lines = input.split('\n');
  const [headerLine, ...rows] = lines;
  const headers = headerLine.split(',');
  return rows.map(rowStr => {
    const row = new Map<string, string>();
    rowStr.split(',').forEach((cell, i) => {
      row.set(headers[i], cell);
    });
    return row;
  });
}
```

Now the fields have to be accessed using the get method, and the result always includes undefined as a possibility:

```
const rockets = parseCSVMap(csvData);
const superHeavy = rockets[2];
const thrust_kN = superHeavy.get('thrust_kN');  // 74,500
//      ^? const thrust_kN: string | undefined
```

If you want to get an object type out of a Map, you'll need to write some parsing code:

```
function parseRocket(map: Map<string, string>): Rocket {
  const name = map.get('name');
  const variant = map.get('variant');
  const thrust_kN = Number(map.get('thrust_kN'));
  if (!name || !variant || isNaN(thrust_kN)) {
    throw new Error(`Invalid rocket: ${map}`);
  }
  return {name, variant, thrust_kN};
}
```

```
const rockets = parseCSVMap(csvData).map(parseRocket);
//    ^? const rockets: Rocket[]
```

While this may feel tedious, it does ensure that your data actually has the shape you expect. This will flag errors when you load your data, rather than at some later point when you try to use it. This pattern of doing data validation on a broad type (Map<string, string>) to get a more specific one (Rocket) is common in Type-Script. Item 74 will explore more systematic ways of doing runtime type validation.

In addition to being a better model of dynamic data, Maps work around some famous gotchas involving the prototype chain.

If your type has a limited set of possible fields, don't model this with an index signature. For instance, if you know your data will have keys like A, B, C, D, but you don't know how many of them there will be, you could model the type either with optional fields or a union:

```
interface Row1 { [column: string]: number }  // Too broad
interface Row2 { a: number; b?: number; c?: number; d?: number }  // Better
type Row3 =
    | { a: number; }
    | { a: number; b: number; }
    | { a: number; b: number; c: number;  }
    | { a: number; b: number; c: number; d: number };  // Also better
```

The last form is the most precise, but it may be less convenient to work with. See Item 29 for more on crafting types to disallow invalid states.

If the problem with using an index signature is that string is too broad, then you can use a Record. This is a generic type that gives you more flexibility in the key type. In particular, you can pass in subsets of string:

```
type Vec3D = Record<'x' | 'y' | 'z', number>;
//    ^? type Vec3D = {
//        x: number;
//        y: number;
//        z: number;
//       }
```

Record is a built-in wrapper around a mapped type (Item 15).

Finally, you can use an index type to disable excess property checking (Item 11). For example, you might define a few known properties on a ButtonProps type but still want to allow it to have any others:

```
declare function renderAButton(props: ButtonProps): void;
interface ButtonProps {
  title: string;
  onClick: () => void;
}
```

```
renderAButton({
  title: 'Roll the dice',
  onClick: () => alert(1 + Math.floor(6 * Math.random())),
  theme: 'Solarized',
// ~~~~ Object literal may only specify known properties...
});
```

Adding an index signature makes this error go away:

```
interface ButtonProps {
  title: string;
  onClick: () => void;
  [otherProps: string]: unknown;
}

renderAButton({
  title: 'Roll the dice',
  onClick: () => alert(1 + Math.floor(20 * Math.random())),
  theme: 'Solarized',  // ok
});
```

Crucially, both `title` and `onClick` still have the same types as before. Passing a `number` as the `title` will result in a type error.

You can also constrain these additional properties to match a certain pattern. For example, some web components allow arbitrary properties but only if they start with `"data-"`. You can model this using an index signature and a template literal type. Item 54 will show you how.

In conclusion, think twice before you add an index signature to your data type. Is there a more precise alternative available? Could you use an `interface` without an index type? Could you use a `Map` instead? A mapped type? If nothing else, can you at least constrain the type of the keys?

Things to Remember

- Understand the drawbacks of index signatures: much like `any`, they erode type safety and reduce the value of language services.
- Prefer more precise types to index signatures when possible: `interfaces`, `Map`, `Records`, mapped types, or index signatures with a constrained key space.

Item 17: Avoid Numeric Index Signatures

JavaScript is a famously quirky language. Some of the most notorious quirks involve implicit type coercions:

```
> "0" == 0
true
```

These can usually be avoided by using === and !== instead of their more coercive cousins.

JavaScript's object model also has its quirks, and these are more important to understand because some of them are modeled by TypeScript's type system. You've already seen one such quirk in Item 10, which discussed object wrapper types. This item discusses another.

What is an object? In JavaScript it's a collection of key/value pairs. The keys are usually strings (in ES2015 and later they can also be symbols). The values can be anything.

This is more restrictive than what you find in many other languages. JavaScript does not have a notion of "hashable" objects like you find in Python or Java. If you try to use a more complex object as a key, it is converted into a string by calling its toString method:

```
> x = {}
{}
> x[[1, 2, 3]] = 2
2
> x
{ '1,2,3': 2 }
```

In particular, *numbers* cannot be used as keys. If you try to use a number as a property name, the JavaScript runtime will convert it to a string:

```
> { 1: 2, 3: 4}
{ '1': 2, '3': 4 }
```

So what are arrays, then? They are certainly objects:

```
> typeof []
'object'
```

And yet it's quite normal to use numeric indices with them:

```
> x = [1, 2, 3]
[ 1, 2, 3 ]
> x[0]
1
```

Are these being converted into strings? In one of the oddest quirks of all, the answer is "yes." You can also access the elements of an array using string keys:

```
> x['1']
2
```

If you use Object.keys to list the keys of an array, you get strings back:

```
> Object.keys(x)
[ '0', '1', '2' ]
```

TypeScript models this by allowing numeric keys and distinguishing between these and strings. If you dig into the type declarations for Array (Item 6), you'll find this in *lib.es5.d.ts*:

```
interface Array<T> {
  // ...
  [n: number]: T;
}
```

This is purely a fiction—string keys are accepted at runtime as the ECMAScript standard dictates that they must—but it is a helpful one that can catch mistakes:

```
const xs = [1, 2, 3];
const x0 = xs[0];  // OK
const x1 = xs['1'];  // stringified numeric constants are also OK

const inputEl = document.getElementsByTagName('input')[0];
const xN = xs[inputEl.value];
//           ~~~~~~~~~~~~~~ Index expression is not of type 'number'.
```

In this case, inputEl.valueAsNumber would be more appropriate and would fix the type error.

While the fiction of numeric keys is helpful, it's important to remember that it is just a fiction. Like all aspects of TypeScript's type system, it is erased at runtime (Item 3). This means that constructs like Object.keys still return strings:

```
const keys = Object.keys(xs);
//    ^? const keys: string[]
```

The pattern here is that a number index signature means that what you put in generally has to be a number, but what you get out is a string.

If this sounds confusing, it's because it is! As a general rule, there's not much reason to use number as the index signature of a type. If you want to specify something that will be indexed using numbers, you probably want to use an Array or tuple type instead. Using number as an index type can create the misconception that numeric properties are a real thing in JavaScript, either for yourself or for readers of your code.

If you object to accepting an Array type because they have many other properties (from their prototype) that you might not use, such as push and concat, then that's good—you're thinking structurally! (If you need a refresher on this, refer to Item 4.) If you truly want to accept tuples of any length or any array-like construct, TypeScript has an ArrayLike type you can use:

```
function checkedAccess<T>(xs: ArrayLike<T>, i: number): T {
  if (i >= 0 && i < xs.length) {
    return xs[i];
  }
  throw new Error(`Attempt to access ${i} which is past end of array.`)
}
```

(TypeScript also has a noUncheckedIndexedAccess option you can set for safe array access. See Item 48.)

ArrayLike has just a length and numeric index signature. As the name implies, this allows array-like structures such as a NodeList to be passed in. In the rare cases that this is what you want, you should use it instead of a normal array. But remember that the keys are still really strings!

```
const tupleLike: ArrayLike<string> = {
  '0': 'A',
  '1': 'B',
  length: 2,
}; // OK
```

If you just need something you can iterate over, you can use the Iterable type instead, which allows you to pass generator expressions to your function (see Item 30).

Object keys in JavaScript (and TypeScript) are either strings or symbols. Numeric index types are best thought of as a concession to make the Array type convenient to use in TypeScript. But remember that numeric indices aren't real. Avoid using them in your own types.

Things to Remember

- Understand that arrays are objects, so their keys are strings, not numbers. number as an index signature is a purely TypeScript construct designed to help catch bugs.
- Prefer Array, tuple, ArrayLike, or Iterable types to using number in an index signature yourself.

CHAPTER 3

Type Inference and Control Flow Analysis

For programming languages used in industry, "statically typed" and "explicitly typed" have traditionally been synonymous. C, C++, Java: they all made you write out your types. But academic languages never conflated these two things: languages like ML and Haskell have long had sophisticated type inference systems, and this has begun to work its way into industry languages. C++ has added auto, and Java has added var. Newer languages like Rust and Swift have had type inference from the start.

TypeScript makes extensive use of type inference. Used well, this can dramatically reduce the number of type annotations your code requires to get full type safety. One of the easiest ways to tell a TypeScript beginner from a more experienced developer is by the number of type annotations. An experienced TypeScript developer will use relatively few annotations (but use them to great effect), while a beginner may drown their code in redundant type annotations.

In most languages, a variable has a type and it never changes. TypeScript is a bit different. A variable has a type *at a location* in your code. The process by which its type changes due to surrounding code is known as *control flow analysis*.

This chapter teaches you how to think about type inference and control flow analysis, shows you some of the problems that can arise with them, and tells you how to fix them. After reading it, you should have a good understanding of how TypeScript infers types, when you still need to write explicit type annotations, and when it's still a good idea to write type annotations even when a type can be inferred.

Item 18: Avoid Cluttering Your Code with Inferable Types

The first thing that many new TypeScript developers do when they convert a codebase from JavaScript is fill it with type annotations. TypeScript is about *types*, after all! But in TypeScript, many annotations are unnecessary. Declaring types for all your variables is counterproductive and is considered poor style.

Don't write:

```
let x: number = 12;
```

Instead, just write:

```
let x = 12;
```

If you mouse over x in your editor, you'll see that its type has been inferred as number (as shown in Figure 3-1).

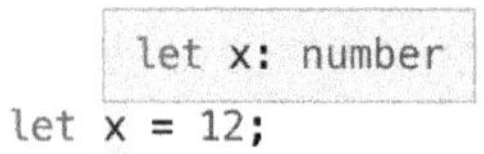

```
              ┌─────────────────┐
              │ let x: number   │
              └─────────────────┘
        let x = 12;
```

Figure 3-1. A text editor showing that the inferred type of x is number.

The explicit type annotation is redundant. Writing it just adds noise. If you're unsure of the type, you can check it in your editor.

TypeScript will also infer the types of more complex objects. Instead of:

```
const person: {
  name: string;
  born: {
    where: string;
    when: string;
  };
  died: {
    where: string;
    when: string;
  }
} = {
  name: 'Sojourner Truth',
  born: {
    where: 'Swartekill, NY',
    when: 'c.1797',
  },
  died: {
    where: 'Battle Creek, MI',
    when: 'Nov. 26, 1883'
  }
};
```

you can just write:

```
const person = {
  name: 'Sojourner Truth',
  born: {
    where: 'Swartekill, NY',
    when: 'c.1797',
  },
  died: {
    where: 'Battle Creek, MI',
    when: 'Nov. 26, 1883'
  }
};
```

Again, the types are exactly the same. Writing the type in addition to the value just adds noise here. (Item 20 will explain how TypeScript infers types for object literals.)

What's true for objects is also true for arrays. TypeScript has no trouble figuring out the return type of this function based on its inputs and operations:

```
function square(nums: number[]) {
  return nums.map(x => x * x);
}
const squares = square([1, 2, 3, 4]);
//    ^? const squares: number[]
```

TypeScript may infer something more precise than what you expected. This is generally a good thing. For example:

```
const axis1: string = 'x';
//    ^? const axis1: string
const axis2 = 'y';
//    ^? const axis2: "y"
```

"y" is a more precise type for the axis2 variable. The explicit string annotation on axis1 adds noise and reduces type safety.

Allowing types to be inferred can also facilitate refactoring. Say you have a Product type and a function to log it:

```
interface Product {
  id: number;
  name: string;
  price: number;
}

function logProduct(product: Product) {
  const id: number = product.id;
  const name: string = product.name;
  const price: number = product.price;
  console.log(id, name, price);
}
```

At some point you learn that product IDs might have letters in them in addition to numbers. So you change the type of id in Product:

```
interface Product {
  id: string;
  name: string;
  price: number;
}
```

Because you included explicit annotations on all the variables in logProduct, this produces an error:

```
function logProduct(product: Product) {
  const id: number = product.id;
      // ~~ Type 'string' is not assignable to type 'number'
  const name: string = product.name;
  const price: number = product.price;
  console.log(id, name, price);
}
```

Had you left off all the annotations in the logProduct function body, the code would have passed the type checker without modification (and worked correctly at runtime, too).

Here's a better implementation of logProduct that allows the types of all local variables to be inferred (it also switches to destructuring assignment):

```
function logProduct(product: Product) {
  const {id, name, price} = product;
  console.log(id, name, price);
}
```

The corresponding version with explicit type annotations is repetitive and cluttered:

```
function logProduct(product: Product) {
  const {id, name, price}: {id: string; name: string; price: number } = product;
  console.log(id, name, price);
}
```

You can't put type annotations directly inside the destructuring because, as Item 8 explained, they would be interpreted as renaming directives in value space. Destructuring assignment is a great way to make your code more concise. It encourages consistent naming and it works much better with inferred types.

Explicit type annotations are still required in some situations where TypeScript doesn't have enough context to determine a type on its own. You have seen one of these before: function parameters.

Some languages will infer types for parameters based on their eventual usage, but TypeScript does not. In TypeScript, a variable's type is generally determined when it is first introduced. (Item 25 discusses an important exception to this rule.)

Ideal TypeScript code includes type annotations for function/method signatures but not for the local variables created in their bodies. This keeps noise to a minimum and lets readers focus on the implementation logic.

There are some situations where you can leave the type annotations off of function parameters, too. When there's a default value, for example:

```
function parseNumber(str: string, base=10) {
  //                              ^? (parameter) base: number
  // ...
}
```

Here the type of base is inferred as number because of the default value of 10.

Parameter types can usually be inferred when the function is used as a callback for a library with type declarations. The declarations on request and response in this example using the express HTTP server library are not required:

```
// Don't do this:
app.get('/health', (request: express.Request, response: express.Response) => {
  response.send('OK');
});

// Do this:
app.get('/health', (request, response) => {
  //                 ^? (parameter) request: Request<...>
  response.send('OK');
  // ^? (parameter) response: Response<...>
});
```

Item 24 has more to say about how context is used in type inference.

There are a few situations where you may still want to specify a type even where it can be inferred.

One is when you define an object literal:

```
const elmo: Product = {
  name: 'Tickle Me Elmo',
  id: '048188 627152',
  price: 28.99,
};
```

When you specify a type on a definition like this, you enable excess property checking (Item 11). This can help catch errors, particularly for types with optional fields.

You also increase the odds that an error will be reported in the right place. If you leave off the annotation, a mistake in the object's definition will result in a type error where it's used, rather than where it's defined:

```
const furby = {
  name: 'Furby',
  id: 630509430963,
```

```
    price: 35,
};
logProduct(furby);
//          ~~~~~ Argument ... is not assignable to parameter of type 'Product'
//                Types of property 'id' are incompatible
//                Type 'number' is not assignable to type 'string'
```

In a larger codebase, this type error could appear in a different file with no clear connection to the object definition. With an annotation, you get a more concise error in the exact place where the mistake was made:

```
const furby: Product = {
    name: 'Furby',
    id: 630509430963,
// ~~ Type 'number' is not assignable to type 'string'
    price: 35,
};
logProduct(furby);
```

Similar considerations apply to a function's return type. You may still want to annotate this even when it can be inferred to ensure that implementation errors don't leak out into uses of the function. This is particularly important for exported functions that are part of a public API.

Say you have a function that retrieves a stock quote:

```
function getQuote(ticker: string) {
    return fetch(`https://quotes.example.com/?q=${ticker}`)
        .then(response => response.json());
}
```

You decide to add a cache to avoid duplicating network requests:

```
const cache: {[ticker: string]: number} = {};
function getQuote(ticker: string) {
    if (ticker in cache) {
        return cache[ticker];
    }
    return fetch(`https://quotes.example.com/?q=${ticker}`)
        .then(response => response.json())
        .then(quote => {
            cache[ticker] = quote;
            return quote as number;
        });
}
```

There's a mistake in this implementation, which you can see if you look at the inferred return type for getQuote:

```
getQuote;
// ^? function getQuote(ticker: string): number | Promise<number>
```

You should really be returning `Promise.resolve(cache[ticker])` so that `getQuote` always returns a Promise. The mistake will most likely produce an error…but in the code that calls `getQuote`, rather than in `getQuote` itself:

```
getQuote('MSFT').then(considerBuying);
//               ~~~~ Property 'then' does not exist on type
//                    'number | Promise<number>'
```

Had you annotated the intended return type (`Promise<number>`), the error would have been reported in the correct place:

```
const cache: {[ticker: string]: number} = {};
function getQuote(ticker: string): Promise<number> {
  if (ticker in cache) {
    return cache[ticker];
    // ~~~ Type 'number' is not assignable to type 'Promise<number>'
  }
  // ...
}
```

When you annotate the return type, it keeps implementation errors from manifesting as errors in user code. This is a particularly good idea for functions like `getQuote` that have multiple `return` statements. If you want TypeScript to check that all the `returns` return the same type, you'll need to provide a type annotation to tell it your intent.

(Item 27 explains how async functions are an effective way to avoid this particular mistake.)

Writing out the return type may also help you think more clearly about your function: you should know what its input and output types are *before you implement it*. While the implementation may shift around a bit, the function's contract (its type signature) generally should not. This is similar in spirit to test-driven development (TDD), in which you write the tests that exercise a function before you implement it. Writing the full type signature first helps get you the function you want, rather than the one the implementation makes expedient.

Another reason to annotate return types is if you want to use a named type. You might choose not to write a return type for this function, for example:

```
interface Vector2D { x: number; y: number; }
function add(a: Vector2D, b: Vector2D) {
  return { x: a.x + b.x, y: a.y + b.y };
}
```

TypeScript infers the return type as `{ x: number; y: number; }`. This is compatible with `Vector2D`, but it may be surprising to users of your code when they see `Vector2D` as a type of the input and not of the output (Figure 3-2).

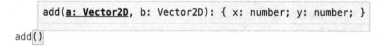

```
add(a: Vector2D, b: Vector2D): { x: number; y: number; }
add()
```

Figure 3-2. The parameters to the add function have named types, but the inferred return value does not.

If you annotate the return type, the presentation is more straightforward. And if you've written documentation on the type (Item 68), it will be associated with the returned value as well. As the complexity of the inferred return type increases, it becomes increasingly helpful to provide a name.

Finally, annotating your return types means that TypeScript has less work to do figuring them out. For large codebases, this can have an impact on compiler performance. Item 78 has more guidance on what to do when your build gets slow.

So should you annotate return types? To reduce code and facilitate refactoring, the default answer is "no." But it shouldn't take much to tip you over to "yes.". If the function has multiple `return` statements, if it's part of a public API, or if you want to use a named return type, then add the annotation.

If you are using a linter, the typescript-eslint rule `no-inferrable-types` (note the variant spelling) can help ensure that all your type annotations are really necessary.

Things to Remember

- Avoid writing type annotations when TypeScript can infer the same type.
- Ideal TypeScript code has type annotations in function/method signatures but not on local variables in their bodies.
- Consider using explicit annotations for object literals to enable excess property checking and ensure errors are reported close to where they occur.
- Don't annotate function return types unless the function has multiple returns, is part of a public API, or you want it to return a named type.

Item 19: Use Different Variables for Different Types

In JavaScript, it's no problem to reuse a variable to hold a differently typed value for a different purpose:

```
let productId = "12-34-56";
fetchProduct(productId);  // Expects a string

productId = 123456;
fetchProductBySerialNumber(productId);  // Expects a number
```

In TypeScript, this results in two errors:

```
let productId = "12-34-56";
fetchProduct(productId);

productId = 123456;
//  ~~~~~~ Type 'number' is not assignable to type 'string'
fetchProductBySerialNumber(productId);
//                         ~~~~~~~~~~~
// Argument of type 'string' is not assignable to parameter of type 'number'
```

Hovering over the first productId in your editor gives a hint as to what's going on (see Figure 3-3).

```
let productId: string
let productId = "12-34-56";
```

Figure 3-3. The inferred type of productId is string.

Based on the value "12-34-56", TypeScript has inferred productId's type as string. You can't assign a number to a string, hence the error.

This leads us to a key insight about variables in TypeScript: *while a variable's value can change, its type generally does not.* The one common way a type can change is to narrow (Item 22), but this involves a type getting smaller, not expanding to include new values. Item 25 presents a notable exception to this rule, but it is an exception and not the rule.

How can you use this idea to fix the example? For productId's type to not change, it must be broad enough to encompass both strings and numbers. This is the very definition of the union type, string|number:

```
let productId: string | number = "12-34-56";
fetchProduct(productId);

productId = 123456;  // OK
fetchProductBySerialNumber(productId);  // OK
```

This fixes the errors. It's interesting that TypeScript has been able to determine that id is really a string in the first call and really a number in the second. It has narrowed the union type based on the assignment.

While a union type does work, it may create more issues down the road. Union types are harder to work with than simple types like string or number because you usually have to check what they are before you do anything with them.

The better solution is to introduce a new variable:

```
const productId = "12-34-56";
fetchProduct(productId);

const serial = 123456;  // OK
fetchProductBySerialNumber(serial);  // OK
```

In the previous version, the first and second `productId` were not semantically related to one another. They were only related by the fact that you reused a variable. This was confusing for the type checker and would be confusing for a human reader, too.

The version with two variables is better for a number of reasons:

- It disentangles two unrelated concepts (ID and serial number).
- It allows you to use more specific variable names.
- It improves type inference. No type annotations are needed.
- It results in simpler types (string and number literals, rather than `string| number`).
- It lets you declare the variables `const` rather than `let`. This makes them easier for people and the type checker to reason about.

The general theme, which will come up repeatedly in this chapter, is that mutation makes it harder for the type checker to follow along with your code. Try to avoid type-changing variables. If you can use different names for different concepts, it will make your code clearer both to human readers and to the type checker. You should have far more `const` than `let`.

This is not to be confused with "shadowed" variables, as in this example:

```
const productId = "12-34-56";
fetchProduct(productId);

{
  const productId = 123456;  // OK
  fetchProductBySerialNumber(productId);  // OK
}
```

While these two `productId`s share a name, they are actually two distinct variables with no relationship to one another. It's fine for them to have different types. While TypeScript is not confused by this, your human readers might be. In general it's better to use different names for different concepts. Many teams choose to disallow this sort of shadowing via linter rules such as eslint's `no-shadow`.

This item focused on scalar values, but similar considerations apply to objects. For more on that, see Item 21.

Things to Remember

- While a variable's value can change, its type generally does not.
- To avoid confusion, both for human readers and for the type checker, avoid reusing variables for differently typed values.

Item 20: Understand How a Variable Gets Its Type

As Item 7 explained, at runtime every variable has a single value. But at static analysis time, when TypeScript is checking your code, a variable has a set of *possible* values, namely, its type. When you initialize a variable with a constant but don't provide a type, the type checker needs to decide on one. In other words, it needs to decide on a set of possible values from the single value that you specified. In TypeScript, this process is known as *widening*. Understanding it will help you make sense of errors and make more effective use of type annotations.

Suppose you're writing a library to work with vectors. You write out a type for a 3D vector and a function to get the value of any of its components:

```
interface Vector3 { x: number; y: number; z: number; }
function getComponent(vector: Vector3, axis: 'x' | 'y' | 'z') {
  return vector[axis];
}
```

But when you try to use it, TypeScript flags an error:

```
let x = 'x';
let vec = {x: 10, y: 20, z: 30};
getComponent(vec, x);
//                ~ Argument of type 'string' is not assignable
//                    to parameter of type '"x" | "y" | "z"'
```

This code runs fine, so why the error?

The issue is that x's type is inferred as string, whereas the getComponent function expected a more specific type for its second argument. This is widening at work, and here it has led to a type error.

Widening is ambiguous in the sense that there are many possible types for any given value. In this statement, for example:

```
const mixed = ['x', 1];
```

what should the type of mixed be? Here are a few possibilities:

- ('x' | 1)[]
- ['x', 1]
- [string, number]

- readonly [string, number]
- (string|number)[]
- readonly (string|number)[]
- [any, any]
- any[]

Without more context, TypeScript has no way to know which one is "right." It has to guess at your intent. (In this case, it guesses (string|number)[].) And smart as it is, TypeScript can't read your mind. It won't get this right 100% of the time. The result is inadvertent errors like the one we just saw.

In the initial example, the type of x is inferred as string because TypeScript chooses to allow code like this:

```
let x = 'x';
x = 'a';
x = 'Four score and seven years ago...';
```

But it would also be valid JavaScript to write:

```
let x = 'x';
x = /x|y|z/;
x = ['x', 'y', 'z'];
```

In inferring the type of x as string, TypeScript attempts to strike a balance between specificity and flexibility. A variable's type won't change to something completely different after it's declared (Item 19), so string makes more sense than string|RegExp or string|string[] or any.

The general rule for primitive values assigned with let is that they expand to their "base type": "x" expands to string, 39 expands to number, true expands to boolean and so on. (null and undefined are handled differently, see Item 25.)

TypeScript gives you a few ways to control the process of widening. One is const. If you declare a variable with const instead of let, it gets a narrower type. In fact, using const fixes the error in our original example:

```
const x = 'x';
//    ^? const x: "x"
let vec = {x: 10, y: 20, z: 30};
getComponent(vec, x);  // OK
```

Because x cannot be reassigned, TypeScript is able to infer a more precise type without risk of inadvertently flagging errors on subsequent assignments. And because the string literal type "x" is assignable to "x"|"y"|"z", the code passes the type checker.

`const` isn't a panacea, however. For objects and arrays, there is still ambiguity. The mixed example illustrated the issue for arrays: should TypeScript infer a tuple type? What type should it infer for the elements?

Similar issues arise with objects. This code is fine in JavaScript:

```
const obj = {
  x: 1,
};
obj.x = 3;
obj.x = '3';
obj.y = 4;
obj.z = 5;
obj.name = 'Pythagoras';
```

The type of `obj` could be inferred anywhere along the spectrum of specificity. At the specific end is `{readonly x: 1}`. More general is `{x: number}`. More general still would be `{[key: string]: number}`, `object` or, most general of all, `any`, or `unknown`.

In the case of objects, TypeScript infers what it calls the "best common type." It determines this by treating each property as though it were assigned with `let`. So the type of `obj` comes out as `{x: number}`. This lets you reassign `obj.x` to a different number, but not to a `string`. And it prevents you from adding other properties via direct assignment. (This is a good reason to build objects all at once, as explained in Item 21.)

So the last four statements are errors:

```
const obj = {
  x: 1,
};
obj.x = 3;  // OK
obj.x = '3';
//  ~ Type 'string' is not assignable to type 'number'
obj.y = 4;
//  ~ Property 'y' does not exist on type '{ x: number; }'
obj.z = 5;
//  ~ Property 'z' does not exist on type '{ x: number; }'
obj.name = 'Pythagoras';
//  ~~~~ Property 'name' does not exist on type '{ x: number; }'
```

Again, TypeScript is trying to strike a balance between specificity and flexibility. It needs to infer a specific enough type to catch errors, but not such a specific type that it creates false positives. It does this by inferring a type of `number` for a property initialized to a value like 1.

If you know better, there are a few ways to override TypeScript's default behavior. One is to supply an explicit type annotation:

```
const obj: { x: string | number } = { x: 1 };
//     ^? const obj: { x: string | number; }
```

Another is to provide additional context to the type checker, e.g., by passing the value as an argument to a function (Item 24).

A third way is with a `const` assertion. This is not to be confused with `let` and `const`, which introduce symbols in value space. This is a purely type-level construct. Look at the different inferred types for these variables:

```
const obj1 = { x: 1, y: 2 };
//    ^? const obj1: { x: number; y: number; }

const obj2 = { x: 1 as const, y: 2 };
//    ^? const obj2: { x: 1; y: number; }

const obj3 = { x: 1, y: 2 } as const;
//    ^? const obj3: { readonly x: 1; readonly y: 2; }
```

When you write `as const` after a value, TypeScript will infer the narrowest possible type for it. There is *no* widening. For true constants, this is typically what you want. You can also use `as const` with arrays to infer a tuple type:

```
const arr1 = [1, 2, 3];
//    ^? const arr1: number[]
const arr2 = [1, 2, 3] as const;
//    ^? const arr2: readonly [1, 2, 3]
```

Despite the similar syntax, a `const` assertion should not be confused with a type assertion (`as T`). While type assertions are best avoided (Item 9), a `const` assertion doesn't compromise type safety and is always OK.

There's a handy trick if you want TypeScript to infer a tuple type instead of an array type, but still allow the type of each element in the tuple to widen to its base type / best common type:

```
function tuple<T extends unknown[]>(...elements: T) { return elements; }

const arr3 = tuple(1, 2, 3);
//    ^? const arr3: [number, number, number]
const mix = tuple(4, 'five', true);
//    ^? const mix: [number, string, boolean]
```

The `tuple` function here serves no purpose at runtime, but guides TypeScript toward inferring the type you want. Another function that can guide inference is JavaScript's `Object.freeze`:

```
const frozenArray = Object.freeze([1, 2, 3]);
//    ^? const frozenArray: readonly number[]
const frozenObj = Object.freeze({x: 1, y: 2});
//    ^? const frozenObj: Readonly<{ x: 1; y: 2; }>
```

Like a `const` assertion, `Object.freeze` has introduced some `readonly` modifiers into the inferred types (though it displays differently, the type of `frozenObj` is exactly the same as obj3). Unlike a const assertion, the "freeze" will be enforced by your Java-Script runtime. But it's a shallow freeze/readonly, whereas a const assertion is deep. Item 14 discusses readonly and how it can help prevent mistakes.

Finally, a fourth way to control widening is the satisfies operator. This ensures that a value, well, satisfies the requirements of a type and guides inference by preventing TypeScript from inferring a wider type. Here's how it works:

```
type Point = [number, number];
const capitals1 = { ny: [-73.7562, 42.6526], ca: [-121.4944, 38.5816] };
//    ^? const capitals1: { ny: number[]; ca: number[]; }

const capitals2 = {
  ny: [-73.7562, 42.6526], ca: [-121.4944, 38.5816]
} satisfies Record<string, Point>;
capitals2
// ^? const capitals2: { ny: [number, number]; ca: [number, number]; }
```

Left to its own devices, TypeScript takes the keys from the object literal and widens the values to number[], just as it would with let. With satisfies, we prevent the values from being widened beyond the Point type.

Compare this to what you get from an annotation using the same type:

```
const capitals3: Record<string, Point> = capitals2;
capitals3.pr;  // undefined at runtime
//        ^? Point
capitals2.pr;
//         ~~ Property 'pr' does not exist on type '{ ny: ...; ca: ...; }'
```

The type coming from satisfies has precise keys, which helps to catch errors.

The satisfies operator will report an error if part of the object isn't assignable to the type:

```
const capitalsBad = {
    ny: [-73.7562, 42.6526, 148],
// ~~ Type '[number, number, number]' is not assignable to type 'Point'.
    ca: [-121.4944, 38.5816, 26],
// ~~ Type '[number, number, number]' is not assignable to type 'Point'.
} satisfies Record<string, Point>;
```

This is an improvement over a const assertion because it will report the error where you define the object, rather than where you use it.

If you're getting incorrect errors that you think are due to widening, consider changing let to const, adding some explicit type annotations, using a helper function like tuple or Object.freeze, or using a const assertion or a satisfies clause. As always, inspecting types in your editor is the key to building an intuition for how this works (see Item 6).

Things to Remember

- Understand how TypeScript infers a type from a literal by widening it.

- Familiarize yourself with the ways you can affect this behavior: `const`, type annotations, context, helper functions, `as const`, and `satisfies`.

Item 21: Create Objects All at Once

As Item 19 explained, while a variable's value may change, its type in TypeScript generally does not. This makes some JavaScript patterns easier to model in TypeScript than others. In particular, it means that you should prefer creating objects all at once, rather than piece by piece.

Here's one way to create an object representing a two-dimensional point in JavaScript:

```
const pt = {};
pt.x = 3;
pt.y = 4;
```

In TypeScript, this will produce errors on each assignment:

```
const pt = {};
//    ^? const pt: {}
pt.x = 3;
// ~ Property 'x' does not exist on type '{}'
pt.y = 4;
// ~ Property 'y' does not exist on type '{}'
```

This is because the type of pt on the first line is inferred based on its value {}, and you may only assign to known properties.

You get the opposite problem if you define a `Point` interface:

```
interface Point { x: number; y: number; }
const pt: Point = {};
   // ~~ Type '{}' is missing the following properties from type 'Point': x, y
pt.x = 3;
pt.y = 4;
```

A type assertion seems to offer a solution:

```
const pt = {} as Point;
//    ^? const pt: Point
pt.x = 3;
pt.y = 4;  // OK
```

The problem with this pattern is that TypeScript won't check that you've assigned all the properties to pt before using it. If you dropped the assignment to pt.y, for example, the code would still pass the type checker but might lead to NaNs or runtime exceptions. As Item 9 explained, type assertions shouldn't be the first tool you reach for.

The best solution is to define the object all at once with a type declaration:

```
const pt: Point = {
  x: 3,
  y: 4,
};
```

If you need to build a larger object from smaller ones, avoid doing it in multiple steps:

```
const pt = {x: 3, y: 4};
const id = {name: 'Pythagoras'};
const namedPoint = {};
Object.assign(namedPoint, pt, id);
namedPoint.name;
        // ~~~~ Property 'name' does not exist on type '{}'
```

You can build the larger object all at once instead using *object spread syntax*, ...:

```
const namedPoint = {...pt, ...id};
//    ^? const namedPoint: { name: string; x: number; y: number; }
namedPoint.name;   // OK
//          ^? (property) name: string
```

You can also use object spread syntax to build up objects field by field in a type-safe way. The key is to use a new variable on every update so that each gets a new type (Item 19):

```
const pt0 = {};
const pt1 = {...pt0, x: 3};
const pt: Point = {...pt1, y: 4};   // OK
```

The type declaration on the final line ensures that we've added all the necessary properties. While this is a roundabout way to build up such a simple object, it can be a useful technique for adding properties to an object and allowing TypeScript to infer a new type.

To conditionally add a property in a type-safe way, you can use spread syntax with {} or any falsy value (null, undefined, false, etc.), which add no properties:

```
declare let hasMiddle: boolean;
const firstLast = {first: 'Harry', last: 'Truman'};
const president = {...firstLast, ...(hasMiddle ? {middle: 'S'} : {})};
//    ^? const president: {
//         middle?: string;
//         first: string;
//         last: string;
//       }
// or: const president = {...firstLast, ...(hasMiddle && {middle: 'S'})};
```

As you can see, the inferred type has an optional property.

You can also use spread syntax to add multiple fields conditionally:

```
declare let hasDates: boolean;
const nameTitle = {name: 'Khufu', title: 'Pharaoh'};
const pharaoh = { ...nameTitle, ...(hasDates && {start: -2589, end: -2566})};
//    ^? const pharaoh: {
//        start?: number;
//        end?: number;
//        name: string;
//        title: string;
//    }
```

In this case, both `start` and `end` have become optional fields. If you read `start` off this type, you'll have to consider the possibility that it's `undefined`:

```
const {start} = pharaoh;
//    ^? const start: number | undefined
```

Sometimes you want to build an object or array by transforming another one. In this case, the equivalent of "building objects all at once" is using built-in functional constructs or utility libraries like Lodash rather than loops. See Item 26 for more on this.

Things to Remember

- Prefer to build objects all at once rather than piecemeal.
- Use multiple objects and object spread syntax (`{...a, ...b}`) to add properties in a type-safe way.
- Know how to conditionally add properties to an object.

Item 22: Understand Type Narrowing

Narrowing, or "refinement," is the process by which TypeScript goes from a broad type to a more specific one. Perhaps the most common example of this is null checking:

```
const elem = document.getElementById('what-time-is-it');
//    ^? const elem: HTMLElement | null
if (elem) {
  elem.innerHTML = 'Party Time'.blink();
  // ^? const elem: HTMLElement
} else {
  elem
  // ^? const elem: null
  alert('No element #what-time-is-it');
}
```

If elem is null, then the code in the first branch won't execute. So TypeScript is able to exclude null from the union type within this block, resulting in a narrower type which is much easier to work with. Because the compiler is following the paths of execution of your code, this is also known as control flow analysis. The type checker is generally quite good at following your logic and narrowing types in conditionals like these, though it can occasionally be thwarted by aliasing (Item 23).

Notice how the same symbol, elem, has different static types at different locations in your code. This is a somewhat unusual ability amongst programming languages: in C++, Java, and Rust, for example, a variable has a single type for its entire lifetime. If you want to narrow its type, you also need to create a new variable. But in TypeScript, a symbol has a type *at a location*. Learn to take advantage of this and you'll write more concise, idiomatic TypeScript.

There are many ways that you can narrow a type. Throwing or returning from a branch will narrow a variable's type for the rest of a block:

```
const elem = document.getElementById('what-time-is-it');
//    ^? const elem: HTMLElement | null
if (!elem) throw new Error('Unable to find #what-time-is-it');
elem.innerHTML = 'Party Time'.blink();
// ^? const elem: HTMLElement
```

You can also use instanceof:

```
function contains(text: string, search: string | RegExp) {
  if (search instanceof RegExp) {
    return !!search.exec(text);
    //         ^? (parameter) search: RegExp
  }
  return text.includes(search);
  //                   ^? (parameter) search: string
}
```

A property check also works:

```
interface Apple { isGoodForBaking: boolean; }
interface Orange { numSlices: number; }
function pickFruit(fruit: Apple | Orange) {
  if ('isGoodForBaking' in fruit) {
    fruit
    // ^? (parameter) fruit: Apple
  } else {
    fruit
    // ^? (parameter) fruit: Orange
  }
  fruit
  // ^? (parameter) fruit: Apple | Orange
}
```

Some built-in functions such as `Array.isArray` are also able to narrow types:

```
function contains(text: string, terms: string | string[]) {
  const termList = Array.isArray(terms) ? terms : [terms];
  //    ^? const termList: string[]
  // ...
}
```

TypeScript is generally quite good at tracking types through conditionals. Think twice before adding a type assertion—it might be on to something that you're not! For example, this is the wrong way to exclude `null` from a union type:

```
const elem = document.getElementById('what-time-is-it');
//    ^? const elem: HTMLElement | null
if (typeof elem === 'object') {
  elem;
  // ^? const elem: HTMLElement | null
}
```

Because `typeof null` is `"object"` in JavaScript, you have not, in fact, excluded `null` with this check![1] Similar surprises can come from falsy primitive values:

```
function maybeLogX(x?: number | string | null) {
  if (!x) {
    console.log(x);
    //          ^? (parameter) x: string | number | null | undefined
  }
}
```

Because the empty string and 0 are both falsy, `x` could still be a `string` or `number` in that branch. TypeScript is right!

Another common way to help the type checker narrow your types is by putting an explicit "tag" on them:

```
interface UploadEvent { type: 'upload'; filename: string; contents: string }
interface DownloadEvent { type: 'download'; filename: string; }
type AppEvent = UploadEvent | DownloadEvent;

function handleEvent(e: AppEvent) {
  switch (e.type) {
    case 'download':
      console.log('Download', e.filename);
      //                      ^? (parameter) e: DownloadEvent
      break;
    case 'upload':
```

---

1 Why this quirk? The original JavaScript implementation represented objects with a type tag and a value. The tag for objects was 0, and `null` was represented as a null pointer (0x0), hence its type tag was 0, and `typeof null` was `"object"`. The standards committee attempted to fix this bug in 2011 but it broke too many websites.

```
        console.log('Upload', e.filename, e.contents.length, 'bytes');
        //                    ^? (parameter) e: UploadEvent
        break;
    }
}
```

This is known as a "tagged union" or "discriminated union," and it is ubiquitous in TypeScript. Chapter 4 will revisit this pattern. When you write switch statements, it's a good idea to test that you've covered all possibilities. Item 59 shows you how.

If TypeScript isn't able to figure out a type, you can introduce a special function to help it out:

```
function isInputElement(el: Element): el is HTMLInputElement {
  return 'value' in el;
}

function getElementContent(el: HTMLElement) {
  if (isInputElement(el)) {
    return el.value;
    //     ^? (parameter) el: HTMLInputElement
  }
  return el.textContent;
  //     ^? (parameter) el: HTMLElement
}
```

This is known as a "user-defined type guard," and the el is HTMLInputElement clause is called a "type predicate." As a return type, this type tells the type checker that it can narrow the type of the parameter if the function returns true.

Some functions are able to use type guards to narrow types in arrays or objects, notably the filter method on Arrays:

```
const formEls = document.querySelectorAll('.my-form *');
const formInputEls = [...formEls].filter(isInputElement);
//    ^? const formInputEls: HTMLInputElement[]
```

It's important to note user-defined type guards are no safer than a type assertion (el as HTMLInputElement): there's nothing checking that the body of a type guard corresponds to the type predicate it returns. (In this case, in fact, there are a few Elements with a value property that are not HTMLInputElements.)

You can often rework your code slightly to help TypeScript follow along. This code using a Map is correct but produces a type error:

```
const nameToNickname = new Map<string, string>();
declare let yourName: string;
let nameToUse: string;
if (nameToNickname.has(yourName)) {
  nameToUse = nameToNickname.get(yourName);
  // ~~~~~~ Type 'string | undefined' is not assignable to type 'string'.
} else {
  nameToUse = yourName;
}
```

The issue is that TypeScript doesn't understand the relationship between the `has` and `get` methods of a `Map`. It doesn't know that checking `has` eliminates the possibility of `undefined` in a subsequent lookup with `get`. A slight change eliminates the type error (and preserves the behavior):

```
const nickname = nameToNickname.get(yourName);
let nameToUse: string;
if (nickname !== undefined) {
  nameToUse = nickname;
} else {
  nameToUse = yourName;
}
```

This pattern is common and can be written more concisely using the "nullish coalescing" operator (`??`):

```
const nameToUse = nameToNickname.get(yourName) ?? yourName;
```

If you find yourself fighting with the type checker in a conditional, think about whether you can rework it to help TypeScript follow along.

It's also helpful to understand when types *don't* narrow. One notable example is in callbacks:

```
function logLaterIfNumber(obj: { value: string | number }) {
  if (typeof obj.value === "number") {
    setTimeout(() => console.log(obj.value.toFixed()));
    //                                      ~~~~~~~
    // Property 'toFixed' does not exist on type 'string | number'.
  }
}
```

We've done a `typeof` check which should narrow the type of `obj.value`. So why did it revert back to the union type, which produced a type error?

It's because the calling code might look like this:

```
const obj: { value: string | number } = { value: 123 };
logLaterIfNumber(obj);
obj.value = 'Cookie Monster';
```

By the time the callback runs, the type of `obj.value` has changed, invalidating the refinement. This code throws an exception at runtime, and TypeScript is right to warn you about it.

Understanding how types narrow will help you build an intuition for how type inference works, make sense of errors, and generally have a more productive relationship with the type checker.

Things to Remember

- Understand how TypeScript narrows types based on conditionals and other types of control flow.
- Use tagged/discriminated unions and user-defined type guards to help the process of narrowing.
- Think about whether code can be refactored to let TypeScript follow along more easily.

Item 23: Be Consistent in Your Use of Aliases

When you introduce a new name for a value:

```
const place = {name: 'New York', latLng: [41.6868, -74.2692]};
const loc = place.latLng;
```

you have created an *alias*. Changes to properties on the alias will be visible on the original value as well:

```
> loc[0] = 0;
0
> place.latLng
[ 0, -74.2692 ]
```

If you've used a language that has pointer or reference types, this is the same idea. There are two variables that point to the same underlying object.

Aliases are the bane of compiler writers in all languages because they make control flow analysis difficult. If you're deliberate in your use of aliases, TypeScript will be able to understand your code better and help you find more real errors.

Suppose you have a data structure that represents a polygon:

```
interface Coordinate {
  x: number;
  y: number;
}

interface BoundingBox {
  x: [number, number];
  y: [number, number];
```

```
    }

interface Polygon {
  exterior: Coordinate[];
  holes: Coordinate[][];
  bbox?: BoundingBox;
}
```

The geometry of the polygon is specified by the exterior and holes properties. (The holes array lets you represent doughnut shapes, which have holes in the interior.) The bbox property is an optimization that may or may not be present. You can use it to speed up a point-in-polygon check:

```
function isPointInPolygon(polygon: Polygon, pt: Coordinate) {
  if (polygon.bbox) {
    if (pt.x < polygon.bbox.x[0] || pt.x > polygon.bbox.x[1] ||
        pt.y < polygon.bbox.y[0] || pt.y > polygon.bbox.y[1]) {
      return false;
    }
  }

  // ... more complex check
}
```

This code works (and type checks) but is a bit repetitive: polygon.bbox appears five times in three lines! Here's an attempt to factor out an intermediate variable to reduce duplication:

```
function isPointInPolygon(polygon: Polygon, pt: Coordinate) {
  const box = polygon.bbox;
  if (polygon.bbox) {
    if (pt.x < box.x[0] || pt.x > box.x[1] ||
    //      ~~~                   ~~~ 'box' is possibly 'undefined'
        pt.y < box.y[0] || pt.y > box.y[1]) {
    //      ~~~                   ~~~ 'box' is possibly 'undefined'
      return false;
    }
  }
  // ...
}
```

This code still works, so why the error? By factoring out the box variable, you've created an alias for polygon.bbox, and this has thwarted the control flow analysis that quietly worked in the first example.

You can inspect the types of box and polygon.bbox to see what's happening:

```
function isPointInPolygon(polygon: Polygon, pt: Coordinate) {
  polygon.bbox
  //      ^? (property) Polygon.bbox?: BoundingBox | undefined
  const box = polygon.bbox;
  //    ^? const box: BoundingBox | undefined
```

```
    if (polygon.bbox) {
      console.log(polygon.bbox);
      //                          ^? (property) Polygon.bbox?: BoundingBox
      console.log(box);
      //               ^? const box: BoundingBox | undefined
    }
  }
```

The property check refines the type of polygon.bbox but not the type of box, hence
the errors. This leads us to the golden rule of aliasing: *if you introduce an alias, use it
consistently.*

Using box in the property check fixes the error:

```
function isPointInPolygon(polygon: Polygon, pt: Coordinate) {
  const box = polygon.bbox;
  if (box) {
    if (pt.x < box.x[0] || pt.x > box.x[1] ||
        pt.y < box.y[0] || pt.y > box.y[1]) {  // OK
      return false;
    }
  }
  // ...
}
```

The type checker is happy now, but there's an issue for human readers. We're using
two names for the same thing: box and bbox. This is a distinction without a difference
(Item 41).

Object destructuring syntax rewards consistent naming by letting us write more concise code. You can even use it on arrays and nested structures:

```
function isPointInPolygon(polygon: Polygon, pt: Coordinate) {
  const {bbox} = polygon;
  if (bbox) {
    const {x, y} = bbox;
    if (pt.x < x[0] || pt.x > x[1] || pt.y < y[0] || pt.y > y[1]) {
      return false;
    }
  }
  // ...
}
```

A few other points:

- This code would have required more property checks if the x and y properties
  had been optional, rather than the whole bbox property. We benefited from following the advice of Item 33, which discusses the importance of pushing null values to the perimeter of your types.

- An optional property was appropriate for bbox but would not have been appropriate for holes. If holes was optional, then it would be possible for it to be either missing or an empty array ([]). This would be a distinction without a difference. An empty array is a fine way to indicate "no holes."

In your interactions with the type checker, don't forget that aliasing can introduce confusion at runtime, too:

```
const {bbox} = polygon;
if (!bbox) {
  calculatePolygonBbox(polygon);  // Fills in polygon.bbox
  // Now polygon.bbox and bbox refer to different values!
}
```

TypeScript's control flow analysis tends to be quite good for local variables. But for properties you should be on guard:

```
function expandABit(p: Polygon) { /* ... */ }

polygon.bbox
//      ^? (property) Polygon.bbox?: BoundingBox | undefined
if (polygon.bbox) {
  polygon.bbox
  //      ^? (property) Polygon.bbox?: BoundingBox
  expandABit(polygon);
  polygon.bbox
  //      ^? (property) Polygon.bbox?: BoundingBox
}
```

The call to expandABit(polygon) could very well un-set polygon.bbox, so it would be safer for the type to revert to BoundingBox | undefined. But this would get frustrating: you'd have to repeat your property checks every time you called a function. So TypeScript makes the pragmatic choice to assume the function does not invalidate its type refinements. Item 48 discusses other situations like this where TypeScript trades safety for convenience.

If you'd factored out a local bbox variable instead of using polygon.bbox, the type of bbox would remain accurate, but it might no longer be the same value as polygon.bbox. If you're concerned about these sorts of side effects, the best option is to pass a read-only version of polygon to the function (Item 14). By preventing mutation, we also improve type safety. This is a concern specifically for object types (including arrays) because they are mutable. Primitive values (numbers, strings, etc.) are already immutable.

Things to Remember

- Aliasing can prevent TypeScript from narrowing types. If you create an alias for a variable, use it consistently.
- Be aware of how function calls can invalidate type refinements on properties. Trust refinements on local variables more than on properties.

Item 24: Understand How Context Is Used in Type Inference

TypeScript doesn't just infer types based on values. It also considers the context in which the value occurs. This usually works well but can sometimes lead to surprises. Understanding how context is used in type inference will help you identify and work around these surprises when they do occur.

In JavaScript, you can factor out an expression into a constant without changing the behavior of your code (so long as you don't alter execution order). In other words, these two statements are equivalent:

```
// Inline form
setLanguage('JavaScript');

// Reference form
let language = 'JavaScript';
setLanguage(language);
```

In TypeScript, this refactor still works:

```
function setLanguage(language: string) { /* ... */ }

setLanguage('JavaScript');  // OK

let language = 'JavaScript';
setLanguage(language);  // OK
```

Now suppose you take to heart the advice of Item 35 and replace the string type with a more precise union of string literal types:

```
type Language = 'JavaScript' | 'TypeScript' | 'Python';
function setLanguage(language: Language) { /* ... */ }

setLanguage('JavaScript');  // OK

let language = 'JavaScript';
setLanguage(language);
//          ~~~~~~~~ Argument of type 'string' is not assignable
//                   to parameter of type 'Language'
```

What went wrong? With the inline form, TypeScript knows from the function declaration that the parameter is supposed to be of type Language. The string literal 'JavaScript' is assignable to this type, so this is OK. But when you factor out a variable, TypeScript must infer its type at the time of assignment. It applies the usual algorithm (Item 20) and infers string, which is not assignable to Language. Hence the error.

 Some languages are able to infer types for variables based on their eventual usage. But this can also be confusing. Anders Hejlsberg, the creator of TypeScript, refers to it as "spooky action at a distance." By and large, TypeScript determines the type of a variable when it is first introduced. For a notable exception to this rule, see Item 25.

There are two good ways to solve this problem. One is to constrain the possible values of language with a type annotation:

```
let language: Language = 'JavaScript';
setLanguage(language);  // OK
```

This also has the benefit of flagging an error if there's a typo in the language—for example 'Typescript' (it should be a capital "S").

The other solution is to make the variable constant:

```
const language = 'JavaScript';
//      ^? const language: "JavaScript"
setLanguage(language);  // OK
```

By using const, we've told the type checker that this variable cannot change. So TypeScript can infer a more precise type for language, namely the string literal type "JavaScript". This is assignable to Language so the code type checks. Of course, if you do need to reassign language, then you'll need to use the type annotation.

The fundamental issue here is that we've separated the value from the context in which it's used. Sometimes this is OK, but often it is not. The rest of this item walks through a few cases where this loss of context can cause errors and shows you how to fix them.

Tuple Types

In addition to string literal types, problems can come up with tuple types. Suppose you're working with a map visualization that lets you programmatically pan the map:

```
// Parameter is a (latitude, longitude) pair.
function panTo(where: [number, number]) { /* ... */ }

panTo([10, 20]);  // OK
```

```
const loc = [10, 20];
//    ^? const loc: number[]
panTo(loc);
//    ~~~ Argument of type 'number[]' is not assignable to
//        parameter of type '[number, number]'
```

As before, you've separated a value from its context. In the first instance, [10, 20] is assignable to the tuple type [number, number]. In the second, TypeScript infers the type of loc as number[] (i.e., an array of numbers of unknown length). This is not assignable to the tuple type, since many arrays have the wrong number of elements.

So how can you fix this error without resorting to any? You've already declared it const, so that won't help. But you can still provide a type annotation to let TypeScript know precisely what you mean:

```
const loc: [number, number] = [10, 20];
panTo(loc);  // OK
```

As Item 20 explained, another way is to provide a "const context." This tells Type-Script that you intend the value to be deeply constant, rather than the shallow constant that const gives:

```
const loc = [10, 20] as const;
//    ^? const loc: readonly [10, 20]
panTo(loc);
//    ~~~ The type 'readonly [10, 20]' is 'readonly'
//        and cannot be assigned to the mutable type '[number, number]'
```

The type of loc is now inferred as readonly [10, 20], rather than number[]. Unfortunately this is *too* precise! The type signature of panTo makes no promises that it won't modify the contents of its where parameter. Since the loc parameter has a readonly type, this won't do.

The best solution here is to add a readonly annotation to the panTo function:

```
function panTo(where: readonly [number, number]) { /* ... */ }
const loc = [10, 20] as const;
panTo(loc);  // OK
```

If the type signature is outside your control, then you'll need to use an annotation. (Item 14 has more to say about readonly and type safety.)

const contexts can neatly solve issues around losing context in inference, but they do have an unfortunate downside: if you make a mistake in the definition (say you add a third element to the tuple), then the error will be flagged at the call site, not at the definition. This may be confusing, especially if the error occurs in a deeply nested object that's used far from where it's defined:

```
const loc = [10, 20, 30] as const;  // error is really here.
panTo(loc);
```

```
//     ~~~ Argument of type 'readonly [10, 20, 30]' is not assignable to
//         parameter of type 'readonly [number, number]'
//             Source has 3 element(s) but target allows only 2.
```

For this reason, it's preferable to use the inline form or apply a type declaration.

Objects

The problem of separating a value from its context also comes up when you factor out a constant from a larger object that contains some string literals or tuples. For example:

```
type Language = 'JavaScript' | 'TypeScript' | 'Python';
interface GovernedLanguage {
  language: Language;
  organization: string;
}

function complain(language: GovernedLanguage) { /* ... */ }

complain({ language: 'TypeScript', organization: 'Microsoft' });  // OK

const ts = {
  language: 'TypeScript',
  organization: 'Microsoft',
};
complain(ts);
//       ~~ Argument of type '{ language: string; organization: string; }'
//             is not assignable to parameter of type 'GovernedLanguage'
//          Types of property 'language' are incompatible
//             Type 'string' is not assignable to type 'Language'
```

In the ts object, the type of language is inferred as string. As before, the solution is to add a type annotation (const ts: GovernedLanguage = ...), use a const assertion (as const), or the satisfies operator (Item 20).

Callbacks

When you pass a callback to another function, TypeScript uses context to infer the parameter types of the callback:

```
function callWithRandomNumbers(fn: (n1: number, n2: number) => void) {
  fn(Math.random(), Math.random());
}

callWithRandomNumbers((a, b) => {
  //                   ^? (parameter) a: number
  console.log(a + b);
  //             ^? (parameter) b: number
});
```

The types of a and b are inferred as number because of the type declaration for callWithRandomNumbers. If you factor the callback out into a constant, you lose that context and get noImplicitAny errors:

```
const fn = (a, b) => {
  //          ~      Parameter 'a' implicitly has an 'any' type
  //          ~ Parameter 'b' implicitly has an 'any' type
  console.log(a + b);
}
callWithRandomNumbers(fn);
```

The solution is either to add type annotations to the parameters:

```
const fn = (a: number, b: number) => {
  console.log(a + b);
}
callWithRandomNumbers(fn);
```

or to apply a type declaration to the entire function expression if one is available (see Item 12). If the function is only used in one place, prefer the inline form since it reduces the need for annotations.

Things to Remember

- Be aware of how context is used in type inference.
- If factoring out a variable introduces a type error, maybe add a type annotation.
- If the variable is truly a constant, use a const assertion (as const). But be aware that this may result in errors surfacing at use, rather than definition.
- Prefer inlining values where it's practical to reduce the need for type annotations.

Item 25: Understand Evolving Types

In TypeScript, a variable's type is generally determined when it is declared. After this, it can be *narrowed* (by checking if it is null, for instance; see Item 22), but it cannot expand to include new values. There is one notable exception to this, however, and that is "evolving types." Understanding how these work will reduce the need for type annotations in your code and help you read TypeScript code that uses this convenient pattern.

In JavaScript, you might write a function to generate a range of numbers, like this:

```
function range(start, limit) {
  const nums = [];
  for (let i = start; i < limit; i++) {
    nums.push(i);
  }
  return nums;
}
```

When you convert this to TypeScript, it works exactly as you'd expect:

```
function range(start: number, limit: number) {
  const nums = [];
  for (let i = start; i < limit; i++) {
    nums.push(i);
  }
  return nums;
  //     ^? const nums: number[]
}
```

Upon closer inspection, however, it's surprising that this works! How does TypeScript know that the type of nums is number[] when it's initialized as [], which could be an array of any type? Clearly TypeScript is not following its usual rules for deriving a type from a literal value (Item 20). Inspecting each of the three occurrences of nums to reveal its inferred type starts to tell the story:

```
function range(start: number, limit: number) {
  const nums = [];
  //     ^? const nums: any[]
  for (let i = start; i < limit; i++) {
    nums.push(i);
    // ^? const nums: any[]
  }
  return nums;
  //     ^? const nums: number[]
}
```

The type of nums starts as any[], an undifferentiated array. But after we push number values onto it, its type "evolves" to become number[].

This is distinct from narrowing (aka "refinement"). An empty array's type can expand by pushing different elements onto it:

```
const result = [];
//     ^? const result: any[]
result.push('a');
result
// ^? const result: string[]
result.push(1);
result
// ^? const result: (string | number)[]
```

With conditionals, the type can even vary across branches. Here you can see the same behavior with a simple value, rather than an array:

```
let value;
// ^? let value: any
if (Math.random() < 0.5) {
  value = /hello/;
  value
  // ^? let value: RegExp
} else {
```

```
  value = 12;
  value
  // ^? let value: number
}
value
// ^? let value: number | RegExp
```

 This behavior can be confusing to follow in your editor since the type is only "evolved" *after* you assign or push an element. Inspecting the type on the line with the assignment still shows any or any[].

This construct is a convenient way to reduce the need for type annotations. You can use it in your own code, and you should recognize it in code that you read. It's sometimes known as "evolving any" because the variable implicitly has an any type, but this is not a dangerous any (more on that momentarily). It's also sometimes called "evolving let" or "evolving arrays."

Another case that triggers this "evolving" behavior is if a variable is initially set to null or undefined. This often comes up when you set a value in a try/catch block:

```
let value = null;
//  ^? let value: any
try {
  value = doSomethingRiskyAndReturnANumber();
  value
  // ^? let value: number
} catch (e) {
  console.warn('alas!');
}
value
// ^? let value: number | null
```

If you try to use an evolving type before you set it or push values onto it, you'll get an implicit any error:

```
function range(start: number, limit: number) {
  const nums = [];
  //    ~~~~ Variable 'nums' implicitly has type 'any[]' in some
  //         locations where its type cannot be determined
  if (start === limit) {
    return nums;
    //     ~~~~ Variable 'nums' implicitly has an 'any[]' type
  }
  for (let i = start; i < limit; i++) {
    nums.push(i);
  }
  return nums;
}
```

Put another way, evolving types are only any when you *write* to them. If you try to *read* from them while they're still any, you'll get an error. This isn't the scary any that Item 5 warned you about. It won't spread through your application like other any types.

Implicit any types do not evolve through function calls. The arrow function here trips up inference:

```
function makeSquares(start: number, limit: number) {
  const nums = [];
  //    ~~~~ Variable 'nums' implicitly has type 'any[]' in some locations
  range(start, limit).forEach(i => {
    nums.push(i * i);
  });
  return nums;
  //     ~~~~ Variable 'nums' implicitly has an 'any[]' type
}
```

Improved type inference is a good reason to prefer for-of loops to forEach loops in TypeScript. For this specific case, though, it would be better to use the built-in array map method to transform the array in a single statement, avoiding iteration and evolving types entirely. See Item 26 for more on how functional constructs can help types flow.

Evolving types come with all the usual caveats about type inference. Is the correct type for your array really (string|number)[]? Or should it be number[] and you incorrectly pushed a string? You may still want to provide an explicit type annotation to get better error checking instead of using an evolving type, or at least annotate the return type of your function to make sure that implementation errors don't escape into the type signature (Item 18).

When you build an array by pushing elements onto it or set a value conditionally, consider whether you can use the evolving type construct to reduce the need for type annotations and to help types flow through your code.

Things to Remember

- While TypeScript types typically only *refine*, the types of values initialized to null, undefined, or [ ] are allowed to *evolve*.
- Recognize and understand this construct where it occurs, and use it to reduce the need for type annotations in your own code.
- For better error checking, consider providing an explicit type annotation instead of using evolving types.

Item 26: Use Functional Constructs and Libraries to Help Types Flow

JavaScript has never included the sort of standard library you find in Python, C, or Java. Over the years, many libraries have tried to fill the gap. jQuery provided helpers not just for interacting with the DOM but also for iterating and mapping over objects and arrays. Underscore focused more on providing general utility functions, and Lodash built on this effort. Today libraries like Ramda continue to bring ideas from functional programming into the JavaScript world.

Some features from these libraries, such as `map`, `flatMap`, `filter`, and `reduce`, have made it into the JavaScript language itself. While these constructs (and the other ones provided by Lodash) are helpful in JavaScript and often preferable to a hand-rolled loop, this advantage tends to get even more lopsided when you add TypeScript to the mix. This is because their type declarations ensure that types flow through these constructs. With hand-rolled loops, you're responsible for the types yourself.

For example, consider parsing some CSV data. You could do it in plain JavaScript in a somewhat imperative style:

```
const csvData = "...";
const rawRows = csvData.split('\n');
const headers = rawRows[0].split(',');

const rows = rawRows.slice(1).map((rowStr) => {
  const row = {};
  rowStr.split(",").forEach((val, j) => {
    row[headers[j]] = val;
  });
  return row;
});
```

More functionally minded JavaScripters might prefer to build the row objects with `reduce`:

```
const rows = rawRows.slice(1)
  .map((rowStr) =>
    rowStr
      .split(",")
      .reduce((row, val, i) => ((row[headers[i]] = val), row), {})
  );
```

This version saves a few characters but may be more cryptic depending on your sensibilities. Lodash's `zipObject` function, which forms an object by "zipping" up arrays of keys and values, can tighten it even further:

```
import _ from 'lodash';
const rows = rawRows.slice(1)
    .map(rowStr => _.zipObject(headers, rowStr.split(',')));
```

Personally, I find this the clearest of all. But is it worth the cost of adding a dependency on a third-party library to your project and requiring all your coworkers to learn how to use it?

When you add TypeScript to the mix, it starts to tip the balance more strongly in favor of the Lodash solution.

Both vanilla JavaScript versions of the CSV parser produce the same error in TypeScript:

```
const rowsImperative = rawRows.slice(1).map(rowStr => {
  const row = {};
  rowStr.split(',').forEach((val, j) => {
    row[headers[j]] = val;
    // ~~~~~~~~~~~~ No index signature with a parameter of
    //             type 'string' was found on type '{}'
  });
  return row;
});
const rowsFunctional = rawRows.slice(1)
  .map((rowStr) =>
    rowStr
      .split(",")
      .reduce(
        (row, val, i) => ((row[headers[i]] = val), row),
        //                   ~~~~~~~~~~~~~~~~ No index signature with a parameter of
        //                                   type 'string' was found on type '{}'
        {}
      )
  );
```

The solution in each case is to provide a type annotation for {}, either {[column: string]: string} or Record<string, string>.

The Lodash version, on the other hand, passes the type checker without modification:

```
const rowsLodash =
  rawRows.slice(1).map(rowStr => _.zipObject(headers, rowStr.split(',')));
rowsLodash
// ^? const rowsLodash: _.Dictionary<string>[]
```

Dictionary is a Lodash type alias. Dictionary<string> is the same as {[key: string]: string} or Record<string, string>. The important thing here is that the type of rows is exactly correct, no type annotations needed.

These advantages get more pronounced as your data munging gets more elaborate. For example, suppose you have an object containing a list of the players on each team in the NBA:

```
interface BasketballPlayer {
  name: string;
  team: string;
```

```
  salary: number;
}
declare const rosters: {[team: string]: BasketballPlayer[]};
```

To build a flat list using a loop, you might use concat with an array. This code runs fine but does not type check:

```
let allPlayers = [];
//  ~~~~~~~~~~ Variable 'allPlayers' implicitly has type 'any[]'
//             in some locations where its type cannot be determined
for (const players of Object.values(rosters)) {
  allPlayers = allPlayers.concat(players);
  //           ~~~~~~~~~~ Variable 'allPlayers' implicitly has an 'any[]' type
}
```

(The concat method does not trigger the "evolving" behavior described in Item 25.)

To fix the error you need to add a type annotation to allPlayers:

```
let allPlayers: BasketballPlayer[] = [];
for (const players of Object.values(rosters)) {
  allPlayers = allPlayers.concat(players);  // OK
}
```

But a better solution is to use Array.prototype.flat:

```
const allPlayers = Object.values(rosters).flat(); // OK
//    ^? const allPlayers: BasketballPlayer[]
```

The flat method flattens a multidimensional array. Its type signature is something like T[][] => T[].[2] This version is the most concise and requires no type annotations. As an added bonus you can use const instead of let to prevent future mutations to the allPlayers variable.

Say you want to start with allPlayers and make a list of the highest-paid players on each team, ordered by salary.

Here's a solution without Lodash. It requires a type annotation wherever you don't use functional constructs:

```
const teamToPlayers: {[team: string]: BasketballPlayer[]} = {};
for (const player of allPlayers) {
  const {team} = player;
  teamToPlayers[team] = teamToPlayers[team] || [];
  teamToPlayers[team].push(player);
}

for (const players of Object.values(teamToPlayers)) {
  players.sort((a, b) => b.salary - a.salary);
}
```

---

2 The flat method also takes a depth parameter which complicates the type declarations.

```
const bestPaid = Object.values(teamToPlayers).map(players => players[0]);
bestPaid.sort((playerA, playerB) => playerB.salary - playerA.salary);
console.log(bestPaid);
```

Here's the output:

```
[
  { team: 'GSW', salary: 51915615, name: 'Stephen Curry' },
  { team: 'PHO', salary: 47649433, name: 'Kevin Durant' },
  { team: 'DEN', salary: 47607350, name: 'Nikola Jokić' },
  { team: 'PHI', salary: 47607350, name: 'Joel Embiid' },
  { team: 'LAL', salary: 47607350, name: 'LeBron James' },
  ...
]
```

Here's the equivalent with Lodash:

```
const bestPaid = _(allPlayers)
  .groupBy(player => player.team)
  .mapValues(players => _.maxBy(players, p => p.salary)!)
  .values()
  .sortBy(p => -p.salary)
  .value();
console.log(bestPaid.slice(0, 10));
//              ^? const bestPaid: BasketballPlayer[]
```

In addition to being half the length, this code only requires a single non-null assertion (the type checker doesn't know that the players array passed to _.maxBy is non-empty). It makes use of a "chain," a concept in Lodash and Underscore that lets you write a sequence of operations in a more natural order. Instead of writing:

```
_.c(_.b(_.a(v)))
```

you write:

```
_(v).a().b().c().value()
```

The _(v) "wraps" the value, and the .value() "unwraps" it.

You can inspect each function call in the chain to see the type of the wrapped value. It's always correct.

It's not a coincidence that types flow so well through built-in functional constructs and those in libraries like Lodash. By avoiding mutation and returning new values from every call, they are able to produce new types as well (Item 19). To a large extent, the development of TypeScript has been driven by an attempt to accurately model the behavior of JavaScript libraries in the wild. Take advantage of all this work and use them!

Things to Remember

- Use built-in functional constructs and those in utility libraries like Lodash instead of hand-rolled constructs to improve type flow, increase legibility, and reduce the need for explicit type annotations.

Item 27: Use async Functions Instead of Callbacks to Improve Type Flow

Classic JavaScript modeled asynchronous behavior using callbacks. This led to the infamous "pyramid of doom":

```
declare function fetchURL(
  url: string, callback: (response: string) => void
): void;

fetchURL(url1, function(response1) {
  fetchURL(url2, function(response2) {
    fetchURL(url3, function(response3) {
      // ...
      console.log(1);
    });
    console.log(2);
  });
  console.log(3);
});
console.log(4);

// Logs:
// 4
// 3
// 2
// 1
```

This code is heavily nested and, as you can see from the logs, the execution order is the opposite of the code order. This makes callback code hard to read. It gets even more confusing if you want to run the requests concurrently or bail when an error occurs.

ES2015 introduced the concept of a Promise to break the pyramid of doom. A Promise represents something that will be available in the future (they're also sometimes called "futures"). Here's the same code using Promises:

```
const page1Promise = fetch(url1);
page1Promise.then(response1 => {
  return fetch(url2);
}).then(response2 => {
  return fetch(url3);
}).then(response3 => {
```

```
      // ...
    }).catch(error => {
      // ...
    });
```

Now there's less nesting, and the execution order more directly matches the code order. It's also easier to consolidate error handling and use higher-order tools like `Promise.all`.

ES2017 introduced the `async` and `await` keywords to make things even more concise:

```
    async function fetchPages() {
      const response1 = await fetch(url1);
      const response2 = await fetch(url2);
      const response3 = await fetch(url3);
      // ...
    }
```

The `await` keyword pauses execution of the `fetchPages` function until each Promise resolves. Within an `async` function, awaiting a Promise that rejects will throw an exception. This lets you use the usual `try/catch` machinery:

```
    async function fetchPages() {
      try {
        const response1 = await fetch(url1);
        const response2 = await fetch(url2);
        const response3 = await fetch(url3);
        // ...
      } catch (e) {
        // ...
      }
    }
```

Just like exceptions, Promise rejections in TypeScript are untyped.

`async` and `await` are supported by all recent JavaScript runtimes, but even if you target ES5 or earlier, the TypeScript compiler will perform some elaborate transformations to make `async` and `await` work. In other words, whatever your runtime, with TypeScript you can use async/await.

There are a few good reasons to prefer Promises or `async`/`await` to callbacks:

- Promises are easier to compose than callbacks.
- Types are able to flow through Promises more easily than callbacks.

If you want to fetch the pages concurrently, for example, you can compose Promises with `Promise.all`:

```
async function fetchPages() {
  const [response1, response2, response3] = await Promise.all([
    fetch(url1), fetch(url2), fetch(url3)
  ]);
  // ...
}
```

Using destructuring assignment with `await` is particularly nice in this context.

TypeScript is able to infer the types of each of the three `response` variables as `Response`. The equivalent code to issue the requests concurrently with callbacks requires more machinery and a type annotation:

```
function fetchPagesWithCallbacks() {
  let numDone = 0;
  const responses: string[] = [];
  const done = () => {
    const [response1, response2, response3] = responses;
    // ...
  };
  const urls = [url1, url2, url3];
  urls.forEach((url, i) => {
    fetchURL(url, r => {
      responses[i] = url;
      numDone++;
      if (numDone === urls.length) done();
    });
  });
}
```

Extending this to include error handling or to be as generic as `Promise.all` is challenging.

Type inference also works well with `Promise.race`, which resolves when the first of its input Promises resolves. You can use this to add timeouts to Promises in a general way:

```
function timeout(timeoutMs: number): Promise<never> {
  return new Promise((resolve, reject) => {
    setTimeout(() => reject('timeout'), timeoutMs);
  });
}

async function fetchWithTimeout(url: string, timeoutMs: number) {
  return Promise.race([fetch(url), timeout(timeoutMs)]);
}
```

The return type of `fetchWithTimeout` is inferred as `Promise<Response>`, no type annotations required. It's interesting to dig into why this works: the return type of `Promise.race` is the union of the types of its inputs, in this case `Promise<Response | never>`. But taking a union with `never` (the empty set) is a no-op, so this gets simplified to `Promise<Response>`. When you work with Promises, all of TypeScript's type inference machinery works to get you the right types.

You may occasionally need to use raw Promises, notably when you are wrapping a callback API like `setTimeout`. But if you have a choice, you should generally prefer `async`/`await` to raw Promises for two reasons:

- It typically produces more concise and straightforward code.
- It enforces that `async` functions always return Promises.

This latter property helps avoid a confusing class of bugs. By definition, an `async` function always returns a `Promise`. This is true even if it doesn't `await` anything. TypeScript can help you build an intuition for this:

```
async function getNumber() { return 42; }
//             ^? function getNumber(): Promise<number>
```

You can also create `async` arrow functions:

```
const getNumber = async () => 42;
//    ^? const getNumber: () => Promise<number>
```

The raw Promise equivalent is:

```
const getNumber = () => Promise.resolve(42);
//    ^? const getNumber: () => Promise<number>
```

While it may seem odd to return a Promise for an immediately available value, this actually helps enforce an important rule: a function should either always be run synchronously or always be run asynchronously. It should never mix the two.

To see how breaking this rule can lead to chaos, let's try to add a cache to the `fetch` URL function:

```
// Don't do this!
const _cache: {[url: string]: string} = {};
function fetchWithCache(url: string, callback: (text: string) => void) {
  if (url in _cache) {
    callback(_cache[url]);
  } else {
    fetchURL(url, text => {
      _cache[url] = text;
      callback(text);
    });
  }
}
```

While invoking the callback immediately may seem like an optimization, the function is now extremely difficult for a client to use:

```
let requestStatus: 'loading' | 'success' | 'error';
function getUser(userId: string) {
```

```
  fetchWithCache(`/user/${userId}`, profile => {
    requestStatus = 'success';
  });
  requestStatus = 'loading';
}
```

What will the value of requestStatus be after calling getUser? It depends entirely on whether the profile is cached. If it's not, requestStatus will be set to "success." If it is, it'll get set to "success" and then set back to "loading." Oops!

Using async for both functions enforces consistent behavior:

```
const _cache: {[url: string]: string} = {};
async function fetchWithCache(url: string) {
  if (url in _cache) {
    return _cache[url];
  }
  const response = await fetch(url);
  const text = await response.text();
  _cache[url] = text;
  return text;
}

let requestStatus: 'loading' | 'success' | 'error';
async function getUser(userId: string) {
  requestStatus = 'loading';
  const profile = await fetchWithCache(`/user/${userId}`);
  requestStatus = 'success';
}
```

Now it's completely transparent that requestStatus will end in "success." It's easy to accidentally produce half-synchronous code with callbacks or raw Promises, but difficult with async.[3]

Note that if you return a Promise from an async function, it will not get wrapped in another Promise: the return type will be Promise<T> rather than Promise <Promise<T>>. Again, TypeScript will help you build an intuition for this:

```
async function getJSON(url: string) {
  const response = await fetch(url);
  const jsonPromise = response.json();
  return jsonPromise;
  //      ^? const jsonPromise: Promise<any>
}
getJSON
// ^? function getJSON(url: string): Promise<any>
```

---

3 There's still a more subtle bug in this version: if you call fetchWithCache twice in a row with the same URL, it will issue two requests. How would you fix this?

Things to Remember

- Prefer Promises to callbacks for better composability and type flow.

- Prefer `async` and `await` to raw Promises when possible. They produce more concise, straightforward code and eliminate whole classes of errors.

- If a function returns a Promise, declare it `async`.

Item 28: Use Classes and Currying to Create New Inference Sites

Suppose you define an API using a TypeScript `interface`:

```
export interface SeedAPI {
  '/seeds': Seed[];
  '/seed/apple': Seed;
  '/seed/strawberry': Seed;
  // ...
}
```

This says that our API has a `/seeds` endpoint that returns an array of `Seed` objects. The `/seed/apple` and `/seed/strawberry` endpoints return one `Seed` object.

Let's write a function that issues requests to our API endpoints. This function should check that the endpoints exist, and it should return the correct type of data. This will be extremely helpful for making safe API calls from the client.

Here's how that function should work:

```
// Correct usage:
const berry = await fetchAPI<SeedAPI>('/seed/strawberry'); // OK, returns Seed

// Incorrect usage; these should be errors:
fetchAPI<SeedAPI>('/seed/chicken');  // endpoint doesn't exist
const seed: Seed = await fetchAPI<SeedAPI>('/seeds'); // wrong return type
```

Here's how you might declare `fetchAPI` (we're not concerned about the implementation here, just the types):

```
declare function fetchAPI<
  API, Path extends keyof API
>(path: Path): Promise<API[Path]>;
```

Unfortunately, when you try to use this, you'll get an error:

```
fetchAPI<SeedAPI>('/seed/strawberry');
//       ~~~~~~~ Expected 2 type arguments, but got 1.
```

The problem is that type inference in TypeScript is an all or nothing affair: either you can let TypeScript infer *all* the type parameters from usage, or you can specify all of them explicitly. There's no in-between. (You can provide a default value for a type parameter, but this can only reference other type parameters; it can't be inferred from usage.)

The API type parameter could be anything: since we'd like fetchAPI to work with any API, it can't possibly be inferred. It has to be specified explicitly. So it would seem the only solution here is to write the Path type explicitly, too:

```
const berry = fetchAPI<SeedAPI, '/seed/strawberry'>('/seed/strawberry');  // ok
//      ^? const berry: Promise<Seed>
```

This works, but it's frustratingly repetitive. Surely there's a better way. We need to somehow separate the place where we explicitly write the API type parameter from the place where we infer the Path type parameter.

There are two standard ways to do this: classes and currying.

Classes

Classes are very good at capturing bits of state. They spare you from having to repeatedly pass the same state to a set of related functions (the class's methods). In TypeScript, it turns out that classes are also very good at capturing *types*.

Here's how you can define a class to solve this problem:

```
declare class ApiFetcher<API> {
  fetch<Path extends keyof API>(path: Path): Promise<API[Path]>;
}
```

And here's how you use it:

```
const fetcher = new ApiFetcher<SeedAPI>();
const berry = await fetcher.fetch('/seed/strawberry'); // OK
//      ^? const berry: Seed

fetcher.fetch('/seed/chicken');
//             ~~~~~~~~~~~~~~~
// Argument of type '"/seed/chicken"' is not assignable to type 'keyof SeedAPI'

const seed: Seed = await fetcher.fetch('/seeds');
//          ~~~~ Seed[] is not assignable to Seed
```

This produces exactly the errors we were hoping for. (You also need to implement the class, of course! We're just focusing on the types here.)

What used to be a function that needed two generic type parameters is now a class with one generic type parameter that you specify explicitly, and a method with one generic type parameter that's inferred. TypeScript is perfectly happy to let you bind the API type parameter when you call the class's constructor (new ApiFetcher<SeedAPI>()) and then infer Path when you call the fetch method.

Using classes to create a distinct binding site is particularly effective when you have multiple methods that all require the same type parameter.

Currying

Fun fact: programming languages don't really need functions with more than one parameter. Instead of:

```
declare function getDate(mon: string, day: number): Date;
getDate('dec', 25);
```

you could write a function that returns another function:

```
declare function getDate(mon: string): (day: number) => Date;
getDate('dec')(25);
```

Note the slightly different syntax to call the second version. This practice is known as *currying*, after the logician Haskell Curry, who always disavowed having come up with the technique.

Currying gives us the flexibility we need to introduce as many inference sites as we like. Each function call can infer new type parameters.

Here's how you can rework `fetchAPI` using functions that return functions:

```
declare function fetchAPI<API>():
  <Path extends keyof API>(path: Path) => Promise<API[Path]>;
```

Now `fetchAPI` takes *no* parameters, but it returns a function that takes one. Here's how you use it:

```
const berry = await fetchAPI<SeedAPI>()('/seed/strawberry'); // OK
//      ^? const berry: Seed

fetchAPI<SeedAPI>()('/seed/chicken');
//                    ~~~~~~~~~~~~~~~
// Argument of type '"/seed/chicken"' is not assignable to type 'keyof SeedAPI'
//
const seed: Seed = await fetchAPI<SeedAPI>()('/seeds');
//    ~~~~ Seed[] is not assignable to Seed
```

Just like the class solution, this works in the case where we want it to and produces the desired error in the others. You can use an intermediate variable to separate out the two function calls to reduce repetition:

```
const fetchSeedAPI = fetchAPI<SeedAPI>();
const berry = await fetchSeedAPI('/seed/strawberry');
//      ^? const berry: Seed
```

The currying approach isn't as distinct from the class approach as it might initially appear. If you use a different name and return an object type instead of a function, they look nearly identical:

```
declare function apiFetcher<API>(): {
  fetch<Path extends keyof API>(path: Path): Promise<API[Path]>;
}

const fetcher = apiFetcher<SeedAPI>();
fetcher.fetch('/seed/strawberry');  // ok
```

The only difference in usage between this and the class example is the keyword new.

If you want to specify some generic parameters explicitly while allowing others to be inferred, classes and currying are your two options.

So which one should you prefer? Ultimately it's up to you. Whichever one feels most comfortable and produces the API you find most convenient is the way to go. The currying approach does have at least one advantage in the context of TypeScript, however: it creates a scope in which you can define local type aliases:

```
function fetchAPI<API>() {
  type Routes = keyof API & string;  // local type alias

  return <Path extends Routes>(
    path: Path
  ): Promise<API[Path]> => fetch(path).then(r => r.json());
}
```

You can't do this with just a declaration: only the implementation introduces a new scope. Local type aliases like Routes can cut down on repetition involving complex type expressions. There is no equivalent of this for classes.

Things to Remember

- For functions with multiple type parameters, inference is all or nothing: either all type parameters are inferred or all must be specified explicitly.
- To get partial inference, use either classes or currying to create a new inference site.
- Prefer the currying approach if you'd like to create a local type alias.

CHAPTER 4

Type Design

> Show me your flowcharts and conceal your tables, and I shall continue to be mystified.
> Show me your tables, and I won't usually need your flowcharts; they'll be obvious.
>
> —Fred Brooks, *The Mythical Man Month* (Addison-Wesley Professional)

The language in Fred Brooks's quote is dated, but the sentiment remains true: code is difficult to understand if you can't see the data or data types on which it operates. This is one of the great advantages of a type system: by writing out types, you make them visible to readers of your code. And this makes your code understandable.

Other chapters cover the nuts and bolts of TypeScript types: using them, inferring them, transforming them, and writing declarations with them. This chapter discusses the design of the types themselves. The examples in this chapter are all written with TypeScript in mind, but most of the ideas are more broadly applicable.

If you write your types well, then with any luck your flowcharts will be obvious, too.

Item 29: Prefer Types That Always Represent Valid States

If you design your types well, your code should be straightforward to write. But if you design your types poorly, no amount of cleverness or documentation will save you. Your code will be confusing and prone to bugs.

A key to effective type design is crafting types that can only represent a valid state. This item walks through a few examples of how this can go wrong and shows you how to fix them.

Suppose you're building a web application that lets you select a page, loads the content of that page, and then displays it. You might write the state like this:

```
interface State {
  pageText: string;
  isLoading: boolean;
  error?: string;
}
```

When you write your code to render the page, you need to consider all of these fields:

```
function renderPage(state: State) {
  if (state.error) {
    return `Error! Unable to load ${currentPage}: ${state.error}`;
  } else if (state.isLoading) {
    return `Loading ${currentPage}...`;
  }
  return `<h1>${currentPage}</h1>\n${state.pageText}`;
}
```

Is this right, though? What if isLoading and error are both set? What would that mean? Is it better to display the loading message or the error message? It's hard to say! There's not enough information available.

Or what if you're writing a changePage function? Here's an attempt:

```
async function changePage(state: State, newPage: string) {
  state.isLoading = true;
  try {
    const response = await fetch(getUrlForPage(newPage));
    if (!response.ok) {
      throw new Error(`Unable to load ${newPage}: ${response.statusText}`);
    }
    const text = await response.text();
    state.isLoading = false;
    state.pageText = text;
  } catch (e) {
    state.error = '' + e;
  }
}
```

There are many problems with this! Here are a few:

- We forgot to set state.isLoading to false in the error case.
- We didn't clear out state.error, so if the previous request failed, then you'll keep seeing that error message instead of a loading message or the new page.
- If the user changes pages again while the page is loading, who knows what will happen. They might see a new page and then an error, or the first page and not the second, depending on the order in which the responses come back.

The problem is that the state includes both too little information (which request failed? which is loading?) and too much: the State type allows both isLoading and error to be set, even though this represents an invalid state. This makes both render() and changePage() impossible to implement well.

Here's a better way to represent the application state:

```
interface RequestPending {
  state: 'pending';
}
interface RequestError {
  state: 'error';
  error: string;
}
interface RequestSuccess {
  state: 'ok';
  pageText: string;
}
type RequestState = RequestPending | RequestError | RequestSuccess;

interface State {
  currentPage: string;
  requests: {[page: string]: RequestState};
}
```

This uses a tagged union (also known as a "discriminated union") to explicitly model the different states that a network request can be in. This version of the state is three to four times longer, but it has the enormous advantage of not admitting invalid states. The current page is modeled explicitly, as is the state of every request that you issue. As a result, the renderPage and changePage functions are easy to implement:

```
function renderPage(state: State) {
  const {currentPage} = state;
  const requestState = state.requests[currentPage];
  switch (requestState.state) {
    case 'pending':
      return `Loading ${currentPage}...`;
    case 'error':
      return `Error! Unable to load ${currentPage}: ${requestState.error}`;
    case 'ok':
      return `<h1>${currentPage}</h1>\n${requestState.pageText}`;
  }
}

async function changePage(state: State, newPage: string) {
  state.requests[newPage] = {state: 'pending'};
  state.currentPage = newPage;
  try {
    const response = await fetch(getUrlForPage(newPage));
    if (!response.ok) {
      throw new Error(`Unable to load ${newPage}: ${response.statusText}`);
    }
    const pageText = await response.text();
    state.requests[newPage] = {state: 'ok', pageText};
```

```
  } catch (e) {
    state.requests[newPage] = {state: 'error', error: '' + e};
  }
}
```

The ambiguity from the first implementation is entirely gone: it's clear what the current page is, and every request is in exactly one state. If the user changes the page after a request has been issued, that's no problem either. The old request still completes, but it doesn't affect the UI.

For a simpler but more dire example, consider the fate of Air France Flight 447, an Airbus 330 that disappeared over the Atlantic on June 1, 2009. The Airbus was a fly-by-wire aircraft, meaning that the pilots' control inputs went through a computer system before affecting the physical control surfaces of the plane. In the wake of the crash, many questions were raised about the wisdom of relying on computers to make such life-and-death decisions. Two years later when the black box recorders were recovered from the bottom of the ocean, they revealed many factors that led to the crash. A key factor was bad state design.

The cockpit of the Airbus 330 had a separate set of controls for the pilot and copilot. The "side sticks" controlled the angle of attack. Pulling back would send the airplane into a climb, while pushing forward would make it dive. The Airbus 330 used a system called "dual input" mode, which let the two side sticks move independently. Here's how you might model its state in TypeScript:

```
interface CockpitControls {
  /** Angle of the left side stick in degrees, 0 = neutral, + = forward */
  leftSideStick: number;
  /** Angle of the right side stick in degrees, 0 = neutral, + = forward */
  rightSideStick: number;
}
```

Suppose you were given this data structure and asked to write a `getStickSetting` function that computed the current stick setting. How would you do it?

One way would be to assume that the pilot (who sits on the left) is in control:

```
function getStickSetting(controls: CockpitControls) {
  return controls.leftSideStick;
}
```

But what if the copilot has taken control? Maybe you should use whichever stick is away from zero:

```
function getStickSetting(controls: CockpitControls) {
  const {leftSideStick, rightSideStick} = controls;
  if (leftSideStick === 0) {
    return rightSideStick;
  }
  return leftSideStick;
}
```

But there's a problem with this implementation: we can only be confident returning the left setting if the right one is neutral. So you should check for that:

```
function getStickSetting(controls: CockpitControls) {
  const {leftSideStick, rightSideStick} = controls;
  if (leftSideStick === 0) {
    return rightSideStick;
  } else if (rightSideStick === 0) {
    return leftSideStick;
  }
  // ???
}
```

What do you do if they're both non-zero? Hopefully they're about the same, in which case you could just average them:

```
function getStickSetting(controls: CockpitControls) {
  const {leftSideStick, rightSideStick} = controls;
  if (leftSideStick === 0) {
    return rightSideStick;
  } else if (rightSideStick === 0) {
    return leftSideStick;
  }
  if (Math.abs(leftSideStick - rightSideStick) < 5) {
    return (leftSideStick + rightSideStick) / 2;
  }
  // ???
}
```

But what if they're not? Can you throw an error? Not really: the wing flaps need to be set at some angle!

On Air France 447, the copilot silently pulled back on his side stick as the plane entered a storm. It gained altitude but eventually lost speed and entered a stall, a condition in which the plane is moving too slowly to effectively generate lift. It began to drop.

To escape a stall, pilots are trained to push the controls forward to make the plane dive and regain speed. This is exactly what the pilot did. But the copilot was still silently pulling back on his side stick. And the Airbus function looked like this:

```
function getStickSetting(controls: CockpitControls) {
  return (controls.leftSideStick + controls.rightSideStick) / 2;
}
```

Even though the pilot pushed the stick fully forward, it averaged out to nothing. He had no idea why the plane wasn't diving. By the time the copilot revealed what he'd done, the plane had lost too much altitude to recover and it crashed into the ocean, killing all 228 people on board.

The point of all this is that there is no good way to implement getStickSetting given that input! The function has been set up to fail. In most planes the two sets of controls are mechanically connected. If the copilot pulls back, the pilot's controls will also pull back. The state of these controls is simple to express:

```
interface CockpitControls {
  /** Angle of the stick in degrees, 0 = neutral, + = forward */
  stickAngle: number;
}
```

And now, as in the Fred Brooks quote from the start of the chapter, our flowcharts are obvious. You don't need a `getStickSetting` function at all.

As you design your types, take care to think about which values you are including and which you are excluding. If you only allow values that represent valid states, your code will be easier to write and TypeScript will have an easier time checking it. This is a very general principle, and several of the other items in this chapter will cover specific manifestations of it.

Things to Remember

- Types that represent both valid and invalid states are likely to lead to confusing and error-prone code.
- Prefer types that only represent valid states. Even if they are longer or harder to express, they will save you time and pain in the end!

Item 30: Be Liberal in What You Accept and Strict in What You Produce

This idea is known as the *robustness principle* or *Postel's Law*, after Jon Postel, who wrote it in the context of the TCP networking protocol:

> TCP implementations should follow a general principle of robustness: be conservative in what you do, be liberal in what you accept from others.

A similar rule applies to the contracts for functions. It's fine for your functions to be broad in what they accept as inputs, but they should generally be more specific in what they produce as outputs.

As an example, a 3D mapping API might provide a way to position the camera and calculate a viewport for a bounding box:

```
declare function setCamera(camera: CameraOptions): void;
declare function viewportForBounds(bounds: LngLatBounds): CameraOptions;
```

It is convenient that the result of `viewportForBounds` can be passed directly to `setCamera` to position the camera.

Let's look at the definitions of these types:

```
interface CameraOptions {
  center?: LngLat;
  zoom?: number;
  bearing?: number;
  pitch?: number;
}
type LngLat =
  { lng: number; lat: number; } |
  { lon: number; lat: number; } |
  [number, number];
```

The fields in CameraOptions are all optional because you might want to set just the center or zoom without changing the bearing or pitch. The LngLat type also makes setCamera liberal in what it accepts: you can pass in a {lng, lat} object, a {lon, lat} object, or a [lng, lat] pair if you're confident you got the order right. These accommodations make the function easy to call.

The viewportForBounds function takes in another "liberal" type:

```
type LngLatBounds =
  {northeast: LngLat, southwest: LngLat} |
  [LngLat, LngLat] |
  [number, number, number, number];
```

You can specify the bounds either using named corners, a pair of lat/lngs, or a four-tuple if you're confident you got the order right. Since LngLat already accommodates three forms, there are no fewer than 19 possible forms for LngLatBounds (3 × 3 + 3 × 3 + 1). Liberal indeed!

Now let's write a function that adjusts the viewport to accommodate a GeoJSON feature and stores the new viewport in the URL (we'll assume we have a helper function to calculate the bounding box of a GeoJSON feature):

```
function focusOnFeature(f: Feature) {
  const bounds = calculateBoundingBox(f); // helper function
  const camera = viewportForBounds(bounds);
  setCamera(camera);
  const {center: {lat, lng}, zoom} = camera;
          //        ~~~      Property 'lat' does not exist on type ...
          //            ~~~ Property 'lng' does not exist on type ...
  zoom;
  // ^? const zoom: number | undefined
  window.location.search = `?v=@${lat},${lng}z${zoom}`;
}
```

Whoops! Only the zoom property exists, but its type is inferred as number|undefined, which is also problematic. The issue is that the type declaration for viewportFor Bounds indicates that it is liberal not just in what it accepts but also in what it *produces.* The only type-safe way to use the `camera` result is to introduce a code branch for each component of the union type.

The return type with lots of optional properties and union types makes `viewportFor Bounds` difficult to use. Its broad parameter type is convenient, but its broad return type is not. A more convenient API would be strict in what it produces.

One way to do this is to distinguish a canonical format for coordinates. Following JavaScript's convention of distinguishing "array" and "array-like" (Item 17), you can draw a distinction between `LngLat` and `LngLatLike`. You can also distinguish between a fully defined `Camera` type and the partial version accepted by `setCamera`:

```
interface LngLat { lng: number; lat: number; };
type LngLatLike = LngLat | { lon: number; lat: number; } | [number, number];

interface Camera {
  center: LngLat;
  zoom: number;
  bearing: number;
  pitch: number;
}
interface CameraOptions extends Omit<Partial<Camera>, 'center'> {
  center?: LngLatLike;
}
type LngLatBounds =
  {northeast: LngLatLike, southwest: LngLatLike} |
  [LngLatLike, LngLatLike] |
  [number, number, number, number];

declare function setCamera(camera: CameraOptions): void;
declare function viewportForBounds(bounds: LngLatBounds): Camera;
```

The loose `CameraOptions` type adapts the stricter `Camera` type. Using `Partial <Camera>` as the parameter type in `setCamera` would not work here since you do want to allow `LngLatLike` objects for the `center` property. And you can't write `"Camera Options extends Partial<Camera>"` since `LngLatLike` is a supertype of `LngLat`, not a subtype. (If this feels backwards, head over to Item 7 for a refresher.)

If this seems too complicated, you could also write the type out explicitly at the cost of some repetition:

```
interface CameraOptions {
  center?: LngLatLike;
  zoom?: number;
  bearing?: number;
  pitch?: number;
}
```

In either case, with these new type declarations the `focusOnFeature` function passes the type checker:

```
function focusOnFeature(f: Feature) {
  const bounds = calculateBoundingBox(f);
  const camera = viewportForBounds(bounds);
  setCamera(camera);
  const {center: {lat, lng}, zoom} = camera;  // OK
  //                         ^? const zoom: number
  window.location.search = `?v=@${lat},${lng}z${zoom}`;
}
```

This time the type of `zoom` is `number`, rather than `number|undefined`. The `viewport ForBounds` function is now much easier to use. If there were any other functions that produced bounds, you would also need to introduce a canonical form and a distinction between `LngLatBounds` and `LngLatBoundsLike`.

Is allowing 19 possible forms of bounding box a good design? Perhaps not. But if you're writing type declarations for a library that does this, you need to model its behavior. Just don't have 19 return types!

One of the most common applications of this pattern is to functions that take arrays as parameters. For example, here's a function that sums the elements of an array:

```
function sum(xs: number[]): number {
  let sum = 0;
  for (const x of xs) {
    sum += x;
  }
  return sum;
}
```

The return type of `number` is quite strict. Great! But what about the parameter type of `number[]`? We're not using many of its capabilities, so it could be looser. Item 17 discussed the `ArrayLike` type, and `ArrayLike<number>` would work well here. Item 14 discussed `readonly` arrays, and `readonly number[]` would also work well as a parameter type.

But if you only need to iterate over the parameter, then `Iterable` is the broadest type of all:

```
function sum(xs: Iterable<number>): number {
  let sum = 0;
  for (const x of xs) {
    sum += x;
  }
  return sum;
}
```

This works as you'd expect with an array:

```
const six = sum([1, 2, 3]);
//    ^? const six: number
```

The advantage of using `Iterable` here instead of `Array` or `ArrayLike` is that it also allows generator expressions:

```
function* range(limit: number) {
  for (let i = 0; i < limit; i++) {
    yield i;
  }
}
const zeroToNine = range(10);
//    ^? const zeroToNine: Generator<number, void, unknown>
const fortyFive = sum(zeroToNine);  // ok, result is 45
```

If your function just needs to iterate over its parameter, use `Iterable` to make it work with generators as well. If you're using `for-of` loops then you won't need to change a single line of your code.

Things to Remember

- Input types tend to be broader than output types. Optional properties and union types are more common in parameter types than return types.

- Avoid broad return types since these will be awkward for clients to use.

- To reuse types between parameters and return types, introduce a canonical form (for return types) and a looser form (for parameters).

- Use `Iterable<T>` instead of `T[]` if you only need to iterate over your function parameter.

Item 31: Don't Repeat Type Information in Documentation

What's wrong with this code?

```
/**
 * Returns a string with the foreground color.
 * Takes zero or one arguments. With no arguments, returns the
 * standard foreground color. With one argument, returns the foreground color
 * for a particular page.
 */
function getForegroundColor(page?: string) {
  return page === 'login' ? {r: 127, g: 127, b: 127} : {r: 0, g: 0, b: 0};
}
```

The code and the comment disagree! Without more context it's hard to say which is right, but something is clearly amiss. As a professor of mine used to say, "when your code and your comments disagree, they're both wrong!"

Let's assume that the code represents the desired behavior. There are a few issues with this comment:

- It says that the function returns the color as a `string` when it actually returns an `{r, g, b}` object.
- It explains that the function takes zero or one arguments, which is already clear from the type signature.
- It's needlessly wordy: the comment is longer than the function declaration *and* implementation!

TypeScript's type annotation system is designed to be compact, descriptive, and readable. Its developers are language experts with decades of experience. It's almost certainly a better way to express the types of your function's inputs and outputs than your prose!

And because your type annotations are checked by the TypeScript compiler, they'll never get out of sync with the implementation. Perhaps `getForegroundColor` used to return a string but was later changed to return an object. The person who made the change might have forgotten to update the long comment.

Nothing stays in sync unless it's forced to. With type annotations, TypeScript's type checker is that force! If you put type information in annotations rather than documentation, you greatly increase your confidence that it will remain correct as the code evolves.

A better comment might look like this:

```
/** Get the foreground color for the application or a specific page. */
function getForegroundColor(page?: string): Color {
  // ...
}
```

If you want to describe a particular parameter, use an `@param` JSDoc annotation. See Item 68 for more on this.

Comments about a lack of mutation are also suspect:

```
/** Sort the strings by numeric value (i.e. "2" < "10"). Does not modify nums. */
function sortNumerically(nums: string[]): string[] {
  return nums.sort((a, b) => Number(a) - Number(b));
}
```

The comment *says* that this function doesn't modify its parameter, but the `sort` method on Arrays operates in place, so it very much does. Claims in comments don't count for much.

If you declare the parameter `readonly` instead (Item 14), then you can let TypeScript enforce the contract:

```
/** Sort the strings by numeric value (i.e. "2" < "10"). */
function sortNumerically(nums: readonly string[]): string[] {
  return nums.sort((a, b) => Number(a) - Number(b));
  //              ~~~~ ~ ~ Property 'sort' does not exist on 'readonly string[]'.
}
```

A correct implementation of this function would either copy the array or use the immutable `toSorted` method:

```
/** Sort the strings by numeric value (i.e. "2" < "10"). */
function sortNumerically(nums: readonly string[]): string[] {
  return nums.toSorted((a, b) => Number(a) - Number(b));  // ok
}
```

What's true for comments is also true for variable names. Avoid putting types in them: rather than naming a variable `ageNum`, name it `age` and make sure it's really a `number`.

An exception to this is for numbers with units. If it's not clear what the units are, you may want to include them in a variable or property name. For instance, `timeMs` is a much clearer name than just `time`, and `temperatureC` is a much clearer name than `temperature`. Item 64 describes "brands," which provide a more type-safe approach to modeling units.

Things to Remember

- Avoid repeating type information in comments and variable names. In the best case it is duplicative of type declarations, and in the worst case it will lead to conflicting information.
- Declare parameters `readonly` rather than saying that you don't mutate them.
- Consider including units in variable names if they aren't clear from the type (e.g., `timeMs` or `temperatureC`).

Item 32: Avoid Including null or undefined in Type Aliases

In this code, is the optional chain (`?.`) necessary? Could `user` ever be null?

```
function getCommentsForUser(comments: readonly Comment[], user: User) {
  return comments.filter(comment => comment.userId === user?.id);
}
```

Even assuming `strictNullChecks`, it's impossible to say without seeing the definition of `User`. If it's a type alias that allows `null` or `undefined`, then the optional chain is needed:

```
type User = { id: string; name: string; } | null;
```

On the other hand, if it's a simple object type, then it's not:

```
interface User {
  id: string;
  name: string;
}
```

As a general rule, it's better to avoid type aliases that allow `null` or `undefined` values. While the type checker won't be confused if you break this rule, human readers of your code will be. When we read a type name like `User`, we assume that it represents a user, rather than *maybe* representing a user.

If you must include `null` in a type alias for some reason, do readers of your code a favor and use a name that's unambiguous:

```
type NullableUser = { id: string; name: string; } | null;
```

But why do that when `User|null` is a more succinct and universally recognizable syntax?

```
function getCommentsForUser(comments: readonly Comment[], user: User | null) {
  return comments.filter(comment => comment.userId === user?.id);
}
```

This rule is about the top level of type aliases. It's not concerned with a `null` or `undefined` (or optional) property in a larger object:

```
type BirthdayMap = {
  [name: string]: Date | undefined;
};
```

Just don't do this:

```
type BirthdayMap = {
  [name: string]: Date | undefined;
} | null;
```

There are also reasons to avoid `null` values and optional fields in object types, but that's a topic for Items 33 and 37. For now, avoid type aliases that will be confusing to readers of your code. Prefer type aliases that represent something, rather than representing something *or* `null` or `undefined`.

Things to Remember

- Avoid defining type aliases that include `null` or `undefined`.

Item 33: Push Null Values to the Perimeter of Your Types

When you first turn on `strictNullChecks`, it may seem as though you have to add scores of `if` statements checking for `null` and `undefined` values throughout your code. This is often because the relationships between null and non-null values are implicit: when variable A is non-null, you know that variable B is also non-null and vice versa. These implicit relationships are confusing both for human readers of your code and for the type checker.

Values are easier to work with when they're either completely null or completely non-null, rather than a mix. You can model this by pushing the null values out to the perimeter of your structures.

Suppose you want to calculate the min and max of a list of numbers. We'll call this the "extent." Here's an attempt:

```
// @strictNullChecks: false
function extent(nums: Iterable<number>) {
  let min, max;
  for (const num of nums) {
    if (!min) {
      min = num;
      max = num;
    } else {
      min = Math.min(min, num);
      max = Math.max(max, num);
    }
  }
  return [min, max];
}
```

The code type checks (without `strictNullChecks`) and has an inferred return type of `number[]`, which seems fine. But it has a bug and a design flaw:

- If the min or max is zero, it may get overridden. For example, `extent([0, 1, 2])` will return `[1, 2]` rather than `[0, 2]`.

- If the `nums` array is empty, the function will return `[undefined, undefined]`.

This sort of object with several `undefined`s will be difficult for clients to work with and is exactly the sort of type that this item discourages. We know from reading the source code that either both `min` and `max` will be `undefined` or neither will be, but that information isn't represented in the type system.

Turning on `strictNullChecks` makes the issue with `undefined` more apparent:

```
function extent(nums: Iterable<number>) {
  let min, max;
  for (const num of nums) {
    if (!min) {
      min = num;
      max = num;
    } else {
      min = Math.min(min, num);
      max = Math.max(max, num);
      //                ~~~ Argument of type 'number | undefined' is not
      //                    assignable to parameter of type 'number'
    }
  }
  return [min, max];
}
```

The return type of `extent` is now inferred as `(number | undefined)[]`, which makes the design flaw more apparent. This is likely to manifest as a type error wherever you call `extent`:

```
const [min, max] = extent([0, 1, 2]);
const span = max - min;
//           ~~~   ~~~ Object is possibly 'undefined'
```

The error in the implementation of `extent` comes about because you've excluded `undefined` as a value for `min` but not `max`. The two are initialized together, but this information isn't present in the type system. You could make it go away by adding a check for `max`, too, but this would be doubling down on the bug.

A better solution is to put `min` and `max` in the same object and make this object either fully `null` or fully non-`null`:

```
function extent(nums: Iterable<number>) {
  let minMax: [number, number] | null = null;
  for (const num of nums) {
    if (!minMax) {
      minMax = [num, num];
    } else {
      const [oldMin, oldMax] = minMax;
      minMax = [Math.min(num, oldMin), Math.max(num, oldMax)];
    }
  }
  return minMax;
}
```

The return type is now [number, number] | null, which is easier for clients to work with. min and max can be retrieved with either a non-null assertion:

```
const [min, max] = extent([0, 1, 2])!;
const span = max - min;  // OK
```

or a single check:

```
const range = extent([0, 1, 2]);
if (range) {
  const [min, max] = range;
  const span = max - min;  // OK
}
```

By using a single object to track the extent, we've improved our design, helped Type-Script understand the relationship between null values, and fixed the bug: the if (!minMax) check is now problem free.

(A next step might be to prevent passing non-empty lists to extent, which would remove the possibility of returning null altogether. Item 64 presents a way you might represent a non-empty list in TypeScript's type system.)

A mix of null and non-null values can also lead to problems in classes. For instance, suppose you have a class that represents both a user and their posts on a forum:

```
class UserPosts {
  user: UserInfo | null;
  posts: Post[] | null;

  constructor() {
    this.user = null;
    this.posts = null;
  }

  async init(userId: string) {
    return Promise.all([
      async () => this.user = await fetchUser(userId),
      async () => this.posts = await fetchPostsForUser(userId)
    ]);
  }

  getUserName() {
    // ...?
  }
}
```

While the two network requests are loading, the user and posts properties will be null. At any time, they might both be null, one might be null, or they might both be non-null. There are four possibilities. This complexity will seep into every method on the class. This design is almost certain to lead to confusion, a proliferation of null checks, and bugs.

A better design would wait until all the data used by the class is available:

```
class UserPosts {
  user: UserInfo;
  posts: Post[];

  constructor(user: UserInfo, posts: Post[]) {
    this.user = user;
    this.posts = posts;
  }

  static async init(userId: string): Promise<UserPosts> {
    const [user, posts] = await Promise.all([
      fetchUser(userId),
      fetchPostsForUser(userId)
    ]);
    return new UserPosts(user, posts);
  }

  getUserName() {
    return this.user.name;
  }
}
```

Now the UserPosts class is fully non-null, and it's easy to write correct methods on it. Of course, if you need to perform operations while data is partially loaded, then you'll need to deal with the multiplicity of null and non-null states.

Don't be tempted to replace nullable properties with Promises. This tends to lead to even more confusing code and forces all your methods to be async. Promises clarify the code that loads data but tend to have the opposite effect on the class that uses that data.

Things to Remember

- Avoid designs in which one value being null or not null is implicitly related to another value being null or not null.

- Push null values to the perimeter of your API by making larger objects either null or fully non-null. This will make code clearer both for human readers and for the type checker.

- Consider creating a fully non-null class and constructing it when all values are available.

Item 34: Prefer Unions of Interfaces to Interfaces with Unions

If you create an interface whose properties are union types, you should ask whether the type would make more sense as a union of more precise interfaces.

Suppose you're building a vector drawing program and want to define an interface for layers with specific geometry types:

```
interface Layer {
  layout: FillLayout | LineLayout | PointLayout;
  paint: FillPaint | LinePaint | PointPaint;
}
```

The `layout` field controls how and where the shapes are drawn (rounded corners? straight?), while the `paint` field controls styles (is the line blue? thick? thin? dashed?).

The intention is that a `Layer` will have matching `layout` and `paint` properties. A `Fill Layout` should go with a `FillPaint`, and a `LineLayout` should go with a `LinePaint`. But this version of the `Layer` type also allows a `FillLayout` with a `LinePaint`. This possibility makes using the library more error prone and makes this interface difficult to work with.

A better way to model this is with separate interfaces for each type of layer:

```
interface FillLayer {
  layout: FillLayout;
  paint: FillPaint;
}
interface LineLayer {
  layout: LineLayout;
  paint: LinePaint;
}
interface PointLayer {
  layout: PointLayout;
  paint: PointPaint;
}
type Layer = FillLayer | LineLayer | PointLayer;
```

By defining `Layer` in this way, you've excluded the possibility of mixed `layout` and `paint` properties. This is an example of following Item 29's advice to prefer types that only represent valid states.

By far the most common example of this pattern is the "tagged union" (or "discriminated union"). In this case, one of the properties is a union of string literal types:

```
interface Layer {
  type: 'fill' | 'line' | 'point';
  layout: FillLayout | LineLayout | PointLayout;
  paint: FillPaint | LinePaint | PointPaint;
}
```

As before, would it make sense to have type: 'fill' but then a LineLayout and
PointPaint? Certainly not. Convert Layer to a union of interfaces to exclude this
possibility:

```
interface FillLayer {
  type: 'fill';
  layout: FillLayout;
  paint: FillPaint;
}
interface LineLayer {
  type: 'line';
  layout: LineLayout;
  paint: LinePaint;
}
interface PointLayer {
  type: 'paint';
  layout: PointLayout;
  paint: PointPaint;
}
type Layer = FillLayer | LineLayer | PointLayer;
```

The type property is the "tag" or "discriminant." It can be accessed at runtime and
gives TypeScript just enough information to determine which element of the union
type you're working with. Here, TypeScript is able to narrow the type of Layer in an
if statement based on the tag:

```
function drawLayer(layer: Layer) {
  if (layer.type === 'fill') {
    const {paint} = layer;
    //      ^? const paint: FillPaint
    const {layout} = layer;
    //      ^? const layout: FillLayout
  } else if (layer.type === 'line') {
    const {paint} = layer;
    //      ^? const paint: LinePaint
    const {layout} = layer;
    //      ^? const layout: LineLayout
  } else {
    const {paint} = layer;
    //      ^? const paint: PointPaint
    const {layout} = layer;
    //      ^? const layout: PointLayout
  }
}
```

By correctly modeling the relationship between the properties in this type, you help TypeScript check your code's correctness. The same code involving the initial Layer definition would have been cluttered with type assertions.

Because they work so well with TypeScript's type checker, tagged unions are ubiquitous in TypeScript code. Recognize this pattern and apply it when you can. If you can represent a data type in TypeScript with a tagged union, it's usually a good idea to do so.

If you think of optional fields as a union of their type and undefined, then they fit the "interface of unions" pattern as well. Consider this type:

```
interface Person {
  name: string;
  // These will either both be present or not be present
  placeOfBirth?: string;
  dateOfBirth?: Date;
}
```

As Item 31 explained, the comment with type information is a strong sign that there might be a problem. There is a relationship between the placeOfBirth and dateOf Birth fields that you haven't told TypeScript about.

A better way to model this is to move both of these properties into a single object. This is akin to moving null values to the perimeter (Item 33):

```
interface Person {
  name: string;
  birth?: {
    place: string;
    date: Date;
  }
}
```

Now TypeScript complains about values with a place but no date of birth:

```
const alanT: Person = {
  name: 'Alan Turing',
  birth: {
// ~~~~ Property 'date' is missing in type
//      '{ place: string; }' but required in type
//      '{ place: string; date: Date; }'
    place: 'London'
  }
}
```

Additionally, a function that takes a Person object only needs to do a single check:

```
function eulogize(person: Person) {
  console.log(person.name);
  const {birth} = person;
  if (birth) {
```

```
      console.log(`was born on ${birth.date} in ${birth.place}.`);
    }
  }
```

If the structure of the type is outside your control (perhaps it's coming from an API), then you can still model the relationship between these fields using a now-familiar union of interfaces:

```
interface Name {
  name: string;
}

interface PersonWithBirth extends Name {
  placeOfBirth: string;
  dateOfBirth: Date;
}

type Person = Name | PersonWithBirth;
```

Now you get some of the same benefits as with the nested object:

```
function eulogize(person: Person) {
  if ('placeOfBirth' in person) {
    person
    // ^? (parameter) person: PersonWithBirth
    const {dateOfBirth} = person;  // OK
    //       ^? const dateOfBirth: Date
  }
}
```

In both cases, the type definition makes the relationship between the properties more clear.

While optional properties are often useful, you should think twice before adding one to an interface. Item 37 explores more of the downsides of optional fields.

Things to Remember

- Interfaces with multiple properties that are union types are often a mistake because they obscure the relationships between these properties.

- Unions of interfaces are more precise and can be understood by TypeScript.

- Use tagged unions to facilitate control flow analysis. Because they are so well supported, this pattern is ubiquitous in TypeScript code.

- Consider whether multiple optional properties could be grouped to more accurately model your data.

Item 35: Prefer More Precise Alternatives to String Types

Recall from Item 7 that the *domain* of a type is the set of values assignable to that type. The domain of the `string` type is enormous: `"x"` and `"y"` are in it, but so is the complete text of *Moby Dick* (it starts with `"Call me Ishmael…"` and is about 1.2 million characters long). When you declare a variable of type `string`, you should ask whether a narrower type would be more appropriate.

Suppose you're building a music collection and want to define a type for an album. Here's an attempt:

```
interface Album {
  artist: string;
  title: string;
  releaseDate: string;  // YYYY-MM-DD
  recordingType: string;  // E.g., "live" or "studio"
}
```

The prevalence of `string` types and the type information in comments (Item 31) are strong indications that this `interface` isn't quite right. Here's what can go wrong:

```
const kindOfBlue: Album = {
  artist: 'Miles Davis',
  title: 'Kind of Blue',
  releaseDate: 'August 17th, 1959',  // Oops!
  recordingType: 'Studio',  // Oops!
}; // OK
```

The `releaseDate` field is incorrectly formatted (according to the comment) and `'Studio'` is capitalized where it should be lowercase. But these values *are* both strings, so this object is assignable to `Album` and the type checker doesn't complain.

These broad `string` types can mask errors for valid `Album` objects, too. For example:

```
function recordRelease(title: string, date: string) { /* ... */ }
recordRelease(kindOfBlue.releaseDate, kindOfBlue.title);  // OK, should be error
```

The parameters are reversed in the call to `recordRelease` but both are strings, so the type checker doesn't complain. Because of the prevalence of `string` types, code like this is sometimes called "stringly typed." (Item 38 explores how repeated positional parameters of *any* type can be problematic, not just `string`.)

Can you make the types narrower to prevent these sorts of issues? While the complete text of *Moby Dick* would be a ponderous artist name or album title, it's at least plausible. So `string` is appropriate for these fields. For the `releaseDate` field, it's better to use a `Date` object and avoid issues around formatting. Finally, for the `recordingType` field, you can define a union type with just two values (you could also use an `enum`, but I generally recommend avoiding these; see Item 72):

```
type RecordingType = 'studio' | 'live';

interface Album {
  artist: string;
  title: string;
  releaseDate: Date;
  recordingType: RecordingType;
}
```

With these changes, TypeScript is able to do a more thorough check for errors:

```
const kindOfBlue: Album = {
  artist: 'Miles Davis',
  title: 'Kind of Blue',
  releaseDate: new Date('1959-08-17'),
  recordingType: 'Studio'
// ~~~~~~~~~~~~ Type '"Studio"' is not assignable to type 'RecordingType'
};
```

There are advantages to this approach beyond stricter checking. First, explicitly defining the type ensures that its meaning won't get lost as it's passed around. If you wanted to find albums of just a certain recording type, for instance, you might define a function like this:

```
function getAlbumsOfType(recordingType: string): Album[] {
  // ...
}
```

How does the caller of this function know what `recordingType` is expected to be? It's just a `string`. The comment explaining that it's `'studio'` or `'live'` is hidden in the definition of `Album`, where the user might not think to look.

Second, explicitly defining a type allows you to attach documentation to it (see Item 68):

```
/** What type of environment was this recording made in? */
type RecordingType = 'live' | 'studio';
```

When you change `getAlbumsOfType` to take a `RecordingType`, the caller is able to click through and see the documentation (see Figure 4-1).

Figure 4-1. Using a named type instead of `string` makes it possible to attach documentation to the type that is surfaced in your editor.

Another common misuse of `string` is in function parameters. Say you want to write a function that pulls out all the values for a single field in an array. The Underscore and Ramda utility libraries call this `pluck`:

```
function pluck(records, key) {
  return records.map(r => r[key]);
}
```

How would you type this? Here's an initial attempt:

```
function pluck(records: any[], key: string): any[] {
  return records.map(r => r[key]);
}
```

This type checks but isn't great. The `any` types are problematic, particularly on the return value (see Item 43). The first step to improving the type signature is introducing a generic type parameter:

```
function pluck<T>(records: T[], key: string): any[] {
  return records.map(r => r[key]);
  //                      ~~~~~~ Element implicitly has an 'any' type
  //                             because type '{}' has no index signature
}
```

TypeScript is now complaining that the `string` type for `key` is too broad. And it's right to do so: if you pass in an array of `Albums` then there are only four valid values for key ("artist," "title," "releaseDate," and "recordingType"), as opposed to the vast set of strings. This is precisely what the `keyof Album` type is:

```
type K = keyof Album;
//   ^? type K = keyof Album
//      (equivalent to "artist" | "title" | "releaseDate" | "recordingType")
```

So the fix is to replace `string` with `keyof T`:

```
function pluck<T>(records: T[], key: keyof T) {
  return records.map(r => r[key]);
}
```

This passes the type checker. We've also let TypeScript infer the return type. How does it do? If you mouse over `pluck` in your editor, the inferred type is:

```
function pluck<T>(record: T[], key: keyof T): T[keyof T][];
```

`T[keyof T]` is the type of any possible value in `T`. If you're passing in a single string as the key, this is too broad. For example:

```
const releaseDates = pluck(albums, 'releaseDate');
//    ^? const releaseDates: (string | Date)[]
```

The type should be Date[], not (string | Date)[]. While keyof T is much narrower than string, it's *still* too broad. To narrow it further, we need to introduce a second type parameter that is a subtype of keyof T (probably a single value):

```
function pluck<T, K extends keyof T>(records: T[], key: K): T[K][] {
  return records.map(r => r[key]);
}
```

The type signature is now completely correct. We can check this by calling pluck in a few different ways:

```
const dates = pluck(albums, 'releaseDate');
//    ^? const dates: Date[]
const artists = pluck(albums, 'artist');
//    ^? const artists: string[]
const types = pluck(albums, 'recordingType');
//    ^? const types: RecordingType[]
const mix = pluck(albums, Math.random() < 0.5 ? 'releaseDate' : 'artist');
//    ^? const mix: (string | Date)[]
const badDates = pluck(albums, 'recordingDate');
//                             ~~~~~~~~~~~~~~~
// Argument of type '"recordingDate"' is not assignable to parameter of type ...
```

The language service is even able to offer autocomplete on the keys of Album (as shown in Figure 4-2).

Figure 4-2. Using a parameter type of keyof Album instead of string results in better autocomplete in your editor.

string has some of the same problems as any: when used inappropriately, it permits invalid values and hides relationships between types. This thwarts the type checker and can hide real bugs. TypeScript's ability to define subsets of string is a powerful way to bring type safety to JavaScript code. Using more precise types will both catch errors and improve the readability of your code.

This item focused on finite sets of strings, but TypeScript also lets you model infinite sets, for example, all the strings that start with "http:". For these, you'll want to use template literal types, which are the subject of Item 54.

Things to Remember

- Avoid "stringly typed" code. Prefer more appropriate types where not every `string` is a possibility.

- Prefer a union of string literal types to `string` if that more accurately describes the domain of a variable. You'll get stricter type checking and improve the development experience.

- Prefer `keyof T` to `string` for function parameters that are expected to be properties of an object.

Item 36: Use a Distinct Type for Special Values

JavaScript's string `split` method is a handy way to break a string around a delimiter:

```
> 'abcde'.split('c')
[ 'ab', 'de' ]
```

Let's write something like `split`, but for arrays. Here's an attempt:

```
function splitAround<T>(vals: readonly T[], val: T): [T[], T[]] {
  const index = vals.indexOf(val);
  return [vals.slice(0, index), vals.slice(index+1)];
}
```

This works as you'd expect:

```
> splitAround([1, 2, 3, 4, 5], 3)
[ [ 1, 2 ], [ 4, 5 ] ]
```

If you try to `splitAround` an element that's not in the list, however, it does something quite unexpected:

```
> splitAround([1, 2, 3, 4, 5], 6)
[ [ 1, 2, 3, 4 ], [ 1, 2, 3, 4, 5 ] ]
```

While it's not entirely clear what the function *should* do in this case, it's definitely not that! How did such simple code result in such strange behavior?

The root issue is that `indexOf` returns `-1` if it can't find the element in the array. This is a special value: it indicates a failure rather than success. But `-1` is just an ordinary `number`. You can pass it to the Array `slice` method and you can do arithmetic on it. When you pass a negative number to `slice`, it interprets it as counting back from the end of the array. And when you add 1 to `-1`, you get 0. So this evaluates as:

```
[vals.slice(0, -1), vals.slice(0)]
```

The first `slice` returns all but the last element of the array, and the second `slice` returns a complete copy of the array.

This behavior is a bug. Moreover, it's unfortunate that TypeScript wasn't able to help us find this problem. The root issue was that indexOf returned -1 when it couldn't find the element, rather than, say null. Why is that?

Without hopping in a time machine and visiting the Netscape offices in 1995, it's hard to know the answer for sure. But we can speculate! JavaScript was heavily influenced by Java, and its indexOf has this same behavior. In Java (and C), a function can't return a primitive *or* null. Only objects (or pointers) are nullable. So this behavior may derive from a technical limitation in Java that JavaScript does not share.

In JavaScript (and TypeScript), there's no problem having a function return a number or null. So we can wrap indexOf:

```
function safeIndexOf<T>(vals: readonly T[], val: T): number | null {
  const index = vals.indexOf(val);
  return index === -1 ? null : index;
}
```

If we plug that into our original definition of splitAround, we immediately get two type errors:

```
function splitAround<T>(vals: readonly T[], val: T): [T[], T[]] {
  const index = safeIndexOf(vals, val);
  return [vals.slice(0, index), vals.slice(index+1)];
  //                    ~~~~~               ~~~~~ 'index' is possibly 'null'
}
```

This is exactly what we want! There are always two cases to consider with indexOf. With the built-in version, TypeScript can't distinguish them, but with the wrapped version, it can. And it sees here that we've only considered the case where the array contained the value.

The solution is to handle the other case explicitly:

```
function splitAround<T>(vals: readonly T[], val: T): [T[], T[]] {
  const index = safeIndexOf(vals, val);
  if (index === null) {
    return [[...vals], []];
  }
  return [vals.slice(0, index), vals.slice(index+1)];  // ok
}
```

Whether this is the right behavior is debatable, but at least TypeScript has forced us to have that debate!

The root problem with the first implementation was that indexOf had two distinct cases, but the return value in the special case (-1) had the same type as the return value in the regular case (number). This meant that from TypeScript's perspective there was just a single case, and it wasn't able to detect that we didn't check for -1.

This situation comes up frequently when you're designing types. Perhaps you have a type for describing merchandise:

```
interface Product {
  title: string;
  priceDollars: number;
}
```

Then you realize that some products have an unknown price. Making this field optional or changing it to number|null might require a migration and lots of code changes, so instead you introduce a special value:

```
interface Product {
  title: string;
  /** Price of the product in dollars, or -1 if price is unknown */
  priceDollars: number;
}
```

You ship it to production. A week later your boss is irate and wants to know why you've been crediting money to customer cards. Your team works to roll back the change and you're tasked with writing the postmortem. In retrospect, it would have been much easier to deal with those type errors!

Choosing in-domain special values like -1, 0, or "" is similar in spirit to turning off strictNullChecks. When strictNullChecks is off, you can assign null or undefined to any type:

```
// @strictNullChecks: false
const truck: Product = {
  title: 'Tesla Cybertruck',
  priceDollars: null, // ok
};
```

This lets a huge class of bugs slip through the type checker because TypeScript doesn't distinguish between number and number|null. null is a valid value in all types. When you enable strictNullChecks, TypeScript *does* distinguish between these types and it's able to detect a whole host of new problems. When you choose an in-domain special value like -1, you're effectively carving out a non-strict niche in your types. Expedient, yes, but ultimately not the best choice.

null and undefined may not always be the right way to represent special cases since their exact meaning may be context dependent. If you're modeling the state of a network request, for example, it would be a bad idea to use null to mean an error state and undefined to mean a pending state. Better to use a tagged union to represent these special states more explicitly. Item 29 explores this example in more detail.

Things to Remember

- Avoid special values that are assignable to regular values in a type. They will reduce TypeScript's ability to find bugs in your code.

- Prefer null or undefined as a special value instead of 0, -1, or "".

- Consider using a tagged union rather than null or undefined if the meaning of those values isn't clear.

Item 37: Limit the Use of Optional Properties

As your types evolve, you'll inevitably want to add new properties to them. To avoid invalidating existing code or data, you might choose to make these properties optional. While this is sometimes the right choice, optional properties do come at a cost and you should think twice before adding them.

Imagine you have a UI component that displays numbers with a label and units. Think "Height: 12 ft" or "Speed: 10 mph":

```
interface FormattedValue {
  value: number;
  units: string;
}
function formatValue(value: FormattedValue) { /* ... */ }
```

You build a big web application using this component. Perhaps part of it displays formatted information about a hike you've taken ("5 miles at 2 mph"):

```
interface Hike {
  miles: number;
  hours: number;
}
function formatHike({miles, hours}: Hike) {
  const distanceDisplay = formatValue({value: miles, units: 'miles'});
  const paceDisplay = formatValue({value: miles / hours, units: 'mph'});
  return `${distanceDisplay} at ${paceDisplay}`;
}
```

One day you learn about the metric system and decide to support it. To support both metric and imperial, you add a corresponding option to FormattedValue. If needed, the component will do a unit conversion before displaying the value. To minimize changes to existing code and tests, you decide to make the property optional:

```
type UnitSystem = 'metric' | 'imperial';
interface FormattedValue {
  value: number;
  units: string;
  /** default is imperial */
  unitSystem?: UnitSystem;
}
```

To let the user configure this, we'll also want to specify a unit system in our app-wide configuration:

```
interface AppConfig {
  darkMode: boolean;
  // ... other settings ...
  /** default is imperial */
  unitSystem?: UnitSystem;
}
```

Now we can update `formatHike` to support the metric system:

```
function formatHike({miles, hours}: Hike, config: AppConfig) {
  const { unitSystem } = config;
  const distanceDisplay = formatValue({
    value: miles, units: 'miles', unitSystem
  });
  const paceDisplay = formatValue({
    value: miles / hours, units: 'mph'  // forgot unitSystem, oops!
  });
  return `${distanceDisplay} at ${paceDisplay}`;
}
```

We set `unitSystem` in one call to `formatValue` but not the other. This is a bug that means our metric users will see a mix of imperial and metric units.

In fact, our design is a recipe for exactly this sort of bug. In every place that we use the `formatValue` component, we need to remember to pass in a `unitSystem`. Whenever we don't, metric users will see confusing imperial units like yards, acres, or foot-pounds.

It would be nice if there were a way to automatically find every place where we forgot to pass in a `unitSystem`. This is exactly the sort of thing that type checking is good at, but we've kept it from helping us by making the `unitSystem` property optional.

If you make it required instead, you'll get a type error everywhere you forgot to set it. You'll have to fix these one by one, but it's much better to have TypeScript find these mistakes than to hear about them from confused users!

The "default is imperial" documentation comment is also worrisome. In TypeScript, the default value of an optional property on an object is always `undefined`. To implement an alternative default, our code is likely to be littered with lines like this:

```
declare let config: AppConfig;
const unitSystem = config.unitSystem ?? 'imperial';
```

Every one of these is an opportunity for a bug. Perhaps another developer on your team forgets that imperial is the default (why is it the default anyway?) and assumes it should be metric:

```
const unitSystem = config.unitSystem ?? 'metric';
```

Once again the result will be inconsistent display.

If you need to support old values of the AppConfig interface (perhaps they're saved as JSON on disk or in a database) then you can't make the new field required. What you can do instead is split the type in two: one type for un-normalized configurations read from disk, and another with fewer optional properties for use in your app:

```
interface InputAppConfig {
  darkMode: boolean;
  // ... other settings ...
  /** default is imperial */
  unitSystem?: UnitSystem;
}
interface AppConfig extends InputAppConfig {
  unitSystem: UnitSystem;  // required
}
```

If changing an optional property to required in a subtype feels strange, see Item 7. You could also use Required<InputAppConfig> here.

You'll want to add some normalization code:

```
function normalizeAppConfig(inputConfig: InputAppConfig): AppConfig {
  return {
    ...inputConfig,
    unitSystem: inputConfig.unitSystem ?? 'imperial',
  };
}
```

This split solves a few problems:

1. It allows the config to evolve and maintain backward compatibility without adding complexity throughout the application.

2. It centralizes the application of default values.

3. It makes it hard to use an InputAppConfig where an AppConfig is expected.

These sorts of "under construction" types come up frequently with network code. See UserPosts in Item 33 for another example.

As you add more optional properties to an interface, you'll run into a new problem: if you have N optional properties then there are 2^N possible combinations of them. That's a lot of possibilities! If you have 10 optional properties, have you tested all 1,024 combinations? Do all the combinations even make sense? It's likely that there's some structure to these options, perhaps some that are mutually exclusive. If so, then your state should model this (see Item 29). This is a problem with options in general, not just optional properties.

Finally, optional properties are a possible source of unsoundness in TypeScript. Item 48 discusses this in more detail.

As you've seen, there are lots of reasons to avoid optional properties. So when *should* you use them? They're largely unavoidable when describing existing APIs or evolving APIs while maintaining backward compatibility. For huge configurations, it may be prohibitively expensive to fill in all optional fields with default values. And some properties truly are optional: not everyone has a middle name, so an optional middle Name property on a Person type is an accurate model. But be aware of the many drawbacks of optional properties, know how to mitigate them, and think twice before adding an optional property if there's a valid alternative.

Things to Remember

- Optional properties can prevent the type checker from finding bugs and can lead to repeated and possibly inconsistent code for filling in default values.
- Think twice before adding an optional property to an interface. Consider whether you could make it required instead.
- Consider creating distinct types for un-normalized input data and normalized data for use in your code.
- Avoid a combinatorial explosion of options.

Item 38: Avoid Repeated Parameters of the Same Type

What does this function call do?

```
drawRect(25, 50, 75, 100, 1);
```

Without looking at the function's parameter list, it's impossible to say. Here are a few possibilities:

- It draws a 75 × 100 rectangle with its top left at (25, 50) with an opacity of 1.0.
- It draws a 50 × 50 rectangle with corners at (25, 50) and (75, 100), with a stroke width of one pixel.

Without more context, it's hard to know whether this function is being called correctly. And because all the parameters are of the same type, number, the type checker won't be able to help you if you mix up the order or pass in a width and height instead of a second coordinate.

Suppose this was the function declaration:

```
function drawRect(x: number, y: number, w: number, h: number, opacity: number) {
  // ...
}
```

Any function that takes consecutive parameters of the same type is error prone because the type checker won't be able to catch incorrect invocations. One way to improve the situation would be to take in distinct `Point` and `Dimension` types:

```
interface Point {
  x: number;
  y: number;
}
interface Dimension {
  width: number;
  height: number;
}
function drawRect(topLeft: Point, size: Dimension, opacity: number) {
  // ...
}
```

Because the function now takes three parameters with three different types, the type checker is able to distinguish between them. An incorrect invocation that passes in two points will be an error:

```
drawRect({x: 25, y: 50}, {x: 75, y: 100}, 1.0);
//                        ~
// Argument ... is not assignable to parameter of type 'Dimension'.
```

An alternative fix would be to combine all the parameters into a single object:

```
interface DrawRectParams extends Point, Dimension {
  opacity: number;
}
function drawRect(params: DrawRectParams) { /* ... */ }

drawRect({x: 25, y: 50, width: 75, height: 100, opacity: 1.0});
```

Refactoring a function to take an object rather than positional parameters improves clarity for human readers. And, by associating names with each `number`, it helps the type checker catch incorrect invocations as well.

As your code evolves, functions may be modified to take more and more parameters. Even if positional parameters worked well at first, at some point they will become a problem. As the saying goes, "If you have a function with 10 parameters, you probably missed some." Once a function takes more than three or four parameters, you should refactor it to take fewer. (typescript-eslint's `max-params` rule can enforce this.)

When the types of the parameters are the same, you should be even more wary of positional parameters. Even two parameters might be a problem.

There are a few exceptions to this rule:

- If the arguments are commutative (the order doesn't matter), then there's no problem. `max(a, b)` and `isEqual(a, b)`, for example, are unambiguous.
- If there's a "natural" order to the parameters, then the potential for confusion is reduced. `array.slice(start, stop)` makes more sense than `stop, start`, for example. Be careful with this, though: developers might not always agree what a "natural" order is. (Is it year, month, day? Month, day, year? Day, month, year?)

As Scott Meyers wrote in *Effective C++*, "Make interfaces easy to use correctly and hard to use incorrectly." It's hard to argue with that!

Things to Remember

- Avoid writing functions that take consecutive parameters with the same Type-Script type.
- Refactor functions that take many parameters to take fewer parameters with distinct types, or a single object parameter.

Item 39: Prefer Unifying Types to Modeling Differences

TypeScript's type system gives you powerful tools to map between types. Item 15 and Chapter 6 explain how to use many of them. Once you realize that you can model a transformation using the type system, you may feel an overwhelming urge to do so. And this will feel productive. So many types! So much safety!

If it's available to you, though, a better option than *modeling* the difference between two types is to *eliminate* the difference between those two types. Then no type-level machinery is required, and the cognitive burden of keeping track of which version of a type you're working with goes away.

To make this more concrete, imagine you have an interface that derives from a database table. Databases typically use snake_case for column names, so this is how your data comes out:

```
interface StudentTable {
  first_name: string;
  last_name: string;
  birth_date: string;
}
```

TypeScript code typically uses camelCase property names. To make the `Student` type more consistent with the rest of your code, you might introduce an alternate version of `Student`:

```
interface Student {
  firstName: string;
  lastName: string;
  birthDate: string;
}
```

You can write a function to convert between these two types. More interestingly, you can use template literal types to *type* this function. Item 54 walks through how to do this, but the end result is that you can generate one type from the other:

```
type Student = ObjectToCamel<StudentTable>;
//   ^? type Student = {
//        firstName: string;
//        lastName: string;
//        birthDate: string;
//      }
```

Amazing! After the thrill of finding a compelling use case for fancy type-level programming wears off, you may find yourself running into lots of errors from passing one version of the type to a function that's expecting the other:

```
async function writeStudentToDb(student: Student) {
  await writeRowToDb(db, 'students', student);
  //                                 ~~~~~~~
  // Type 'Student' is not assignable to parameter of type 'StudentTable'.
}
```

It's not obvious from the error message, but the problem is that you've forgotten to call your conversion code:

```
async function writeStudentToDb(student: Student) {
  await writeRowToDb(db, 'students', objectToSnake(student));  // ok
}
```

While it's helpful that TypeScript flagged this mistake before it caused a runtime error, it would be simpler to have just a single version of the Student type in your code so that this error is impossible to make.

There are two versions of the Student type. Which should you choose?

- To adopt the camelCase version, you'll need to set up some kind of adapter to make sure your database returns camelCased version of the columns. You'll also need to make sure that whatever tool you use to generate TypeScript types from your database knows about this transformation. The advantage of this approach is that your database interfaces will look just like all your other types.

- To adopt the snake_case version, you don't need to do anything at all. You just need to accept a superficial inconsistency in the naming convention for a deeper consistency in your types.

Either of these approaches is feasible, but the latter is simpler.

The general principle is that you should prefer unifying types to modeling small differences between them. That being said, there are some caveats to this rule.

First, unification isn't always an option. You may need the two types if the database and the API aren't under your control. If this is the case, then modeling these sorts of differences systematically in the type system will help you find bugs in your transformation code. It's better than creating types ad hoc and hoping they stay in sync.

Second, don't unify types that aren't actually representing the same thing! "Unifying" the different types in a tagged union would be counterproductive, for example, because they presumably represent different states that you want to keep separate.

Things to Remember

- Having distinct variants of the same type creates cognitive overhead and requires lots of conversion code.
- Rather than modeling slight variations on a type in your code, try to eliminate the variation so that you can unify to a single type.
- Unifying types may require some adjustments to runtime code.
- If the types aren't in your control, you may need to model the variations.
- Don't unify types that aren't representing the same thing.

Item 40: Prefer Imprecise Types to Inaccurate Types

In writing type declarations you'll inevitably find situations where you can model behavior in a more precise or less precise way. Precision in types is generally a good thing because it will help your users catch bugs and take advantage of the tooling that TypeScript provides. But take care as you increase the precision of your type declarations: it's easy to make mistakes, and incorrect types can be worse than no types at all.

Suppose you are writing type declarations for GeoJSON, a format we've seen before in Item 33. A GeoJSON geometry can be one of a few types, each of which has differently shaped coordinate arrays:

```
interface Point {
  type: 'Point';
  coordinates: number[];
}
interface LineString {
  type: 'LineString';
  coordinates: number[][];
}
interface Polygon {
  type: 'Polygon';
```

```
    coordinates: number[][][];
  }
  type Geometry = Point | LineString | Polygon;  // Also several others
```

This is fine, but number[] for a coordinate is a bit imprecise. Really these are latitudes and longitudes, so perhaps a tuple type would be better:

```
  type GeoPosition = [number, number];
  interface Point {
    type: 'Point';
    coordinates: GeoPosition;
  }
  // Etc.
```

You publish your more precise types to the world and wait for the adulation to roll in. Unfortunately, a user complains that your new types have broken everything. Even though you've only ever used latitude and longitude, a position in GeoJSON is allowed to have a third element, an elevation, and potentially more. In an attempt to make the type declarations more precise, you've gone too far and made the types inaccurate! To continue using your type declarations, your user will have to introduce type assertions or silence the type checker entirely with **as any**. Perhaps they'll give up and start writing their own declarations.

As another example, consider trying to write type declarations for a Lisp-like language defined in JSON:

```
  12
  "red"
  ["+", 1, 2]  // 3
  ["/", 20, 2]  // 10
  ["case", [">", 20, 10], "red", "blue"]  // "red"
  ["rgb", 255, 0, 127]  // "#FF007F"
```

The Mapbox library uses a system like this to determine the appearance of map features across many devices. There's a whole spectrum of precision with which you could try to type this:

1. Allow anything.

2. Allow strings, numbers, and arrays.

3. Allow strings, numbers, and arrays starting with known function names.

4. Make sure each function gets the correct number of arguments.

5. Make sure each function gets the correct type of arguments.

The first two options are straightforward:

```
  type Expression1 = any;
  type Expression2 = number | string | any[];
```

A type system is said to be "complete" if it allows all valid programs. These two types *will* allow all valid Mapbox expressions. There will be no false positive errors. But with such simple types there will be many false negatives: invalid expressions that aren't flagged as such. In other words, the types are not very precise.

Let's see if we can improve the precision without losing the completeness property. To avoid regressions, we should introduce a test set of expressions that are valid and expressions that are not. (Item 55 is all about testing types.)

```
const okExpressions: Expression2[] = [
  10,
  "red",
  ["+", 10, 5],
  ["rgb", 255, 128, 64],
  ["case", [">", 20, 10], "red", "blue"],
];
const invalidExpressions: Expression2[] = [
  true,
// ~~~ Type 'boolean' is not assignable to type 'Expression2'
  ["**", 2, 31],  // Should be an error: no "**" function
  ["rgb", 255, 0, 127, 0],  // Should be an error: too many values
  ["case", [">", 20, 10], "red", "blue", "green"],  // (Too many values)
];
```

To go to the next level of precision, you can use a union of string literal types as the first element of a tuple:

```
type FnName = '+' | '-' | '*' | '/' | '>' | '<' | 'case' | 'rgb';
type CallExpression = [FnName, ...any[]];
type Expression3 = number | string | CallExpression;

const okExpressions: Expression3[] = [
  10,
  "red",
  ["+", 10, 5],
  ["rgb", 255, 128, 64],
  ["case", [">", 20, 10], "red", "blue"],
];
const invalidExpressions: Expression3[] = [
  true,
  // Error: Type 'boolean' is not assignable to type 'Expression3'
  ["**", 2, 31],
  // ~~ Type '"**"' is not assignable to type 'FnName'
  ["rgb", 255, 0, 127, 0],  // Should be an error: too many values
  ["case", [">", 20, 10], "red", "blue", "green"],  // (Too many values)
];
```

There's one new caught error and no regressions. Pretty good! One complication is that our type declarations have become more closely related to our Mapbox version. If Mapbox adds a new function, then the type declarations need to add it, too. These types are more precise, but they're also higher maintenance.

What if you want to make sure that each function gets the correct number of arguments? This gets trickier since the types now need to be recursive to reach down into all the function calls. TypeScript allows this, though we do need to take some care to convince the type checker that our recursion isn't infinite. There are a few ways to do this. One is to define `CaseCall` (which must be an array of even length) with an `interface` rather than a `type`.

This is possible, if a bit awkward:

```
type Expression4 = number | string | CallExpression;

type CallExpression = MathCall | CaseCall | RGBCall;

type MathCall = [
  '+' | '-' | '/' | '*' | '>' | '<',
  Expression4,
  Expression4,
];

interface CaseCall {
  0: 'case';
  [n: number]: Expression4;
  length: 4 | 6 | 8 | 10 | 12 | 14 | 16; // etc.
}

type RGBCall = ['rgb', Expression4, Expression4, Expression4];
```

Let's see how we've done:

```
const okExpressions: Expression4[] = [
  10,
  "red",
  ["+", 10, 5],
  ["rgb", 255, 128, 64],
  ["case", [">", 20, 10], "red", "blue"],
];
const invalidExpressions: Expression4[] = [
  true,
// ~~~ Type 'boolean' is not assignable to type 'Expression4'
  ["**", 2, 31],
// ~~~~ Type '"**"' is not assignable to type '"+" | "-" | "/" | ...
  ["rgb", 255, 0, 127, 0],
  //                      ~ Type 'number' is not assignable to type 'undefined'.
  ["case", [">", 20, 10], "red", "blue", "green"],
  // ~~~~~~~~~~~~~~~~~~~~~~~~~~~~~~~~~~~~~~~~~~~~
  // Types of property 'length' are incompatible.
  //     Type '5' is not assignable to type '4 | 6 | 8 | 10 | 12 | 14 | 16'.
];
```

Now all the invalid expressions produce errors. And it's interesting that you can express something like "an array of even length" using a TypeScript `interface`. But some of these error messages are a bit confusing, particularly the one about Type `'5'`.

Is this an improvement over the previous, less precise types? The fact that you get errors for more incorrect usages is definitely a win, but confusing error messages will make this type more difficult to work with. As Item 6 explained, language services are as much a part of the TypeScript experience as type checking, so it's a good idea to look at the error messages resulting from your type declarations and try autocomplete in situations where it should work. If your new type declarations are more precise but break autocomplete, then they'll make for a less enjoyable TypeScript development experience.

The complexity of this type declaration has also increased the odds that a bug will creep in. For example, `Expression4` requires that all math operators take two parameters, but the Mapbox expression spec says that + and * can take more. Also, - can take a single parameter, in which case it negates its input. `Expression4` incorrectly flags errors in all of these:

```
const moreOkExpressions: Expression4[] = [
  ['-', 12],
  // ~~~~~ Type '["-", number]' is not assignable to type 'MathCall'.
  //         Source has 2 element(s) but target requires 3.
  ['+', 1, 2, 3],
  //             ~ Type 'number' is not assignable to type 'undefined'.
  ['*', 2, 3, 4],
  //             ~ Type 'number' is not assignable to type 'undefined'.
];
```

Once again, in trying to be more precise we've overshot and become inaccurate. These inaccuracies can be corrected, but you'll want to expand your test set to convince yourself that you haven't missed anything else. Complex code generally requires more tests, and the same is true of types.

As you refine types, it can be helpful to think of the "uncanny valley" metaphor. As a cartoonish drawing becomes more true to life, we tend to perceive it as becoming more realistic. But only up to a point. If it goes for too much realism, we tend to hyperfocus on the few remaining inaccuracies.

In the same way, refining very imprecise types like `any` is almost always helpful. You and your coworkers will perceive this as an improvement to type safety and productivity. But as your types get more precise, the expectation that they'll also be accurate increases. You'll start to trust the types to catch most errors, and so the inaccuracies will stand out more starkly. If you spend hours tracking down a type error, only to find that the types are inaccurate, it will undermine confidence in your **type declarations** and perhaps TypeScript itself. It certainly won't boost your productivity!

Things to Remember

- Avoid the uncanny valley of type safety: complex but inaccurate types are often worse than simpler, less precise types. If you cannot model a type accurately, do not model it inaccurately! Acknowledge the gaps using any or unknown.

- Pay attention to error messages and autocomplete as you make typings increasingly precise. It's not just about correctness: developer experience matters, too.

- As your types grow more complex, your test suite for them should expand.

Item 41: Name Types Using the Language of Your Problem Domain

> There are only two hard problems in Computer Science: cache invalidation and naming things.
>
> —Phil Karlton

This book has had much to say about the *shape* of types and the sets of values in their domains, but much less about what you *name* your types. But this is an important part of type design, too. Well-chosen type, property, and variable names can clarify intent and raise the level of abstraction of your code and types. Poorly chosen types can obscure your code and lead to incorrect mental models.

Suppose you're building out a database of animals. You create an interface to represent one:

```
interface Animal {
  name: string;
  endangered: boolean;
  habitat: string;
}

const leopard: Animal = {
  name: 'Snow Leopard',
  endangered: false,
  habitat: 'tundra',
};
```

There are a few issues here:

- name is a very general term. What sort of name are you expecting? A scientific name? A common name?

- The boolean endangered field is also ambiguous. What if an animal is extinct? Is the intent here "endangered or worse"? Or does it literally mean endangered?

- The `habitat` field is very ambiguous, not just because of the overly broad `string` type (Item 35), but also because it's unclear what's meant by "habitat."

- The variable name is `leopard`, but the value of the `name` property is "Snow Leopard." Is this distinction meaningful?

Here's a type declaration and value with less ambiguity:

```
interface Animal {
  commonName: string;
  genus: string;
  species: string;
  status: ConservationStatus;
  climates: KoppenClimate[];
}
type ConservationStatus = 'EX' | 'EW' | 'CR' | 'EN' | 'VU' | 'NT' | 'LC';
type KoppenClimate = |
  'Af' | 'Am' | 'As' | 'Aw' |
  'BSh' | 'BSk' | 'BWh' | 'BWk' |
  'Cfa' | 'Cfb' | 'Cfc' | 'Csa' | 'Csb' | 'Csc' | 'Cwa' | 'Cwb' | 'Cwc' |
  'Dfa' | 'Dfb' | 'Dfc' | 'Dfd' |
  'Dsa' | 'Dsb' | 'Dsc' | 'Dwa' | 'Dwb' | 'Dwc' | 'Dwd' |
  'EF' | 'ET';
const snowLeopard: Animal = {
  commonName: 'Snow Leopard',
  genus: 'Panthera',
  species: 'Uncia',
  status: 'VU',  // vulnerable
  climates: ['ET', 'EF', 'Dfd'],  // alpine or subalpine
};
```

This makes a number of improvements:

- `name` has been replaced with more specific terms: `commonName`, `genus`, and `species`.

- `endangered` has become `status`, a `ConservationStatus` type that uses a standard classification system from the IUCN.

- `habitat` has become `climates` and uses another standard taxonomy, the Köppen climate classification.

If you needed more information about the fields in the first version of this type, you'd have to go find the person who wrote them and ask. In all likelihood, they've left the company or don't remember. Worse yet, you might run `git blame` to find out who wrote these lousy types, only to find that it was you!

The situation is much improved with the second version. If you want to learn more about the Köppen climate classification system or track down what the precise meaning of a conservation status is, then there are a myriad of resources online to help you.

Every domain has specialized vocabulary to describe its subject. Rather than inventing your own terms, try to reuse terms from the domain of your problem. These vocabularies have often been honed over years, decades, or centuries and are well understood by people in the field. Using these terms will help you communicate with users and increase the clarity of your types.

Take care to use domain vocabulary accurately: co-opting the language of a domain to mean something different is even more confusing than inventing your own.

These same considerations apply to other labels as well, such as function parameter names, tuple labels, and index type labels.

Here are a few other rules to keep in mind as you name types, properties, and variables:

- Make distinctions meaningful. In writing and speech it can be tedious to use the same word over and over. We introduce synonyms to break the monotony. This makes prose more enjoyable to read, but it has the opposite effect on code. If you use two different terms, make sure you're drawing a meaningful distinction. If not, you should use the same term.

- Avoid vague, meaningless names like "data," "info," "thing," "item," "object," or the ever-popular "entity." If Entity has a specific meaning in your domain, fine. But if you're using it because you don't want to think of a more meaningful name, then you'll eventually run into trouble: there may be multiple distinct types called "Entity" in your project, and can you remember what's an Item and what's an Entity?

- Name things for what they are, not for what they contain or how they are computed. `Directory` is more meaningful than `INodeList`. It allows you to think about a directory as a concept, rather than in terms of its implementation. Good names can increase your level of abstraction and decrease your risk of inadvertent collisions.

Things to Remember

- Reuse names from the domain of your problem where possible to increase the readability and level of abstraction of your code. Make sure you use domain terms accurately.

- Avoid using different names for the same thing: make distinctions in names meaningful.
- Avoid vague names like "Info" or "Entity." Name types for what they are, rather than for their shape.

Item 42: Avoid Types Based on Anecdotal Data

The other items in this chapter have discussed the many benefits of good type design and shown what can go wrong without it. A well-designed type makes TypeScript a pleasure to use, while a poorly designed one can make it miserable to use. But this does put quite a bit of pressure on type design. Wouldn't it be nice if you didn't have to do this yourself?

At least some of your types are likely to come from outside your program: specifications, file formats, APIs, or database schemas. It's tempting to write declarations for these types yourself based on the data you've seen, perhaps the rows in your test database or the responses you've seen from a particular API endpoint.

Resist this urge! It's far better to import types from another source or generate them from a specification. When you write types yourself based on anecdotal data, you're only considering the examples you've seen. You might be missing important edge cases that could break your program. When you use more official types, TypeScript will help ensure that this doesn't happen.

In Item 30 we used a function that calculated the bounding box of a GeoJSON feature. Here's what a definition might look like:

```
function calculateBoundingBox(f: GeoJSONFeature): BoundingBox | null {
  let box: BoundingBox | null = null;

  const helper = (coords: any[]) => {
    // ...
  };

  const {geometry} = f;
  if (geometry) {
    helper(geometry.coordinates);
  }

  return box;
}
```

How would you define the GeoJSONFeature type? You could look at some GeoJSON features in your repo and sketch out an interface:

```
interface GeoJSONFeature {
  type: 'Feature';
  geometry: GeoJSONGeometry | null;
```

```
    properties: unknown;
}
interface GeoJSONGeometry {
  type: 'Point' | 'LineString' | 'Polygon' | 'MultiPolygon';
  coordinates: number[] | number[][] | number[][][] | number[][][][];
}
```

The function passes the type checker with this definition. But is it really correct? This check is only as good as our homegrown type declarations.

A better approach would be to use the formal GeoJSON spec.[1] Fortunately for us, there are already TypeScript type declarations for it on DefinitelyTyped. You can add these in the usual way:[2]

```
$ npm install --save-dev @types/geojson
+ @types/geojson@7946.0.14
```

With these declarations, TypeScript flags an error:

```
import {Feature} from 'geojson';

function calculateBoundingBox(f: Feature): BoundingBox | null {
  let box: BoundingBox | null = null;

  const helper = (coords: any[]) => {
    // ...
  };

  const {geometry} = f;
  if (geometry) {
    helper(geometry.coordinates);
    //               ~~~~~~~~~~~
    //    Property 'coordinates' does not exist on type 'Geometry'
    //      Property 'coordinates' does not exist on type 'GeometryCollection'
  }

  return box;
}
```

The problem is that this code assumes that a geometry will have a coordinates property. This is true for many geometries, including points, lines, and polygons. But a GeoJSON geometry can also be a GeometryCollection, a heterogeneous collection of other geometries. Unlike the other geometry types, it does not have a coordinates property.

---

1 GeoJSON is also known as RFC 7946. The very readable spec is at *http://geojson.org*.

2 The unusually large major version number matches the RFC number. This was cute at the time but has proven a nuisance in practice.

If you call `calculateBoundingBox` on a feature whose geometry is a `Geometry Collection`, it will throw an error about not being able to read property 0 of `undefined`. This is a real bug! And we caught it by sourcing types from the community.

One option for fixing the bug is to explicitly disallow `GeometryCollections`:

```
const {geometry} = f;
if (geometry) {
  if (geometry.type === 'GeometryCollection') {
    throw new Error('GeometryCollections are not supported.');
  }
  helper(geometry.coordinates);  // OK
}
```

TypeScript is able to refine the type of `geometry` based on the check, so the reference to `geometry.coordinates` is allowed. If nothing else, this results in a clearer error message for the user.

But the better solution is to support `GeometryCollections`! You can do this by pulling out another helper function:

```
const geometryHelper = (g: Geometry) => {
  if (g.type === 'GeometryCollection') {
    g.geometries.forEach(geometryHelper);
  } else {
    helper(g.coordinates);  // OK
  }
}

const {geometry} = f;
if (geometry) {
  geometryHelper(geometry);
}
```

Our handwritten GeoJSON types were based only on our own experience with the format, which did not include `GeometryCollections`. This led to a false sense of security about our code's correctness. Using community types based on a spec gives you confidence that your code will work with *all* values, not just the ones you happen to have seen.

Similar considerations apply to API calls. If there's an official TypeScript client for the API you're working with, use that! But even if not, you may be able to generate TypeScript types from an official source.

If you're using a GraphQL API, for example, it includes a schema that describes all its queries and mutations, as well as all the types. There are many tools available to add TypeScript types to GraphQL queries. Head to your favorite search engine and you'll quickly be on the path to type safety.

Many REST APIs publish an OpenAPI schema. This is a file that describes all the endpoints, HTTP verbs (GET, POST, etc.), and types using JSON Schema.

Say we're using an API that lets us post comments on a blog. Here's what an OpenAPI schema might look like:

```
// schema.json
{
  "openapi": "3.0.3",
  "info": { "version": "1.0.0", "title": "Sample API" },
  "paths": {
    "/comment": {
      "post": {
        "requestBody": { "content": { "application/json": {
          "schema": { "$ref": "#/components/schemas/Comment" }
        }}}
      },
      "responses": {
        "200": { /* ... */ }
      }
    }
  },
  "components": {
    "schemas": {
      "CreateCommentRequest": {
        "properties": {
            "body": { "type": "string" },
            "postId": { "type": "string" },
            "title": { "type": "string" }
        },
        "type": "object",
        "required": ["postId", "title", "body"]
      }
    }
  }
}
```

The `paths` section defines the endpoints and associates them with types, which are found in the `components/schemas` section. All the information we need to generate types is here. There are many ways to get types out of an OpenAPI Schema. One is to extract the schemas and run them through `json-schema-to-typescript`:

```
$ jq .components.schemas.CreateCommentRequest schema.json > comment.json
$ npx json-schema-to-typescript comment.json > comment.ts
$ cat comment.ts
// ....
export interface CreateCommentRequest {
  body: string;
  postId: string;
  title: string;
}
```

This results in nice, clean `interfaces` that will help you interact with this API in a type-safe way. TypeScript will flag type errors in your request bodies and the response types will flow through your code. The important thing is that you didn't write the types yourself. Rather, they're generated from a reliable source of truth. If a field is optional or can be `null`, TypeScript will know about it and force you to handle that possibility.

A next step here would be to add runtime validation and connect the types directly to the endpoints with which they're associated. There are many tools that can help you with this, and Item 74 will return to this example.

When you generate types, you do need to ensure that they stay in sync with the API schema. Item 58 discusses strategies for handling this.

What if there's no spec or official schema available? Then you'll have to generate types from data. Tools like `quicktype` can help with this. But be aware that your types may not match reality: there may be edge cases that you've missed. (An exception would be if your data set is finite, for example, a directory of 1,000 JSON files. Then you know that you haven't missed anything!)

Even if you're not aware of it, you are already benefiting from code generation. TypeScript's type declarations for the browser DOM API, which are explored in Item 75, are generated from the API descriptions on MDN. This ensures that they correctly model a complicated system and helps TypeScript catch errors and misunderstandings in your own code.

Things to Remember

- Avoid writing types by hand based on data that you've seen. It's easy to misunderstand a schema or get nullability wrong.
- Prefer types sourced from official clients or the community. If these don't exist, generate TypeScript types from schemas.

CHAPTER 5

Unsoundness and the any Type

Type systems were traditionally binary affairs: either a language had a fully static type system or a fully dynamic one. TypeScript blurs the line, because its type system is *optional* and *gradual*. You're free to add types to parts of your program but not others.

This is essential for migrating existing JavaScript codebases to TypeScript bit by bit (Chapter 10). Key to this is the any type, which effectively disables type checking for parts of your code. It is both powerful and prone to abuse. Learning to use any wisely is essential for writing effective TypeScript. This chapter walks you through how to limit the downsides of any while still retaining its benefits.

The any type is just the most extreme example of the more general problem of *unsoundness*: when a symbol's static type does not match its runtime type. Even if you eliminate all the anys from your code, you may still fall into soundness traps. Item 48 presents a few of these and shows you how to avoid them.

Item 43: Use the Narrowest Possible Scope for any Types

Consider this code:

```
declare function getPizza(): Pizza;
function eatSalad(salad: Salad) { /* ... */ }

function eatDinner() {
  const pizza = getPizza();
  eatSalad(pizza);
  //       ~~~~~
  // Argument of type 'Pizza' is not assignable to parameter of type 'Salad'
  pizza.slice();
}
```

If you somehow know that this call to eatSalad is OK, the best way forward is to adjust your types so that TypeScript understands that, too. (An arugula pizza with parmesan and lemon is kind of like a salad!) But if, for whatever reason, you can't do that, you can use any to force TypeScript to accept this code in two ways:

```
function eatDinner1() {
  const pizza: any = getPizza();  // Don't do this
  eatSalad(pizza);  // ok
  pizza.slice();  // This call is unchecked!
}

function eatDinner2() {
  const pizza = getPizza();
  eatSalad(pizza as any);  // This is preferable
  pizza.slice();  // this is safe
}
```

Of these, the second form is vastly preferable. Why? Because the any type is scoped to a single expression in a function argument. It has no effect outside this argument or this line. When code after the eatSalad call references pizza, its type is still Pizza, and it can still trigger type errors; whereas in the first example, its type is any for its entire lifetime until it goes out of scope at the end of the function. This means that the pizza.slice() call is completely unchecked. A spelling mistake or incorrect parameter type will pass the type checker but throw an exception when you run it.

It would also have been bad to make eatSalad accept an any type. While this would have left pizza with a Pizza type in eatDinner, it would have prevented type checking on this parameter for all calls to eatSalad in your program, not just this one.

The stakes become significantly higher if you *return* pizza from eatDinner. Look what happens:

```
function eatDinner1() {
  const pizza: any = getPizza();
  eatSalad(pizza);
  pizza.slice();
  return pizza;  // unsafe pizza!
}

function spiceItUp() {
  const pizza = eatDinner1();
  //      ^? const pizza: any
  pizza.addRedPepperFlakes();  // This call is also unchecked!
}
```

An any return type is "contagious" in that it can spread throughout a codebase. As a result of our changes to eatDinner1, an any type has quietly appeared in spiceItUp. This would not have happened with the more narrowly scoped any in eatDinner2.

This is a good reason to consider including explicit return type annotations, even when the return type can be inferred. It prevents an any type from inadvertently "escaping." You'd have to explicitly write any. See Item 18 for more on the pros and cons of annotating return types. There are a few functions in the standard library that return an any type, notably JSON.parse. These are quite dangerous! Item 71 explores ways to protect yourself.

We used any here to suppress an error that we believed to be incorrect. Another way to do this is with @ts-ignore or @ts-expect-error:

```
function eatDinner1() {
  const pizza = getPizza();
  // @ts-ignore
  eatSalad(pizza);
  pizza.slice();
}

function eatDinner2() {
  const pizza = getPizza();
  // @ts-expect-error
  eatSalad(pizza);
  pizza.slice();
}
```

These silence an error on the next line, leaving the type of pizza unchanged. Of these two forms, @ts-expect-error is preferable because if the error goes away later (perhaps the signature of eatSalad changed), TypeScript will tell you, and you'll be able to remove the directive.

Because they're explicitly scoped to one line, @ts-ignore and @ts-expect-error aren't "contagious" in the way that any can be. Still, try not to lean too heavily on these directives: the type checker usually has a good reason to complain and, if the error on the next line changes to something more problematic, you'll have prevented TypeScript from letting you know. And if a second error appears on the same line, you'll never find out about it.

You may also run into situations where you get a type error for just one property in a larger object:

```
const config: Config = {
  a: 1,
  b: 2,
  c: {
    key: value
// ~~~ Property ... missing in type 'Bar' but required in type 'Foo'
  }
};
```

You can silence errors like this by throwing an `as any` around the whole `config` object:

```
const config: Config = {
  a: 1,
  b: 2,
  c: {
    key: value
  }
} as any;  // Don't do this!
```

But this has the side effect of disabling type checking for the other properties (a and b) as well. Using a more narrowly scoped any limits the damage:

```
const config: Config = {
  a: 1,
  b: 2,  // These properties are still checked
  c: {
    key: value as any
  }
};
```

If the first example involved limiting the scope of any in time, this is limiting the scope in space. In both cases the goal is the same: if you must use any, reduce its scope as much as you possibly can to avoid collateral damage.

If you adopt typescript-eslint's `recommended-type-checked` preset, you'll enable a set of rules such as `no-unsafe-assignment` and `no-unsafe-return` that help to highlight the spread of any types.

Things to Remember

- Make your uses of any as narrowly scoped as possible to avoid undesired loss of type safety elsewhere in your code.

- Never return an any type from a function. This will silently lead to the loss of type safety for code that calls the function.

- Use `as any` on individual properties of a larger object instead of the whole object.

Item 44: Prefer More Precise Variants of any to Plain any

The any type encompasses all values that can be expressed in JavaScript. This is a vast domain! It includes not just all numbers and strings, but all arrays, objects, regular expressions, functions, classes, and DOM elements, not to mention `null` and `undefined`. When you use an any type, ask whether you really had something more specific in mind. Would it be OK to pass in a regular expression or a function?

Often the answer is "no," in which case you might be able to retain some type safety by using a more specific type:

```
function getLengthBad(array: any) {  // Don't do this!
  return array.length;
}

function getLength(array: any[]) {  // This is better
  return array.length;
}
```

The latter version, which uses any[] instead of any, is better in three ways:

- The reference to array.length in the function body is type checked.

- The function's return type is inferred as number instead of any.

- Calls to getLength will be checked to ensure that the parameter is an array:

```
getLengthBad(/123/);  // No error, returns undefined
getLength(/123/);
//        ~~~~~
// Argument of type 'RegExp' is not assignable to parameter of type 'any[]'.

getLengthBad(null);  // No error, throws at runtime
getLength(null);
//        ~~~~
// Argument of type 'null' is not assignable to parameter of type 'any[]'.
```

If you expect a parameter to be an array of arrays but don't care about the type, you can use any[][].

If you expect some sort of object but don't know what the values will be, you can use {[key: string]: any} or Record<string, any>:

```
function hasAKeyThatEndsWithZ(o: Record<string, any>) {
  for (const key in o) {
    if (key.endsWith('z')) {
      console.log(key, o[key]);
      return true;
    }
  }
  return false;
}
```

You could also use the object type in this situation, which includes all nonprimitive types. This is slightly different in that, while you can still enumerate keys, you can't access the values of any of them:

```
function hasAKeyThatEndsWithZ(o: object) {
  for (const key in o) {
    if (key.endsWith('z')) {
      console.log(key, o[key]);
```

```
//                    ~~~~~~ Element implicitly has an 'any' type
//                           because type '{}' has no index signature
    return true;
  }
}
return false;
}
```

Iterating over object types is particularly tricky in TypeScript. Item 60 goes into much more detail about how to work around this particular issue.

Avoid using any if you expect a function type. You have several options here depending on how specific you want to get:

```
type Fn0 = () => any;  // any function callable with no params
type Fn1 = (arg: any) => any;  // With one param
type FnN = (...args: any[]) => any;  // With any number of params
                                     // same as "Function" type
```

All of these are more precise than any and hence preferable to it. Note the use of any[] as the type for the rest parameter in the last example. any would also work here but would be less precise:

```
const numArgsBad = (...args: any) => args.length;
//    ^? const numArgsBad: (...args: any) => any
const numArgsBetter = (...args: any[]) => args.length;
//    ^? const numArgsBetter: (...args: any[]) => number
```

Note the differing return types. Rest parameters are perhaps the most common use of the any[] type.

If you want an array but don't care about the type of the elements, you may be able to use unknown[] instead of any[]. This is preferable because it is safer. See Item 46 for more on the unknown type.

Things to Remember

- When you use any, think about whether any JavaScript value is truly permissible.

- Prefer more precise forms of any such as any[] or {[id: string]: any} or () => any if they more accurately model your data.

Item 45: Hide Unsafe Type Assertions in Well-Typed Functions

In an ideal world, your functions have exactly the type signatures you want and their implementations (also in TypeScript) pass the type checker, contain no type assertions or any types, and don't fall into any other soundness traps (Item 48). Fortunately, this is the case for most functions you'll write. But this is the chapter on any and unsoundness, so you won't be surprised to hear that things aren't always ideal.

If you have to choose between a safe, assertion-free function implementation and the type signature that you want, choose the type signature. It's the public API of your function, and it's visible to the rest of your code and your users. The function's implementation is a detail that's hidden from your users. Your assertions and any types will be hidden from view there. Much better to have an unsafe (but well-tested) implementation than to adopt a type signature that makes life hard for your users.

To see how this might come up, consider this code that fetches information about mountain peaks:

```
interface MountainPeak {
  name: string;
  continent: string;
  elevationMeters: number;
  firstAscentYear: number;
}

async function checkedFetchJSON(url: string): Promise<unknown> {
  const response = await fetch(url);
  if (!response.ok) {
    throw new Error(`Unable to fetch! ${response.statusText}`);
  }
  return response.json();
}

export async function fetchPeak(peakId: string): Promise<MountainPeak> {
  return checkedFetchJSON(`/api/mountain-peaks/${peakId}`);
//       ~~~~~ Type 'unknown' is not assignable to type 'MountainPeak'.
}
```

The checkedFetchJSON wrapper provides two services here. First, it checks whether the fetch succeeded and throws (thus rejecting the Promise) if it did not. Second, it gives the JSON response an unknown type (Item 46) which is safer than the any type that you'd get by default.

Unfortunately, there's a type error because unknown is not assignable to MountainPeak. If you want to avoid type assertions or any types in your fetchPeak implementation, you'll have to change the return type to match:

```
export async function fetchPeak(peakId: string): Promise<unknown> {
  return checkedFetchJSON(`/api/mountain-peaks/${peakId}`);  // ok
}
```

This passes the type checker and contains no unsafe assertions (good!), but this comes at a significant cost. The `fetchPeak` function is now extremely hard to use:

```
const sevenPeaks = [
  'aconcagua', 'denali', 'elbrus', 'everest', 'kilimanjaro', 'vinson', 'wilhelm'
];
async function getPeaksByHeight(): Promise<MountainPeak[]> {
  const peaks = await Promise.all(sevenPeaks.map(fetchPeak));
  return peaks.toSorted(
  // ~~~ Type 'unknown' is not assignable to type 'MountainPeak'.
    (a, b) => b.elevationMeters - a.elevationMeters
    //          ~                        ~ 'b' and 'a' are of type 'unknown'
  );
}
```

Any code that calls it will likely have to use a type assertion:

```
async function getPeaksByDate(): Promise<MountainPeak[]> {
  const peaks = await Promise.all(sevenPeaks.map(fetchPeak)) as MountainPeak[];
  return peaks.toSorted((a, b) => b.firstAscentYear - a.firstAscentYear);
}
```

This will result in type assertions scattered throughout your code whenever you call `fetchPeak`. This is duplicative, tedious, and introduces the possibility that you'll assert different types in different places.

Rather than changing the return type of `fetchPeak` to placate the type checker, a better approach would be to keep the type signature as it was and add an assertion in the function body:

```
export async function fetchPeak(peakId: string): Promise<MountainPeak> {
  return checkedFetchJSON(
    `/api/mountain-peaks/${peakId}`,
  ) as Promise<MountainPeak>;
}
```

With the type assertion hidden away in the function implementation, calling code can be written cleanly without any knowledge of our unsafe secret:

```
async function getPeaksByContinent(): Promise<MountainPeak[]> {
  const peaks = await Promise.all(sevenPeaks.map(fetchPeak));  // no assertion!
  return peaks.toSorted((a, b) => a.continent.localeCompare(b.continent));
}
```

By localizing the type assertion, we've also made it easier to increase its safety. Here's a version that checks at least some of the shape of the response:

```
export async function fetchPeak(peakId: string): Promise<MountainPeak> {
  const maybePeak = checkedFetchJSON(`/api/mountain-peaks/${peakId}`);
  if (
    !maybePeak ||
    typeof maybePeak !== 'object' ||
    !('firstAscentYear' in maybePeak)
```

```
  ) {
    throw new Error(`Invalid mountain peak: ${JSON.stringify(maybePeak)}`);
  }
  return checkedFetchJSON(
    `/api/mountain-peaks/${peakId}`,
  ) as Promise<MountainPeak>;
}
```

You're unlikely to do this sort of shape checking at every single call site, but it's easy enough to do with the type assertion in one place. (If you find yourself writing this sort of validation code often, Item 74 introduces some more systematic approaches for validating TypeScript types at runtime. All these approaches hide type assertions in well-typed functions!)

Another way to hide a type assertion is by providing a single overload of the function:

```
export async function fetchPeak(peakId: string): Promise<MountainPeak>;
export async function fetchPeak(peakId: string): Promise<unknown> {
  return checkedFetchJSON(`/api/mountain-peaks/${peakId}`);  // OK
}

const denali = fetchPeak('denali');
//    ^? const denali: Promise<MountainPeak>
```

In this case, the overload presents a different type signature to callers of the function than the one used in the implementation. There is some safety here: TypeScript will check that the two signatures are compatible. But this isn't fundamentally any different than a type assertion, and you'd still be well served to do some kind of data validation.

You might also find yourself pushed into using a type assertion because TypeScript's type checker can't follow along with your code. For example, this function checks if two objects are shallowly equal to each other:

```
function shallowObjectEqual(a: object, b: object): boolean {
  for (const [k, aVal] of Object.entries(a)) {
    if (!(k in b) || aVal !== b[k]) {
      //                        ~~~~ Element implicitly has an 'any' type
      //                             because type '{}' has no index signature
      return false;
    }
  }
  return Object.keys(a).length === Object.keys(b).length;
}
```

It's a bit surprising that TypeScript complains about the b[k] access despite your having just checked that k in b is true. But it does, so you'll need to resort to either @ts-expect-error or an any type.

This would be the wrong way to fix the type error:

```
function shallowObjectEqualBad(a: object, b: any): boolean {
  for (const [k, aVal] of Object.entries(a)) {
    if (!(k in b) || aVal !== b[k]) {  // ok
      return false;
    }
  }
  return Object.keys(a).length === Object.keys(b).length;
}
```

By changing b's type to any, we allow code that will crash at runtime:

```
shallowObjectEqual({x: 1}, null)
//                        ~~~~ Type 'null' is not assignable to type 'object'.
shallowObjectEqualBad({x: 1}, null);  // ok, throws at runtime
```

Better to hide the any type inside the function implementation:

```
function shallowObjectEqualGood(a: object, b: object): boolean {
  for (const [k, aVal] of Object.entries(a)) {
    if (!(k in b) || aVal !== (b as any)[k]) {
      // `(b as any)[k]` is OK because we've just checked `k in b`
      return false;
    }
  }
  return Object.keys(a).length === Object.keys(b).length;
}
```

This any is narrowly scoped (Item 43), does not affect the type signature of the function, and even includes a comment explaining why it's valid. This is a fine use of an any type and a type assertion. Your code is correct, the type signature is clear, and your users will be none the wiser.

You should unit test all your code, of course, but this is especially true when it uses type assertions. Since you've told TypeScript to trust you, everything's OK, and the burden of proof is on you to show that. Comments explaining why a type assertion is valid are helpful, but thorough tests are an even better demonstration of correctness.

Things to Remember

- Sometimes unsafe type assertions and any types are necessary or expedient. When you need to use one, hide it inside a function with a correct signature.

- Don't compromise a function's type signature to fix type errors in the implementation.

- Make sure you explain why your type assertions are valid, and unit test your code thoroughly.

Item 46: Use unknown Instead of any for Values with an Unknown Type

Suppose you want to write a YAML parser (YAML can represent the same set of values as JSON but allows a superset of JSON's syntax). What should the return type of your parseYAML method be? It's tempting to make it any (like JSON.parse):

```
function parseYAML(yaml: string): any {
  // ...
}
```

But this flies in the face of Item 43's advice to avoid "contagious" any types, specifically by not returning them from functions. (Item 71 will explore how to "fix" JSON.parse so that it doesn't return any.)

Ideally, you'd like your users to immediately assign the result to another type:

```
interface Book {
  name: string;
  author: string;
}
const book: Book = parseYAML(`
  name: Wuthering Heights
  author: Emily Brontë
`);
```

Without the type annotation, though, the book variable would quietly get an any type, thwarting type checking wherever it's used:

```
const book = parseYAML(`
  name: Jane Eyre
  author: Charlotte Brontë
`);
console.log(book.title);  // No error, logs "undefined" at runtime
book('read');  // No error, throws "book is not a function" at runtime
```

A safer alternative would be to have parseYAML return an unknown type:

```
function safeParseYAML(yaml: string): unknown {
  return parseYAML(yaml);
}
const book = safeParseYAML(`
  name: The Tenant of Wildfell Hall
  author: Anne Brontë
`);
console.log(book.title);
//          ~~~~ 'book' is of type 'unknown'
book("read");
// Error: 'book' is of type 'unknown'
```

To understand the unknown type, it helps to think about any in terms of assignability. The power and danger of any come from two properties:

- All types are assignable to the any type.
- The any type is assignable to all other types.[1]

If we "think of types as sets of values" (Item 7), the first property means that any is a supertype of all other types, while the second means that it is a subtype. This is strange! It means that any doesn't fit into the type system, since a set can't simultaneously be both a subset and a superset of all other sets. This is the source of any's power but also the reason it's problematic. Since the type checker is set based, the use of any effectively disables it.

The unknown type is an alternative to any that *does* fit into the type system. It has the first property (any type is assignable to unknown) but not the second (unknown is only assignable to unknown and, of course, any). It's known as a "top" type since it's at the top of the type hierarchy. The never type is the opposite: it has the second property (can be assigned to any other type) but not the first (no other type can be assigned to never). It's known as a "bottom" type.

Attempting to access a property on a value with the unknown type is an error. So is attempting to call it or do arithmetic with it. You can't do much of anything with unknown, which is exactly the point. The errors about an unknown type will encourage you to pick something more specific:

```
const book = safeParseYAML(`
  name: Villette
  author: Charlotte Brontë
`) as Book;
console.log(book.title);
//               ~~~~ Property 'title' does not exist on type 'Book'
book('read');
// Error: This expression is not callable
```

These errors are more sensible. Since unknown is not assignable to other types, you'll need a type assertion. But it is also appropriate: we really do know more about the type of the resulting object than TypeScript does.

unknown is appropriate whenever you know that there will be a value but you either don't know or don't care about its type. The result of parseYAML is one example, but there are others. In the GeoJSON spec, for example, the properties property of a feature is a grab bag of anything JSON serializable. So unknown makes sense:

---

1 With the exception of never.

```
interface Feature {
  id?: string | number;
  geometry: Geometry;
  properties: unknown;
}
```

If you write a function to check if an array has fewer than 10 elements, you don't particularly care about the type of the elements. So unknown makes sense here, too:

```
function isSmallArray(arr: readonly unknown[]): boolean {
  return arr.length < 10;
}
```

As you've seen, you can get a more specific type from unknown using a type assertion. But this isn't the only way. An instanceof check will do:

```
function processValue(value: unknown) {
  if (value instanceof Date) {
    value
    // ^? (parameter) value: Date
  }
}
```

You can also use a user-defined type guard:

```
function isBook(value: unknown): value is Book {
  return (
      typeof(value) === 'object' && value !== null &&
      'name' in value && 'author' in value
  );
}
function processValue(value: unknown) {
  if (isBook(value)) {
    value;
    // ^? (parameter) value: Book
  }
}
```

TypeScript requires quite a bit of proof to narrow an unknown type: in order to avoid errors on the in checks, you first have to demonstrate that val is an object type and that it is non-null (since typeof null === 'object'). As with any user-defined type guard, remember that it's no safer than a type assertion. Nothing checks that you've implemented the guard correctly or kept it in sync with your type. (Item 74 discusses solutions to this conundrum.)

You'll sometimes see a type parameter used instead of unknown. You could have declared the safeParseYAML function this way:

```
function safeParseYAML<T>(yaml: string): T {
  return parseYAML(yaml);
}
```

This is generally considered bad style in TypeScript, however. It looks different than a type assertion, but it is no safer and is functionally the same. Better to just return unknown and force your users to use an assertion, or narrow to the type they want. This is a common example of an unnecessary use of generics, which is the subject of Item 51.

unknown can also be used instead of any in "double assertions":

```
declare const foo: Foo;
let barAny = foo as any as Bar;
let barUnk = foo as unknown as Bar;
```

These are functionally equivalent, but the unknown version prevents the visceral reaction you and your coworkers might have at seeing as any.

As a final note, you may see code that uses object or {} in a similar way to how unknown has been described in this item. They are also broad types but are slightly narrower than unknown:

- The {} type consists of all values except null and undefined.
- The Object type (capital "O") is the nearly the same as {}. Strings, numbers, booleans, and other primitives are assignable to Object.
- The object type (lowercase "o") consists of all nonprimitive types. This doesn't include true or 12 or "foo", but does include objects, arrays, and functions.

It's quite rare that you really want to permit any value except null and undefined, so unknown is generally preferable to {} or Object.

Things to Remember

- The unknown type is a type-safe alternative to any. Use it when you know you have a value but do not know or do not care what its type is.
- Use unknown to force your users to use a type assertion or other form of narrowing.
- Avoid return-only type parameters, which can create a false sense of security.
- Understand the difference between {}, object, and unknown.

Item 47: Prefer Type-Safe Approaches to Monkey Patching

One of the most famous features of JavaScript is that its objects and classes are "open" in the sense that you can add arbitrary properties to them. This is occasionally used to create global variables on web pages by assigning to window or document:

```
window.monkey = 'Tamarin';
document.monkey = 'Howler';
```

or to attach data to DOM elements:

```
const el = document.getElementById('colobus');
el.home = 'tree';
```

Adding properties to built-in objects at runtime is known as "monkey patching" and is particularly common with code that uses jQuery or D3.

You can even attach properties to the prototypes of built-ins, with sometimes surprising results:

```
> RegExp.prototype.monkey = 'Capuchin'
'Capuchin'
> /123/.monkey
'Capuchin'
```

These approaches are generally not good designs. When you attach data to `window` or a DOM node, you are essentially turning it into a global variable. This makes it easy to inadvertently introduce dependencies between far-flung parts of your program, and means that you have to think about side effects whenever you call a function. Outside of `strict` mode, JavaScript makes it very easy to introduce global variables: just drop the `let`, `var`, or `const` from an assignment.

Adding TypeScript introduces another problem: while the type checker knows about built-in properties of `Document` and `HTMLElement`, it certainly doesn't know about the ones you've added:

```
document.monkey = 'Tamarin';
//       ~~~~~~ Property 'monkey' does not exist on type 'Document'
```

The most straightforward way to fix this error is with an `any` assertion:

```
(document as any).monkey = 'Tamarin';  // OK
```

This satisfies the type checker, but, as should be no surprise by now, it has some downsides. As with any use of `any`, you lose type safety and language services:

```
(document as any).monky = 'Tamarin';  // Also OK, misspelled
(document as any).monkey = /Tamarin/;  // Also OK, wrong type
```

The best solution is to move your data out of `window`, `document`, or the DOM. But if you can't (perhaps you're using a library that requires it or are in the process of migrating a JavaScript application), then the monkey patch is part of your environment (Item 76) and you should model it with TypeScript. There's no perfect way to do this, but `as any` sets a low bar for safety and developer experience, and there are ways to do considerably better.

Imagine you're building a web application and you have an object with information about the currently logged-in user. You fetch this on page load via an API and store it as a global variable for convenient access throughout your code:

```
interface User {
  name: string;
}

document.addEventListener("DOMContentLoaded", async () => {
  const response = await fetch('/api/users/current-user');
  const user = (await response.json()) as User;
  window.user = user;
  //     ~~~~ Property 'user' does not exist
  //          on type 'Window & typeof globalThis'.
});

// ... elsewhere ...
export function greetUser() {
  alert(`Hello ${window.user.name}!`);
  //                    ~~~~ Property 'user' does not exist on type Window...
}
```

The type errors arise because TypeScript doesn't know about our patch to the global object. Rather than writing (window as any), one option is to use an augmentation, one of the special abilities of interface (Item 13):

```
declare global {
  interface Window {
    /** The currently logged-in user */
    user: User;
  }
}
```

This tells TypeScript that Window has another property that it didn't know about from the built-in DOM types. With the augmentation in place, our code passes the type checker:

```
document.addEventListener("DOMContentLoaded", async () => {
  const response = await fetch('/api/users/current-user');
  const user = (await response.json()) as User;
  window.user = user;  // OK
});

// ... elsewhere ...
export function greetUser() {
  alert(`Hello ${window.user.name}!`);  // OK
}
```

This is an improvement over using any in a few ways:

- You get type safety. The type checker will flag misspellings or assignments of the wrong type.
- You can attach documentation to the property (Item 68).
- You get autocomplete and other language services on the property.
- There is a record of precisely what the monkey patch is.

There are a few problems with the augmentation approach. In cases (such as user) where a global is set while your application is running, there's no way to introduce the augmentation only after this has happened. This masks a race condition in our code. What happens if we call greetUser() before window.user is set?

To avoid issues like this, you may want to include undefined as a possibility on your global. This will force you to handle the possibility that user isn't available wherever you access it:

```
declare global {
  interface Window {
    /** The currently logged-in user */
    user: User | undefined;
  }
}

// ...
export function greetUser() {
  alert(`Hello ${window.user.name}!`);
  //                ~~~~~~~~~~~ 'window.user' is possibly 'undefined'.
}
```

There's a trade-off here between correctness and convenience.

If your serving infrastructure allows it, another solution for this specific situation would be to inline the user variable into the HTML of the page:

```
<script type="text/javascript">
window.user = { name: 'Bill Withers' };
</script>
<script src="your-code.js"></script>
```

This way you can safely remove the undefined possibility since user has been unconditionally set before any of your code runs and there's no possibility of a race condition.

Another issue with augmentation is that, as the declare global suggests, it applies globally. You can't hide it from other parts of your code or from libraries. If your app includes multiple pages and user is only available on some of them, the global augmentation won't be able to model that accurately.

An alternative approach that doesn't pollute the global scope is to use a narrower type assertion. Rather than (window as any), we can define another type with our added property:

```
type MyWindow = (typeof window) & {
  /** The currently logged-in user */
  user: User | undefined;
}

document.addEventListener("DOMContentLoaded", async () => {
  const response = await fetch('/api/users/current-user');
  const user = (await response.json()) as User;
  (window as MyWindow).user = user;  // OK
});

// ...
export function greetUser() {
  alert(`Hello ${(window as MyWindow).user.name}!`);
  //                ~~~~~~~~~~~~~~~~~~~~~~~~ Object is possibly 'undefined'.
}
```

TypeScript is OK with the type assertion because Window and MyWindow share properties (Item 9). And you get type safety in the assignment. The scope issues are also more manageable: there's no global modification of the Window type, just the introduction of a new type (which is only in scope if you import it).

The downside is that you have to write an assertion (or introduce a new variable) whenever you reference the monkey-patched property. And you'll want to enforce that no one sneaks in a (window as any), perhaps using a linter rule.

But you can take this all as encouragement to refactor into something more structured. Monkey patching shouldn't be *too* easy!

Things to Remember

- Prefer structured code to storing data in globals or on the DOM.
- If you must store data on built-in types, use one of the type-safe approaches (augmentation or asserting a custom interface).
- Understand the scoping issues of augmentations. Include undefined if that's a possibility at runtime.

Item 48: Avoid Soundness Traps

Hang out on the internet much and you'll hear gripes about how TypeScript isn't "sound," and that this makes it a poor choice of language. This item will explain what this means and walk you through common sources of unsoundness in TypeScript.

Rest assured, TypeScript is a great language, and it's never a good idea to listen to people on the internet!

A language is called "sound" if the static type of every symbol is guaranteed to be compatible with its runtime value. Using the terminology from Item 7, this means that every symbol's runtime value remains in the domain of that symbol's static type.

Here's an example of a sound type:

```
const x = Math.random();
//    ^? const x: number
```

TypeScript infers a static type of number for x, and this is sound: whatever value Math.random() returns at runtime, it will be a number. This doesn't mean that x could be any number at runtime: a more precise type would be the half-open interval [0, 1), but TypeScript has no way to express this. number is good enough. Soundness is more about accuracy than precision.

Here's an example of unsoundness in TypeScript:

```
const xs = [0, 1, 2];
//    ^? const xs: number[]
const x = xs[3];
//    ^? const x: number
```

The static type of x is inferred as number, but at runtime its value is undefined, which is not a number. So this is unsound and can lead to problems at runtime, for example, if you try to call a method on x:

```
console.log(x.toFixed(1));
```

There are no type errors, but when you run this code it will throw an error:

```
console.log(x.toFixed(1));
            ^

TypeError: Cannot read properties of undefined (reading 'toFixed')
```

Unsound types can easily lead to runtime errors, so a sound type system is generally considered to be a desirable property of a programming language.

Soundness comes with trade-offs, however. It's easier for less expressive type systems to achieve soundness. If TypeScript didn't support generic types, for example, it would eliminate many of the sources of unsoundness that you'll read about later. But generic types are useful! This hypothetical version of TypeScript would have a harder time modeling JavaScript patterns and would catch fewer bugs.

In other words, there's a trade-off among a type system's expressiveness, its soundness, and its convenience. TypeScript gives you some choices about where you want to be on this spectrum: by enabling strictNullChecks (Item 2), you accept some inconvenience (needing to annotate `null` types and do `null` checks) in exchange for increased expressiveness.

As we saw previously, TypeScript as a whole is emphatically *not* sound. In fact, soundness is not a design goal of TypeScript at all. Instead, it favors convenience and the ability to work with existing JavaScript libraries.

Still, unsoundness can lead to crashes, bugs, or even data corruption, and you should avoid it when you can. Unchecked array accesses are one well-known soundness trap, but there are many others in TypeScript. The rest of this item will go through some of the sources of unsoundness in TypeScript and show how you can rework your code to avoid them.

any

If you "put an `any` on it," then anything goes. The static types may or may not have anything to do with real runtime types:

```
function logNumber(x: number) {
  console.log(x.toFixed(1));  // x is a string at runtime
  //           ^? (parameter) x: number
}
const num: any = 'forty two';
logNumber(num);  // no error
```

There are no type errors here, but this code will throw an exception at runtime.

The solution is simple: limit your use of `any` or, better, don't use it at all! This chapter has lots of advice about how to mitigate and avoid the static type disaster that is `any`, but the highlights are to limit the scope of `any` and to use `unknown` as a safer alternative when possible. For built-ins like `JSON.parse` that return `any` types, Item 71 shows you how to use declaration merging to get a safer alternative.

Type Assertions

The slightly less offensive cousin of `any` is the "type assertion." We've already covered this in Item 9, but here's a refresher on what this looks like:

```
function logNumber(x: number) {
  console.log(x.toFixed(1));
}
const hour = (new Date()).getHours() || null;
//    ^? const hour: number | null
logNumber(hour);
//        ~~~~ ... Type 'null' is not assignable to type 'number'.
logNumber(hour as number);  // type checks, but might blow up at runtime
```

The `as number` in the last line is the type assertion, and it makes the error go away.

What can you do about this? You can replace many assertions with conditionals (if statements or ternary operators):

```
if (hour !== null) {
  logNumber(hour);  // ok
  //           ^? const hour: number
}
```

Within the if block, the static type of hour is narrowed based on the condition, so the type assertion isn't needed (see Item 22 for more on narrowing).

Type assertions often come up in the context of input validation. It's a good idea to adopt a systematic approach to keeping your TypeScript types and your runtime validation logic in sync. Item 74 will walk you through your options.

Object and Array Lookups

Even in strict mode, TypeScript doesn't do any sort of bounds checking on array lookups. As we saw in the introduction to this item, this can lead directly to unsoundness and runtime errors.

The same can happen when you reference a property on an object with an index type:

```
type IdToName = { [id: string]: string };
const ids: IdToName = {'007': 'James Bond'};
const agent = ids['008'];  // undefined at runtime.
//    ^? const agent: string
```

Why does TypeScript allow this sort of code? Because it's extremely common and because it's quite difficult to prove whether any particular index/array access is valid. If you'd like TypeScript to try, there's a noUncheckedIndexedAccess option. If you turn it on, it finds the error in the example from the introduction but also flags perfectly valid code:

```
const xs = [1, 2, 3];
alert(xs[3].toFixed(1));  // invalid code
//    ~~~~~ Object is possibly 'undefined'.
alert(xs[2].toFixed(1));  // valid code
//    ~~~~~ Object is possibly 'undefined'.
```

This option moves you to a different place on the spectrum of soundness versus convenience: TypeScript is able to catch more errors, but it is less convenient to work with because it also flags code that's not an error. noUncheckedIndexedAccess is at least smart enough to understand some common array constructs:

```
const xs = [1, 2, 3];
for (const x of xs) {
  console.log(x.toFixed(1));  // OK
}
const squares = xs.map(x => x * x);  // also OK
```

If you're concerned about unsafe access to specific arrays or objects, you can explicitly add undefined to their value types:

```
const xs: (number | undefined)[] = [1, 2, 3];
alert(xs[3].toFixed(1));
//     ~~~~~ Object is possibly 'undefined'.

type IdToName = { [id: string]: string | undefined };
const ids: IdToName = {'007': 'James Bond'};
const agent = ids['008'];
//    ^? const agent: string | undefined
alert(agent.toUpperCase());
//    ~~~~~ 'agent' is possibly 'undefined'.
```

The advantage of this approach over noUncheckedIndexedAccess is that it lets you limit the scope (and presumably false positives) of that flag. The disadvantage is that it lacks the smarts of the flag: the for-of loop will give you errors with this approach. It also introduces the possibility that you push an undefined onto the array.

Finally, it's often possible to rework your code to reduce the need for these sorts of lookups. Rather than passing indices or keys to functions, try to work with the objects that they refer to.

Inaccurate Type Definitions

The type declarations for a JavaScript library are like a giant type assertion: they claim to statically model the runtime behavior of the library but there's nothing that guarantees this. (Unless, that is, the library is written in TypeScript, the declarations are generated by tsc, and the library has no unsound types!)

It's hard to show a current example here since these kinds of bugs tend to get fixed once you highlight them, particularly for declarations on DefinitelyTyped (@types). But a famous historic one was the React.FC definition in @types/react, which made UI components accept children, even when this didn't make logical sense.

How do you work around this? The best way is to fix the bug! For types on DefinitelyTyped, the turnaround time on this is usually a week or less. If this isn't an option, you can work around some issues via augmentation or, in the worst case, a type assertion.

It's also worth noting that some functions have types that are just very hard to model statically. Take a look at the parameter list for String.prototype.replace for a head-scratching example:

```
'foo'.replace(/f(.)/, (fullMatch, group1, offset, fullString, namedGroups) => {
  console.log(fullMatch); // "fo"
  console.log(group1); // "o"
  console.log(offset); // 0
  console.log(fullString); // "foo"
```

```
    console.log(namedGroups);  // undefined
    return fullMatch;
  });
```

If you're interested in the `offset` parameter, its position will depend on the number of capture groups (parenthesized expressions) in your regular expression. TypeScript has no concept of a regex literal type, so there's no way to determine the number of capture groups statically. So the callback parameters get an `any` type.

There are also some functions that are incorrectly typed for historical reasons, e.g., `Object.assign`. If this is causing you trouble, Item 71 has a fix.

Type declarations model more than just JavaScript libraries. They also describe the environment in which your code runs: the expected JavaScript runtime and other global environments. Item 76 has more to say about the importance of creating an accurate model of your environment.

Bivariance in Class Hierarchies

Assignability is tricky to think about with function types. It works a bit differently for the return type and the parameter types. For the return type, assignability works exactly like any other type:

```
declare function f(): number | string;
const f1: () => number | string | boolean = f;  // OK
const f2: () => number = f;
//     ~~ Type '() => string | number' is not assignable to type '() => number'.
//         Type 'string | number' is not assignable to type 'number'.
```

This makes sense: if you call a function expecting it to return a `number` but the function could also return a `string`, then trouble will ensue. We say that functions are *covariant* in their return types.

Parameter types go the opposite way:

```
declare function f(x: number | string): void;
const f1: (x: number | string | boolean) => void = f;
//     ~~
// Type 'string | number | boolean' is not assignable to type 'string | number'.
const f2: (x: number) => void = f;  // OK
```

This also makes sense: you shouldn't be able to call a function expecting number|string with a boolean. Functions are *contravariant* in their parameter types.

Now let's see what happens when we apply this to classes:

```
class Parent {
  foo(x: number | string) {}
  bar(x: number) {}
}
class Child extends Parent {
```

```
    foo(x: number) {}  // OK
    bar(x: number | string) {}  // OK
}
```

Recall from Item 7 that extends on a class or interface can be read as "subtype of." But in that case, given what we've just learned about function assignability, surely one of the two methods on Child should be an error. Since functions are contravariant in their parameter types, the Child foo method should not be assignable to the Parent foo.

You can adapt this form of unsoundness to get an undetected exception:

```
class FooChild extends Parent {
  foo(x: number) {
    console.log(x.toFixed());
  }
}
const p: Parent = new FooChild();
p.foo('string');  // No type error, crashes at runtime
```

TypeScript models methods on classes as *bivariant*: if either the parent or the child method is assignable to the other, then it's valid. Historically this was how *all* function assignments were modeled. But with strictFunctionTypes, which was introduced in TypeScript 2.6 way back in 2017, standalone function types are treated more accurately.

In practice this means that when you're inheriting from a class, you need to take extra care to get the method signatures correct. Typically, child classes should have the exact same method signature as their parents. But they can get out of sync over time if you change the parent's signature and expect to get a type error for all child implementations. Be on the lookout for this! When you change a method signature on a class in a hierarchy, check the same method on any parent or child classes.

TypeScript's Inaccurate Model of Variance for Objects and Arrays

This one has been widely discussed online. Here's the standard example of how it works:

```
function addFoxOrHen(animals: Animal[]) {
  animals.push(Math.random() > 0.5 ? new Fox() : new Hen());
}

const henhouse: Hen[] = [new Hen()];
addFoxOrHen(henhouse);  // oh no, a fox in the henhouse!
```

The issue is that it's only safe to assign Hen[] to Animal[] if you don't modify the array. In other words, only readonly Hen[] should be assignable to readonly Animal[]. TypeScript hasn't always had readonly, though, and in the early days it chose to allow this sort of code. Perhaps in the future there will be a new strict option to handle this source of unsoundness.

What can *you* do about it? It's best not to mutate function parameters, which you can enforce with a readonly annotation (Item 14):

```
function addFoxOrHen(animals: readonly Animal[]) {
  animals.push(Math.random() > 0.5 ? new Fox() : new Hen());
  //       ~~~~ Property 'push' does not exist on type 'readonly Animal[]'.
}
```

You can dodge the issue entirely by rewriting the initial example so that the function returns an Animal, rather than adding it to an array:

```
function foxOrHen(): Animal {
  return Math.random() > 0.5 ? new Fox() : new Hen();
}

const henhouse: Hen[] = [new Hen(), foxOrHen()];
//                                  ~~~~~~~~~~ error, yay! Chickens are safe.
// Type 'Animal' is missing the following properties from type 'Hen': ...
```

You can run into similar issues with any object mutated by a function, not just arrays. If you create an alias for your object (Item 23) and mutate it, then you can run into trouble even without a function call.

While variance can be tricky to think about, the lesson here is straightforward: avoid mutating function parameters! And to make sure you don't, declare them readonly or Readonly.

Function Calls Don't Invalidate Refinements

Here's some code that doesn't look too suspicious at first glance (at least from a type safety perspective):

```
interface FunFact {
  fact: string;
  author?: string;
}

function processFact(fact: FunFact, processor: (fact: FunFact) => void) {
  if (fact.author) {
    processor(fact);
    console.log(fact.author.blink());  // ok
    //                ^? (property) FunFact.author?: string
  }
}
```

Depending on what processor does, however, the call to blink() might throw at runtime:

```
processFact(
  {fact: 'Peanuts are not actually nuts', author: 'Botanists'},
  f => delete f.author
);
// Type checks, but throws `Cannot read property 'blink' of undefined`.
```

The issue is that if (fact.author) refines the type of fact.author from string|
undefined to string. This is sound. However, the call to processor(fact) *should*
invalidate this refinement. The type of fact.author should revert back to string|
undefined because TypeScript has no way of knowing what the callback will do to
our refined fact.

Why does TypeScript allow this? Because most functions don't mutate their parameters, and this sort of pattern is common in JavaScript.

How can you avoid this? Again, don't mutate your function parameters! You can
enforce that callbacks do this by passing them a Readonly version of the object
(Item 14).

Assignability and Optional Properties

It's important to remember that object types in TypeScript types aren't "sealed": they
could have properties other than the ones you've declared (Item 4). When combined
with optional properties, this can lead to unsoundness.

Here's how this might happen:

```
interface Person {
  name: string;
}
interface PossiblyAgedPerson extends Person {
  age?: number;
}
const p1 = { name: "Serena", age: "42 years" };
const p2: Person = p1;
const p3: PossiblyAgedPerson = p2;
console.log(`${p3.name} is ${p3.age?.toFixed(1)} years old.`);
```

The assignment from p1 to p2 circumvents excess property checking (Item 11). p2 has
a static type of Person. This is sound because the type {name: string; age:
string} is assignable to Person. With structural typing, it's OK to have extra
properties.

The assignment to p3 is where we lose soundness. If you think of types as being
sealed, without having extra properties, then this assignment should be allowed: a
Person wouldn't have an age property and, since this property is optional on
PossiblyAgedPerson, that would be OK. But types aren't sealed and, as happened
here, it's possible that they have additional properties that are incompatible with the
optional property's type.

If you run into this issue, it may be because you've had a name collision between overly generic property names (e.g., type). Try choosing more specific property names. Naming the properties ageInYears and ageFormatted in this example would have prevented this error.

Unsoundness is just one of the problems with optional properties. Item 37 discusses other reasons why you should think carefully before adding one.

There are a few other sources of unsoundness in TypeScript, but these are some of the ones that you're most likely to come across in practice. Remember, unsoundness isn't a flaw in the language. It reflects a choice about where TypeScript wants to be positioned along the spectrum of convenience, expressiveness, and safety. If you want to move to a different point along that spectrum, you have some knobs that let you do so (e.g., strictNullChecks and noUncheckedIndexedAccess). Otherwise, be aware of the common patterns that lead to unsoundness and try to avoid them.

Things to Remember

- "Unsoundness" is when a symbol's value at runtime diverges from its static type. It can lead to crashes and other bad behavior without type errors.
- Be aware of some of the common ways that unsoundness can arise: any types, type assertions (as, is), object and array lookups, and inaccurate type definitions.
- Avoid mutating function parameters as this can lead to unsoundness. Mark them as read-only if you don't intend to mutate them.
- Make sure child classes match their parent's method declarations.
- Be aware of how optional properties can lead to unsound types.

Item 49: Track Your Type Coverage to Prevent Regressions in Type Safety

You've enabled noImplicitAny and added type annotations to all the values that had implicit any types. Are you safe from the problems associated with any types? The answer is "no"; any types can still enter your program in two main ways:

Through explicit any *types*
Even if you follow the advice of Items 43 and 44, making your any types both narrow and specific, they remain any types. In particular, types like any[ ] and {[key: string]: any} become plain anys once you index into them, and the resulting any types can flow through your code.

From third-party type declarations

This is particularly insidious since any types from an @types declaration file enter silently: even though you have noImplicitAny enabled and you never wrote the word "any," you still have any types flowing through your code.

Because of the negative effects any types can have on type safety and developer experience (Item 5), it's a good idea to keep track of the number of them in your codebase. There are many ways to do this, including the type-coverage package on npm:

```
$ npx type-coverage
9985 / 10117 98.69%
```

This means that, of the 10,117 symbols in this project, 9,985 (98.69%) had a type other than any or an alias to any. If a change inadvertently introduces an any type and it flows through your code, you'll see a corresponding drop in this percentage.

In some ways, this percentage is a way of keeping score on how well you've followed the advice of the other items in this chapter. Using narrowly scoped any will reduce the number of symbols with any types, and so will using more specific forms like any[]. Tracking this numerically helps you make sure things only get better over time.

Even collecting type coverage information once can be informative. Running type-coverage with the --detail flag will print where every any type occurs in your code:

```
$ npx type-coverage --detail
path/to/code.ts:1:10 getColumnInfo
path/to/module.ts:7:1 pt2
...
```

These are worth investigating because they're likely to turn up sources of anys that you hadn't considered. Let's look at a few examples.

Explicit any types are often the result of choices you made for expediency earlier on. Perhaps you were getting a type error that you didn't want to take the time to sort out. Maybe the type was one that you hadn't written out yet. Or you might have just been in a rush.

Type assertions with any can prevent types from flowing where they otherwise would. Perhaps you've built an application that works with tabular data and needed a single-parameter function that built up some kind of column description:

```
function getColumnInfo(name: string): any {
  return utils.buildColumnInfo(appState.dataSchema, name);  // Returns any
}
```

The utils.buildColumnInfo function returned any at some point. As a reminder, you added a comment and an explicit : any annotation to the function.

However, in the intervening months you've also added a type for `ColumnInfo`, and `utils.buildColumnInfo` no longer returns `any`. The `any` annotation is now throwing away valuable type information. Get rid of it!

Third-party `any` types can come in a few forms, but the most extreme is when you give an entire module an `any` type:

```
declare module 'my-module';
```

Now you can import anything from `my-module` without error. These symbols all have `any` types and will lead to more `any` types if you pass values through them:

```
import {someMethod, someSymbol} from 'my-module';  // OK

const pt1 = { x: 1, y: 2 };
//    ^? const pt1: { x: number; y: number; }
const pt2 = someMethod(pt1, someSymbol);  // OK
//    ^? const pt2: any
```

Since the usage looks identical to a well-typed module, it's easy to forget that you stubbed out the module. Or maybe a coworker did it and you never knew in the first place. It's worth revisiting these from time to time. Maybe there are official type declarations for the module. Or perhaps after reading Chapter 8 you've gained enough understanding of the module to write types yourself and contribute them back to the community.

Another common source of `any`s with third-party declarations is when there's a bug in the types. Maybe the declarations didn't follow the advice of Item 30 and declared a function to return a union type when in fact it returns something much more specific. When you first used the function, this didn't seem worth fixing so you used an `any` assertion. But maybe the declarations have been fixed since then. Or maybe it's time to fix them yourself!

If you'd like to continually be aware of the `any` types in your code, you can set up `type-coverage` as a TypeScript Language Service plug-in. This is like having X-ray vision, letting you see all the `any` types hiding in plain sight in your code (Figure 5-1).

```
import {someMethod, someSymbol} from 'my-module';

         The type of 'pt2' is 'any' ts-plugin-type-coverage(1)

         const pt2: any

const     View Problem (⌥F8)    No quick fixes available
const pt2 = someMethod(pt1, someSymbol);
```

Figure 5-1. Symbols with an any type highlighted in your editor. None of these would have been noImplicitAny errors.

If you add `type-coverage` to your continuous integration system, you'll find out about surprising drops in type safety as soon as they happen.

The considerations that led you to use an any type may no longer apply. Maybe there's a type you can plug in now where previously you used any. Maybe an unsafe type assertion is no longer necessary. Maybe the bug in the type declarations you were working around has been fixed. Tracking your type coverage highlights these choices and encourages you to keep revisiting them.

Things to Remember

- Even with `noImplicitAny` set, any types can make their way into your code either through explicit anys or third-party type declarations (`@types`).
- Consider tracking how well-typed your program is using a tool like `type-coverage`. This will encourage you to revisit decisions about using any and increase type safety over time.

CHAPTER 6

Generics and Type-Level Programming

TypeScript's type system is designed to model the runtime behavior of JavaScript code. Because JavaScript is so dynamic and permissive, this has pushed TypeScript's type system to develop increasingly powerful capabilities. As Item 15 explained, this includes logic for mapping between types.

When you add generic type aliases to the mix, TypeScript's type system becomes powerful enough that you can think of it as its own independent programming language. (TypeScript's type system is Turing Complete (*https://oreil.ly/snlm0*), so this is true in a formal sense.) Rather than programming with values, as you do in JavaScript, you're now programming with types. In other words, type-level programming. This is distinct from metaprogramming (writing programs that operate on programs), though the two terms are sometimes conflated.

Learning new languages is fun, and you can find all sorts of wild applications built using TypeScript's type system, ranging from games to SQL parsers. This has been driven in part by the Type Challenges (*https://tsch.js.org*) project, which includes hundreds of increasingly difficult puzzles to solve in the type system. Solving these as you read this chapter is a great way to cement what you've learned.

This chapter also includes a few cautionary notes. Just because TypeScript includes a programming language for types doesn't mean it's a particularly intuitive, ergonomic, or pleasant language to work with. Just because you *can* write logic at the type level doesn't mean it's always a good idea. Overuse of generic types can lead to cryptic, hard-to-maintain code. Josh Goldberg puts it well in *Learning TypeScript* (O'Reilly):

> Although generics can give us a lot of flexibility in describing types in code, they can become rather complex quite quickly. Programmers new to TypeScript often go through a phase of overusing generics to the point of making code confusing to read and overly complex to work with. TypeScript best practice is generally to use generics only when necessary, and to be clear about what they're used for when they are.

This chapter will help you decide whether it's necessary to use generic types and presents some alternatives. Used well, type-level code can improve other developers' experiences without their ever needing to know that there's fancy type-level code involved.

Item 50: Think of Generics as Functions Between Types

Item 15 showed how you can use type operations (`extends`, mapped types, indexing, `keyof`) to reduce repetition between related types. In value-land, functions are one of the key ways to factor out repeated code. In type-land, the equivalent of a function is a *generic type*. A generic type takes one or more *type parameters* and produces a concrete, nongeneric type. Whereas you "call" a function, you "instantiate" a generic type.

The built-in `Partial` generic type makes all the properties of another type optional. Here's how you might define that yourself:

```
type MyPartial<T> = {[K in keyof T]?: T[K]};
```

Here `T` is the type parameter. You can see that this works exactly the same as the built-in `Partial` type:

```
interface Person {
  name: string;
  age: number;
}

type MyPartPerson = MyPartial<Person>;
//     ^? type MyPartPerson = { name?: string; age?: number; }

type PartPerson = Partial<Person>;
//     ^? type PartPerson = { name?: string; age?: number; }
```

By defining this generic type, we've encapsulated the type-level operations required to optionalize all the properties on another type. This is exactly analogous to how a function might encapsulate the logic of taking one value and producing another. You don't need to know the details of how `Math.cos` is implemented to know that it calculates the cosine of a number.

You can write generic types that take multiple type parameters. Here's how you might try to define the equivalent of the built-in `Pick` generic:

```
type MyPick<T, K> = {
  [P in K]: T[P]
  //   ~        Type 'K' is not assignable to type 'string | number | symbol'.
  //       ~~~~ Type 'P' cannot be used to index type 'T'.
};
```

Even when you're programming at the type level, TypeScript applies all the same tools of static analysis to check for assignability and other errors in your code. Here it's found two problems:

- We're mapping over K, but TypeScript has no reason to believe that it contains types that can be used as property keys, namely string, number, or symbol.
- Even if it were a valid property key, TypeScript has no reason to believe that P can be used to index into T. T might not be an object type, and it might not have that key.

There are many ways to deal with type-level errors, just as there are many ways to deal with type errors in nongeneric code. Perhaps the simplest is to ignore them. This works surprisingly well!

```
// @ts-expect-error (don't do this!)
type MyPick<T, K> = { [P in K]: T[P] };
type AgeOnly = MyPick<Person, 'age'>;
//   ^? type AgeOnly = { age: number; }
```

You can think of this as the type-level equivalent of TypeScript emitting JavaScript, even in the presence of type errors (Item 3). Just because it doesn't like your implementation of a generic type doesn't mean that TypeScript won't let you use it.

Of course, TypeScript is right to complain. This version of MyPick is quite error prone:

```
type FirstNameOnly = MyPick<Person, 'firstName'>;
//   ^? type FirstNameOnly = { firstName: unknown; }
type Flip = MyPick<'age', Person>;
//   ^? type Flip = {}
```

Rather than getting a type error, incorrect uses of MyPick just return the wrong type. It's almost like programming in JavaScript!

Another way to make the error go away is to add intersections with the types that TypeScript is expecting. Here's what that looks like:

```
type MyPick<T, K> = { [P in K & PropertyKey]: T[P & keyof T] };

type AgeOnly = MyPick<Person, 'age'>;
//   ^? type AgeOnly = { age: number; }
type FirstNameOnly = MyPick<Person, 'firstName'>;
//   ^? type FirstNameOnly = { firstName: never; }
```

PropertyKey is a built-in alias for string | number | symbol. You can think of this sort of intersection as a kind of type-level equivalent of as any. It has made the type errors in the implementation go away and left the correct uses unchanged. The incorrect uses come out slightly differently, and this is perhaps an improvement: never is often an indication that something has gone wrong.

But keeping with the analogy, as any is rarely the right choice in value-land, and these intersections are not typically the best choice at the type level, either. You often solve type errors by making a function accept a narrower type for its parameters, and that's exactly what we want to do here. You can add a constraint on type parameters using the extends keyword:

```
type MyPick<T extends object, K extends keyof T> = {[P in K]: T[P]};

type AgeOnly = MyPick<Person, 'age'>;
//    ^? type AgeOnly = { age: number; }
type FirstNameOnly = MyPick<Person, 'firstName'>;
//                                   ~~~~~~~~~~~
//               Type '"firstName"' does not satisfy the constraint 'keyof Person'.
type Flip = MyPick<'age', Person>;
//                 ~~~~ Type 'string' does not satisfy the constraint 'object'.
```

By constraining T to be an object type and constraining K to be a subtype of the keys of T, we've solved two problems at once: we've eliminated the type errors in the implementation and we've produced type errors on the invalid instantiations of MyPick.

When you have noImplicitAny set, TypeScript requires that you provide type annotations for all function parameters. There's no equivalent of this for type parameters. If you don't specify a constraint, it defaults to unknown, which allows users to pass in any type whatsoever. When you're defining a generic type, consider whether you want to give your users a bit less freedom and a bit more safety.

When you write a function, you choose descriptive parameter names and write TSDoc comments (Item 68). You should do that for generic types as well. There's a convention of using one-letter names for type parameters (as this item has), but you should be just as wary of these in type-level code as you would be of one-letter variable names.

The general rule of thumb in naming is that the length of a name should match its scope. Long-lived globals should have long, descriptive names, whereas short names like i, k, or v can actually improve legibility in a concise arrow function with limited scope. For a short generic like MyPick, T and K are fine. But for a longer definition where the type parameter has broader scope (a generic class, say), a longer, more meaningful name will improve clarity.

You can write TSDoc for generic types and the TypeScript language service will surface it in relevant situations, just as it would for functions. The type-level equivalent of @param is @template:[1]

---

1 This name makes more sense if you're coming from the C++ world, where generic types are known as "template types" and developers talk about "template metaprogramming."

```
/**
 * Construct a new object type using a subset of the properties of another one
 * (same as the built-in `Pick` type).
 * @template T The original object type
 * @template K The keys to pick, typically a union of string literal types.
 */
type MyPick<T extends object, K extends keyof T> = {
  [P in K]: T[P]
};
```

If you inspect MyPick at an instantiation site, you'll get the full documentation. And if you mouse over T or K in the definition, you'll see the documentation for just that type parameter (Figure 6-1).

```
/**
 * Construct a new object type using a subset of the properties of another one
 * (same as the built-in `Pick` type)
 * @temp  (type parameter) K in type MyPick<T extends object, K extends keyof T>
 * @temp  The keys to pick, typically a union of string literal types.
 */
type MyP  @template K — The keys to pick, typically a union of string literal types.
  [P in K]: T[P]
};
```

Figure 6-1. The @template TSDoc tag can be used to document a type parameter.

TypeScript types are best thought of as sets of values (Item 7), so generic types inherently operate on sets. This is quite distinct from JavaScript functions where you know that each parameter will have a single value every time the function is called. In practice this means that you always need to think about how your generic type will behave with union types. Item 53 shows you how to do this.

You write tests for your value-level code, what about for your type-level code? You absolutely should test your types! This is an interesting and deep enough topic that it warrants its own item. Check out Item 55.

You can also add type parameters to some value-level constructs such as functions and classes. We might accompany our Pick generic type with a corresponding pick function, for example:

```
function pick<T extends object, K extends keyof T>(
  obj: T, ...keys: K[]
): Pick<T, K> {
  const picked: Partial<Pick<T, K>> = {};
  for (const k of keys) {
    picked[k] = obj[k];
  }
  return picked as Pick<T, K>;
}
```

```
const p: Person = { name: 'Matilda', age: 5.5 };
const age = pick(p, 'age');
//    ^? const age: Pick<Person, "age">
console.log(age);  // logs { age: 5.5 }
```

Just looking at the type and ignoring the bits between the parentheses, this looks a lot like the definition of the `MyPick` type from earlier:

```
type P = typeof pick;
//    ^? type P = <T extends object, K extends keyof T>(
//         obj: T, ...keys: K[]
//       ) => Pick<T, K>
```

You can think of generic functions as conceptually defining an associated generic type. The beauty of generic functions, however, is that TypeScript can often infer the type parameters from the values when the function is called. In the previous example, we just wrote `pick(p, 'age')`. This is significantly more concise than (and produces the exact same results as) writing out the types explicitly:

```
const age = pick<Person, 'age'>(p, 'age');
//    ^? const age: Pick<Person, "age">
```

Another advantage is that the user of your `pick` function needn't know that they're working with generic types or type-level operations at all. They can just enjoy the accurate, precise types. The type of `age` is a hint that there's type-level programming at work, but this, too, can be hidden if you like. Item 56 shows how.

Classes can also take type parameters, and these, too, can be inferred from usage:

```
class Box<T> {
  value: T;
  constructor(value: T) {
    this.value = value;
  }
}

const dateBox = new Box(new Date());
//    ^? const dateBox: Box<Date>
```

Recall from Item 8 that `class` is one of the few constructs in TypeScript that introduces both a type and a value. For a generic class, it introduces a generic type that relates the type parameter (`T`) to the properties and methods of that class.

Just as classes are good at capturing related bits of state that you'd otherwise have to track yourself, generic classes are a good way to capture types. A generic class's type parameters are set when it's constructed and they don't need to be passed to its methods when you call them (though its methods can have type parameters of their own). Item 28 explored how this could be used to gain more fine-grained control over type inference.

In value-land, you can write "higher order functions" like `map`, `filter`, and `reduce` that take other functions as parameters. This gives you enormous flexibility to factor out shared behaviors. Is there a type-level equivalent of these?

At the time of this writing, the answer is no. These would be "functions on functions on types" or "higher-kinded types" as they're usually known. They would let you factor out common operations, like applying a generic type to the value types in an object:

```
type MapValues<T extends object, F> = {
  [K in keyof T]: F<T[K]>;
  //                  ~~~~~~~ Type 'F' is not generic.
};
```

The good news is that this doesn't limit what you can do with generic types. It only limits the way you express yourself. In this case, you need to use a mapped type instead of `MapValues`. Similarly, there's no such thing as an anonymous generic type.

Generic types are best thought of as functions between types. Keep this in mind as you write them. You're working at the type level now and it's exciting and new. But you're still coding, and all the best practices you've learned for writing value-level code still apply.

Things to Remember

- Think of generic types as functions between types.
- Use `extends` to constrain the domain of type parameters, just as you'd use a type annotation to constrain a function parameter.
- Choose type parameter names that increase the legibility of your code, and write TSDoc for them.
- Think of generic functions and classes as conceptually defining generic types that are conducive to type inference.

Item 51: Avoid Unnecessary Type Parameters

Here's what the official *TypeScript Handbook* (*https://oreil.ly/j7PWM*) has to say about generic functions:

> Writing generic functions is fun, and it can be easy to get carried away with type parameters. Having too many type parameters or using constraints where they aren't needed can make inference less successful, frustrating callers of your function.

It goes on to offer a few specific pieces of advice about how to use generics, including one that is sometimes called the "Golden Rule of Generics":

Type Parameters Should Appear Twice

Type parameters are for relating the types of multiple values. If a type parameter is only used once in the function signature, it's not relating anything.

Rule: If a type parameter only appears in one location, strongly reconsider if you actually need it.

This rule gives you a specific way to tell whether any type parameter is good or bad, but it's not always obvious how to apply it, and it doesn't offer much guidance about how to rework your code if you're using generics poorly. In this item we'll go through a few examples of good and bad uses of generics to illustrate how the rule works, and we'll rewrite the bad ones.

Let's start with the `identity` function:

```
function identity<T>(arg: T): T {
  return arg;
}
```

This function takes a single parameter and returns it, leaving its type unaltered. Here's how you might use it:

```
const date = identity(new Date());
//    ^? const date: Date
const nums = [1, 2, 3];
//    ^? const nums: number[]
const numsCopy = nums.map(identity);
//    ^? const numsCopy: number[]
```

This function can be useful in practice if you're required to pass in a callback but you don't want to alter your data. Thinking about the Golden Rule, is this a good use of generics or a bad use? In this example, the type parameter T appears in two places after its declaration:

```
function identity<T>(arg: T): T {
//                (decl.)   1   2
  return arg;
}
```

So this passes the test and is a good use of generics. And rightly so: it relates two types because it says that the input parameter's type and the function's return type are the same.

How about this one?

```
function third<A, B, C>(a: A, b: B, c: C): C {
  return c;
}
```

The type parameter C appears twice, so it's fine. But A and B only appear once (other than in their declarations), so this function fails the test. You can rewrite it using only one type parameter:

```
function third<C>(a: unknown, b: unknown, c: C): C {
  return c;
}
```

Here's a type declaration for a function that parses YAML:

```
declare function parseYAML<T>(input: string): T;
```

Is this a good use of generics or a bad use of generics? The type parameter T only appears once, so it must be bad. How to fix it? It depends what your goal is. These so-called "return-only generics" are dangerous because they're equivalent to a type assertion (Item 9), but don't use the word as:

```
interface Weight {
  pounds: number;
  ounces: number;
}

const w: Weight = parseYAML('');
```

At first blush, this code looks safe because there are no type assertions or any types. But this is an illusion. You could replace Weight with any other type and this code would still type check. Setting a default value for the type parameter doesn't change this:

```
declare function parseYAML<T=null>(input: string): T;
const w: Weight = parseYAML('');  // still allowed
```

It's better to make this function return unknown instead (see Item 46 for a refresher on the unknown type):

```
declare function parseYAML(input: string): unknown;
```

This will force users of the function to perform a type assertion on the result:

```
const w = parseYAML('') as Weight;
```

This is actually a good thing since it forces you to be explicit about your unsafe type assertion. There are no illusions of type safety here![2]

How about this one?

```
function printProperty<T, K extends keyof T>(obj: T, key: K) {
  console.log(obj[key]);
}
```

---

2 There are a few any-returning functions in the standard library, such as JSON.parse. See Item 71 for a discussion of how to make them return unknown instead.

Since K only appears once, this is a bad use of generics (T is fine because it appears both as a parameter type and as a constraint on K). Fix it by moving the keyof T into the parameter type and eliminating K:

```
function printProperty<T>(obj: T, key: keyof T) {
  console.log(obj[key]);
}
```

This function looks superficially similar:

```
function getProperty<T, K extends keyof T>(obj: T, key: K) {
  return obj[key];
}
```

This one, however, is actually a good use of generics. To see why, we need to look at the inferred return type of the function. If you inspect getProperty in your editor, you'll see that its return type is T[K]. That means this signature is equivalent to:

```
function getProperty<T, K extends keyof T>(obj: T, key: K): T[K] {
  return obj[key];
}
```

So K *does* appear twice! This is a good use of generics: K is related to T, and the return type is related to both K and T.

What about a class?

```
class ClassyArray<T> {
  arr: T[];
  constructor(arr: T[]) { this.arr = arr; }

  get(): T[] { return this.arr; }
  add(item: T) { this.arr.push(item); }
  remove(item: T) {
    this.arr = this.arr.filter(el => el !== item)
  }
}
```

This is fine since T appears many times in the implementation (I count 5). When you instantiate a ClassyArray, you bind the type parameter and it relates the types of all the properties and methods on the class. (This can be useful for creating inference sites, as we saw in Item 28.)

This class, on the other hand, fails the test:

```
class Joiner<T extends string | number> {
  join(els: T[]) {
    return els.map(el => String(el)).join(',');
  }
}
```

First of all, T only applies to join, so it can be moved down onto the method, rather than the class:

```
class Joiner {
  join<T extends string | number>(els: T[]) {
    return els.map(el => String(el)).join(',');
  }
}
```

By moving the declaration of T closer to its use, we make it possible for TypeScript to infer the type of T. Generally, this is what you want! But in this case, since T only appears once, you should make it nongeneric:

```
class Joiner {
  join(els: (string | number)[]) {
    return els.map(el => String(el)).join(',');
  }
}
```

Finally, why does this need to be a class at all? These sorts of wrapper classes are common in Java (which doesn't support standalone functions) but they're unnecessary in JavaScript.[3] Make it a standalone function instead:

```
function join(els: (string|number)[]) {
  return els.map(el => String(el)).join(',');
}
```

How about this function to get the length of any array-like object?

```
interface Lengthy {
  length: number;
}
function getLength<T extends Lengthy>(x: T) {
  return x.length;
}
```

Since T only appears once after its definition, this is a bad use of generics. It could be written as:

```
function getLength(x: Lengthy) {
  return x.length;
}
```

or even:

```
function getLength(x: {length: number}) {
  return x.length;
}
```

Or, since TypeScript has a built-in ArrayLike type:

```
function getLength(x: ArrayLike<unknown>) {
  return x.length;
}
```

---

3 There's a famous adage for object-oriented programmers: "Don't make objects that end with *er*."

Every rule has exceptions, so are there any exceptions to this one? There are some rare cases where extraneous type parameters can help you get an implementation right. For example, both type parameters in this function are bad:

```
declare function processUnrelatedTypes<A, B>(a: A, b: B): void;
```

The fix is to rewrite it this way:

```
declare function processUnrelatedTypes(a: unknown, b: unknown): void;
```

This has a consequence for the implementation of the function, however. In the first declaration, a and b were not assignable to one another in the body of the function:

```
function processUnrelatedTypes<A, B>(a: A, b: B) {
    a = b;
// ~ Type 'B' is not assignable to type 'A'.
    b = a;
// ~ Type 'A' is not assignable to type 'B'.
}
```

With the improved type signature, they are:

```
function processUnrelatedTypes(a: unknown, b: unknown) {
  a = b;  // ok
  b = a;  // ok
}
```

A workaround is to use a single overload to create a distinct type signature for callers versus the implementation. Item 52 shows what this looks like. As a general rule, however, this sort of situation is rare, and you should avoid generic type parameters that only appear once.

By now you should have a good sense for how to apply the golden rule of generics and how to fix the declarations that break it. As you read and write generic functions, think about whether they follow this rule! If a function or class doesn't need to be generic, then it will be easier to understand and maintain if it isn't.

Put another way, the first rule of generics is "don't."

Things to Remember

- Avoid adding type parameters to functions and classes that don't need them.
- Since type parameters relate types, every type parameter must appear two or more times to establish a relationship.
- Remember that a type parameter may appear in an inferred type.
- Avoid "return-only generics."
- Unneeded type parameters can often be replaced with the unknown type.

Item 52: Prefer Conditional Types to Overload Signatures

How would you write a type declaration for this JavaScript function?

```
function double(x) {
  return x + x;
}
```

`double` can be passed either a `string` or a `number`. So you might use a union type:

```
declare function double(x: string | number): string | number;
```

While this declaration is accurate, it's a bit imprecise:

```
const num = double(12);
//    ^? const num: string | number
const str = double('x');
//    ^? const str: string | number
```

When `double` is passed a `number`, it returns a `number`. And when it's passed a `string`, it returns a `string`. This declaration misses that nuance and will produce types that are inconvenient to work with.

You might try to capture this relationship by making the function generic:

```
declare function double<T extends string | number>(x: T): T;

const num = double(12);
//    ^? const num: 12
const str = double('x');
//    ^? const str: "x"
```

Unfortunately, in our zeal for precision we've overshot. The types are now a little *too* precise. When passed a `string` type, this `double` declaration will result in a `string` type, which is correct. But when passed a string *literal* type, the return type is the same string literal type. This is wrong: doubling `'x'` results in `'xx'`, not `'x'`. As Item 40 explained, imprecise types are preferable to inaccurate types, so this is a step in the wrong direction. How can we do better?

Another option is to provide multiple type declarations, also known as "overload signatures" (see Item 3 for a refresher). While JavaScript only allows you to write one implementation of a function, TypeScript allows you to write any number of type signatures. You can use this to improve the type of `double`:

```
declare function double(x: number): number;
declare function double(x: string): string;

const num = double(12);
//    ^? const num: number
const str = double('x');
//    ^? const str: string
```

This is progress! But there's still a subtle bug. This type declaration will work with values that are either a string or a number, but not with values that could be either:

```
function f(x: string | number) {
  return double(x);
  //             ~ Argument of type 'string | number' is not assignable
  //               to parameter of type 'string'
}
```

This call to double is safe and should return string|number. When you provide overload signatures, TypeScript processes them one by one until it finds a match. The error you're seeing is a result of the last overload (the string version) failing, because string|number is not assignable to string.

While you could fix this by adding a third string|number overload, a better solution is to use a *conditional type*. Conditional types are like if statements (conditionals) in type space. They're perfect for situations like this one where there are a few possibilities that you need to cover:

```
declare function double<T extends string | number>(
  x: T
): T extends string ? string : number;
```

This is similar to the first attempt to type double using a generic function, but with a more elaborate return type. You read the conditional type like you'd read a ternary (?:) operator in JavaScript:

- If T is a subtype of string (i.e., string, or a string literal, or a union of string literals, or a template literal type), then the return type is string.

- Otherwise return number.

With this declaration, all of our examples work:

```
const num = double(12);
//    ^? const num: number
const str = double('x');
//    ^? const str: string

function f(x: string | number) {
  //    ^? function f(x: string | number): string | number
  return double(x);  // ok
}
```

The string|number example works because conditional types *distribute* over unions. When T is string|number, TypeScript resolves the conditional type as follows:

```
  (string|number) extends string ? string : number
→ (string extends string ? string : number) |
  (number extends string ? string : number)
→ string | number
```

The way that conditional types distribute over unions is part of the design of TypeScript's type system. It didn't have to be this way. But in many cases (such as this one), this behavior is correct and extremely convenient.

While the type declaration using overload signatures was simpler to write, the version using conditional types is more correct because it generalizes to the union of the individual cases. This is often the case for overload signatures. Whereas overloads are treated independently, the type checker can analyze conditional types as a single expression, distributing them over unions.

Whenever you write a conditional type, you should think about whether you want it to distribute over unions. Usually you do, but this isn't always the case. Item 53 presents a situation where distribution is incorrect and shows how you can gain some control over it.

Are there any situations where you should prefer overloads? If the union case is implausible, or if your function really acts as two or more very distinct functions with completely different signatures, then it may not be worth the effort to handle it, and keeping the distinct overloads separate will result in more readable code.

If you find yourself in this situation, though, think about whether it would be clearer to have two different functions. An example of this comes from the Node standard library, which offers both callback- and Promise-based versions of filesystem functions like readFile. This *could* be a single function that behaves differently depending on its arguments. But you generally know in advance whether you're using callbacks or Promises, so it's clearer and simpler to have two distinct functions.

Since this is a chapter on type-level programming, we've focused entirely on the types. But it's worth briefly discussing how to *implement* overloaded functions and functions that return conditional types. This can often be awkward and require type assertions in the function body. TypeScript will not infer a conditional type for a variable.

One strategy is to define a single overload to present a different type signature to callers than you use to implement the function. For example:

```
function double<T extends string | number>(
  x: T
): T extends string ? string : number;
function double(x: string | number): string | number {
  return typeof x === 'string' ? x + x : x + x;
}
```

Here we use the conditional type for the externally visible API, but use a simpler type for the implementation. (The typeof check looks a bit odd but saves us a type assertion.) TypeScript does some checking that the two signatures are compatible, but it cannot do a perfect job. It's still important to test your types, as explained in Item 55.

Things to Remember

- Prefer conditional types to overloaded type signatures. By distributing over unions, conditional types allow your declarations to support union types without additional overloads.

- If the union case is implausible, consider whether your function would be clearer as two or more functions with different names.

- Consider using the single overload strategy for implementing functions declared with conditional types.

Item 53: Know How to Control the Distribution of Unions over Conditional Types

Item 52 looked at how conditional types distribute over unions, and how this could be helpful in typing a double function:

```
declare function double<T extends number | string>(
  x: T
): T extends string ? string : number;

const num = double(12);
//    ^? const num: number
const str = double('x');
//    ^? const str: string

declare let numOrStr: number | string;
const either = double(numOrStr);
//    ^? const either: number | string
```

In this case, the distribution over unions produced the desired result. This is typically, but not always, the case.

To see an example of where distribution is not desirable, let's define an isLessThan function that determines whether its first argument is less than the second. We'd like it to operate on dates, numbers, and strings. As a convenience, if you pass a Date in as the first argument, we'd like to allow you to pass a number (milliseconds since epoch) as the second argument.

You can model this using a conditional type:

```
type Comparable<T> =
    T extends Date ? Date | number:
    T extends number ? number :
    T extends string ? string :
    never;

declare function isLessThan<T>(a: T, b: Comparable<T>): boolean;
```

This seems to allow and disallow the combinations that we expect:

```
isLessThan(new Date(), new Date());  // ok
isLessThan(new Date(), Date.now());  // ok, Date/number comparison allowed
isLessThan(12, 23);  // ok
isLessThan('A', 'B');  // ok
isLessThan(12, 'B');
//                    ~~~ Argument of type 'string' is not assignable to parameter
//                        of type 'number'.
```

Because of the way it's written, `Comparable` distributes over unions. Is this desirable? Evidently not:

```
let dateOrStr = Math.random() < 0.5 ? new Date() : 'A';
// ^? let dateOrStr: Date | string
isLessThan(dateOrStr, 'B')  // ok, but should be an error
```

The second parameter should really be the intersection of the two possibilities, not the union. And (`Date | number`) & `string` is `never`, so this call shouldn't be allowed at all.

How can we prevent distribution? Unions only distribute over conditional types if the condition is a bare type (`T extends ...`). So to prevent distribution, we need to complicate the expression a bit. The standard way to do this is to wrap `T` in a one-element tuple type, [`T`]:

```
type Comparable<T> =
    [T] extends [Date] ? Date | number:
    [T] extends [number] ? number :
    [T] extends [string] ? string :
    never;
```

The type [`A`] is assignable to [`B`] if and only if A is assignable to B. So on the surface this change doesn't look like it should affect the behavior of `Comparable`. But since [`T`] is not a bare type, unions no longer distribute over `Comparable` and we get the desired errors without breaking the other valid calls:

```
isLessThan(new Date(), new Date());  // ok
isLessThan(new Date(), Date.now());  // ok, Date/number comparison allowed
isLessThan(12, 23);  // ok
isLessThan('A', 'B');  // ok
isLessThan(12, 'B');
//                    ~~~ Argument of type 'string' is not assignable to parameter
//                        of type 'number'.
isLessThan(dateOrStr, 'B');
//                        ~~~ Argument of type 'string' is not assignable to
//                            parameter of type 'never'.
```

Sometimes the situation is reversed and you have a conditional type that doesn't distribute but you'd like it to. This typically occurs as an inadvertent consequence of the way that the generic type was implemented.

To see how this might happen, let's implement a generic type, NTuple<T, N>, that produces a tuple with N elements, all of type T. This is a step up in complexity from the types we've seen before, but we'll talk our way through it. Here's one way to do it using an accumulator:

```
type NTuple<T, N extends number> = NTupleHelp<T, N, []>;

type NTupleHelp<T, N extends number, Acc extends T[]> =
  Acc['length'] extends N
  ? Acc
  : NTupleHelp<T, N, [T, ...Acc]>;
```

The trick here is to keep adding elements to a tuple type until its length property matches the number that we want. Remember that this lookup is happening in the type system. Looking up 'length' on an array type will yield number, but for a tuple type it will yield a more precise numeric literal type like 0, 1, 2, etc.

This generic type works as we'd hope for constructing N-tuples if N is a single number:

```
type PairOfStrings = NTuple<string, 2>;
//   ^? type PairOfStrings = [string, string]
type TripleOfNumbers = NTuple<number, 3>;
//   ^? type TripleOfNumbers = [number, number, number]
```

But it does not work as we'd hope if N is a union:

```
type PairOrTriple = NTuple<bigint, 2 | 3>;
//   ^? type PairOrTriple = [bigint, bigint]
```

This *should* be [bigint, bigint] | [bigint, bigint, bigint]. The immediate issue is that Acc['length'] extends 2 | 3 is true as soon as the accumulator gets to be a pair. But the deeper issue is that our conditional type isn't distributing over unions. We'd like it to. Why isn't it, and how can we fix it?

The problem is that the condition is Acc['length'] extends N, which does not start with the bare "N extends…" that's required for distribution. So the easiest fix is to add an extra conditional type that looks like this:

```
type NTuple<T, N extends number> =
    N extends number
    ? NTupleHelp<T, N, []>
    : never;
```

Because N is constrained to extend number, this conditional will always evaluate to true (you could make it N extends any or N extends unknown if you like). Its sole purpose is to add a conditional type in the right form for distribution. And it works!

```
type PairOrTriple = NTuple<bigint, 2 | 3>;
//   ^? type PairOrTriple = [bigint, bigint] | [bigint, bigint, bigint]
```

This happens because NTupleHelp is instantiated with N = 2 and N = 3 and the results are unioned together. Using an accumulator is a common technique with recursive generic types because it can improve their performance. Item 57 will explain how.[4]

Conditional types have two other surprising behaviors that you should be aware of when they distribute over the boolean and never types.

First, boolean. Let's define a generic type that yields a celebratory message if its argument is true:

```
type CelebrateIfTrue<V> = V extends true ? 'Huzzah!' : never;

type Party = CelebrateIfTrue<true>;
//   ^? type Party = "Huzzah!"
type NoParty = CelebrateIfTrue<false>;
//   ^? type NoParty = never
type SurpriseParty = CelebrateIfTrue<boolean>;
//   ^? type SurpriseParty = "Huzzah!"
```

It's surprising that this last instantiation resolves to "Huzzah!" because you wouldn't expect boolean extends true to be true. What's going on is a bit more subtle. Internally, TypeScript treats boolean as a union:

```
type boolean = true | false;
```

Because boolean is a union, it can distribute over conditional types. So spelling it out a bit, the evaluation looks like this:

```
type SurpriseParty
    = CelebrateIfTrue<boolean>
    = CelebrateIfTrue<true | false>
    = CelebrateIfTrue<true> | CelebrateIfTrue<false>
    = "Huzzah!" | never
    = "Huzzah!";
```

In this case, it's probably not what you wanted. As before, you can prevent distribution by wrapping the condition in a one-tuple:

```
type CelebrateIfTrue<V> = [V] extends [true] ? 'Huzzah!' : never;

type SurpriseParty = CelebrateIfTrue<boolean>;
//   ^? type SurpriseParty = never
```

Another surprise comes with the never type. Looking at this definition, you'd expect AllowIn<T> to always evaluate to either "Yes", "No" or possibly "Yes" | "No":

```
type AllowIn<T> = T extends {password: "open-sesame"} ? "Yes" : "No";
```

---

4 A remaining issue with this definition is that NTuple<string, number> is [], but it should be string[]. Try fixing it without breaking existing behavior.

But there's one other possibility if T is never:

```
type N = AllowIn<never>;
//   ^? type N = never
```

Why does this evaluate to never if neither side of the conditional is never? Again, it's all about distribution over unions. TypeScript treats the never type as an empty union and, if there's nothing to distribute over, you get empty back. This might make a bit more sense if you replace T with T|never (which is the same as T) and see what happens:

```
AllowIn<T>
  = AllowIn<T | never>
  = AllowIn<T> | AllowIn<never>
  = AllowIn<T> | never
  = AllowIn<T>
```

Surely T|never should be treated the same as T. And when distribution applies, this means that F<never> must be never, regardless of how you define F. As before, if you don't want this, one solution is to wrap your condition in a one-tuple.

The way that conditional types distribute over unions is one of their most powerful and useful capabilities. It is usually, but not always, the behavior that you want. When you write a generic type, think about whether you want it to distribute over unions, and be aware of how seemingly innocuous refactors can enable or disable distribution.

Things to Remember

- Think about whether you want unions to distribute over your conditional types.
- Know how to enable or disable distribution by adding conditions or by wrapping conditions in one-tuples.
- Be aware of the surprising behavior of boolean and never types when they distribute over unions.

Item 54: Use Template Literal Types to Model DSLs and Relationships Between Strings

Item 35 suggested using more precise alternatives to string types in your own code. But there are many strings in the world and it's hard to avoid them entirely. In these cases, TypeScript offers its own unique tool for capturing patterns and relationships in strings: template literal types. This item will explore how this feature works and how you can use it to bring safety to code that would be impossible to type otherwise.

Like all programming languages, TypeScript has a `string` type but, as we've seen in previous items, it also has string *literal* types, which are types whose domain consists of a single string value. These are often combined with unions:

```
type MedalColor = 'gold' | 'silver' | 'bronze';
```

With unions of string literal types, you can model finite sets of strings. With `string` itself you can capture the infinite set all possible strings. Template literal types let you model something in between, for example, the set of all strings starting with `pseudo`:

```
type PseudoString = `pseudo${string}`;
const science: PseudoString = 'pseudoscience';  // ok
const alias: PseudoString = 'pseudonym';  // ok
const physics: PseudoString = 'physics';
//    ~~~~~~~ Type '"physics"' is not assignable to type '`pseudo${string}`'.
```

Like `string`, the `PseudoString` type has an infinite domain (Item 7). But unlike `string`, values in the `PseudoString` type have some structure: they all start with `pseudo`. As with other type-level constructs, the syntax for template literal types is deliberately meant to evoke JavaScript's template literals.

JavaScript abounds with structured strings. For example, what if you want to require that an object have some known set of properties, but also allow any others that start with `data-`? (This pattern is common with the DOM.)

```
interface Checkbox {
  id: string;
  checked: boolean;
  [key: `data-${string}`]: unknown;
}

const check1: Checkbox = {
  id: 'subscribe',
  checked: true,
  value: 'yes',
// ~~~~ Object literal may only specify known properties,
//      and 'value' does not exist in type 'Checkbox'.
  'data-listIds': 'all-the-lists',  // ok
};
const check2: Checkbox = {
  id: 'subscribe',
  checked: true,
  listIds: 'all-the-lists',
// ~~~~~~ Object literal may only specify known properties,
//        and 'listIds' does not exist in type 'Checkbox'
};
```

Had we used `string` as the index type, we'd lose the benefit of excess property checking on `check1` (see Item 11) and incorrectly permit the property without a `data-` prefix on `check2`:

```
interface Checkbox {
  id: string;
  checked: boolean;
  [key: string]: unknown;
}

const check1: Checkbox = {
  id: 'subscribe',
  checked: true,
  value: 'yes',  // permitted
  'data-listIds': 'all-the-lists',
};
const check2: Checkbox = {
  id: 'subscribe',
  checked: true,
  listIds: 'all-the-lists'  // also permitted, matches index type
};
```

Template literal types are helpful for modeling subsets of `string`, but their real power comes when we combine them with generics and type inference to capture *relationships* between types.

Consider the `querySelector` function provided by the DOM. TypeScript is already clever enough to give you a more specific subtype of `HTMLElement` if you query for it:

```
const img = document.querySelector('img');
//    ^? const img: HTMLImageElement | null
```

This allows you to access `img.src`, for example, which would not be permitted on the less specific `Element` type. (Item 75 covers TypeScript and the DOM.)

This cleverness is not very deep, though. If you try to query for an image with a specific ID, you'll just get an `Element`:

```
const img = document.querySelector('img#spectacular-sunset');
//    ^? const img: Element | null
img?.src
//    ~~~ Property 'src' does not exist on type 'Element'.
```

With the help of template literal types, we can make this work. TypeScript's type declarations for the DOM (*lib.dom.d.ts*) include a mapping from tag name to type:

```
interface HTMLElementTagNameMap {
  "a": HTMLAnchorElement;
  "abbr": HTMLElement;
  "address": HTMLElement;
  "area": HTMLAreaElement;
  // ... many more ...
  "video": HTMLVideoElement;
  "wbr": HTMLElement;
}
```

as well as a few declarations for `querySelector`:[5]

```
interface ParentNode extends Node {
  // ...
  querySelector<E extends Element = Element>(selectors: string): E | null;
  // ...
}
```

Now we can use a template literal type to add an overload for the `tag#id` case:

```
type HTMLTag = keyof HTMLElementTagNameMap;
declare global {
  interface ParentNode {
    querySelector<
      TagName extends HTMLTag
    >(
      selector: `${TagName}#${string}`
    ): HTMLElementTagNameMap[TagName] | null;
  }
}
```

The example from before now works as you'd hope, returning the more precise image type and allowing access to its `src` property:

```
const img = document.querySelector('img#spectacular-sunset');
//    ^? const img: HTMLImageElement | null
img?.src  // ok
```

This is helpful, but we've slightly missed the mark:

```
const img = document.querySelector('div#container img');
//    ^? const img: HTMLDivElement | null
```

A space in a CSS selector means "descendant of." In this case, our template literal type `${TagName}#${string}` matched "div", then "#", then "container img". In attempting to get more precise types, we've run afoul of Item 40's advice to prefer imprecision to inaccuracy.

While one could imagine building an entire CSS selector parser using template literal types, a less ambitious way to handle this issue is to guard against characters with special meanings in CSS selectors using another overload:

```
type CSSSpecialChars = ' ' | '>' | '+' | '~' | '||' | ',';
type HTMLTag = keyof HTMLElementTagNameMap;

declare global {
  interface ParentNode {
    // escape hatch
    querySelector(
      selector: `${HTMLTag}#${string}${CSSSpecialChars}${string}`
```

---

5 Since E only appears once in this declaration, it's a bad use of a type parameter. See Item 51.

```
  ): Element | null;

  // same as before
  querySelector<
    TagName extends HTMLTag
  >(
    selector: `${TagName}#${string}`
  ): HTMLElementTagNameMap[TagName] | null;
}
}
```

Now you at least get an imprecise type for the more complex selector, rather than an inaccurate type:

```
const img = document.querySelector('img#spectacular-sunset');
//    ^? const img: HTMLImageElement | null
const img2 = document.querySelector('div#container img');
//    ^? const img2: Element | null
```

This will help ensure safe usage. For more on TypeScript and the DOM, see Item 75.

Template literal types are often combined with conditional types to implement parsers for domain-specific languages (DSLs) like CSS selectors. To see how this works, let's try to get precise types for an objectToCamel function that camelCases the keys of a snake_cased object:

```
// e.g. foo_bar -> fooBar
function camelCase(term: string) {
  return term.replace(/_([a-z])/g, m => m[1].toUpperCase());
}

// (return type to be filled in shortly)
function objectToCamel<T extends object>(obj: T) {
  const out: any = {};
  for (const [k, v] of Object.entries(obj)) {
    out[camelCase(k)] = v;
  }
  return out;
}

const snake = {foo_bar: 12};
//    ^? const snake: { foo_bar: number; }
const camel = objectToCamel(snake);
// camel's value at runtime is {fooBar: 12};
// we'd like the type to be {fooBar: number}
const val = camel.fooBar;  // we'd like this to have a number type
const val2 = camel.foo_bar;  // we'd like this to be an error
```

Let's start by defining a type-level ToCamelOnce helper:

```
type ToCamelOnce<S extends string> =
    S extends `${infer Head}_${infer Tail}`
    ? `${Head}${Capitalize<Tail>}`
```

```
    : S;

type T = ToCamelOnce<'foo_bar'>;  // type is "fooBar"
```

Here we've used the `infer` keyword in a conditional type to extract the part of the string before and after an underscore. When `S` is `"foo_bar"`, then `Head` is the string literal type `"foo"` and `Tail` is the string literal type `"bar"`. When we get a match, we construct a new string (using a template literal type) without the underscore and with the first letter of the tail capitalized (`Capitalize` is a built-in helper).

To make this work on strings with multiple underscores like `"foo_bar_baz"`, we need to make it recursive:

```
type ToCamel<S extends string> =
    S extends `${infer Head}_${infer Tail}`
    ? `${Head}${Capitalize<ToCamel<Tail>>}`
    : S;
type T0 = ToCamel<'foo'>;  // type is "foo"
type T1 = ToCamel<'foo_bar'>;  // type is "fooBar"
type T2 = ToCamel<'foo_bar_baz'>;  // type is "fooBarBaz"
```

Now we can give `objectToCamel` a more precise type using a mapped type (Item 15) that rewrites the keys using the helper:

```
type ObjectToCamel<T extends object> = {
  [K in keyof T as ToCamel<K & string>]: T[K]
};

function objectToCamel<T extends object>(obj: T): ObjectToCamel<T> {
  // ... as before ...
}
```

And now the types are exactly what we wanted!

```
const snake = {foo_bar: 12};
//    ^? const snake: { foo_bar: number; }
const camel = objectToCamel(snake);
//    ^? const camel: ObjectToCamel<{ foo_bar: number; }>
//                    (equivalent to { fooBar: number; })
const val = camel.fooBar;
//    ^? const val: number
const val2 = camel.foo_bar;
//                 ~~~~~~~ Property 'foo_bar' does not exist on type
//                         '{ fooBar: number; }'. Did you mean 'fooBar'?
```

This new, more precise type for `objectToCamel` is an excellent example of "fancy" TypeScript features being used to benefit a developer. You don't need to know anything about template literal types, conditional types, or mapped types to use `objectToCamel`. But you still benefit from them in the form of more precise types. Your experience of TypeScript is that it understands this code even if you don't understand precisely how it does that.

One small issue is that the display of the camel's type isn't ideal. Item 56 will explain how to improve it.

Things to Remember

- Use template literal types to model structured subsets of string types and domain-specific languages (DSLs).

- Combine template literal types with mapped and conditional types to capture nuanced relationships between types.

- Take care to avoid crossing the line into inaccurate types. Strive for uses of template literal types that improve developer experience without requiring knowledge of fancy language features.

Item 55: Write Tests for Your Types

Write tests until fear is transformed into boredom.

—Phlip (quoted in Kent Beck, *Test Driven Development: By Example* [Addison-Wesley Professional])

You wouldn't write code without tests (I hope!), and you shouldn't write type declarations without writing tests for them either. But how do you test types? If you're authoring type declarations or a TypeScript library, testing your types is an essential, but surprisingly fraught, undertaking.

This is a particularly acute need for TypeScript compared to most other programming languages for two reasons:

- TypeScript lets you put an enormous amount of logic in the *types*. Where there's logic, there might be bugs, and where there might be bugs, you should write tests.

- For JavaScript libraries and, to some extent, TypeScript code, you can define your types independently of the runtime implementation. This means that the two can get out of sync, and you need to write tests to ensure that this doesn't happen.

There are two main ways to test types: using the type system and using tooling outside the type system. Either approach works, and both have their advantages. This item will first look at some *ineffective* ways to test types, then talk about the pros and cons of the two standard approaches.

Suppose you've written a type declaration for a map function provided by a utility library (the popular Lodash library provides such a function, as do native arrays):

```
declare function map<U, V>(array: U[], fn: (u: U) => V): V[];
```

How can you check that this type declaration results in the expected types? (Presumably, there are separate tests for the implementation.) One common technique is to write a test file that calls the function:

```
map(['2017', '2018', '2019'], v => Number(v));
```

This will do some blunt error checking: if your declaration of map only listed a single parameter, this would catch the mistake. But does it feel like something is missing here?

The equivalent of this style of test for runtime behavior might look something like this:

```
test('square a number', () => {
  square(1);
  square(2);
});
```

Sure, this tests that the square function doesn't throw an error. But it doesn't check the return value, so there's no real test of the behavior. An incorrect implementation of square would still pass this test.

This approach is common in testing type declaration files because it's simple to copy/paste existing unit tests for a library. And while it does provide some value, it would be much better to actually check some types!

One way to do this is to assign the result to a variable with a declared type:

```
const lengths: number[] = map(['john', 'paul'], name => name.length);
```

This is exactly the sort of superfluous type declaration that Item 18 would encourage you to remove. But here it plays an essential role: it provides some confidence that the map declaration is at least doing something sensible with the types. And indeed, you can find many type declarations in DefinitelyTyped that use exactly this approach for testing.

There are a few problems with using assignment for testing, however.

One problem is that you have to create a named variable that is likely to be unused. This adds boilerplate, and also means that you'll have to disable any linter rules that warn about unused variables.

The usual workaround is to define a helper:

```
function assertType<T>(x: T) {}
```

```
assertType<number[]>(map(['john', 'paul'], name => name.length));
```

A second issue is that we're checking *assignability* of the two types rather than equality. Often this works as you'd expect. For example:

```
const n = 12;
assertType<number>(n);  // OK
```

If you inspect the n symbol in your editor, you'll see that its type is actually 12, a numeric literal type. This is a subtype of number, and the assignability check passes, just as you'd expect.

So far, so good. But things get murkier when you start checking the types of objects:

```
const beatles = ['john', 'paul', 'george', 'ringo'];
assertType<{name: string}[]>(
  map(beatles, name => ({
    name,
    inYellowSubmarine: name === 'ringo'
  }))
);  // OK
```

The map call returns an array of {name: string, inYellowSubmarine: boolean} objects. This is assignable to {name: string}[], so the code passes the type checker. But what about the yellow submarine? In this case, we'd really prefer to check for type *equality*.

Testing for assignability can lead to surprising behavior with function types, too:

```
const add = (a: number, b: number) => a + b;
assertType<(a: number, b: number) => number>(add);  // OK

const double = (x: number) => 2 * x;
assertType<(a: number, b: number) => number>(double);  // OK!?
```

It's surprising that the second assertion succeeds since the functions take different numbers of parameters. But this is just how assignability works in TypeScript: a function type is assignable to another function type that takes fewer parameters:

```
const g: (x: string) => any = () => 12;  // OK
```

This reflects the fact that it's perfectly fine to call a JavaScript function with more parameters than it's declared to take. TypeScript chooses to model this behavior rather than bar it, largely because it is pervasive in callbacks. The callback in the Lodash map function, for example, takes up to three parameters:

```
map(array, (element, index, array) => { /* ... */ });
```

While all three are available if you need them, it's very common to use only one or sometimes two, as we have so far in this item. In fact, it's quite rare to use all three. If TypeScript disallowed this assignment, it would report errors in an enormous amount of JavaScript code.

So what can you do? You could break apart the function type and test its pieces using the built-in Parameters and ReturnType types:

```
const double = (x: number) => 2 * x;
declare let p: Parameters<typeof double>;
assertType<[number, number]>(p);
//                              ~ Argument of type '[number]' is not
//                                assignable to parameter of type [number, number]
declare let r: ReturnType<typeof double>;
assertType<number>(r);  // OK
```

But if "this" isn't complicated enough, there's another issue: Lodash's map sets the value of this for its callback. TypeScript can model this behavior (see Item 69), so your type declaration should do so. And you should test it. How can we do that?

Our tests of map so far have been a bit "black box" in style: we've run an array and function through map and tested the type of the result, but we haven't tested the details of the intermediate steps. We can do so by filling out the callback function and verifying the types of its parameters and this directly:

```
const beatles = ['john', 'paul', 'george', 'ringo'];
assertType<number[]>(map(
  beatles,
  function(name, i, array) {
    // ~~~ Argument of type '(name: any, i: any, array: any) => any' is
    //     not assignable to parameter of type '(u: string) => any'
    assertType<string>(name);
    assertType<number>(i);
    assertType<string[]>(array);
    assertType<string[]>(this);
    //                   ~~~~ 'this' implicitly has type 'any'
    return name.length;
  }
));
```

This has surfaced a few issues with our declaration of map from earlier, namely that its callback only takes one parameter and that it doesn't set a type for this. Note the use of a function expression instead of an arrow function so that we could test the type of this.

Here is a declaration that passes the checks:

```
declare function map<U, V>(
  array: U[],
  fn: (this: U[], u: U, i: number, array: U[]) => V
): V[];
```

There remains a final issue, however, and it is a major one. Here's a complete type declaration file for our module that will pass even the most stringent tests for map but is worse than useless:

```
declare module 'your-amazing-module';
```

This assigns an any type to the *entire module*. Your type assertions will all pass, but you won't have any type safety. What's worse, every call to a function in this module will quietly produce an any type, contagiously destroying type safety throughout your code. Even with noImplicitAny, you can still get any types through type declarations files.

One way to address this issue is by adding some "negative" tests: tests that are expected to fail. TypeScript lets you do this via @ts-expect-error comments:

```
// @ts-expect-error only takes two parameters
map([1, 2, 3], x => x * x, 'third parameter');
```

This inverts the usual error checking process: now you'll get a compiler error if there *isn't* a type error. This does give you some protection against any types, but be warned: @ts-expect-error is a very blunt instrument. You can't say exactly which error you expect. For example, the previous snippet still passes with an any type because there will be an implicit any error on the function parameter:

```
declare const map: any;
map([1, 2, 3], x => x * x, 'third parameter');
//               ~ Parameter 'x' implicitly has an 'any' type.
```

One workaround here is to split your code across multiple lines to reduce the scope of the directive:

```
map(
  [1, 2, 3],
  x => x * x,
  // @ts-expect-error only takes two parameters
  'third parameter'
);
```

It would be better if we could adapt assertType to handle these pesky any types, though. With some cleverness, you *can* detect an any type using a type alias. But rather than add complexity to our testing code, let's take this as a cue to pull in a testing library.

One of the more popular choices that works within the type system is expect-type. You can use it on its own or via the vitest testing framework, which bundles it. Here's what it looks like:

```
import {expectTypeOf} from 'expect-type';

const beatles = ['john', 'paul', 'george', 'ringo'];
expectTypeOf(map(
  beatles,
  function(name, i, array) {
    expectTypeOf(name).toEqualTypeOf<string>();
    expectTypeOf(i).toEqualTypeOf<number>();
    expectTypeOf(array).toEqualTypeOf<string[]>();
```

```
      expectTypeOf(this).toEqualTypeOf<string[]>();
      return name.length;
   }
)).toEqualTypeOf<number[]>();
```

As you'd hope, it's able to catch any types, differing function types, and subtle differences like readonly properties:

```
const anyVal: any = 1;
expectTypeOf(anyVal).toEqualTypeOf<number>();
//                   ~~~~~~
//          Type 'number' does not satisfy the constraint 'never'.

const double = (x: number) => 2 * x;
expectTypeOf(double).toEqualTypeOf<(a: number, b: number) => number>();
//                   ~~~~~~~~~~~~~~~~~~~~~~~~~~~~~~~~~~~
//          Type ... does not satisfy '"Expected: function, Actual: never"'

interface ABReadOnly {
  readonly a: string;
  b: number;
}
declare let ab: {a: string, b: number};
expectTypeOf(ab).toEqualTypeOf<ABReadOnly>();
//               ~~~~~~~~~~~~~
//          Arguments for the rest parameter 'MISMATCH' were not provided.
expectTypeOf(ab).toEqualTypeOf<{a: string, b: number}>();  // OK
```

Testing types in this way offers a number of advantages:

- It doesn't require any additional tooling. All type testing is done via tsc, which you're using already.

- Since types are tested structurally, it won't get tripped up by meaningless differences like 1|2 versus 2|1.

- TypeScript's language service will help with refactoring. If you rename an interface, for example, its name will also get updated in any type assertions.

- Your assertions will get formatted in the same way as your code if you're using a formatting tool like prettier.

There are also a few downsides to this approach:

- The error message for mismatched types ('MISMATCH') doesn't give much guidance about what the mismatch is or where it occurs.

- Because it's testing the structure of types, it cannot detect issues around how they display. As Item 56 will explain, you have some control over this and should care about it.

That being said, this is a great way to test your types and it's a vast improvement over the hand-rolled attempts we saw earlier in this item.

Another approach in this vein was popularized by the Type Challenges repo (*https:// tsch.js.org*). It looks like this:

```
export type Equals<X, Y> =
  (<T>() => T extends X ? 1 : 2) extends
  (<T>() => T extends Y ? 1 : 2) ? true : false;

export type Expect<T extends true> = T;

const double = (x: number) => 2 * x;
type Test1 = Expect<Equals<typeof double, (x: number) => number>>;
type Test2 = Expect<Equals<typeof double, (x: string) => number>>;
//                  ~~~~~~~~~~~~~~~~~~~~~~~~~~~~~~~~~~~~~~~~~~~~~~~~
//                  Type 'false' does not satisfy the constraint 'true'.
```

Recall from Item 48 that function types are covariant with respect to their return types. But the only way the first conditional type could reliably be assignable to the second is if X is equal to Y. (Try plugging in a few concrete types for X, Y, and T to convince yourself of this.) Rather than relying on type-level logic to test for equality, this is the rare case where we can get TypeScript itself to compare types for equality.

While this is slightly more robust than expect-type, it has many of the same advantages and disadvantages. The error messages for failed tests aren't particularly illuminating. And type equality is such a rare concept in TypeScript that the semantics are a bit murky. Some parts of the type's display matter, while others don't:

```
type Test3 = Expect<Equals<1 | 2, 2 | 1>>;  // good!
type Test4 = Expect<Equals<[a: 1, b: 2], [1, 2]>>;  // maybe not so good
type Test5 = Expect<Equals<{x: 1} & {y: 2}, {x: 1, y: 2}>>;  // surprising
//                  ~~~~~~~~~~~~~~~~~~~~~~~~~~~~~~~~~~~~~~~~
//                  Type 'false' does not satisfy the constraint 'true'.
```

So much for testing types within the type system. What if you want to test types using an external tool? Two common ones are dtslint and eslint-plugin-expect-type. As the names suggest, these both operate as linters.

dtslint was built to test type declarations in the DefinitelyTyped repository. It operates through specially formatted comments. Here's how you might write the last test for the map function using dtslint:

```
const beatles = ['john', 'paul', 'george', 'ringo'];
map(beatles, function(
  name, // $ExpectType string
  i,    // $ExpectType number
  array // $ExpectType string[]
) {
  this  // $ExpectType string[]
```

```
      return name.length;
}); // $ExpectType number[]
```

Rather than checking assignability, `dtslint` inspects the type of each symbol and does a textual comparison. This matches how you'd manually test the type declarations in your editor: `dtslint` essentially automates this process. This approach does have some drawbacks: despite being fundamentally the same type, `number|string` and `string|number` are textually different. But so are `string` and `any`, despite being assignable to each other, which is really the point.

`eslint-plugin-expect-type` works in a similar way, but as an ESLint plugin. This is more convenient if you want to test your own TypeScript types, rather than type declarations on DefinitelyTyped. In addition to `$ExpectType` comments, it will check the types in Twoslash-style comments:

```
const spiceGirls = ['scary', 'sporty', 'baby', 'ginger', 'posh'];
//    ^? const spiceGirls: string[]
```

This should look familiar: it's the same syntax used for code samples in this book! You can also use Twoslash-style comments on the TypeScript playground (see Figure P-1 in the Preface to the Second Edition).

Testing types using an external tool has a number of strengths:

- It matches the way you interact with types in your editor. There's no type-level fanciness required to do a character-by-character comparison of type displays.
- Since it tests the string representation of a type, it's able to catch issues around how types display (Item 56).
- The ESLint plugin's auto-fixer makes it easy to update tests.

There are some downsides, though:

- It requires setting up another tool (though it's likely you're already using ESLint).
- It can be too sensitive; e.g., saying that `1|2` and `2|1` are different types because they display differently.
- You miss out on type formatting / refactoring since the types are in comments.

Some tools take a hybrid approach. `tsd`, for example, is a type testing tool that operates within the type system but also includes an external tool to provide the stricter type checks that are hard to get otherwise.

Finally, there are some things you might like to test that neither tool can help you with. For example, here's a popular trick for providing autocomplete on a few values while still allowing any `string`:

```
type Game = 'wordle' | 'crossword' | (string & {});
const spellingBee: Game = 'spelling bee';
let g: Game = '';
```

If you hit Ctrl-Space inside that last empty string, TypeScript will suggest "wordle" or "crossword." But it will still allow any string to be assigned to a Game. If you want to write a test that this works as you expect, neither of the two approaches described in this item will help (Figure 6-2).

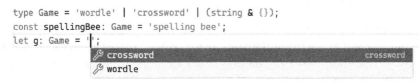

Figure 6-2. TypeScript offers autocomplete for two values, but accepts all strings.

Testing type declarations is tricky business. You *should* test them. But be aware of the pitfalls of some of the common techniques. Don't roll your own type testing system. If you're writing type declarations on DefinitelyTyped, you should use `dtslint` because that's the standard tool in that setting. If you're testing your own code, use a library like `vitest`, `expect-type`, or `tsd`. If you want to write tests that are sensitive to the way a type displays, not just its structure, use `eslint-plugin-expect-type`.

Things to Remember

- When testing types, be aware of the difference between equality and assignability, particularly for function types.
- For functions that use callbacks, test the inferred types of the callback parameters. Don't forget to test the type of `this` if it's part of your API.
- Avoid writing your own type testing code. Use one of the standard tools instead.
- For code on DefinitelyTyped, use `dtslint`. For your own code, use **vitest**, `expect-type`, or the Type Challenges approach. If you want to test type display, use `eslint-plugin-expect-type`.

Item 56: Pay Attention to How Types Display

Usually, we care about what types *are* and which values are assignable to them. But when you're using a TypeScript library, the way it chooses to *display* types can make a big difference in your experience of using it. This means that, as a library author, you need to pay attention to how your types display.

For any type, there are many valid ways to display it. For example, union types typically display their constituents in the order in which you listed them:

```
type T123 = '1' | '2' | '3';
//   ^? type T123 = "1" | "2" | "3"
```

But if you happen to have introduced an overlapping union earlier, you might get a different display:

```
type T21 = '2' | '1';
//   ^? type T21 = "2" | "1"

type T123 = '1' | '2' | '3';
//   ^? type T123 = "2" | "1" | "3"
```

Is it 1, 2, 3 or 2, 1, 3? They're two equally valid representations of the exact same type. In this case the legibility is about the same for both, but sometimes it can vary substantially between multiple representations.

To see an example of an undesirable type display, let's implement a `PartiallyPartial` generic that makes a few of the properties of an object optional but not the others. Here's an implementation:

```
type PartiallyPartial<T, K extends keyof T> =
  Partial<Pick<T, K>> & Omit<T, K>;
```

Here's what it might look like in practice:

```
interface BlogComment {
  commentId: number;
  title: string;
  content: string;
}

type PartComment = PartiallyPartial<BlogComment, 'title'>;
//   ^? type PartComment =
//          Partial<Pick<BlogComment, "title">> &
//          Omit<BlogComment, "title">
```

The generic type is implemented correctly, and this is a perfectly valid display of the result of this instantiation. But it leaves a few things to be desired for a user inspecting `PartComment`: what is the type of `title`? Is it nullable? And what other fields are there behind that `Omit`? The whole thing feels implementation-y, as though it's telling the user more about how the generic type was defined than what the resulting type is.

We'd like to tell TypeScript to do a little more work to resolve those generic types. There's a widespread trick to do exactly that:

```
type Resolve<T> = T extends Function ? T : {[K in keyof T]: T[K]};
```

We'll talk about how this works momentarily. But first, here's how you use it:

```
type PartiallyPartial<T, K extends keyof T> =
  Resolve<Partial<Pick<T, K>> & Omit<T, K>>;

type PartComment = PartiallyPartial<BlogComment, 'title'>;
//   ^? type PartComment = {
//         title?: string | undefined;
//         commentId: number;
//         content: string;
//      }
```

By wrapping the generic type with `Resolve`, we've magically told TypeScript to flatten out the display of all its properties. It's much clearer what this type is now. Even better, all traces of the implementation are gone. The user of this type doesn't need to know that it's been implemented using `Partial`, `Pick`, or `Omit`.

So how does `Resolve` work? If you ignore the conditional type, you're left with an expression that looks it should be the identity for object types:

```
type ObjIdentity<T> = {[K in keyof T]: T[K]};
```

And indeed, this does work to "resolve" some types. Because it's a homomorphic mapped type (see Item 15), it allows primitive types to pass through unmodified:

```
type S = ObjIdentity<string>;
//   ^? type S = string
type N = ObjIdentity<number>;
//   ^? type N = number
type U = ObjIdentity<'A' | 'B' | 'C'>;
//   ^? type U = "A" | "B" | "C"
```

It's not the identity for functions, however, which is why we need the conditional type guarding `Resolve`:

```
type F = ObjIdentity<(a: number) => boolean>;
//   ^? type F = {}
```

This helper is ubiquitous in TypeScript code that uses lots of generic types. `Resolve` is my choice of names, but you may also see it called `Simplify`, `NOP`, `NOOP`, or `Merge Insertions`.

You can make a `DeepResolve` that recursively resolves object types, but this typically isn't a good idea because `Resolve` winds up being too aggressive on classes:

```
type D = Resolve<Date>;
//   ^? type D = {
//         toLocaleString: {
//            (locales?: Intl.LocalesArgument,
//             options?: Intl.DateTimeFormatOptions | undefined): string;
//            (): string;
//            (locales?: string | string[] | undefined,
//             options?: Intl.DateTimeFormatOptions | undefined): string;
```

```
//          };
//          ... 42 more ...;
//          [Symbol.toPrimitive]: {
//              ...;
//          };
//      }
```

The inlining has backfired here. Better to just let this type display as `Date`.

You can also use `Resolve` to inline `keyof` expressions if you feel that improves their legibility:

```
interface Color { r: number; g: number; b: number; a: number };
type Chan = keyof Color;
//   ^? type Chan = keyof Color
type ChanInline = Resolve<keyof Color>;
//   ^? type ChanInline = "r" | "g" | "b" | "a"
```

Sometimes there are particularly important cases for which you'd like to have types display cleanly. For `PartiallyPartial`, this might be when the type parameter K is `never` (in which case none of the fields are optional). Here's how that case is handled with our current definition:

```
type FullComment = PartiallyPartial<BlogComment, never>;
//   ^? type FullComment = {
//          title: string;
//          commentId: number;
//          content: string;
//      }
```

This result is correct and it's a valid way of displaying this type. But there's a more concise representation available: `FullComment` is just `BlogComment`. We can get a more concise type by checking for this case:

```
type PartiallyPartial<T extends object, K extends keyof T> =
  [K] extends [never]
  ? T  // special case
  : T extends unknown  // extra conditional to preserve distribution over unions
  ? Resolve<Partial<Pick<T, K>> & Omit<T, K>>
  : never;

type FullComment = PartiallyPartial<BlogComment, never>;
//   ^? type FullComment = BlogComment
```

See Item 53 for an explanation of why we've wrapped the condition in a tuple type (`[K]` instead of K) and added a `T extends unknown` clause. Adding this special case does not change the behavior of `PartiallyPartial` at all, it just improves the way it displays its result in one situation.

You may see some other techniques used to adjust type display, for example:

- `Exclude<keyof T, never>` to inline `keyof` expressions
- `unknown & T` or `{} & T` to inline object types

These can both be replaced by `Resolve`, which has the same effect and is less brittle.

When you change the display of your types, make sure you don't sacrifice legibility in one case for the sake of another. Since these manipulations are subtle and don't affect assignability, it's easy for regressions to go unnoticed. New versions of TypeScript can also affect how types display. For this reason, it's important to have a system in place for testing the display of types. Item 55 shows you how.

Things to Remember

- There are many valid ways to display the same type. Some are clearer than others.
- TypeScript gives you some tools to control how types display, notably the `Resolve` generic. Make judicious use of this to clarify type display and hide implementation details.
- Consider handling important special cases of generic types to improve type display.
- Write tests for your generic types and their display to avoid regressions.

Item 57: Prefer Tail-Recursive Generic Types

The history of computing is filled with accidental programming languages. You add some customizability to a system. Your users like it and ask for more. You add a few more useful features. You keep giving your users more control. Soon enough, someone points out that you're Turing Complete![6] Famous examples of this dynamic include Microsoft Excel, the C preprocessor, C++ templates, and TypeScript generic types.

These accidental programming languages are often purely functional because this paradigm gives you tremendous control with a minimum of concepts. All you need is function composition and some sort of branching. In the case of TypeScript's type system, function composition means instantiating a generic type. And you can get branching either by looking up keys in an object type or by using a conditional type.

Purely functional languages typically implement looping via recursion. As we saw in Item 54, this can be used to great effect to process string types.

---

6 For TypeScript, see *https://oreil.ly/C5EzQ*.

But while recursion is conceptually efficient, it comes with some real-world drawbacks because each recursive call requires a new entry on the stack.

To see how this can be a problem, let's write a JavaScript function to sum all the numbers in a list. One way is with recursion:

```
function sum(nums: readonly number[]): number {
  if (nums.length === 0) {
    return 0;
  }
  return nums[0] + sum(nums.slice(1));
}

console.log(sum([0, 1, 2, 3, 4]));
```

As you'd expect, this prints:

```
10
```

This is not a very efficient way to sum a list of numbers. Each number in the list entails another recursive call that uses stack space and will eventually overflow. For me, using Node.js, this happens when the array has somewhere between 7,000 and 8,000 elements:

```
const arr = Array(7875).fill(1);
console.log(sum(arr));

    return nums[0] + sum(nums.slice(1));
                     ^

RangeError: Maximum call stack size exceeded
```

A version of sum implemented using a for-of loop would have no such limitation. So are loops inherently better than recursion? Not so fast! Long ago, functional programmers came up with a clever solution to this problem. If the last thing a function does is call itself recursively and return that value, it can give up its space on the stack: its work is done and it doesn't need it any more. This is known as *Tail Call Optimization* (TCO) and functions with this form are called *tail recursive*.

Here's a tail-recursive version of sum that uses an accumulator:

```
function sum(nums: readonly number[], acc=0): number {
  if (nums.length === 0) {
    return acc;
  }
  return sum(nums.slice(1), nums[0] + acc);
}
```

Running this quickly produces the correct result without a stack overflow:[7]

```
$ bun sum-tail-rec.js
7875
```

The same concerns apply to recursive TypeScript type aliases. TypeScript limits the number of recursive instantiations of a type alias to prevent infinite loops and sluggishness in the type checker. But it supports Tail Call Optimization and gives tail-recursive type aliases a much greater depth limit. Because they are more efficient and more capable, you should make recursive type aliases tail recursive whenever possible.

This is particularly relevant for generics that process string literal types one character at a time. For example, here's a generic type that converts a string literal type to the union of the characters in the string:

```
type GetChars<S extends string> =
    S extends `${infer FirstChar}${infer RestOfString}`
    ? FirstChar | GetChars<RestOfString>
    : never;

type ABC = GetChars<"abc">;
//   ^? type ABC = "a" | "b" | "c"
```

This performs an operation (a union with FirstChar) after its recursive call, so it is not tail recursive. For string literal types longer than about 50 characters, you'll get an overflow:

```
type Long = GetChars<"abcdefghijklmnopqrstuvwxyzABCDEFGHIJKLMNOPQRSTUVWX">;
//          ~~~~~~~~~~~~~~~~~~~~~~~~~~~~~~~~~~~~~~~~~~~~~~~~~~~~~~~~~~~~~~~
//                   Type instantiation is excessively deep and possibly infinite.
```

For a more realistic example of how this could cause a problem, let's revisit objectTo Camel from Item 54. That function took an object with snake_cased properties ({foo_bar: 0}) and returned an equivalent object with camelCased properties ({fooBar: 0}). We developed a ToCamel generic to convert the string literal type "foo_bar" into "fooBar".

Now let's go in the opposite direction and implement ToSnake. There's no delimiter ("_") in this case, so we'll process the string type character by character.

Here's an implementation:

```
type ToSnake<T extends string> =
    string extends T
```

---

7 Although ES2015 requires that JavaScript engines support Tail Call Optimization, at the time of this writing only Safari does. This means that to see TCO in action, you need to use a runtime like bun that's based on JavaScriptCore (Safari) rather than one like Node that's based on V8 (Chrome)

```
    ? string   // We want ToSnake<string> = string
    : T extends `${infer First}${infer Rest}`
    ? (First extends Uppercase<First>  // Is First a capital letter?
      ? `_${Lowercase<First>}${ToSnake<Rest>}`  // e.g. "B" -> "_b"
      : `${First}${ToSnake<Rest>}`)
    : T;

type S = ToSnake<'fooBarBaz'>;
//    ^? type S = "foo_bar_baz"

type Two = ToSnake<'className' | 'tagName'>;
//    ^? type Two = "class_name" | "tag_name"
```

There are two recursive calls here, depending on whether the first character of the string literal type is a capital letter. If so, we want to replace it with an underscore and a lowercase letter and keep going. Otherwise we leave it as is and keep going. The second example shows that it distributes over unions correctly (Item 53).

This type alias does work after the recursive call in each branch of the conditional (string concatenation, lowercasing), so it's not tail recursive. And, as you might expect by now, it's easy for it to overflow the stack:

```
type Long = ToSnake<'reallyDescriptiveNamePropThatsALittleTooLoquacious'>;
//          ~~~~~~~~~~~~~~~~~~~~~~~~~~~~~~~~~~~~~~~~~~~~~~~~~~~~~~~~~~~~~~~~
//          Type instantiation is excessively deep and possibly infinite.
```

If you try to snake_case an object with a long key using this helper, your type will blow up. While 50 characters might seem like enough for a property name, there are many examples of properties that are much longer, particularly in the Java world.[8]

We can lift the limitation for long string literal types and speed up type checking for all instantiations by refactoring ToSnake to be tail recursive:

```
type ToSnake<T extends string, Acc extends string = ""> =
  string extends T
  ? string   // We want ToSnake<string> = string
  : T extends `${infer First}${infer Rest}`
  ? ToSnake<
      Rest,
      First extends Uppercase<First>
      ? `${Acc}_${Lowercase<First>}`
      : `${Acc}${First}`
    >
  : Acc;

type S = ToSnake<'fooBarBaz'>;
//    ^? type S = "foo_bar_baz"
```

---

8 Try Googling "VirtualMachineDeviceRuntimeInfoVirtualEthernetCardRuntimeStateVmDirectPathGen2Inac-
tiveReasonOther."

```
type Two = ToSnake<'className' | 'tagName'>;
//   ^? type Two = "class_name" | "tag_name"

type Long = ToSnake<'reallyDescriptiveNamePropThatsALittleTooLoquacious'>;
//   ^? type Long = "really_descriptive_name_prop_thats_a_little_too_loquacious"
```

As with the tail-recursive version of sum, we've added an accumulator to track the work we've done so far. This allows us to shift the recursive instantiation into a tail position and lift the limit. You'll be able to snake_case whatever wordy property names your Java coworkers throw at you!

Things to Remember

- Aim to make your recursive generic types tail recursive. They're more efficient and have greater depth limits.

- Recursive type aliases can often be made tail recursive by rewriting them to use an accumulator.

Item 58: Consider Codegen as an Alternative to Complex Types

Beware of the Turing tar-pit in which everything is possible but nothing of interest is easy.
—Alan Perlis

This chapter has explored programming at the type level in TypeScript. This means implementing logic and functions that operate on types rather than values (Item 50). Just like regular programs, we can write tests (Item 55) and think about their performance (Item 57). Especially with tools for working with template literal types (Item 54), type-level programs in TypeScript can do some truly impressive things.

TypeScript's type system is Turing complete, so in theory you can represent any computation with it. As the quote at the start of this item warns, though, just because something is possible does not mean it's easy. Or wise.

Suppose your TypeScript program interacts with a database and includes some SQL:

```
async function getBooks(db: Database) {
  const result = await db.query(
    `SELECT title, author, year, publisher FROM books`
  );
  return result.rows;
}
```

With some cleverness, you may be able to use template literal types and conditional types to parse that query in TypeScript's type system. Combine this with a type representing your database schema, and you may actually be able to infer the result type of

---

that query from the query SQL itself. This is an impressive achievement, and you'll certainly get more precise types from it.

But what if your program also includes this query?

```
async function getLatestBookByAuthor(db: Database, publisher: string) {
  const result = await db.query(
    `SELECT author, MAX(year) FROM books GROUP BY author WHERE publisher=$1`,
    [publisher]
  );
  return result.rows;
}
```

Getting the right types for this query is substantially harder. Your SQL query parser will need to understand GROUP BY clauses, MAX expressions, and know that the $1 placeholder means that you need to pass a second parameter with a single string in an array. Even if you were able to build a parser for the first query, this one will likely push your code into the "Turing tar-pit", where everything is possible but nothing is easy. You may also find it increasingly hard to be sure you're following the advice of Item 40 to prefer imprecise types to inaccurate types. With more complex programs, it's easier to make mistakes.

There's an alternative that's considerably simpler, though: code generation, or codegen. Codegen is metaprogramming in the true sense: programs that operate on code and generate other code. The beauty of codegen is that it lets you write your type manipulations in any language you like. Yes, TypeScript's type system is powerful and capable, but it's probably not your first choice for getting a job done. With codegen, you can write your type manipulation code in ordinary TypeScript. You could also use Python or Rust. Even a shell script might do the job.

For our SQL queries, one option is to use the PgTyped library. It finds appropriately-tagged SQL queries in your TypeScript, examines them against a live database, and writes out a type declaration file with the input and output types. Here's how you'd write your query in TypeScript using PgTyped:

```
// books-queries.ts
import { sql } from '@pgtyped/runtime';
const selectLatest = sql`
    SELECT author, MAX(year)
    FROM books
    GROUP BY author
    WHERE publisher=$publisher
`;

async function getLatestBookByAuthor(db: Database, publisher: string) {
  const result = await selectLatest.run({publisher}, db);
  //    ^? const result: any[]
  return result;
}
```

Then you run the pgtyped command to do codegen:

```
$ npx pgtyped -c pgtyped.config.json
```

(*pgtyped.config.json* is a file that tells PgTyped how to connect to your database)

This results in a new file containing some types:

```
// books-queries.types.ts
/** Types generated for queries found in "books-queries.ts" */

/** 'selectLatest' parameters type */
export interface selectLatestParams {
  publisher: string;
}

/** 'selectLatest' return type */
export interface selectLatestResult {
  author: string;
  year: number;
}

/** 'selectLatest' query type */
export interface selectLatestQuery {
  params: selectLatestParams;
  result: selectLatestResult;
}
```

and some changes to *books-queries.ts*:

```
// books-queries.ts
import { sql } from '@pgtyped/runtime';
import { selectLatestQuery } from './books-queries.types';
export const selectLatestBookByAuthor = sql<selectLatestQuery>`
    SELECT author, MAX(year)
    FROM books
    GROUP BY author
    WHERE publisher=$publisher
`;

async function getLatestBookByAuthor(db: Database, publisher: string) {
  const result = await selectLatestBookByAuthor.run({publisher}, db);
  //    ^? const result: selectLatestResult[]
  return result;
}
```

Our query is now correctly typed! PgTyped is certainly not a simple program, but it's written in TypeScript, uses standard database and testing libraries, and is surely less painful to develop than any equivalently powerful tool written in TypeScript's type system would be.

In addition to allowing you to work in a more conventional programming system, the codegen approach gives you complete control over how the types display. The tricks described in Item 56 won't be needed with your generated types. You can make them look exactly the way you like. Don't like the snake_case type names? Just pipe them through sed or your text processing tool of choice.

The resulting types are also likely to be much less taxing on the TypeScript compiler and language services than your hand-rolled SQL parser.

The one notable cost of code generation is that it adds another build step that must be run regularly to ensure that the generated code stays in sync. In the SQL case, that means that the pgtyped command would need to be rerun whenever a query changes or the database schema changes. The usual way to enforce this is by doing codegen on your continuous integration (CI) system and running git diff to make sure nothing has changed. You might also add this as a pre-push check.

Software engineering is a constant battle against complexity. Major programming languages like TypeScript and the ecosystems around them have been built to give you a fighting chance. Type-level TypeScript, while an impressive tool, is not the best weapon in this battle. If you write some fancy type-level code in TypeScript and feel like you're wading through the Turing tar-pit, consider whether you could generate types instead and write your code in a more conventional language.

Items 42 and 74 explore other ways in which codegen can be used to improve type safety and reduce maintenance overhead.

Things to Remember

- While type-level TypeScript is an impressively powerful tool, it's not always the best tool for the job.
- For complex type manipulations, consider generating code and types as an alternative to writing type-level code. Your code generation tool can be written in ordinary TypeScript or any other language.
- Run codegen and git diff on your continuous integration system to make sure generated code stays in sync.

CHAPTER 7

TypeScript Recipes

As the TypeScript community has grown, developers have come up with more and more tricks for solving specific problems. Some of these "recipes" leverage TypeScript's type checker to catch new categories of mistakes, such as values getting out of sync or nonexhaustive conditionals. Others are tricks for modeling patterns that TypeScript struggles with on its own: iterating over objects, filtering null values from Arrays, or modeling variadic functions.

By applying the recipes in this chapter, you'll help TypeScript catch more real problems with fewer false positives. If you enjoy these, you'll find many more recipes in Stefan Baumgartner's *TypeScript Cookbook*.

Item 59: Use Never Types to Perform Exhaustiveness Checking

Static type analysis is a great way to find places where you do something that you shouldn't. When you assign the wrong type of value, reference a nonexistent property, or call a function with the wrong number of arguments, you'll get a type error.

But there are also errors of omission: times when you should do something but you don't. While TypeScript won't always catch these on its own, there's a popular trick that can be used to convert a missing case in a switch or if statement into a type error. This is known as "exhaustiveness checking." Let's see how it works.

Suppose you're building a drawing program, perhaps using the HTML <canvas> element. You might define the set of shapes you can draw using a tagged union:

```
type Coord = [x: number, y: number];
interface Box {
  type: 'box';
  topLeft: Coord;
  size: Coord;
}
interface Circle {
  type: 'circle';
  center: Coord;
  radius: number;
}
type Shape = Box | Circle;
```

You can draw these using built-in canvas methods:

```
function drawShape(shape: Shape, context: CanvasRenderingContext2D) {
  switch (shape.type) {
    case 'box':
      context.rect(...shape.topLeft, ...shape.size);
      break;
    case 'circle':
      context.arc(...shape.center, shape.radius, 0, 2 * Math.PI);
      break;
  }
}
```

So far, so good. Now you decide to add a third shape:

```
interface Line {
  type: 'line';
  start: Coord;
  end: Coord;
}
type Shape = Box | Circle | Line;
```

There are no type errors, but this change has introduced a bug: drawShape will silently ignore any line shapes. This is an error of omission. How can we get Type-Script to catch this kind of mistake?

If you look at the type of shape after an exhaustive switch statement, there's a clue:

```
function processShape(shape: Shape) {
  switch (shape.type) {
    case 'box': break;
    case 'circle': break;
    case 'line': break;
    default:
      shape
      // ^? (parameter) shape: never
  }
}
```

Recall from Item 7 that the never type is a "bottom" type whose domain is the empty set. When we've covered all the possible types of Shape, this is all that's left. If we missed a case, then the type would be something other than never:

```
function processShape(shape: Shape) {
  switch (shape.type) {
    case 'box': break;
    case 'circle': break;
    // (forgot 'line')
    default:
      shape
      // ^? (parameter) shape: Line
  }
}
```

No value is assignable to the never type, and we can use this to turn an omission into a type error:

```
function assertUnreachable(value: never): never {
  throw new Error(`Missed a case! ${value}`);
}

function drawShape(shape: Shape, context: CanvasRenderingContext2D) {
  switch (shape.type) {
    case 'box':
      context.rect(...shape.topLeft, ...shape.size);
      break;
    case 'circle':
      context.arc(...shape.center, shape.radius, 0, 2 * Math.PI);
      break;
    default:
      assertUnreachable(shape);
      //                ~~~~~
      // ... type 'Line' is not assignable to parameter of type 'never'.
  }
}
```

We'll get into the details of assertUnreachable momentarily, but first let's fix the error by covering the missing case:

```
function drawShape(shape: Shape, context: CanvasRenderingContext2D) {
  switch (shape.type) {
    case 'box':
      context.rect(...shape.topLeft, ...shape.size);
      break;
    case 'circle':
      context.arc(...shape.center, shape.radius, 0, 2 * Math.PI);
      break;
    case 'line':
      context.moveTo(...shape.start);
      context.lineTo(...shape.end);
      break;
```

```
      default:
        assertUnreachable(shape); // ok
    }
  }
```

It's important to leave the `assertUnreachable` call in place, even if it is, as the name suggests, unreachable. It protects you from future errors of omission should you introduce additional shapes.

Why throw an exception in `assertUnreachable`? Isn't this code unreachable? That may be the case for well-typed TypeScript, but it's always possible that `drawShape` will be called from JavaScript, or with an `any` or other unsound type (Item 48). Throwing an exception protects us from surprise values at runtime, not just during type checking.

The exhaustiveness check was especially helpful for `drawShape` because it didn't have a return value. It was only run for side effects. If your function does return a value, then annotating the return type gives you some protection against missing cases:

```
function getArea(shape: Shape): number {
  //                            ~~~~~ Function lacks ending return statement and
  //                                  return type does not include 'undefined'.
  switch (shape.type) {
    case 'box':
      const [width, height] = shape.size;
      return width * height;
    case 'circle':
      return Math.PI * shape.radius ** 2;
  }
}
```

If we'd omitted the return type annotation, TypeScript would have inferred it as `number | undefined` rather than producing an error. It's likely that this would have produced errors elsewhere in your code, where you call `getArea`, but it's better to get errors close to where the mistake was made. As Item 18 explained, it's a good idea to add a return type annotation to any function with multiple `return`s.

(You'll only get this error when `strictNullChecks` is set, since otherwise, `undefined` is part of the `number` type. This is a great reason to use `strictNullChecks`!)

As the error says, if `undefined` is a legitimate return value, then this check won't protect you. Even when a function returns a value, it can be a good idea to do exhaustiveness checking.

That's why we added `never` as the return type for `assertUnreachable` earlier. Since `never` is assignable to all other types, you can safely return it, regardless of the return type of the function:

```
function getArea(shape: Shape): number {
  switch (shape.type) {
```

```
    case 'box':
      const [width, height] = shape.size;
      return width * height;
    case 'circle':
      return Math.PI * shape.radius ** 2;
    case 'line':
      return 0;
    default:
      return assertUnreachable(shape);   // ok
  }
}
```

The `assertUnreachable` pattern is common in TypeScript code and you may run into other variations on it, either using a direct assignment to `never`:

```
function processShape(shape: Shape) {
  switch (shape.type) {
    case 'box': break;
    case 'circle': break;
    default:
      const exhaustiveCheck: never = shape;
      //    ~~~~~~~~~~~~~~~ Type 'Line' is not assignable to type 'never'.
      throw new Error(`Missed a case: ${exhaustiveCheck}`);
  }
}
```

or using the `satisfies` operator:

```
function processShape(shape: Shape) {
  switch (shape.type) {
    case 'box': break;
    case 'circle': break;
    default:
      shape satisfies never
      //    ~~~~~~~~~ Type 'Line' does not satisfy the expected type 'never'.
      throw new Error(`Missed a case: ${shape}`);
  }
}
```

All of these patterns work in the same way. Use whichever one you like best.

With some cleverness, the same trick can be extended to make sure you handle all *pairs* of two types, i.e., the cross-product. For example, say you write some code to play "rock, paper, scissors":

```
type Play = 'rock' | 'paper' | 'scissors';

function shoot(a: Play, b: Play) {
  if (a === b) {
    console.log('draw');
  } else if (
    (a === 'rock' && b === 'scissors') ||
    (a === 'paper' && b === 'rock')
```

```
    ) {
      console.log('A wins');
    } else {
      console.log('B wins');
    }
  }
```

Unfortunately, we've missed a case. If A plays scissors on B's paper, then, much to player A's surprise, this function will report that B has won. We can use a template literal type (Item 54) and exhaustiveness checking to force ourselves to cover every possible case explicitly:

```
function shoot(a: Play, b: Play) {
  const pair = `${a},${b}` as `${Play},${Play}`;  // or: as const
  //    ^? const pair: "rock,rock" | "rock,paper" | "rock,scissors" |
  //                   "paper,rock" | "paper,paper" | "paper,scissors" |
  //                   "scissors,rock" | "scissors,paper" | "scissors,scissors"
  switch (pair) {
    case 'rock,rock':
    case 'paper,paper':
    case 'scissors,scissors':
      console.log('draw');
      break;
    case 'rock,scissors':
    case 'paper,rock':
      console.log('A wins');
      break;
    case 'rock,paper':
    case 'paper,scissors':
    case 'scissors,rock':
      console.log('B wins');
      break;
    default:
      assertUnreachable(pair);
      //                ~~~~ Argument of type "scissors,paper" is not
      //                     assignable to parameter of type 'never'.
  }
}
```

By default, `${a},${b}` would have a type of string. `${Play},${Play}` is a sub-type of string consisting of the nine possible pairs of plays separated by a comma. We can apply the usual exhaustiveness checking trick to make sure we've covered all nine. In this case, we missed one and it resulted in a type error. The error even included the combination we missed! As before, add the missing case and leave the assertion in place in case you ever add an additional possible play.

While it comes up less frequently than straightforward exhaustiveness checking, this technique is occasionally helpful for modeling transitions between states.

The typescript-eslint rule `switch-exhaustiveness-check` can also be used for exhaustiveness checking. Whereas `assertUnreachable` is opt-in, the linter rule is opt-out. If you enable it, you may find that some of your `switch` statements were not intended to be exhaustive, or that they are exhaustive for reasons that are hard to capture in the type system. And you can use `assertUnreachable` in other situations that are intended to be exhaustive, such as `if` statements. But you may find some bugs, too, so the linter rule is worth a try!

Errors of omission are just as important as errors of commission. Use `never` types and the `assertUnreachable` trick to let TypeScript help you avoid them.

Things to Remember

- Use an assignment to the `never` type to ensure that all possible values of a type are handled (an "exhaustiveness check").
- Add a return type annotation to functions that return from multiple branches. You may still want an explicit exhaustiveness check, however.
- Consider using template literal types to ensure that every combination of two or more types is handled.

Item 60: Know How to Iterate Over Objects

This code runs fine, and yet TypeScript flags an error in it. Why?

```
const obj = {
  one: 'uno',
  two: 'dos',
  three: 'tres',
};
for (const k in obj) {
  const v = obj[k];
  //        ~~~~~ Element implicitly has an 'any' type
  //              because type ... has no index signature
}
```

Inspecting the `obj` and `k` symbols gives a clue:

```
const obj = { one: 'uno', two: 'dos', three: 'tres' };
//    ^? const obj: {
//         one: string;
//         two: string;
//         three: string;
//       }
for (const k in obj) {
  //        ^? const k: string
  // ...
}
```

The type of k is string, but you're trying to index into an object whose type only has three specific keys: 'one', 'two', and 'three'. There are strings other than these three, so this has to fail.

Using a type assertion to get a narrower type for k fixes the issue:

```
for (const kStr in obj) {
  const k = kStr as keyof typeof obj;
  //    ^? const k: "one" | "two" | "three"
  const v = obj[k];  // OK
}
```

So the real question is: why is the type of k in the first example inferred as string rather than "one" | "two" | "three"?

To understand, let's look at a slightly different example:

```
interface ABC {
  a: string;
  b: string;
  c: number;
}

function foo(abc: ABC) {
  for (const k in abc) {
    //       ^? const k: string
    const v = abc[k];
    //        ~~~~~ Element implicitly has an 'any' type
    //              because type 'ABC' has no index signature
  }
}
```

It's the same error as before. And you can "fix" it using the same sort of type assertion (k as keyof ABC). But in this case TypeScript is right to complain. Here's why:

```
const x = {a: 'a', b: 'b', c: 2, d: new Date()};
foo(x);  // OK
```

The function foo can be called with any value *assignable* to ABC, not just a value with 'a', 'b', and 'c' properties. It's entirely possible that the value will have other properties, too (see Item 4 for a refresher on why). To allow for this, TypeScript gives k the only type it can be confident of, namely, string.[1]

Using a type assertion to keyof ABC would have another downside here:

```
function foo(abc: ABC) {
  for (const kStr in abc) {
    let k = kStr as keyof ABC;
    // ^? let k: keyof ABC (equivalent to "a" | "b" | "c")
```

---

1 Symbols can also be object keys but they are not enumerable.

```
    const v = abc[k];
    //    ^? const v: string | number
  }
}
```

If `"a" | "b" | "c"` is too narrow for k, then `string | number` is certainly too narrow for v. In the preceding example, one of the values is a `Date`, but it could be anything. This could lead to chaos at runtime. As Item 9 explained, type assertions should always make you nervous because TypeScript might be on to something. (Surprisingly, TypeScript will let you declare `let k: keyof ABC` above this `for-in` loop and use k as the iterator, but this is no safer than a type assertion and is less explicit.)

So what if you just want to iterate over the object's keys and values without type errors? `Object.entries` lets you iterate over both simultaneously:

```
function foo(abc: ABC) {
  for (const [k, v] of Object.entries(abc)) {
    //          ^? const k: string
    console.log(v);
    //            ^? const v: any
  }
}
```

While these types may be hard to work with, they are at least honest![2]

Another reason that TypeScript infers `string` in `for-in` loops is *prototype pollution*. This is a security issue where properties defined on `Object.prototype` are inherited by all other objects. These inherited properties will be enumerated by a `for-in` loop, so `string` is a safer choice. (`Object.entries` excludes inherited properties.)

A safe way to get more precise types is to explicitly list the keys you're interested in:

```
function foo(abc: ABC) {
  const keys = ['a', 'b', 'c'] as const;
  for (const k of keys) {
    //        ^? const k: "a" | "b" | "c"
    const v = abc[k];
    //    ^? const v: string | number
  }
}
```

If your intention is to cover all the keys in `ABC`, you'll need some way to keep the keys array in sync with the type.

---

2 The typings for utility functions like Lodash's `_.forEach` and may provide more precise types for k and v, but these are unsound for the reasons mentioned in this item.

While iterating over objects comes with many hazards, iterating over a Map does not:

```
const m = new Map([
  //    ^? const m: Map<string, string>
  ['one', 'uno'],
  ['two', 'dos'],
  ['three', 'tres'],
]);
for (const [k, v] of m.entries()) {
  //         ^? const k: string
  console.log(v);
  //             ^? const v: string
}
```

Maps are easier to iterate over because they don't have the same structural behavior as objects: you'll never put a number value in a Map<string, string> without using a type assertion or going through an any type. But they can be less convenient to work with if your data is coming via JSON or from another API that's already designed to use objects. Item 16 has an example of how replacing an object type with a Map can improve the type safety of your code.

If you want to iterate over the keys and values in an immutable object, you can use an explicit type assertion on the key in a for-in loop. To safely iterate over an object that could have additional properties, use Object.entries. It's always safe, though the key and value types are more difficult to work with. And consider whether a Map might be an appropriate alternative.

Things to Remember

- Be aware that any objects your function receives as parameters might have additional keys.
- Use Object.entries to iterate over the keys and values of any object.
- Use a for-in loop with an explicit type assertion to iterate objects when you know exactly what the keys will be.
- Consider Map as an alternative to objects since it's easier to iterate over.

Item 61: Use Record Types to Keep Values in Sync

Suppose you're writing a UI component for drawing scatter plots. It has a few different types of properties that control its display and behavior:

```
interface ScatterProps {
  // The data
  xs: number[];
  ys: number[];
```

```
  // Display
  xRange: [number, number];
  yRange: [number, number];
  color: string;

  // Events
  onClick?: (x: number, y: number, index: number) => void;
}
```

To avoid unnecessary work, you'd like to redraw the chart only when you need to. Changing data or display properties will require a redraw, but changing the event handler will not.

Here's one way you might implement this optimization:

```
function shouldUpdate(
  oldProps: ScatterProps,
  newProps: ScatterProps
) {
  for (const kStr in oldProps) {
    const k = kStr as keyof ScatterProps;
    if (oldProps[k] !== newProps[k]) {
      if (k !== 'onClick') return true;
    }
  }
  return false;
}
```

(See Item 60 for an explanation of the keyof assertion in this loop. This assertion is safe because we don't care about the value types, only whether they are equal.)

What happens when you or a coworker add a new property? The shouldUpdate function will redraw the chart whenever it changes. You might call this the conservative or "fail open" approach. The upside is that the chart will always look right. The downside is that it might be drawn too often.

A "fail closed" approach might look like this:

```
function shouldUpdate(
  oldProps: ScatterProps,
  newProps: ScatterProps
) {
  return (
    oldProps.xs !== newProps.xs ||
    oldProps.ys !== newProps.ys ||
    oldProps.xRange !== newProps.xRange ||
    oldProps.yRange !== newProps.yRange ||
    oldProps.color !== newProps.color
    // (no check for onClick)
  );
}
```

With this approach there won't be any unnecessary redraws, but there might be some *necessary* draws that get dropped. An important principle in optimization is to "first, do no harm." We shouldn't sacrifice correct behavior for the sake of performance.

Neither approach is ideal. What you'd really like is to force your coworker or future self to make a decision when adding the new property. You might try adding a comment:

```
interface ScatterProps {
  xs: number[];
  ys: number[];
  // ...
  onClick?: (x: number, y: number, index: number) => void;

  // Note: if you add a property here, update shouldUpdate!
}
```

But do you really expect this to work? It would be better if the type checker could enforce this for you.

If you set it up the right way, it can. The key is to use a `Record` type with the right set of keys:

```
const REQUIRES_UPDATE: Record<keyof ScatterProps, boolean> = {
  xs: true,
  ys: true,
  xRange: true,
  yRange: true,
  color: true,
  onClick: false,
};

function shouldUpdate(
  oldProps: ScatterProps,
  newProps: ScatterProps
) {
  for (const kStr in oldProps) {
    const k = kStr as keyof ScatterProps;
    if (oldProps[k] !== newProps[k] && REQUIRES_UPDATE[k]) {
      return true;
    }
  }
  return false;
}
```

The `keyof ScatterProps` annotation tells the type checker that `REQUIRES_UPDATE` should have all the same properties as `ScatterProps`. Critically, these are all required properties.

Now if in the future you add a new property to `ScatterProps`:

```
interface ScatterProps {
  // ...
  onDoubleClick?: () => void;
}
```

then this will produce an error in the definition of REQUIRES_UPDATE:

```
const REQUIRES_UPDATE: Record<keyof ScatterProps, boolean> = {
  //    ~~~~~~~~~~~~~~~ Property 'onDoubleClick' is missing in type ...
  // ...
};
```

This will certainly force the issue! Deleting or renaming a property will cause a similar error. This is excess property checking (Item 11) at work, and it lets us enforce that the object has exactly the set of properties we want, no more, no less. TypeScript has given us a third choice in the classic fail open/fail closed dilemma, namely "just fail."

It's important that we used an object with boolean values here. Had we used an array:

```
const PROPS_REQUIRING_UPDATE: (keyof ScatterProps)[] = [
  'xs',
  'ys',
  // ...
];
```

then we would have been forced into the same fail open/fail closed choice.

Records and mapped types are ideal if you want one object to have exactly the same properties as another. Here we used it to avoid the classic fail open/fail closed dilemma, but there are many other applications, for example, requiring that every property in your application's state have a corresponding URL parameter.

Things to Remember

- Recognize the fail open versus fail closed dilemma.
- Use Record types to keep related values and types synchronized.
- Consider using Record types to force choices when adding new properties to an interface.

Item 62: Use Rest Parameters and Tuple Types to Model Variadic Functions

Sometimes you'd like to have a function take a different number of arguments, depending on a TypeScript type.

To see how this might happen, imagine that you have an interface that describes the query parameters that different routes in a web app can accept:

```
interface RouteQueryParams {
  '/': null,
  '/search': { query: string; language?: string; }
  // ...
}
```

This says that the root page (/) does not take any query parameters, whereas the /search page takes a query param and an optional language param.

You can define a function to construct a URL for a route:

```
function buildURL(route: keyof RouteQueryParams, params?: any) {
  return route + (params ? `?${new URLSearchParams(params)}` : '');
}

console.log(buildURL('/search', {query: 'do a barrel roll', language: 'en'}))
console.log(buildURL('/'))
```

This builds the URLs you'd expect:

```
/search?query=do+a+barrel+roll&language=en
/
```

Unfortunately, it's not very safe thanks to that any on the second parameter. You're free to construct a URL for any route with whatever search parameters you like:

```
buildURL('/', {query: 'recursion'});  // should be an error (no params for root)
buildURL('/search');  // should be an error (missing params)
```

Here's a safer version:

```
function buildURL<Path extends keyof RouteQueryParams>(
  route: Path,
  params: RouteQueryParams[Path]
) {
  return route + (params ? `?${new URLSearchParams(params)}` : '');
}
```

We've made the function generic in the route, which can usually be inferred, and made the parameter type depend on this route.

This new type signature works perfectly for the /search route:

```
buildURL('/search', {query: 'do a barrel roll'})
buildURL('/search', {query: 'do a barrel roll', language: 'en'})
buildURL('/search', {})
//                    ~~ Property 'query' is missing in type '{}'
```

For the root page, however, you need to pass an additional null parameter:

```
buildURL('/', {query: 'recursion'});  // error, good!
//            ~~~~~~~~~~~~~~~~~~~ Argument of type '{ query: string; }' is
//                                not assignable to parameter of type 'null'
buildURL('/', null);  // ok
```

```
buildURL('/');  // we'd like this to be allowed
//  ~~~~ Expected 2 arguments, but got 1.
```

Writing an extra null isn't the end of the world, of course, but it is a nuisance and the old API with its optional parameter looked nicer. We could make the second parameter optional with the new version, but this should only be allowed when the route doesn't take any search parameters. In other words, we want the function to take a variable number of arguments, depending on an inferred type.

The trick to doing this is to use a conditional type (Item 52) and rest parameters:

```
function buildURL<Path extends keyof RouteQueryParams>(
  route: Path,
  ...args: (
     RouteQueryParams[Path] extends null
     ? []
     : [params: RouteQueryParams[Path]]
  )
) {
  const params = args ? args[0] : null;
  return route + (params ? `?${new URLSearchParams(params)}` : '');
}
```

If the query parameter type extends null, then this looks like: (route: Path, ...args: []), which is a one-parameter function. If it doesn't, then it looks like (route: Path, ...args: [params: ...]), which is a two-parameter function.

This works exactly as you'd hope:

```
buildURL('/search', {query: 'do a barrel roll'})
buildURL('/search', {query: 'do a barrel roll', language: 'en'})
buildURL('/search', {})
//                   ~~ Property 'query' is missing in type '{}' ...

buildURL('/', {query: 'recursion'});
//            ~~~~~~~~~~~~~~~~~~~~~ Expected 1 arguments, but got 2.
buildURL('/', null);
//            ~~~~ Expected 1 arguments, but got 2.
buildURL('/');  // ok
```

When you inspect the call sites, it really looks like there are two different functions, depending on the route. The rest parameter is an implementation detail that's hidden from the user. TypeScript has even picked up the name of the second parameter (params) from the label on the tuple element:

```
buildURL('/');
// ^? function buildURL<"/">(route: "/"): string
buildURL('/search', {query: 'do a barrel roll'})
// ^? function buildURL<"/search">(
//       route: "/search", params: { query: string; language?: string; }
//    ): string
```

If you fail to include this label, your users will see a more generic parameter name like `args_0`.

This is the most general technique for modeling variadic functions. You could also use overload signatures to achieve a similar effect, but this would result in code duplication and, as Item 52 explained, conditional types handle unions more naturally than overloads.

Sometimes the number or type of parameters to a function depends on a TypeScript type. When this happens, you can model it using rest parameters with a tuple type.

Things to Remember

- Use rest parameters and tuple types to model functions whose signature depends on the type of an argument.
- Use conditional types to model relationships between the type of one parameter and the number and type of the remaining parameters.
- Remember to label the elements of your tuple types to get meaningful parameter names at call sites.

Item 63: Use Optional Never Properties to Model Exclusive Or

In ordinary speech, "or" means "exclusive or." Only programmers and logicians use an *inclusive* or.

In TypeScript, it's easy to get mixed up between these two:

```
interface ThingOne {
  shirtColor: string;
}
interface ThingTwo {
  hairColor: string;
}
type Thing = ThingOne | ThingTwo;
```

We usually read the last line as "type `Thing` is a `ThingOne` or `ThingTwo`." But just like JavaScript's runtime or (`||`), TypeScript's type-level or (`|`) is an *inclusive* or. There's no reason a thing can't be both a `ThingOne` *and* a `ThingTwo`:

```
const bothThings = {
  shirtColor: 'red',
  hairColor: 'blue',
};
const thing1: ThingOne = bothThings;  // ok
const thing2: ThingTwo = bothThings;  // ok
```

Why does this work? It's because TypeScript has a structural type system (Item 4). Both the ThingOne and ThingTwo types allow additional properties that aren't declared in their interface, though, as Item 11 explains, this is sometimes obscured by excess property checking.

So what if you really do want an exclusive or? What if you want to keep your ThingOnes and ThingTwos separate? How can you model that?

The standard trick is to use an *optional never* type in your interface to disallow a property:

```
interface OnlyThingOne {
  shirtColor: string;
  hairColor?: never;
}
interface OnlyThingTwo {
  hairColor: string;
  shirtColor?: never;
}
type ExclusiveThing = OnlyThingOne | OnlyThingTwo;
```

Now none of the assignments from before pass the type checker:

```
const thing1: OnlyThingOne = bothThings;
//    ~~~~~~ Types of property 'hairColor' are incompatible.
const thing2: OnlyThingTwo = bothThings;
//    ~~~~~~ Types of property 'shirtColor' are incompatible.
const allThings: ExclusiveThing = {
//  ~~~~~~~~~~ Types of property 'hairColor' are incompatible.
  shirtColor: 'red',
  hairColor: 'blue',
};
```

This works because no value is assignable to a never type. But because the property is *optional*, there's exactly one way out: not having that property.

This isn't just useful for unions. Recall from Item 4 that structural typing isn't a good model for two- and three-dimensional vectors. You can use an optional never to directly disallow a z property on a 2D vector:

```
interface Vector2D {
  x: number;
  y: number;
  z?: never;
}
```

With this type, you'll get an error if you accidentally pass a three-dimensional vector to a function like norm that expects a two-dimensional vector:

```
function norm(v: Vector2D) {
  return Math.sqrt(v.x ** 2 + v.y ** 2);
}
const v = {x: 3, y: 4, z: 5};
const d = norm(v);
//                 ~ Types of property 'z' are incompatible.
```

This wouldn't be an error without the z?: never because the call is structurally valid, even though it's semantically incorrect. We'll look at another approach to fixing the Vector2D problem, brands, in Item 64.

You can also use a tagged union (Item 34) to achieve an exclusive or:

```
interface ThingOneTag {
  type: 'one';
  shirtColor: string;
}
interface ThingTwoTag {
  type: 'two';
  hairColor: string;
}
type Thing = ThingOneTag | ThingTwoTag;
```

A string can't be both 'one' *and* 'two', so there's no overlap between these types. This means there's no distinction between inclusive and exclusive or. This is one of many great reasons to use tagged unions when you can.

Rather than adding optional never properties by hand, it's possible to define a generic exclusive or (XOR) helper:

```
type XOR<T1, T2> =
    (T1 & {[k in Exclude<keyof T2, keyof T1>]?: never}) |
    (T2 & {[k in Exclude<keyof T1, keyof T2>]?: never});
```

You can use this to construct ExclusiveThing directly from the interfaces at the start of this item:

```
type ExclusiveThing = XOR<ThingOne, ThingTwo>;
const allThings: ExclusiveThing = {
  //  ~~~~~~~~~ Types of property 'hairColor' are incompatible.
  shirtColor: 'red',
  hairColor: 'blue',
};
```

While tagged unions are a more common way to create exclusive types in TypeScript, the optional never trick can be helpful in situations where you either can't or don't want to add an explicit tag.

Things to Remember

- In TypeScript, "or" is "inclusive or": A | B means either A, B, or both.

- Consider the "both" possibility in your code, and either handle it or disallow it.

- Use tagged unions to model exclusive or where it's convenient. Consider using optional `never` properties where it isn't.

Item 64: Consider Brands for Nominal Typing

Item 4 discussed structural typing and how it can sometimes lead to surprising results:

```
interface Vector2D {
  x: number;
  y: number;
}
function calculateNorm(p: Vector2D) {
  return Math.sqrt(p.x ** 2 + p.y ** 2);
}

calculateNorm({x: 3, y: 4});  // OK, result is 5
const vec3D = {x: 3, y: 4, z: 1};
calculateNorm(vec3D);  // OK! result is also 5
```

What if you'd like `calculateNorm` to reject 3D vectors? This goes against the structural typing model of TypeScript but is certainly more mathematically correct.

Item 63 showed how you can specifically prevent a z field using an optional `never` property. This is a purely type-level fix. It doesn't require you to change the values at runtime.

You can also prevent types from being assignable to one another by adding a "tag" to the value at runtime:

```
interface Vector2D {
  type: '2d';
  x: number;
  y: number;
}
```

Here the `type` property serves as the "tag." This pattern is particularly common with union types. Item 34 explored "tagged unions" in more detail and they are certainly one way to mitigate this problem. They do have a few downsides, however. They add runtime overhead, changing what was previously a very simple type with only numeric properties into one with a mix of strings and numbers. Moreover, you can only add an explicit tag like this to object types.

Interestingly, you can get many of the same benefits as explicit tags while operating only in the type system. In this context, tags are typically known as "brands" (think cows, not Coca-Cola). This types-only approach removes runtime overhead and also lets you brand built-in types like string or number where you can't attach additional properties. This is known as *nominal typing*, as opposed to TypeScript's usual structural typing. With nominal typing, a value is a Vector2D because you say it is, not because it has the right shape.

Let's see how this works using filesystem paths. What if you have a function that operates on the filesystem and requires an absolute (as opposed to a relative) path? This is easy to check at runtime (does the path start with "/"?), but not so easy in the type system.

Here's an approach with brands:

```
type AbsolutePath = string & {_brand: 'abs'};
function listAbsolutePath(path: AbsolutePath) {
  // ...
}
function isAbsolutePath(path: string): path is AbsolutePath {
  return path.startsWith('/');
}
```

You can't construct an object that is a string and has a _brand property. This is purely a game with the type system. (If you think you can assign properties to a string, Item 10 will explain why you're mistaken.)

If you have a string path that could be either absolute or relative, you can check using the type guard, which will refine its type:

```
function f(path: string) {
  if (isAbsolutePath(path)) {
    listAbsolutePath(path);
  }
  listAbsolutePath(path);
  //               ~~~~ Argument of type 'string' is not assignable to
  //                    parameter of type 'AbsolutePath'
}
```

This is helpful documentation about which functions expect absolute or relative paths, and which type of path each variable holds. It is not an ironclad guarantee: path as AbsolutePath will succeed for any string. But if you avoid these sorts of assertions, then the only way to get an AbsolutePath is to be given one or to check, which is exactly what you want.

You can also brand number types—for example, to attach units:

```
type Meters = number & {_brand: 'meters'};
type Seconds = number & {_brand: 'seconds'};
```

```
const meters = (m: number) => m as Meters;
const seconds = (s: number) => s as Seconds;

const oneKm = meters(1000);
//    ^? const oneKm: Meters
const oneMin = seconds(60);
//    ^? const oneMin: Seconds
```

This can be awkward in practice, however, since arithmetic operations make the numbers forget their brands:

```
const tenKm = oneKm * 10;
//    ^? const tenKm: number
const v = oneKm / oneMin;
//    ^? const v: number
```

If your code involves lots of numbers with mixed units, though, this may still be an attractive approach to documenting the expected types of numeric parameters.

There are other techniques for branding types. You may encounter code that uses private fields to brand classes or an intersection with TypeScript string-based enums, which are nominally typed (Item 72).

Another common technique is to use a unique symbol type:

```
declare const brand: unique symbol;
export type Meters = number & {[brand]: 'meters'};
```

The advantage of this technique is that, since the brand symbol isn't exported, users will have to use a type assertion or helper function to get a value with a Meters type. They can't use the brand directly or create another type that's compatible with it.

Regardless of how you construct them, brands can be used to model many properties that cannot be expressed within the type system. For example, using binary search to find an element in a list:

```
function binarySearch<T>(xs: T[], x: T): boolean {
  let low = 0, high = xs.length - 1;
  while (high >= low) {
    const mid = low + Math.floor((high - low) / 2);
    const v = xs[mid];
    if (v === x) return true;
    [low, high] = x > v ? [mid + 1, high] : [low, mid - 1];
  }
  return false;
}
```

This works if the list is sorted, but will result in false negatives if it is not. You can't represent a sorted list in TypeScript's type system. But you can create a brand:

```
type SortedList<T> = T[] & {_brand: 'sorted'};

function isSorted<T>(xs: T[]): xs is SortedList<T> {
```

```
  for (let i = 0; i < xs.length - 1; i++) {
    if (xs[i] > xs[i + 1]) {
      return false;
    }
  }
  return true;
}

function binarySearch<T>(xs: SortedList<T>, x: T): boolean {
  // ...
}
```

To call this version of binarySearch, you either need to be given a SortedList (i.e., have proof that the list is sorted) or prove that it's sorted yourself using isSorted. The linear scan isn't great, but at least you'll be safe!

This is a helpful perspective to have on the type checker in general. To call a method on an object, for instance, you either need to be given a non-null object or prove that it's non-null yourself with a conditional. This is analogous to the two ways of getting a SortedList: you can either be given one, or prove that the list is sorted yourself.

Things to Remember

- With nominal typing, a value has a type because you say it has a type, not because it has the same shape as that type.
- Consider attaching brands to distinguish primitive and object types that are semantically distinct but structurally identical.
- Be familiar with the various techniques for branding: properties on object types, string-based enums, private fields, and unique symbols.

CHAPTER 8

Type Declarations and @types

Dependency management can be confusing in any language, and TypeScript is no exception. In fact, because types are often shipped as separate packages, dependencies in TypeScript can be especially bewildering.

This chapter will help you build a mental model for how dependencies work in Type-Script and show you how to sort through some of the issues that can come up with them. It will also help you craft your own type declaration files to publish and share with others. By writing great type declarations, you can help not just your own project but the entire TypeScript community.

Item 65: Put TypeScript and @types in devDependencies

The Node Package Manager, npm, is ubiquitous in the JavaScript world. It provides both a repository of JavaScript libraries (the npm registry) and a way to specify which versions of them you depend on (*package.json*).

npm draws a distinction between a few types of dependencies, each of which goes in a separate section of *package.json*:

dependencies
> These are packages that are required to run your JavaScript. If you import lodash at runtime, then it should go in dependencies. When you publish your code on npm and another user installs it, it will also install these dependencies. (These are known as transitive dependencies.)

devDependencies
> These packages are used to develop and test your code but are not required at runtime. Your test framework is an example of a devDependency. Unlike depen dencies, these are *not* installed transitively with your packages.

peerDependencies

These are packages that you require at runtime but don't want to be responsible for tracking. If you publish a React component, for example, it will be compatible with a range of versions of React itself. You'd prefer that the user select one, rather than you choosing for them, which could result in multiple versions of React running on the same page.

Of these, `dependencies` and `devDependencies` are by far the most common. As you use TypeScript, be aware of which type of dependency you're adding. Because TypeScript is a development tool and TypeScript types do not exist at runtime (Item 3), packages related to TypeScript generally belong in `devDependencies`.

The first dependency to consider is TypeScript itself. While you can install TypeScript system-wide, this is a bad idea for two main reasons:

- There's no guarantee that you and your coworkers will always have the same version installed.
- It adds a step to your project setup.

Make TypeScript a `devDependency` instead. That way you and your coworkers will always get the correct version when you run `npm install`. You update TypeScript the same way you'd update any other package.

Your IDE and build tools will happily discover a version of TypeScript installed in this way. On the command line, for example, you can use `npx` to run the version of `tsc` installed by npm:

```
$ npx tsc
```

The next type of dependency to consider is *type dependencies* or `@types`. If a library itself does not come with TypeScript type declarations, then you may still be able to find typings on DefinitelyTyped, a community-maintained collection of type definitions for JavaScript libraries. Type definitions from DefinitelyTyped are published on the npm registry under the `@types` scope: `@types/jquery` has type definitions for jQuery, `@types/lodash` has types for Lodash, and so on. These `@types` packages only contain the *types*. They don't contain the implementation.

Your `@types` dependencies should also be `devDependencies`, even if the package itself is a direct dependency. For example, to depend on React and its type declarations, you might run:

```
$ npm install react
```

```
$ npm install --save-dev @types/react
```

This will result in a *package.json* file that looks something like this:

```
{
  "devDependencies": {
    "@types/react": "^18.2.23",
    "typescript": "^5.2.2"
  },
  "dependencies": {
    "react": "^18.2.0"
  }
}
```

The idea here is that you should publish JavaScript, not TypeScript, and your Java-Script does not depend on the `@types` when you run it. (TypeScript users might depend on these `@types`, but transitive types dependencies are best avoided. Item 70 will show you how.)

What if you're building a web app, with no intentions to ever publish it as a library on npm? You may find advice to the effect that it's not worth separating out `devDependencies` in this situation, and that you may as well just make everything a prod dependency. Even for a web app, though, putting `@types` in `devDependencies` has a few advantages:

- If your app has a server component, you can run `npm install --production` to only install prod dependencies in your production image. Assuming you've compiled your TypeScript to JavaScript already, these will be the only dependencies you need to run your code. This will result in a slimmer image that spins up more quickly.

- If you're using an automated dependency update tool (such as Renovate or Dependabot), you can tell it to prioritize production dependencies. These are the ones that are more likely to have important security updates that could affect end users of your code, and these are the ones that you should focus on.

There are a few things that can go wrong with `@types` dependencies, and the next item will delve deeper into this topic.

Things to Remember

- Understand the difference between `dependencies` and `devDependencies` in *package.json*.

- Put TypeScript in your project's `devDependencies`. Don't install TypeScript system-wide.

- Put `@types` dependencies in `devDependencies`, not `dependencies`.

Item 66: Understand the Three Versions Involved in Type Declarations

Dependency management rarely conjures up happy feelings for software developers. Usually, you just want to use a library and not think too much about whether its transitive dependencies are compatible with yours.

The bad news is that TypeScript doesn't make this any better. In fact, it can make dependency management quite a bit *more* complicated. This is because instead of having a single version to worry about, you now have up to three:

- The version of the package
- The version of its type declarations (@types)
- The version of TypeScript

If any of these versions get out of sync with one another, you can run into errors that may not be clearly related to dependency management. But as the saying goes, "make things as simple as possible, but no simpler." Understanding the full complexity of TypeScript package management will help you diagnose and fix problems. And it will help you make more informed decisions when it comes time to publish type declarations of your own.

Here's how dependencies in TypeScript are supposed to work. You install a package as a direct dependency, and you install its types as a dev dependency (see Item 65):

```
$ npm install react
+ react@18.2.0

$ npm install --save-dev @types/react
+ @types/react@18.2.23
```

Note that the major and minor versions (18.2) match but the patch versions (.0 and .23) do not. This is exactly what you want to see. The 18.2 in the @types version means that these type declarations describe the API of version 18.2 of react. Assuming the react module follows good semantic versioning hygiene, the patch versions (18.2.1, 18.2.2, …) will not change its public API and will not require updates to the type declarations. But the type declarations *themselves* might have bugs or omissions. The patch versions of the @types module correspond to these sorts of fixes and additions. In this case, there were many more updates to the type declarations than the library itself (23 versus 0).

Version matching can go wrong in a few ways.

First, you might update a library but forget to update its type declarations. This often happens as a result of automatic dependency updating tools such as Dependabot. In this case you'll get type errors whenever you try to use new features of the library. If there were breaking changes to the library, you might get runtime errors despite your code passing the type checker.

The solution is usually to update your type declarations so that the versions are back in sync. If the type declarations have not been updated, you have a few options. You can use an augmentation in your own project to add new functions and methods that you'd like to use (Item 71 shows you how). Or you can contribute updated type declarations back to the community.

Second, your type declarations might get ahead of your library. This can happen if you've been using a library without its typings (perhaps you gave it an any type using declare module) and try to install them later. If there have been new releases of the library and its type declarations, your versions might be out of sync. The symptoms of this are similar to the first problem, just in reverse. The type checker will be comparing your code against the latest API, while you'll be using an older one at runtime. The solution is to either upgrade the library or downgrade the type declarations until they match.

Third, the type declarations might require a newer version of TypeScript than you're using in your project. Much of the development of TypeScript's type system has been motivated by an attempt to more precisely type popular JavaScript libraries like Lodash, React, and Ramda. It makes sense that the type declarations for these libraries would want to use the latest and greatest features to get you better type safety.

You'll experience this problem as type errors in the @types declarations themselves. The solution is to do one of the following: upgrade your TypeScript version, use an older version of the type declarations, or, if you really can't update TypeScript, stub out the types with declare module. It is possible for a library to provide different type declarations for different versions of TypeScript via typesVersions. This is rare (well under 1% of packages on DefinitelyTyped do so), but you may encounter it in widely used typings like @types/node and @types/react.

To install @types for a specific version of TypeScript, you can use:

```
npm install --save-dev @types/react@ts4.9
```

The version matching between libraries and their types is best effort and may not always be correct. But the more popular the library is, the more likely it is that its type declarations will get this right.

Fourth, you can wind up with duplicate @types dependencies. Say you depend on @types/foo and @types/bar. If @types/bar depends on an incompatible version of @types/foo, then npm will attempt to resolve this by installing both versions, one in a nested folder:

```
node_modules/
  @types/
    foo/
      index.d.ts @1.2.3
    bar/
      index.d.ts
      node_modules/
        @types/
          foo/
            index.d.ts @2.3.4
```

While this is sometimes OK for node modules that are used at runtime, it almost certainly won't be OK for type declarations, which live in a flat global namespace. You'll see this as errors about duplicate declarations or declarations that cannot be merged. You can track down why you have a duplicate type declaration by running npm ls @types/foo. The solution is typically to update your dependency on @types/foo or @types/bar so that they are compatible.

Transitive @types dependencies like these are often a source of trouble. If you're publishing types, see Item 70 for a way to avoid them. If you have a large number of duplicated type declarations, it can even become a performance issue for the TypeScript compiler. Item 78 dives into this topic in more detail.

Some packages, particularly those written in TypeScript, choose to bundle their own type declarations. This is usually indicated by a "types" field in their *package.json* which points to a *.d.ts* file:

```
{
  "name": "left-pad",
  "version": "1.3.0",
  "description": "String left pad",
  "main": "index.js",
  "types": "index.d.ts"
  // ...
}
```

Does this solve all our problems? Would I even be asking if the answer was "yes"?

Bundling types *does* solve the problem of version mismatch, particularly if the library itself is written in TypeScript and the type declarations are generated by tsc (with the declaration setting). But bundling has some problems of its own.

First, what if there's an error in the bundled types that can't be fixed through augmentation (Item 71)? Or the types worked fine when they were published, but a new TypeScript version has since been released which flags an error. With @types, you could depend on the library's implementation but not its type declarations. But with bundled types, you lose this option. One bad type declaration might keep you stuck on an old version of TypeScript. Contrast this with DefinitelyTyped: as TypeScript is developed, Microsoft runs it against all the type declarations on DefinitelyTyped. Breaks are fixed quickly.

Second, what if your types depend on another library's type declarations? Usually, this would be a devDependency (Item 65). But if you publish your module and another user installs it, they won't get your devDependencies. Type errors will result. On the other hand, you probably don't want to make it a direct dependency either, since then your JavaScript users will install @types modules for no reason. Item 70 discusses the standard workaround for this situation. But if you publish your types on Definitely-Typed, this is not a problem at all: you declare your type dependency there, and only your TypeScript users will get it.

Some projects adopt a hybrid solution of publishing their TypeScript types as a separate package. This keeps you in control of your own code while still allowing you to cleanly separate the implementation and type dependency trees.

Third, what if you need to fix an issue with the type declarations of an old version of your library? Would you be able to go back and release a patch update? DefinitelyTyped has mechanisms for simultaneously maintaining type declarations for different versions of the same library, something that might be hard for you to do in your own project.

Fourth, how committed are you to accepting patches for type declarations? Remember, the versions of react and @types/react from the start of this item. There were far more patch updates to the type declarations than the library itself. DefinitelyTyped is community maintained and is able to handle this volume. In particular, if a library maintainer doesn't look at a patch within five days, a global maintainer will. Can you commit to a similar turnaround time for your library?

Managing dependencies in TypeScript can be challenging, but it does come with rewards: well-written type declarations can help you learn how to use libraries correctly and can greatly improve your productivity with them. As you run into issues with dependency management, keep the three versions in mind.

If you are publishing packages, weigh the pros and cons of bundling type declarations versus publishing them on DefinitelyTyped. The official recommendation is to bundle type declarations only if the library is written in TypeScript. This works well in practice since tsc can automatically generate type declarations for you (by using the declaration compiler option). For JavaScript libraries, handcrafted type declarations are more likely to contain errors, and they'll require more updates. If you publish your type declarations on DefinitelyTyped, the community will help you support and maintain them.

Things to Remember

- There are three versions involved in an @types dependency: the library version, the @types version, and the TypeScript version.
- Recognize the symptoms of different types of version mismatch.
- If you update a library, make sure you update the corresponding @types.
- Understand the pros and cons of bundling types versus publishing them on DefinitelyTyped. Prefer bundling types if your library is written in TypeScript, and DefinitelyTyped if it is not.

Item 67: Export All Types That Appear in Public APIs

Use TypeScript long enough and you'll eventually find yourself wanting to use a type or interface from a third-party library, only to find that it isn't exported. This is just a nuisance for library users. As you'll see, any type that's part of a public API is effectively exported anyway, even if not explicitly. As a library author, this means that you ought to just export your types to begin with as a convenience to your users.

Suppose you want to create some private, unexported types:

```
interface SecretName {
  first: string;
  last: string;
}

interface SecretSanta {
  name: SecretName;
  gift: string;
}

export function getGift(name: SecretName, gift: string): SecretSanta {
  // ...
}
```

As a user of your module, I cannot directly import SecretName or SecretSanta, only getGift. But this is more an annoyance than a firm barrier: because those types appear in an exported function signature, I can extract them. One way is to use the Parameters and ReturnType generic types:

```
type MySanta = ReturnType<typeof getGift>;
//   ^? type MySanta = SecretSanta
type MyName = Parameters<typeof getGift>[0];
//   ^? type MyName = SecretName
```

If your goal in not exporting these types was to preserve flexibility, then the jig is up! You've already committed to them by putting them in a public API. Do your users a favor and export them.

Things to Remember

- Export types that appear in any form in any public method. Your users will be able to extract them anyway, so you may as well make it easy for them.

Item 68: Use TSDoc for API Comments

Here's a TypeScript function to generate a greeting:

```
// Generate a greeting. Result is formatted for display.
function greet(name: string, title: string) {
  return `Hello ${title} ${name}`;
}
```

The author was kind enough to leave a comment describing what this function does. But for documentation intended to be read by users of your functions, it's better to use JSDoc-style comments:

```
/** Generate a greeting. Result is formatted for display. */
function greetJSDoc(name: string, title: string) {
  return `Hello ${title} ${name}`;
}
```

The reason is that there is a nearly universal convention in editors to surface JSDoc-style comments when the function is called (see Figure 8-1).

```
(alias) greetJSDoc(name: string, title: string): string
import greetJSDoc

Generate a greeting. Result is formatted for display.
greetJSDoc('John Doe', 'Sir');
```

Figure 8-1. JSDoc-style comments are shown in tooltips in your editor.

The inline comment, in contrast, gets no such treatment (see Figure 8-2).

```
(alias) greet(name: string, title: string): string
import greet
greet('John Doe', 'Sir');
```

Figure 8-2. Inline comments are typically not shown in tooltips.

The TypeScript language service supports this convention, and you should take advantage of it. If a comment describes a public API, it should be JSDoc. In the context of TypeScript, these comments are sometimes called TSDoc. You can use many of the usual conventions like `@param` and `@returns`:

```
/**
 * Generate a greeting.
 * @param name Name of the person to greet
 * @param title The person's title
 * @returns A greeting formatted for human consumption.
 */
function greetFullTSDoc(name: string, title: string) {
  return `Hello ${title} ${name}`;
}
```

This lets editors show the relevant documentation for each parameter as you're writing out a function call (as shown in Figure 8-3). Only the documentation for the name parameter is shown here, not title.

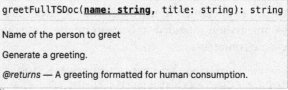

Figure 8-3. *An @param annotation lets your editor show documentation for the current parameter as you type it.*

You can also use TSDoc with type definitions:

```
/** A measurement performed at a time and place. */
interface Measurement {
  /** Where was the measurement made? */
  position: Vector3D;
  /** When was the measurement made? In seconds since epoch. */
  time: number;
  /** Observed momentum */
  momentum: Vector3D;
}
```

As you inspect individual fields in a Measurement object, you'll get contextual documentation (see Figure 8-4).

```
const m: Measurement = {

  (property) Measurement.time: number

  When was the measurement made? In seconds since epoch.

  time: (new Date().getTime()) / 1000,
  position: {x: 0, y: 0, z: 0},
  momentum: {x: 1, y: 2, z: 3},
};
```

Figure 8-4. *TSDoc for a field is shown when you mouse over that field in your editor.*

The documentation on individual fields is carried along through mapped types so long as they are "homomorphic" (see Item 15). This includes helper types such as `Partial` and `Pick`.

You can use the `@template` tag to document type parameters for generic types. Item 50 shows how this works.

TSDoc comments are formatted using Markdown, so if you want to use bold, italic, or bulleted lists, you can (see Figure 8-5).

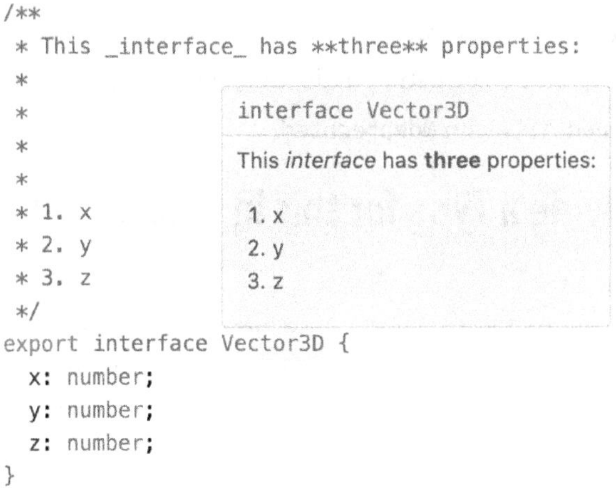

```
/**
 * This _interface_ has **three** properties:
 *
 *
 *
 *
 * 1. x
 * 2. y
 * 3. z
 */
export interface Vector3D {
  x: number;
  y: number;
  z: number;
}
```

interface Vector3D

This *interface* has **three** properties:

1. x
2. y
3. z

Figure 8-5. TSDoc comments can include Markdown formatting.

Try to avoid writing essays in your documentation, though. The best comments are short and to the point.

JSDoc includes some conventions for specifying type information (`@param {string} name ...`), but you should avoid these in favor of TypeScript types (Item 31).

Finally, you should mark deprecated symbols using the `@deprecated` tag. Not only does this provide a clear indication that a function is deprecated, it also enables the most aggressive TSDoc feature of all: `@deprecated` symbols are typically rendered using ~~strikethrough~~ text. This means you don't even need to inspect a symbol to know it's deprecated, as you can see in Figure 8-6.

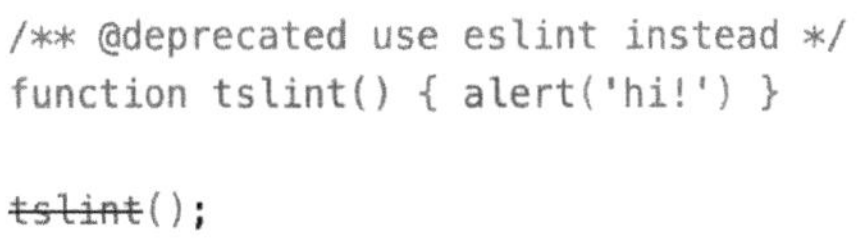

```
/** @deprecated use eslint instead */
function tslint() { alert('hi!') }

tslint();
```

Figure 8-6. Symbols marked with the @deprecated tag are struck through.

If you mark a method as deprecated, do your users a favor and say what the new alternative is. At the very least, include a reference to documentation on the deprecation.

Things to Remember

- Use JSDoc-/TSDoc-formatted comments to document exported functions, classes, and types. This helps editors surface information for your users when it's most relevant.
- Use @param, @returns, and Markdown for formatting.
- Avoid including type information in documentation (see Item 31).
- Mark deprecated APIs with @deprecated.

Item 69: Provide a Type for this in Callbacks if It's Part of Their API

JavaScript's this keyword is one of the most notoriously confusing parts of the language. Unlike variables declared with let or const, which are lexically scoped, this is dynamically scoped: its value depends not on where it appears in your code but on how you get there.

this is most often used in classes, where it typically references the current instance of an object:

```
class C {
  vals = [1, 2, 3];
  logSquares() {
    for (const val of this.vals) {
      console.log(val ** 2);
    }
  }
}

const c = new C();
c.logSquares();
```

This logs:

```
1
4
9
```

Now look what happens if you try to put `logSquares` in a variable and call that:

```
const c = new C();
const method = c.logSquares;
method();
```

This version throws an error at runtime:

```
        for (const val of this.vals) {
                        ^

TypeError: Cannot read properties of undefined (reading 'vals')
```

The problem is that `c.logSquares()` actually does two things: it calls `C.prototype.logSquares` *and* it binds the value of `this` in that function to `c`. By pulling out a reference to `logSquares`, you've separated these, and `this` gets set to `undefined`.

JavaScript gives you complete control over `this` binding. You can use `call` to explicitly set `this` and fix the problem:

```
const c = new C();
const method = c.logSquares;
method.call(c);  // Logs the squares again
```

There's no reason that `this` had to be bound to an instance of C. It could have been bound to anything. So libraries can, and do, make the value of `this` part of their APIs. Even the DOM does this in event handlers, for instance:

```
document.querySelector('input')?.addEventListener('change', function(e) {
  console.log(this);  // Logs the input element on which the event fired.
});
```

`this` binding often comes up in the context of callbacks like this one. If you want to define an `onClick` handler in a class, for example, you might try this:

```
class ResetButton {
  render() {
    return makeButton({text: 'Reset', onClick: this.onClick});
  }
  onClick() {
    alert(`Reset ${this}`);
  }
}
```

When a user clicks the button, it will alert with "Reset undefined." Oops! As usual, the culprit is `this` binding. A common solution is to create a bound version of the method in the constructor:

```
class ResetButton {
  constructor() {
    this.onClick = this.onClick.bind(this);
  }
```

```
    render() {
      return makeButton({text: 'Reset', onClick: this.onClick});
    }
    onClick() {
      alert(`Reset ${this}`);
    }
  }
```

The onClick() { ... } definition defines a property on ResetButton.prototype.
This is shared by all instances of ResetButton. When you bind this.onClick = ...
in the constructor, it creates a property called onClick on the instance of
ResetButton with this bound to that instance. The onClick instance property comes
before the onClick prototype property in the lookup sequence, so this.onClick
refers to the bound function in the render() method.

There is a shorthand for this binding that is extremely convenient:

```
  class ResetButton {
    render() {
      return makeButton({text: 'Reset', onClick: this.onClick});
    }
    onClick = () => {
      alert(`Reset ${this}`); // "this" refers to the ResetButton instance.
    }
  }
```

Here we've replaced onClick with an arrow function. This will define a new function
every time a ResetButton is constructed with this set to the appropriate value. It's
instructive to look at the generated JavaScript:

```
  class ResetButton {
    constructor() {
      this.onClick = () => {
        alert(`Reset ${this}`); // "this" refers to the ResetButton instance.
      };
    }
    render() {
      return makeButton({ text: 'Reset', onClick: this.onClick });
    }
  }
```

So what does this all have to do with TypeScript? Because this binding is part of
JavaScript, TypeScript models it. This means that if you're writing (or typing) a
library that sets the value of this on callbacks, then you should model it, too.

You can do so by adding a this parameter to your callback:

```
  function addKeyListener(
    el: HTMLElement,
    listener: (this: HTMLElement, e: KeyboardEvent) => void
  ) {
```

```
    el.addEventListener('keydown', e => listener.call(el, e));
  }
```

The this parameter is special: it's not just another positional argument. You can see this if you try to call it with two parameters:

```
function addKeyListener(
  el: HTMLElement,
  listener: (this: HTMLElement, e: KeyboardEvent) => void
) {
  el.addEventListener('keydown', e => {
    listener(el, e);
    //                 ~ Expected 1 arguments, but got 2
  });
}
```

Even better, TypeScript will enforce that you call the function with the correct this context:

```
function addKeyListener(
  el: HTMLElement,
  listener: (this: HTMLElement, e: KeyboardEvent) => void
) {
  el.addEventListener('keydown', e => {
    listener(e);
    // ~~~~~~~~ The 'this' context of type 'void' is not assignable
    //          to method's 'this' of type 'HTMLElement'
  });
}
```

As a user of this function, you can reference this in the callback and get full type safety:

```
declare let el: HTMLElement;
addKeyListener(el, function(e) {
  console.log(this.innerHTML);
  //          ^? this: HTMLElement
});
```

Of course, if you use an arrow function here, you'll override the value of this. Type-Script will catch the issue:

```
class Foo {
  registerHandler(el: HTMLElement) {
    addKeyListener(el, e => {
      console.log(this.innerHTML);
      //               ~~~~~~~~~ Property 'innerHTML' does not exist on 'Foo'
    });
  }
}
```

Don't forget about this! If you set the value of this in your callbacks, then it's part of your API, and you should include it in your type declarations.

If you're designing a new API, try not to use dynamic this binding. While it was historically popular, it has always been a source of confusion, and the prevalence of arrow functions makes this sort of API much harder to use in modern JavaScript.

Things to Remember

- Understand how this binding works.
- Provide a type for this in callbacks if it's part of your API.
- Avoid dynamic this binding in new APIs.

Item 70: Mirror Types to Sever Dependencies

Suppose you've written a library for parsing CSV files. Its API is simple: you pass in the contents of the CSV file and get back a list of objects mapping column names to values.

As a convenience for your Node.js users, you allow the contents to be either a string or a Node.js Buffer:

```
// parse-csv.ts
import {Buffer} from 'node:buffer';

function parseCSV(contents: string | Buffer): {[column: string]: string}[]  {
  if (typeof contents === 'object') {
    // It's a buffer
    return parseCSV(contents.toString('utf8'));
  }
  // ...
}
```

The type definition for Buffer comes from the Node.js type declarations, which you must install:

```
npm install --save-dev @types/node
```

Here we're following the advice of Item 65 by making @types dev dependencies rather than production dependencies.

When you publish your CSV parsing library, you generate type declarations using --declaration and bundle them with it. Here's what the generated *.d.ts* file looks like:

```
// parse-csv.d.ts
import { Buffer } from 'node:buffer';
export declare function parseCSV(contents: string | Buffer): {
    [column: string]: string;
}[];
```

If you take this approach, the JavaScript users of your library will be happy, but TypeScript web developers will not be. You'll get complaints from them that they're getting an error from your library:

```
Cannot find module 'node:buffer' or its corresponding type declarations.
```

Because we've made @types/node a devDependency, it's not installed with our package, even though our types, which are part of our package, depend on it.

So should we make @types/node a prod dependency? This will make the error go away, but now you're likely to get a different set of complaints:

- JavaScript developers will wonder what these @types modules are that they're depending on.
- TypeScript web developers will wonder why they're depending on Node.js.
- TypeScript developers using a different version of Node.js will wonder why they have duplicated type definitions.

These complaints are reasonable. The Buffer behavior isn't essential and is only relevant for users who are using Node.js already. And the declaration in @types/node is only relevant to Node.js users who are also using TypeScript. The @types/node package is not small (nearly 100k lines of code), and our library only uses a very tiny part of it.

TypeScript's structural typing (Item 4) can help you out of the jam. Rather than using the declaration of Buffer from @types/node, you can write your own with just the methods and properties you need. In this case that's just a toString method that can accept an encoding:

```
export interface CsvBuffer {
  toString(encoding?: string): string;
}
export function parseCSV(
  contents: string | CsvBuffer
): {[column: string]: string}[]  {
  // ...
}
```

This interface is dramatically shorter than the complete one, but it does capture our (simple) needs from a Buffer. In a Node.js project, calling parseCSV with a real Buffer is still OK because the types are compatible:

```
parseCSV(new Buffer("column1,column2\nval1,val2", "utf-8"));  // OK
```

Looking again at the `CsvBuffer` interface, there's nothing about it that's specific to CSV files. Giving it a more "structural" name can reinforce this:

```
/** Anything convertible to a string with an encoding, e.g. a Node buffer. */
export interface StringEncodable {
  toString(encoding?: string): string;
}
```

Since it's important that a Node `Buffer` is assignable to `StringEncodable` (the comment says as much!), you should write a unit test that verifies this:

```
import {Buffer} from 'node:buffer';
import {parseCSV} from './parse-csv';

test('parse CSV in a buffer', () => {
  expect(
    parseCSV(new Buffer("column1,column2\nval1,val2", "utf-8"))
  ).toEqual(
    [{column1: 'val1', column2: 'val2'}]
  );
});
```

This test verifies both the runtime behavior of your code and the assignability of a Node `Buffer` to `StringEncodable`. The test imports `node:buffer`, but that's fine because `@types/node` can be a `devDependency` without affecting users of your library.

If your code starts using more methods from the `Buffer` interface, then you'll need to add them to your version of this interface as well. This may feel duplicative but, as they say in the Go Language community, "a little copying is better than a little dependency." If you depend on a large portion of another library's types, you may choose to formalize this copying by vendoring the dependency.

In any case, by severing the `@types` dependency you get a good experience for JavaScript and all kinds of TypeScript developers. If the `@types` dependency had dependencies of its own, then you may sever an entire dependency tree, which can have a large positive impact on compiler performance (Item 78).

This technique is also helpful for severing dependencies between your unit tests and production systems. See the `getAuthors` example in Item 4.

Things to Remember

- Avoid transitive type dependencies in published npm modules.
- Use structural typing to sever dependencies that are nonessential.
- Don't force JavaScript users to depend on `@types`. Don't force web developers to depend on Node.js.

Item 71: Use Module Augmentation to Improve Types

JavaScript famously has some "bad parts," like implicit globals and type coercions. Most of these were design decisions made in the halcyon days of the mid-90s that have proven extremely hard to reverse.

TypeScript has a few historical warts of its own. One of these is the type declaration for JSON.parse, which returns any:

```
declare let apiResponse: string;

const response = JSON.parse(apiResponse);
const cacheExpirationTime = response.lastModified + 3600;
//      ^? const cacheExpirationTime: any
```

If you fail to give response a type, it will quietly spread any types throughout your code. As Item 5 explained, this will undermine type safety, thwart language services, and generally give you a poor experience with TypeScript.

It would be better if JSON.parse returned unknown which, as Item 46 explained, can be used as a type-safe alternative to any. So why doesn't it? It's because the unknown type was only introduced in TypeScript 3.0, which came out in July of 2018. Enormous amounts of TypeScript code had been written before then, and changing the return type of JSON.parse would have been extremely disruptive. So the TypeScript team made a concession to pragmatism. Future code will be a bit less safe, but existing code won't break.

But just because the TypeScript team decided to keep this type signature doesn't mean that you have to. Recall from Item 13 that interfaces have a special power that type aliases do not: they participate in "declaration merging," where repeated definitions of the same interface are merged to form a final result.

We can use this to change the type signature of JSON.parse. Here's what it looks like (in *lib.es5.d.ts*):

```
interface JSON {
  parse(
    text: string,
    reviver?: (this: any, key: string, value: any) => any
  ): any;
  // ...
}
declare var JSON: JSON;
```

We're interested in the interface. If you define your own interface JSON in a type declaration file in your project, TypeScript will merge it with the library declarations.

```
// declarations/safe-json.d.ts
interface JSON {
  parse(
```

```
    text: string,
    reviver?: (this: any, key: string, value: any) => any
): unknown;
}
```

Note the changed return type. The result is similar to a TypeScript function overload (Item 52). Since libs are loaded before our code, our overload will always win. The result is that JSON.parse now returns unknown:

```
const response = JSON.parse(apiResponse);
//    ^? const response: unknown
const cacheExpirationTime = response.lastModified + 3600;
//                          ~~~~~~~~ response is of type 'unknown'.
```

Using it requires a type assertion, which is exactly what you want:

```
interface ApiResponse {
  lastModified: number;
}
const response = JSON.parse(apiResponse) as ApiResponse;
const cacheExpirationTime = response.lastModified + 3600;  // ok
//    ^? const cacheExpirationTime: number
```

You can do something similar for the fetch API's Response.prototype.json(), which also returns any. Here's a fix:

```
// declarations/safe-response.d.ts
interface Body {
  json(): Promise<unknown>;
}
```

These changes were clear wins. But since you're only making changes that affect your own code, you're also free to make more controversial changes that would never fly in the broader TypeScript ecosystem.

For example, it's part of the language spec that the Set constructor can take a string. This results in something that might not be what you expect:

```
> new Set('abc')
Set(3) { 'a', 'b', 'c' }
```

If your intention was to create a one-element set containing 'abc', then this might introduce bugs in your code. Since the type of both would be Set<string>, and this is how JavaScript works, TypeScript can't help you catch this mistake.

But there's no reason you can't ban calling the Set constructor with a string in your own code. It's a little more difficult than changing the return type of JSON.parse, but it all comes back to declaration merging.

Here's the declaration of Set from *lib.es2015.collections.d.ts*:

```
interface Set<T> {
  add(value: T): this;
```

```
  delete(value: T): boolean;
  has(value: T): boolean;
  readonly size: number;
  // ...
}

interface SetConstructor {
  new <T = any>(values?: readonly T[] | null): Set<T>;
  readonly prototype: Set<any>;
}
declare var Set: SetConstructor;
```

There's also an overload of the constructor in *lib.es2015.iterable.d.ts*:

```
interface SetConstructor {
  new <T>(iterable?: Iterable<T> | null): Set<T>;
}
```

This is the one we'd like to "knock out." Here's how:

```
// declarations/ban-set-string-constructor.d.ts:
interface SetConstructor {
  new (str: string): void;
}
```

With this in place, constructing a Set with a string still won't produce a type error. But it will return void, so trying to do anything with the result will give you a clue that something is amiss:

```
const s = new Set('abc');
//    ^? const s: void
console.log(s.has('abc'));
//            ~~~ Property 'has' does not exist on type 'void'.
const otherSet: Set<string> = s;
//    ~~~~~~~~ Type 'void' is not assignable to type 'Set<string>'.
```

To give users a stronger hint what's going on, you could have the Set constructor return a string literal type containing an error. You can also mark this constructor @deprecated to make it appear struck-through in your user's editor (Item 68):

```
interface SetConstructor {
  /** @deprecated */
  new (str: string): 'Error! new Set(string) is banned.';
}

const s = new Set('abc');
//    ^? const s: "Error! new Set(string) is banned."
```

None of these is a perfect solution: it would be better if we produced a type error when you constructed the Set, rather than producing an unusable type. But that's not possible in TypeScript, and this is what real-world applications of this technique often wind up looking like.

Of course, with great power comes great responsibility. Here are a few things to be aware of:

- As with all type-level constructs, this only affects type checking. The runtime behavior of `JSON.parse` and the `Set` constructor are not affected, either in your own code or in library code.

- This technique is best used either to make the built-in types stricter and more precise, or to disallow certain things. If you add declarations that don't reflect reality at runtime, you can create a confusing situation. As Item 40 explained, incorrect types can be worse than no types.

- We "knocked out" the `Set` constructor by making it return `void` or an error string. But this won't work as well if you want to ban a function or `method` that already returns `void`.

We used declaration merging to improve built-in types, but the same technique can be used for third-party `@types` and bundled type declarations as well. You can find a collection of improvements to the built-in types in the `ts-reset` npm package.

Things to Remember

- Use declaration merging to improve existing APIs or disallow problematic constructs.
- Use `void` or error string returns to "knock out" methods and mark them `@deprecated`.
- Remember that overloads only apply at the type level. Don't make the types diverge from reality.

CHAPTER 9

Writing and Running Your Code

This chapter is a bit of a grab bag: it covers some issues that come up in writing code (not types) as well as issues you may run into when you run your code.

Item 72: Prefer ECMAScript Features to TypeScript Features

The relationship between TypeScript and JavaScript has changed over time. When Microsoft first started work on TypeScript in 2010, the prevailing attitude around JavaScript was that it was a problematic language that needed to be fixed. It was common for frameworks and source-to-source compilers to add missing features like classes, decorators, and a module system to JavaScript. TypeScript was no different. Early versions included home-grown versions of classes, enums, and modules.

Over time, TC39, the standards body that governs JavaScript, added many of these same features to the core JavaScript language. And the features they added were not compatible with the versions that existed in TypeScript. This left the TypeScript team in an awkward predicament: adopt the new features from the standard or maintain existing code?

TypeScript has largely chosen to do the former and eventually articulated its current governing principle: TC39 defines the runtime, while TypeScript innovates solely in the type space.

There are a few remaining features from before this decision. It's important to recognize and understand these, because they don't fit the pattern of the rest of the language. In general, I recommend avoiding them to keep the relationship between TypeScript and JavaScript as clear as possible. This will also ensure that your code is compatible with alternative TypeScript compilers and won't break as a result of future standards alignment.

If you follow this advice, you can think of TypeScript as "JavaScript with types."

Enums

Many languages model types that can take on a small set of values using *enumerations* or *enums*. TypeScript adds them to JavaScript:

```
enum Flavor {
  Vanilla = 0,
  Chocolate = 1,
  Strawberry = 2,
}

let flavor = Flavor.Chocolate;
//  ^? let flavor: Flavor

Flavor  // Autocomplete shows: Vanilla, Chocolate, Strawberry
Flavor[0]  // Value is "Vanilla"
```

The argument for enums is that they provide more safety and transparency than bare numbers. But enums in TypeScript have some quirks. There are actually several variants on enums that all have subtly different behaviors:

Number-valued enum (like Flavor*)*
> The number type is assignable to this, so it's not very safe. (It was designed this way to make bit flag structures possible.)

String-valued enum
> This does offer type safety, and also more informative values at runtime. But it's not structurally typed, unlike every other type in TypeScript (more on this momentarily).

const enum
> Unlike regular enums, const enums go away completely at runtime. If you changed to const enum Flavor in the previous example, the compiler would rewrite Flavor.Chocolate as 1. This also breaks our expectations around how the compiler behaves and still has the divergent behaviors between string and number-valued enums.

const enum *with the* preserveConstEnums *flag set*
> This emits runtime code for const enums, just like for a regular enum.

That string-valued enums are nominally typed comes as a particular surprise, since every other type in TypeScript uses structural typing for assignability (Item 4):

```
enum Flavor {
  Vanilla = 'vanilla',
  Chocolate = 'chocolate',
  Strawberry = 'strawberry',
}

let favoriteFlavor = Flavor.Chocolate;  // Type is Flavor
favoriteFlavor = 'strawberry';
// ~~~~~~~~~~~~ Type '"strawberry"' is not assignable to type 'Flavor'
```

This has implications when you publish a library. Suppose you have a function that takes a `Flavor`:

```
function scoop(flavor: Flavor) { /* ... */ }
```

Because a `Flavor` at runtime is really just a string, it's fine for your JavaScript users to call it with one:

```
scoop('vanilla');  // OK in JavaScript
```

but your TypeScript users will need to import the `enum` and use that instead:

```
scoop('vanilla');
//     ~~~~~~~~~ '"vanilla"' is not assignable to parameter of type 'Flavor'

import {Flavor} from 'ice-cream';
scoop(Flavor.Vanilla);  // OK
```

These divergent experiences for JavaScript and TypeScript users are a reason to avoid string-valued enums.

TypeScript offers an alternative to enums that is less common in other languages: a union of literal types.

```
type Flavor = 'vanilla' | 'chocolate' | 'strawberry';

let favoriteFlavor: Flavor = 'chocolate';  // OK
favoriteFlavor = 'americone dream';
// ~~~~~~~~~~~~ Type '"americone dream"' is not assignable to type 'Flavor'
```

This offers as much safety as the enum and has the advantage of translating more directly to JavaScript. It also provides autocomplete in your editor, as shown in Figure 9-1.

```
function scoop(flavor: Flavor) {
    if (flavor === 'v') {
    }              ⊟ vanilla
}
```

Figure 9-1. TypeScript offering autocomplete for a union of string literal types.

For more on unions of string literal types, see Item 35.

What about numeric enums, like our initial definition of Flavor? If you have the option, strongly consider using strings for your values instead. Numeric enums don't offer the safety you expect, and they're harder to work with than strings. Which would you rather see in your JavaScript debugger or in a network request, {"flavor": 1} or {"flavor": "chocolate"}?

Parameter Properties

It's common to assign constructor parameters to properties when initializing a class:

```
class Person {
  name: string;
  constructor(name: string) {
    this.name = name;
  }
}
```

TypeScript provides a more compact syntax for this:

```
class Person {
  constructor(public name: string) {}
}
```

This is called a "parameter property," and it is equivalent to the code in the first example. There are a few issues to be aware of with parameter properties:

- They are one of the few constructs that generate code when you compile to JavaScript (enums are another). Generally, compilation just involves erasing types.

- Because the parameter is only used in generated code, the source looks like it has unused parameters.

- A mix of parameter and nonparameter properties can hide the design of your classes.

For example:

```
class Person {
  first: string;
  last: string;
  constructor(public name: string) {
    [this.first, this.last] = name.split(' ');
  }
}
```

This class has three properties (first, last, name), but this is hard to read off the code because only two are listed before the constructor. This gets worse if the constructor takes other parameters, too.

If your class consists *only* of parameter properties and no methods, you might consider making it an `interface` and using object literals. Remember that the two are assignable to one another because of structural typing (Item 4):

```
class PersonClass {
  constructor(public name: string) {}
}
const p: PersonClass = { name: 'Jed Bartlet' };  // OK

interface Person {
  name: string;
}
const jed: Person = new PersonClass('Jed Bartlet');  // also OK
```

Opinions are divided on parameter properties. While I generally avoid them, others appreciate the saved keystrokes. Be aware that they do not fit the pattern of the rest of TypeScript, however, and may in fact obscure that pattern for new developers. Try to avoid hiding the design of your class behind a mix of parameter and nonparameter properties.

Namespaces and Triple-Slash Imports

Before ECMAScript 2015, JavaScript didn't have an official module system. Different environments added this missing feature in different ways: Node.js used `require` and `module.exports`, whereas in the browser, the AMD system used a `define` function with a callback.

TypeScript also filled this gap with its own module system. This was done using a `module` keyword and "triple-slash" imports. After ECMAScript 2015 added an official module system, TypeScript added `namespace` as a synonym for `module`, to avoid confusion:

```
// other.ts
namespace foo {
  export function bar() {}
}
// index.ts
/// <reference path="other.ts"/>
foo.bar();
```

Outside of type declaration files, triple-slash imports and the `module` keyword are just a historical curiosity. In your own code, you should use ECMAScript 2015-style modules (`import` and `export`).

experimentalDecorators

Decorators can be used to annotate or modify classes, methods, and properties. If a symbol is preceded by an @ sign, then it's a decorator. They're common in Angular and several other frameworks.

In 2015, TypeScript added support for a draft proposal of decorators in order to support Angular. This was gated behind the --experimentalDecorators flag.

Eight years later, in 2023, the decorators proposal reached stage 3 in a very different form. You can use standard decorators without any flags. Here's what an ECMAScript standard decorator looks like:

```
class Greeter {
  greeting: string;
  constructor(message: string) {
    this.greeting = message;
  }
  @logged  // <-- this is the decorator
  greet() {
    return `Hello, ${this.greeting}`;
  }
}

function logged(originalFn: any, context: ClassMethodDecoratorContext) {
  return function(this: any, ...args: any[]) {
    console.log(`Calling ${String(context.name)}`);
    return originalFn.call(this, ...args);
  };
}

console.log(new Greeter('Dave').greet());
// Logs:
// Calling greet
// Hello, Dave
```

You can tell which version of decorators you're using by checking for experimental Decorators in your *tsconfig.json*. If it's set, then you're using nonstandard decorators. If you're able to, turn this off! But you may be forced to keep this setting by a library or framework, at least until it adopts the latest standards.

If you are using experimentalDecorators, try not to dig the hole deeper by writing your own nonstandard decorators. You'll eventually have to migrate these to the standard version.

If you don't have this flag set, then feel free to write decorators to your heart's content. Just remember that decorators aren't the best solution to all problems and can sometimes make your code harder to follow. Try to avoid decorators that change a method's type signature, for example.

Member Visibility Modifiers (Private, Protected, and Public)

Historically, JavaScript lacked a way to make the properties and methods of a class private. The usual workaround was a convention that underscore-prefixed fields weren't part of a class's public API:

```
class Foo {
  _private = 'secret123';
}
```

But this only discourages users from accessing private data. It's easy to circumvent:

```
const f = new Foo();
f._private;  // 'secret123'
```

TypeScript adds public, protected, and private field visibility modifiers that seem to provide some enforcement:

```
class Diary {
  private secret = 'cheated on my English test';
}

const diary = new Diary();
diary.secret
//     ~~~~~~ Property 'secret' is private and only accessible within ... 'Diary'
```

But private is a feature of the type system and, as Item 3 explained, features of the type system all go away at runtime. Here's what this snippet looks like when TypeScript compiles it to JavaScript:

```
class Diary {
  constructor() {
    this.secret = 'cheated on my English test';
  }
}
const diary = new Diary();
diary.secret;
```

The private indicator is gone, and your secret is out! Much like the _private convention, TypeScript's visibility modifiers only discourage you from accessing private data. You can even access a private property from within TypeScript using a type assertion or iteration:

```
const diary = new Diary();
(diary as any).secret  // OK

console.log(Object.entries(diary));
// logs [["secret", "cheated on my English test"]]
```

ES2022 officially added support for private fields. Unlike TypeScript's `private`, ECMAScript's private is enforced both for type checking and at runtime. To use it, prefix your class property with a #:

```
class PasswordChecker {
  #passwordHash: number;

  constructor(passwordHash: number) {
    this.#passwordHash = passwordHash;
  }

  checkPassword(password: string) {
    return hash(password) === this.#passwordHash;
  }
}

const checker = new PasswordChecker(hash('s3cret'));
checker.#passwordHash
//      ~~~~~~~~~~~~ Property '#passwordHash' is not accessible outside class
//                   'PasswordChecker' because it has a private identifier.
checker.checkPassword('secret');  // Returns false
checker.checkPassword('s3cret');  // Returns true
```

The `#passwordHash` property is not accessible from outside the class and is not enumerable. Even for targets of that don't natively support private fields (ES2021 or earlier), there's a fallback implementation that will keep your data private. ECMAScript private fields are standard, widely supported, and more secure than TypeScript's `private`. You should use them instead.

What about `public` and `protected`? In JavaScript (and TypeScript), `public` is the default visibility so there's no need to annotate this explicitly. And while `private` implies encapsulation, `protected` implies inheritance. The general rule in object-oriented programming is to prefer composition over inheritance, so practical uses of `protected` are quite rare.

`readonly` as a field modifier is a type-level construct and is fine to use. See Item 14. A field may be both `#private` and `readonly`.

Things to Remember

- By and large, you can convert TypeScript to JavaScript by removing all the types from your code.
- Enums, parameter properties, triple-slash imports, experimental decorators, and member visibility modifiers are historical exceptions to this rule.
- To keep TypeScript's role in your codebase as clear as possible and to avoid future compatibility issues, avoid nonstandard features.

Item 73: Use Source Maps to Debug TypeScript

When you run TypeScript code, you're actually running the JavaScript that the Type-Script compiler generates. This is true of any source-to-source compiler, be it a minifier, a compiler, or a preprocessor. The hope is that this is mostly transparent, that you can pretend that the TypeScript source code is being executed without ever having to look at the JavaScript.

This works well until you have to debug your code. Debuggers generally work on the code you're executing and don't know about the translation process it went through. Since JavaScript is such a popular target language, browser vendors collaborated to solve this problem. The result is source maps. They map positions and symbols in a generated file back to the corresponding positions and symbols in the original source. Most browsers and many IDEs support them. If you're not using them to debug your TypeScript, you're missing out!

Suppose you've created a small script to add a button to an HTML page that increments every time you click it:

```
// index.ts
function addCounter(el: HTMLElement) {
  let clickCount = 0;
  const button = document.createElement('button');
  button.textContent = 'Click me';
  button.addEventListener('click', () => {
    clickCount++;
    button.textContent = `Click me (${clickCount})`;
  });
  el.appendChild(button);
}

addCounter(document.body);
```

If you load this in your browser and open the debugger, you'll see the generated Java-Script (here we're using a target of ES5). This closely matches the original source, so debugging isn't too difficult, as you can see in Figure 9-2.

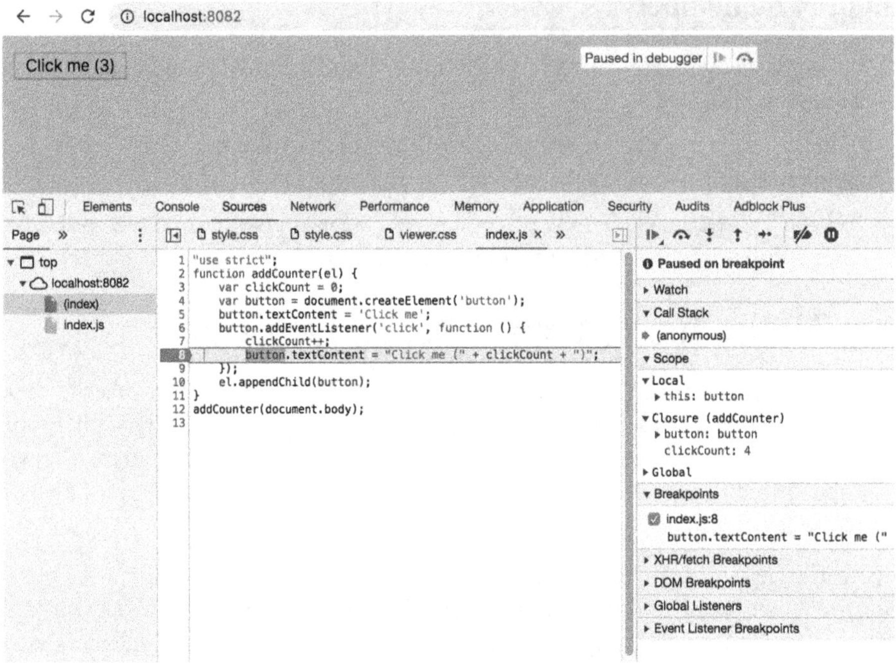

Figure 9-2. Debugging generated JavaScript using Chrome's developer tools. For this simple example, the generated JavaScript closely resembles the TypeScript source.

Let's make the page more fun by fetching an interesting fact about each number from *numbersapi.com*:

```
// index.ts
function addCounter(el: HTMLElement) {
  let clickCount = 0;
  const triviaEl = document.createElement('p');
  const button = document.createElement('button');
  button.textContent = 'Click me';
  button.addEventListener('click', async () => {
    clickCount++;
    const response = await fetch(`http://numbersapi.com/${clickCount}`);
    const trivia = await response.text();
    triviaEl.textContent = trivia;
    button.textContent = `Click me (${clickCount})`;
  });
  el.appendChild(triviaEl);
  el.appendChild(button);
}
```

If you click the button several times quickly, you may discover a race condition! If you open up your browser's debugger to investigate now, you'll see that the generated source has gotten dramatically more complicated (see Figure 9-3).

6 is the number of sides on a cube.

Click me (6)

| Elements | Console | Sources | Network | Performance | Memory | Application | Security | Audits | Adblock Plus |

Page »

▼ ☐ top
  ▼ ◯ localhost:8082
      (index)
      index.js

```
22            case 5: _.label++; y = op[1]; op = [0]; continue
23            case 7: op = _.ops.pop(); _.trys.pop(); continue
24            default:
25                if (!(t = _.trys, t = t.length > 0 && t[t.le
26                if (op[0] === 3 && (!t || (op[1] > t[0] && o
27                if (op[0] === 6 && _.label < t[1]) { _.label
28                if (t && _.label < t[2]) { _.label = t[2]; _
29                if (t[2]) _.ops.pop();
30                _.trys.pop(); continue;
31            }
32            op = body.call(thisArg, _);
33        } catch (e) { op = [6, e]; y = 0; } finally { f = t = 0;
34        if (op[0] & 5) throw op[1]; return { value: op[0] ? op[1
35    }
36 };
37 function addCounter(el) {
38     var _this = this;
39     var clickCount = 0;
40     var triviaEl = document.createElement('p');
41     var button = document.createElement('button');
42     button.textContent = 'Click me';
43     button.addEventListener('click', function () { return __awai
44         var response, trivia;
45         return __generator(this, function (_a) {
46             switch (_a.label) {
47                 case 0:
48                     clickCount++;
49                     return [4 /*yield*/, fetch("http://numbersap
50                 case 1:
51                     response = _a.sent();
52                     return [4 /*yield*/, response.text()];
53                 case 2:
54                     trivia = _a.sent();
55                     triviaEl.textContent = trivia;
56                     button.textContent = "Click me (" + clickCou
57                     return [2 /*return*/];
58             }
59         });
60 
```

{} Line 8, Column 8

Figure 9-3. The TypeScript compiler has generated JavaScript that doesn't closely resemble the original TypeScript source. This will make debugging more difficult.

To support `async` and `await` in older browsers, TypeScript has rewritten the event handler as a state machine. This has the same behavior, but the code no longer bears such a close resemblance to the original source. This is where source maps can help. To tell TypeScript to generate one, set the `sourceMap` option in your *tsconfig.json*:

```
{
  "compilerOptions": {
    "sourceMap": true
  }
}
```

Now when you run `tsc`, it generates two output files for each *.ts* file: a *.js* file and a *.js.map* file. The latter is the source map. With this file in place, a new *index.ts* file appears in your browser's debugger. You can set breakpoints and inspect variables in it, just as you'd hope (see Figure 9-4).

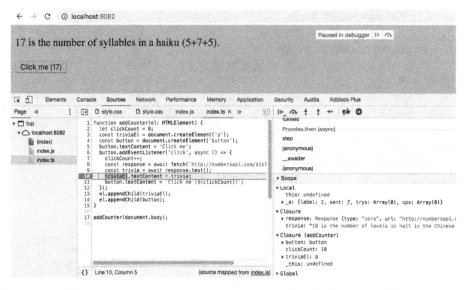

Figure 9-4. When a source map is present, you can work with the original TypeScript source in your debugger, rather than the generated JavaScript.

Note that *index.ts* appears in italics in the file list on the left. This indicates that it isn't a "real" file in the sense that the web page included it. Rather, it was included via the source map. Depending on your settings, *index.js.map* will contain either a reference to *index.ts* (in which case the browser loads it over the network) or an inline copy of it (in which case no request is needed).

There are a few things to be aware of with source maps:

- If you are using a bundler or minifier with TypeScript, it may generate a source map of its own. To get the best debugging experience, you want this to map all the way back to the original TypeScript sources, not the generated JavaScript. If your bundler has built-in support for TypeScript, then this should just work. If not, you may need to hunt down some flags to make it read source map inputs.

- Be aware of whether you're serving source maps in production. If your JS file has a reference to the source map, then the browser will only load it when the debugger is open, so there's no performance impact for end users. (Inline source maps are always downloaded, so you should avoid them in production.) If your source map contains a copy of your original source code, then there may be content that you didn't intend to publicize. Does the world really need to see your snarky comments or internal bug tracker URLs?

You can also debug Node.js programs using source maps. This is typically done via your editor or by connecting to your Node process from a browser's debugger. Here's some code written in TypeScript that's intended to be run in Node.js:

```
// bedtime.ts
async function sleep(ms: number) {
  return new Promise<void>(resolve => setTimeout(resolve, ms));
}

async function main() {
  console.log('Good night!');
  await sleep(1000);
  console.log('Morning already!?');
}

main();
```

(The void in Promise<void> indicates that sleep doesn't resolve to a usable value, similar to returning void from a function.)

To debug this, compile it to JavaScript with sourceMap set in your *tsconfig.json*. Then run it with node using the --inspect-brk flag:

```
$ tsc bedtime.ts
$ node --inspect-brk bedtime.js
Debugger listening on ws://127.0.0.1:9229/587c380b-fdb4-48df-8c09-a83f36d8a2e7
For help, see: https://nodejs.org/en/docs/inspector
```

Now you can open your browser to debug. In Chrome, for example, you navigate to *chrome://inspect*. You should see a remote target that you can "Inspect," as shown in Figure 9-5.

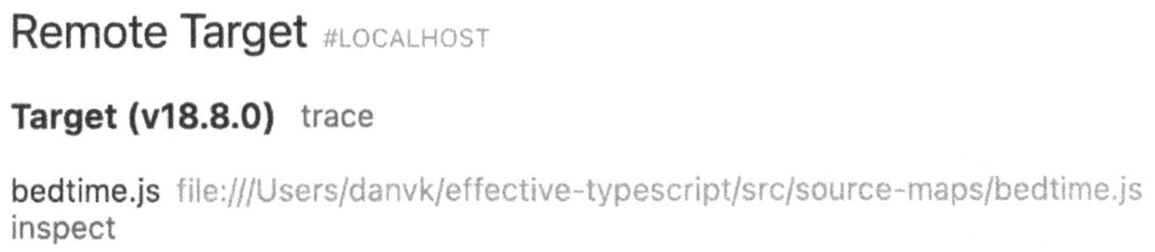

Remote Target #LOCALHOST

Target (v18.8.0) trace

bedtime.js file:///Users/danvk/effective-typescript/src/source-maps/bedtime.js
inspect

Figure 9-5. Selecting a remote debug target to inspect in Google Chrome (chrome:// inspect).

Once you connect, you'll see the usual browser dev tools with the generated Java-Script, as shown in Figure 9-6 (here we're using a target of ES2015).

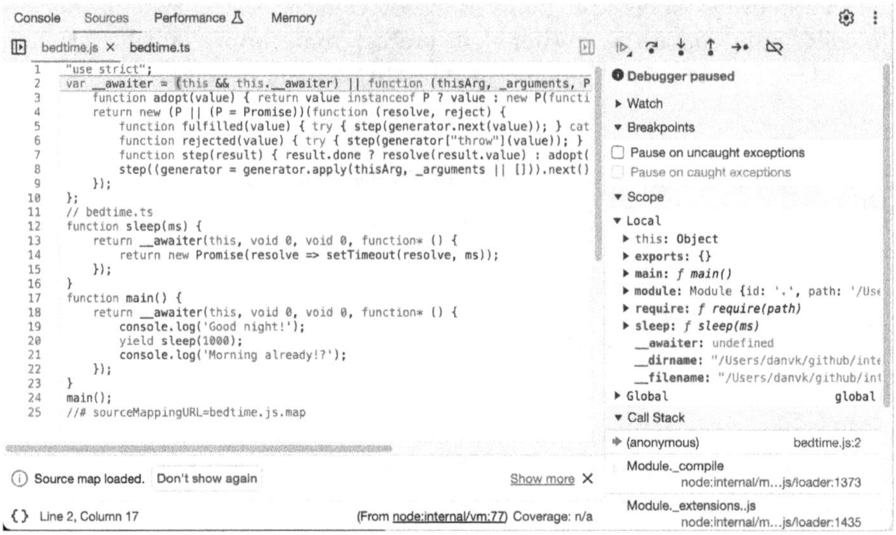

Figure 9-6. Generated JavaScript for a Node.js program in Google Chrome Devtools. Note the source map reference at the bottom.

In addition to opening a websocket running the remote debugging protocol, the `--inspect-brk` flag pauses execution of your code at the very beginning. This is convenient for switching over to the TypeScript view and setting up breakpoints in the original source, as shown in Figure 9-7.

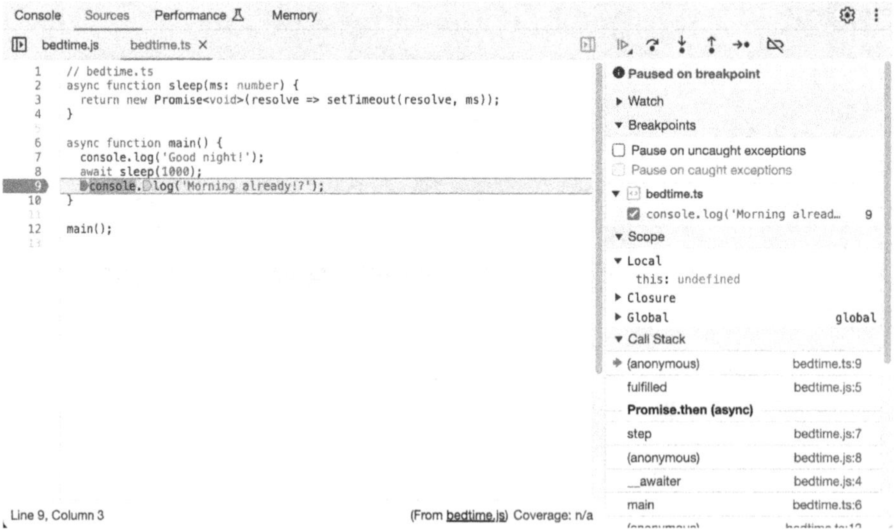

Figure 9-7. Debugging the original TypeScript source for a Node.js program.

JavaScript's `debugger` statement is another convenient way to set a breakpoint exactly where you want.

If you generate *.d.ts* files for your project (by setting the `declaration` option), Type-Script can also generate *.d.ts.map* files that map your type declarations back to the original source. You enable this by setting `declarationMap`. This can be useful for improving languages services like "Go to Definition" in your editor, particularly if you're using project references (Item 78).

The type checker can catch many errors before you run your code, but it is no substitute for a good debugger. Use source maps to get a great TypeScript debugging experience.

Things to Remember

- Don't debug generated JavaScript. Use source maps to debug your TypeScript code at runtime.
- Make sure that your source maps are mapped all the way through to the code that you run.
- Know how to debug Node.js code written in TypeScript.
- Depending on your settings, your source maps might contain an inline copy of your original code. Don't publish them unless you know what you're doing!

Item 74: Know How to Reconstruct Types at Runtime

At some point in the process of learning TypeScript, most developers have an epiphany when they realize that TypeScript types aren't "real": they're erased at runtime (Item 3). This might be accompanied by a feeling of dread: if the types aren't real, how can you trust them?

The independence of types from runtime behavior is a key part of the relationship between TypeScript and JavaScript (Item 1). And most of the time this system works very well. But there are undeniably times when it would be extremely convenient to have access to TypeScript types at runtime. This item explores how this situation might arise and what your options are.

Imagine you're implementing a web server and you define an API endpoint for creating a comment on a blog post (we saw this API before in Item 42). You define a Type-Script type for the request body:

```
interface CreateComment {
  postId: string;
  title: string;
  body: string;
}
```

Your request handler should validate the request. Some of this validation will be at the application level (does `postId` reference a post that exists and that the user can comment on?), but some will be at the type level (does the request have all the properties we expect, are they of the right type, and are there any extra properties?).

Here's what that might look like:

```
app.post('/comment', (request, response) => {
  const {body} = request;
  if (
    !body ||
    typeof body !== 'object' ||
    Object.keys(body).length !== 3 ||
    !('postId' in body) || typeof body.postId !== 'string' ||
    !('title' in body) || typeof body.title !== 'string' ||
    !('body' in body) || typeof body.body !== 'string'
  ) {
    return response.status(400).send('Invalid request');
  }
  const comment = body as CreateComment;
  // ... application validation and logic ...
  return response.status(200).send('ok');
});
```

This is already a lot of validation code, even with just three properties. Worse, there's nothing to ensure that the checks are accurate and in sync with our type. Nothing checks that we spelled the properties correctly. And if we add a new property, we'll need to remember to add a check, too.

This is code duplication at its worst. We have two things (a type and validation logic) that need to stay in sync. It would be better if there was a single source of truth. The `interface` seems like the natural source of truth, but it's erased at runtime so it's unclear how you'd use it in this way.

Let's look at a few possible solutions to this conundrum.

Generate the Types from Another Source

If your API is specified in some other form, perhaps using GraphQL or an OpenAPI schema, then you can use that as the source of truth and generate your TypeScript types from it.

This typically involves running an external tool to generate types and, possibly, validation code. An OpenAPI spec uses JSON Schema, for example, so you can use a tool like `json-schema-to-typescript` to generate the TypeScript types, and a JSON Schema validator such as `Ajv` to validate requests.

The downside of this approach is that it adds some complexity and a build step that must be run whenever your API schema changes. But if you're already specifying your API using OpenAPI or some other system, then this has the enormous advantage of not introducing any new sources of truth, and this is the approach that you should prefer.

If this is a good fit for your situation, then Item 42 includes an example of generating TypeScript types from a schema.

Define Types with a Runtime Library

TypeScript's design makes it impossible to derive runtime values from static types. But going the other direction (from a runtime value to a static type) is straightforward using the type-level `typeof` operator:

```
const val = { postId: '123', title: 'First', body: 'That is all'};
type ValType = typeof val;
//   ^? type ValType = { postId: string; title: string; body: string; }
```

So one option is to define your types using runtime constructs and derive the static types from those. This is typically done using a library. There are many of these, but at the moment the most popular is Zod (React's `PropTypes` is another example).

Here's how the request validation logic would look with Zod:

```
import { z } from 'zod';

// runtime value for type validation
const createCommentSchema = z.object({
  postId: z.string(),
  title: z.string(),
  body: z.string(),
});

// static type
type CreateComment = z.infer<typeof createCommentSchema>;
//   ^? type CreateComment = { postId: string; title: string; body: string; }

app.post('/comment', (request, response) => {
  const {body} = request;
  try {
    const comment = createCommentSchema.parse(body);
    //   ^? const comment: { postId: string; title: string; body: string; }
    // ... application validation and logic ...
    return response.status(200).send('ok');
  } catch (e) {
    return response.status(400).send('Invalid request');
  }
});
```

Zod has completely eliminated the duplication: the value `createCommentSchema` is now the source of truth, and both the static type `CreateComment` and the schema validation (`createCommentSchema.parse`) are derived from that.

Zod and the other runtime type libraries are quite effective at solving this problem. So what are the downsides to using them?

- You now have two ways to define types: Zod's syntax (`z.object`) and TypeScript's (`interface`). While these systems have many similarities, they're not exactly the same. You're already using TypeScript, so presumably your team has committed to learning how to define types using it. Now everyone needs to learn to use Zod as well.

- Runtime type systems tend to be contagious: if `createCommentSchema` needs to reference another type, then that type will also need to be reworked into a runtime type. This may make it hard to interoperate with other sources of types, for example, if you wanted to reference a type from an external library or generate some types from your database (Item 58).

Having a distinct runtime type validation system comes with a few other advantages, too:

- Libraries like Zod can express many constraints that are hard to capture with TypeScript types, for example, "a valid email address" or "an integer." If you don't use a tool like Zod, you'll have to write this sort of validation yourself.

- There's no additional build step. Everything is done through TypeScript. If you expect your schema to change frequently, then this will eliminate a failure mode and tighten your iteration cycle.

Generate Runtime Values from Your Types

If you're willing to introduce a new tool and build step, then there's another possibility: you can reverse the approach from the previous section and generate a runtime value from your TypeScript type. JSON Schema is a popular target.

To make this work we'll put our API types in an *api.ts* file:

```
// api.ts
export interface CreateComment {
  postId: string;
  title: string;
  body: string;
}
```

then we can run `typescript-json-schema` to generate JSON Schema for this type:

```
$ npx typescript-json-schema api.ts '*' > api.schema.json
```

Here's what that file looks like:

```
{
  "$schema": "http://json-schema.org/draft-07/schema#",
  "definitions": {
```

```
      "CreateComment": {
        "type": "object",
        "properties": {
          "body": { "type": "string" },
          "postId": { "type": "string" },
          "title": { "type": "string" }
        }
      }
    }
  }
```

Now we can load *api.schema.json* at runtime. If you enable TypeScript's resolveJson Module option, this can be done with an ordinary import. You can perform validation using any JSON Schema validation library. Here we use the Ajv library:

```
import Ajv from 'ajv';

import apiSchema from './api.schema.json';
import {CreateComment} from './api';

const ajv = new Ajv();

app.post('/comment', (request, response) => {
  const {body} = request;
  if (!ajv.validate(apiSchema.definitions.CreateComment, body)) {
    return response.status(400).send('Invalid request');
  }
  const comment = body as CreateComment;
  // ... application validation and logic ...
  return response.status(200).send('ok');
});
```

The great strength of generating values from your TypeScript types is that you can continue to use all the TypeScript tools you know and love to define your types. You don't need to learn a second way to define types since the JSON Schema is an implementation detail. Your API types can reference types from @types or other sources since they're just TypeScript types.

The downside is that you've introduced a new tool and a new build step. Whenever you change *api.ts*, you'll need to regenerate *api.schema.json*. In practice, you'd want to enforce that these stay in sync using your continuous integration system.

While you don't typically need to access TypeScript types at runtime, there are occasionally situations like input validation where it's extremely useful. We've seen three approaches to this problem. So which one should you choose?

Unfortunately, there's no perfect answer. Each option is a trade-off. If your types are already expressed in some other form, like an OpenAPI schema, then use that as the source of truth for both your types and your validation logic. This will incur some tooling and process overhead, but it's worth it to have a single source of truth.

If not, then the decision is trickier. Would you rather introduce a build step or a second way to define types? If you need to reference types that are only defined using TypeScript types (perhaps they're coming from a library or are generated), then generating JSON Schema from your TypeScript types is the best option. Otherwise, you need to pick your poison!

Things to Remember

- TypeScript types are erased before your code is run. You can't access them at runtime without additional tooling.
- Know your options for runtime types: using a distinct runtime type system (such as Zod), generating TypeScript types from values (`json-schema-to-typescript`), and generating values from your TypeScript types (`typescript-json-schema`).
- If you have another specification for your types (e.g., a schema), use that as the source of truth.
- If you need to reference external TypeScript types, use `typescript-json-schema` or an equivalent.
- Otherwise, weigh whether you prefer another build step or another system for specifying types.

Item 75: Understand the DOM Hierarchy

Most of the items in this book are agnostic about where you run your TypeScript: in a web browser, on a server, or on a phone. This one is different. If you're not working in a browser, skip ahead to Item 76!

The DOM hierarchy is always present when you're running JavaScript in a web browser. When you use `document.getElementById` to get an element, or `document.createElement` to create one, it's always a particular kind of element, even if you're not entirely familiar with the taxonomy. You call the methods and use the properties that you want and hope for the best.

With TypeScript, the hierarchy of DOM elements becomes more visible. Knowing your `Nodes` from your `Elements` and `EventTargets` will help you debug type errors and decide when type assertions are appropriate. Because so many APIs are based on the DOM, this is relevant even if you're using a framework like React or D3.

Suppose you want to track a user's mouse as they drag it across a `<div>`. You write some seemingly innocuous JavaScript:

```
function handleDrag(eDown) {
  const targetEl = eDown.currentTarget;
  targetEl.classList.add('dragging');
  const dragStart = [eDown.clientX, eDown.clientY];
```

```
    const handleUp = (eUp) => {
      targetEl.classList.remove('dragging');
      targetEl.removeEventListener('mouseup', handleUp);
      const dragEnd = [eUp.clientX, eUp.clientY];
      console.log('dx, dy = ', [0, 1].map(i => dragEnd[i] - dragStart[i]));
    }
    targetEl.addEventListener('mouseup', handleUp);
  }
  const surfaceEl = document.getElementById('surface');
  surfaceEl.addEventListener('mousedown', handleDrag);
```

When you add type annotations and run the type checker, it flags no fewer than 11 errors in these 14 lines of code:

```
function handleDrag(eDown: Event) {
  const targetEl = eDown.currentTarget;
  targetEl.classList.add('dragging');
  // ~~~~~              'targetEl' is possibly 'null'
  //        ~~~~~~~~~ Property 'classList' does not exist on type 'EventTarget'
  const dragStart = [
    eDown.clientX, eDown.clientY
    //    ~~~~~~~            ~~~~~~~ Property '...' does not exist on 'Event'
  ];
  const handleUp = (eUp: Event) => {
    targetEl.classList.remove('dragging');
    // ~~~~~              'targetEl' is possibly 'null'
    //        ~~~~~~~~~ Property 'classList' does not exist on type 'EventTarget'
    targetEl.removeEventListener('mouseup', handleUp);
    // ~~~~~ 'targetEl' is possibly 'null'
    const dragEnd = [
      eUp.clientX, eUp.clientY
      //  ~~~~~~~        ~~~~~~~   Property '...' does not exist on 'Event'
    ];
    console.log('dx, dy = ', [0, 1].map(i => dragEnd[i] - dragStart[i]));
  }
  targetEl.addEventListener('mouseup', handleUp);
  // ~~~~~ 'targetEl' is possibly 'null'
}

const surfaceEl = document.getElementById('surface');
surfaceEl.addEventListener('mousedown', handleDrag);
// ~~~~~~ 'surfaceEl' is possibly 'null'
```

What went wrong? What's this EventTarget? And why might everything be null?

To understand the EventTarget errors, it helps to dig into the DOM hierarchy a bit. Here's some HTML:

```
<p id="quote">and <i>yet</i> it moves</p>
```

If you open your browser's JavaScript console and get a reference to the p element, you'll see that it's an HTMLParagraphElement:

```
const p = document.getElementsByTagName('p')[0];
p instanceof HTMLParagraphElement
// true
```

An `HTMLParagraphElement` is a subtype of `HTMLElement`, which is a subtype of `Element`, which is a subtype of `Node`, which is a subtype of `EventTarget`. Note that these are all JavaScript runtime values, not just TypeScript types. Table 9-1 lists some examples of types along the hierarchy.

Table 9-1. Types in the DOM hierarchy

Type	Examples
EventTarget	window, XMLHttpRequest
Node	document, Text, Comment
Element	HTMLElements, SVGElements
HTMLElement	<i>, <b>
HTMLButtonElement	<button>

An `EventTarget` is the most general of all DOM types. All you can do with it is add event listeners, remove them, and dispatch events. With this in mind, the `classList` errors start to make a bit more sense:

```
function handleDrag(eDown: Event) {
  const targetEl = eDown.currentTarget;
  targetEl.classList.add('dragging');
  // ~~~~~          'targetEl' is possibly 'null'
  //       ~~~~~~~~~ Property 'classList' does not exist on type 'EventTarget'
  // ...
}
```

As its name implies, an `Event`'s `currentTarget` property is an `EventTarget`. It could even be `null`. TypeScript has no reason to believe that it has a `classList` property. While `currentTarget` may be an `HTMLElement` in practice, from the type system's perspective there's no reason it couldn't be `window` or an `XMLHttpRequest`. (current Target is the element you registered the listener on, while `target` is the element where the event originated, which could have a different type.)

Moving up the hierarchy we come to `Node`. `Node`s that are not `Element`s include text fragments and comments. For instance, in this HTML:

```
<p>
  And <i>yet</i> it moves
  <!-- quote from Galileo -->
</p>
```

the outermost element is an `HTMLParagraphElement`. As you can see here, it has `children` and `childNodes`:

```
> p.children
HTMLCollection [i]
> p.childNodes
NodeList(5) [text, i, text, comment, text]
```

children returns an HTMLCollection, an array-like structure containing just the child Elements (<i>yet</i>). childNodes returns a NodeList, an array-like collection of Nodes. This includes not just Elements (<i>yet</i>) but also text fragments ("And," "it moves") and comments ("quote from Galileo"). (See Item 17 for a refresher on what "array-like" means.) You can use array spread syntax ([...p.childNodes]) to get a true array if you need one.

What's the difference between an Element and an HTMLElement? There are non-HTML Elements including the whole hierarchy of SVG tags. These are SVGElements, which are another type of Element. What's the type of an <html> or <svg> tag? They're HTMLHtmlElement and SVGSVGElement. If you don't use SVG or MathML then, in practice, all your Elements will be HTMLElements.

Sometimes specialized Element classes will have properties of their own—for example, an HTMLImageElement has a src property, and an HTMLInputElement has a value property. If you want to read one of these properties off a value, its type must be specific enough to have that property.

TypeScript's type declarations for the DOM make liberal use of literal types to try to get you the most specific type possible. For example:

```
const p = document.getElementsByTagName('p')[0];
//    ^? const p: HTMLParagraphElement
const button = document.createElement('button');
//    ^? const button: HTMLButtonElement
const div = document.querySelector('div');
//    ^? const div: HTMLDivElement | null
```

But this is not always possible, notably with document.getElementById:

```
const div = document.getElementById('my-div');
//    ^? const div: HTMLElement | null
```

While type assertions are generally frowned upon (Item 9 explains why), this is a case where you know more than TypeScript does and so they are appropriate. There's nothing wrong with this assertion, so long as you know that #my-div is a div:

```
document.getElementById('my-div') as HTMLDivElement;
```

A runtime check will do the trick if you don't know:

```
const div = document.getElementById('my-div');
if (div instanceof HTMLDivElement) {
  console.log(div);
  //          ^? const div: HTMLDivElement
}
```

(Item 54 explores another way to get more precise types for HTMLElements.)

With strictNullChecks enabled, you'll need to consider the case that document.getElementById returns null. Depending on whether this can really happen, you can either add an if statement or a non-null assertion (!):

```
const div = document.getElementById('my-div')!;
//    ^? const div: HTMLElement
```

These types are not specific to TypeScript. Rather, they are generated from the formal specification of the DOM. This is an example of the advice of Item 42 to generate types from specs when possible.

So much for the DOM hierarchy. What about the clientX and clientY errors?

```
function handleDrag(eDown: Event) {
  // ...
  const dragStart = [
    eDown.clientX, eDown.clientY
    //     ~~~~~~~         ~~~~~~~ Property '...' does not exist on 'Event'
  ];
  // ...
}
```

In addition to the hierarchy for Nodes and Elements, there is also a hierarchy for Events. TypeScript's *lib.dom.d.ts* defines no fewer than 54 subtypes of Event!

Plain Event is the most generic type of event. More specific types include:

UIEvent
> Any sort of user interface event

MouseEvent
> An event triggered by the mouse, such as a click

TouchEvent
> A touch event on a mobile device

KeyboardEvent
> A key press

The problem in handleDrag is that the events are declared as Event, while clientX and clientY exist only on the more specific MouseEvent type.

So how can you fix the example from the start of this item? Item 24 explained how TypeScript makes use of context to infer more precise types, and the DOM declarations make extensive use of this. Inlining the mousedown handler gives TypeScript more context and removes most of the errors. You can also declare the parameter type to be MouseEvent rather than Event.

Here's a complete version of the code sample from the start of this item that passes the type checker:

```
function addDragHandler(el: HTMLElement) {
  el.addEventListener('mousedown', eDown => {
    const dragStart = [eDown.clientX, eDown.clientY];
    const handleUp = (eUp: MouseEvent) => {
      el.classList.remove('dragging');
      el.removeEventListener('mouseup', handleUp);
      const dragEnd = [eUp.clientX, eUp.clientY];
      console.log('dx, dy = ', [0, 1].map(i => dragEnd[i] - dragStart[i]));
    }
    el.addEventListener('mouseup', handleUp);
  });
}

const surfaceEl = document.getElementById('surface');
if (surfaceEl) {
  addDragHandler(surfaceEl);
}
```

The `if` statement at the end handles the possibility that there is no `#surface` element. If you know that this element exists, you could use a non-null assertion instead (`surfaceEl!`). `addDragHandler` requires a non-null `HTMLElement`, following Item 33's advice to push `null` values to the perimeter.

Things to Remember

- The DOM has a type hierarchy that you can usually ignore while writing Java-Script. But these types become more important in TypeScript. Understanding them will help you write TypeScript for the browser.

- Know the differences between `Node`, `Element`, `HTMLElement`, and `EventTarget`, as well as those between `Event` and `MouseEvent`.

- Either use a specific enough type for DOM elements and Events in your code or give TypeScript the context to infer it.

Item 76: Create an Accurate Model of Your Environment

As Item 3 explained, your TypeScript code will eventually get converted to JavaScript and executed. More specifically, it will be executed by a particular runtime (V8, JavaScriptCore, SpiderMonkey) in a particular environment (a web page in a browser, a test runner in Node.js, Deno, Electron, etc.).

For TypeScript to statically model the runtime behavior of your code, it needs a model of that environment. One of your main goals in configuring a TypeScript project is to ensure that this model is as accurate as possible. The more accurately you model your runtime environment, the more effective TypeScript will be at finding errors in your code.

For example, your generated JavaScript might run in a browser where it's included in an HTML page:

```
<script src="path/to/bundle.js"></script>
```

TypeScript gives you a few ways to model this. One is via the `lib` setting in your *tsconfig.json*:

```
{
  "compilerOptions": {
    "lib": ["dom", "es2021"]
  }
}
```

By including `"dom"` in `"lib"`, we tell TypeScript that it should include type declarations for a browser. The `"es2021"` indicates that we expect the browser to have built-in support for everything in the JavaScript standard from that year (either natively or via a polyfill). Using a feature from a newer version (for example, `array.toSorted()`) will result in a type error. You may not know precisely which features are in each ECMAScript version, but TypeScript does. By creating an accurate model of your environment, it can help you catch this particular mistake.

You can also model the types available in a web browser by installing the `@types/web` package, which gives you a bit more control over versioning. Item 75 has much more to say about TypeScript and the DOM.

It's likely that your script tag isn't the only one on your page. Perhaps your HTML actually looks like this:

```
<script type="text/javascript">
window.userInfo = { name: 'Jane Doe', accountId: '123-abc' };
</script>
<script src="https://code.jquery.com/jquery-3.7.1.min.js"></script>
<script type="text/javascript">
// ... load Google Analytics ...
</script>
<script src="path/to/bundle.js"></script>
```

Each of those `<script>` tags modifies the environment in some way, adding global variables that are available to your code. To ensure accurate type checking, you'll need to tell TypeScript about them.

You can model the `userInfo` global with a type declaration file:

```
// user-info-global.d.ts
interface UserInfo {
  name: string;
  accountId: string;
```

```
  }
  declare global {
    interface Window {
      userInfo: UserInfo;
    }
  }
```

See Item 47 for more on more on the `Window` syntax here.

You can model the libraries by installing their type declarations:

```
$ npm install --save-dev @types/google.analytics @types/jquery
```

To get an accurate model, it's essential that the `@types` package models the version of the library that you source on your page. See Item 66 for more on how to match these up. If you get this wrong, TypeScript may report spurious errors or miss some real ones.

Perhaps you're bundling your code using webpack, which lets you import CSS and image files directly from JavaScript. These files are part of the environment, but TypeScript doesn't know about them and will complain:

```
import sunrisePath from './images/beautiful-sunrise.jpg';
//                         ~~~~~~~~~~~~~~~~~~~~~~~~~~~~~~~~
// Cannot find module './images/beautiful-sunrise.jpg' or its type declarations.
```

To make this work, you need to model these types of imports:

```
// webpack-imports.d.ts
declare module '*.jpg' {
  const src: string;
  export default src;
}
```

webpack actually lets you import specific CSS rules from CSS modules. If you use this feature, you'll need to either add it to your model or install one of the npm packages that does this for you.

It's possible that different parts of your application run in different environments. For example, your app might have client code that runs in a browser and server code that runs under Node.js, not to mention test code that runs in its own environment. Since these are distinct environments, you'll want to model them separately. The usual way to do this is with multiple *tsconfig.json* files and project references, which are discussed in Item 78.

As with the browser, make sure you model the Node.js environment accurately. If you run your code using Node.js version 20, make sure you install that version of `@types/node`. This will ensure that you only use the library features that are available to you at runtime.

Things to Remember

- Your code runs in a particular environment. TypeScript will do a better job of checking your code if you create an accurate static model of that environment.
- Model global variables and libraries that are loaded onto a web page along with your code.
- Match versions between type declarations and the libraries and runtime environment that you use.
- Use multiple *tsconfig.json* files and project references to model distinct environments within a single project (for example client and server).

Item 77: Understand the Relationship Between Type Checking and Unit Testing

You sometimes hear claims that adopting TypeScript lets you delete most of your unit tests. Or, flipping the argument around, that there's no point in adding types to your code since you'll still need to write unit tests.

These are both extreme positions, but there is an interesting distinction hiding behind the bluster. Unit tests and type checking are both forms of program verification. So what's the relationship between the two? When should you write tests, and when should you rely on types?

Let's consider a function that adds two numbers:

```
/** Returns the sum of the two numbers. */
function add(a, b) {
  // implementation omitted
}
```

If this seems too simple to test, then take a quick look at the IEEE 754 floating point spec. There are quite a few corner cases! Here's what a unit test might look like:

```
test('add', () => {
  expect(add(0, 0)).toEqual(0);
  expect(add(123, 456)).toEqual(579);
  expect(add(-100, 90)).toEqual(-10);
});
```

Assuming these tests pass, how confident should we be in the correctness of the add function? There are an enormous number of possible inputs. Numbers in JavaScript are 64-bit floats, so there are 2^{64} possible values for each parameter, or 2^{128} possible inputs in total. That's an enormous number: it starts with 3 and is followed by 38 more digits. Our three test cases only cover an infinitesimal fraction of the possibilities.

These gaps create space for bugs to creep in. For example, what if this were the implementation?

```
function add(a, b) {
  if (isNaN(a) || isNaN(b)) {
    return 'Not a number!';
  }
  return (a|0) + (b|0);
}
```

This passes our unit test. But the behavior with NaN values is surprising and probably misguided (it should certainly be called out in the documentation!). The effect of the bitwise operations is to round the inputs toward zero before adding them. Presumably, the function should add nonintegers, too. Unless we specifically wrote unit tests for these cases, we wouldn't be able to catch these bugs.

Now let's see what happens if you add types:

```
function add(a: number, b: number): number {
  if (isNaN(a) || isNaN(b)) {
    return 'Not a number!';
    // ~~~ Type 'string' is not assignable to type 'number'.
  }
  return (a|0) + (b|0);
}
```

Thanks to our type annotations, TypeScript has been able to spot one of the bugs. There are whole classes of implementation errors that it can prevent: returning the wrong type or performing invalid operations on the inputs. You could write a unit test to check that add returns a number, but you'd never be able to test this for all 2^{128} possible inputs. TypeScript has.

Of course, there are many mistakes that the type checker can't catch. It doesn't catch the issue with decimals versus integers. In fact, here's another implementation that passes the type checker but is clearly wrong:

```
function add(a: number, b: number): number {
  return a - b; // oops!
}
```

Any unit test where b is non-zero would catch this bug, but the type checker is blind to it.

Unit tests and type checking are complementary processes. Unit tests demonstrate that your code behaves correctly in at least some situations. In other words, they provide a lower bound on correctness. A type checker can prove that you haven't made a particular class of errors, say returning the wrong type. It provides an upper bound on incorrectness. You can think of the two processes as whittling away at the bugs from both ends until you're satisfied that your code works well enough.

Regardless of what the documentation or types say, in JavaScript, functions can be called with any type of argument. In addition to adding numbers, the simple version of the add function (return a+b) has the following behavior:

```
> add(null, null)
0
> add(null, 12)
12
> add(undefined, null)
NaN
> add('ab', 'cd')
'abcd'
```

Should you test these behaviors? TypeScript is unhappy if you do:

```
test('out-of-domain add', () => {
  expect(add(null, null)).toEqual(0);
  //        ~~~~ Type 'null' is not assignable to parameter of type 'number'.
  expect(add(null, 12)).toEqual(12);
  //        ~~~~ Type 'null' is not assignable to parameter of type 'number'.
  expect(add(undefined, null)).toBe(NaN);
  //        ~~~~~~~~~ Type 'undefined' is not assignable to parameter of ...
  expect(add('ab', 'cd')).toEqual('abcd');
  //        ~~~~ Type 'string' is not assignable to parameter of type 'number'.
});
```

This makes sense. Unit tests are about demonstrating expected behavior. For invalid inputs, there is no expected behavior to demonstrate. You should rely on the type checker to prevent these invalid calls. There's no need to write these sorts of unit tests.

There's an important caveat to this for functions that have potentially harmful side effects. Imagine you have a function that updates a user record in a database:

```
interface User {
  id: string;
  name: string;
  memberSince: string;
}

declare function updateUserById(
  id: string,
  update: Partial<Omit<User, 'id'>> & {id?: never}
): Promise<User>;
```

The intention of the elaborate type on the update parameter is that this function really shouldn't be used to change a user's ID. (Item 63 explains the "optional never" trick.) Doing so might cause a collision or even a security issue if it allows one user to impersonate another. But this is only enforced at the type level. If you call this function from JavaScript, perhaps even with untrusted user input, then it's entirely possible that the update argument will have an id property. It would be better if the function threw an exception (i.e., rejected) rather than corrupting the database.

This is a good behavior to specify and test, even if it's disallowed by the types. You can use an @ts-expect-error directive in your test to assert that it's a type error:

```
test('invalid update', () => {
  // @ts-expect-error Can't call updateUserById to update an ID.
  expect(() => updateUserById('123', {id: '234'})).toReject();
});
```

One of the main goals in software quality assurance (QA) is to find problems as soon as possible, when the cost of fixing them is low. The worst way to learn about a bug is to have an end user (or a security researcher!) report it when it's already in production. Better, but still expensive, is to catch it as part of a manual QA process. Better yet is an automated QA process, say an integration test. Unit tests catch bugs even earlier and more quickly. But type checking is the most immediate of all, reporting bugs right in your editor, hopefully in the exact place that you made a mistake.

To catch bugs as quickly as possible, you should rely on the type checker where you can. TypeScript can catch many errors, but sometimes it requires a bit of help. Items 59, 61, and 64 all present techniques for helping the type checker catch new classes of errors. But when you can't rely on type checking, namely for testing behaviors, unit tests are the next best option.

If your types themselves contain logic (Chapter 6 is all about this), then you absolutely need to write tests for them. Type tests are a different sort of test than unit tests. Item 55 explores the fascinating world of type testing.

Finally, while both types and unit tests will help catch bugs when you refactor, types also power the language services that make programming a more enjoyable experience. As Item 6 explained, they can even do the refactoring for you!

Unit tests and type checking are both forms of program verification, but they work in different and complementary ways. You typically want both. Keep their respective roles clear and avoid repeating the same checks with both.

Things to Remember

- Type checking and unit testing are different, complementary techniques for demonstrating program correctness. You want both.
- Unit tests demonstrate correct behavior on particular inputs, while type checking eliminates whole classes of incorrect behaviors.
- Rely on the type checker to check types. Write unit tests for behaviors that can't be checked with types.
- Avoid testing inputs that would be type errors unless there are concerns about security or data corruption.

Item 78: Pay Attention to Compiler Performance

As Item 3 explained, TypeScript types are erased when you compile your code to JavaScript. So generally speaking, TypeScript has zero impact on the runtime performance of your code.

TypeScript *can* have an impact on the performance of your developer tooling, however. TypeScript comes with two executables, `tsc` and `tsserver` (Item 6). It makes sense to talk about the performance of both of them:

`tsc`, *the TypeScript compiler*
Slow performance here means that your code will take longer to type check as part of a batch process (perhaps on your CI system) and will take longer to produce build artifacts (*.js* and *.d.ts* files).

`tsserver`, *the TypeScript Language Service*
Slow performance here means that your editor might feel sluggish or unresponsive. It may take a frustratingly long time for errors to appear or disappear after you change your code.

If build or editor performance becomes a problem on your project, there are many techniques available that might help. This item will look at a few of the most impactful. For each it will say which type of performance it impacts.

Separate Type Checking from Building

This only affects `tsc` (build) performance, not `tsserver` (editor).

At a high level, TypeScript does two things: it checks your code for type errors and it emits JavaScript. The type checking is typically the more CPU intensive of the two. If you don't need the type checking, then skipping this step can be a huge time saver.

At first blush, this may sound like a strange thing to do. Isn't type checking the whole point of using TypeScript instead of JavaScript? In practice, though, you may be running TypeScript indirectly via some other tool, perhaps a bundler (`webpack`, `vite`, etc.) or `ts-node`. By default, these tools will type check your code and then bundle or run the generated JavaScript. But they don't *need* to do this. You can tell any of them to run in "transpile only" mode to skip the checking.

This can make a noticeable difference even for trivial programs:

```
// hello.ts
console.log('Hello World!');
```

Here's how quickly this runs with and without type checking using `ts-node`:

```
$ time ts-node --transpileOnly hello.ts
Hello World!
```

```
ts-node --transpileOnly hello.ts  0.12s user 0.02s system 110% cpu 0.123 total
$ time ts-node hello.ts
Hello World!
ts-node hello.ts  1.60s user 0.08s system 255% cpu 0.656 total
```

This trivial program took 1.6 seconds to run with type checking but only 0.12 seconds without. If ts-node or a bundler is part of your toolchain, turning off type checking can significantly tighten your iteration cycle and improve your developer experience (DX). You may even be able to plug in an alternative TypeScript compiler, such as swc, to get a bigger speedup.

Of course, type checking is still important! You'll still get type errors as you develop code in your editor (via tsserver), and you should make sure to run tsc on your CI service to make sure you only commit code that passes the type checker.

Prune Unused Dependencies and Dead Code

This affects both build and editor performance.

The less code you have, the faster TypeScript can process it. Fewer types and symbols also means lower RAM usage by tsserver, which will make your editor more responsive.

One good way to shrink your project is via dead code elimination. If you set the noU nusedLocals flag, TypeScript will detect some unused code and types:

```
function foo() {}
//       ~~~ 'foo' is declared but its value is never read.

export function bar() {}
```

This works well for un-exported symbols. But an exported symbol might be unused, too, if it's never imported anywhere. To detect that, you'll need a more sophisticated tool like knip. This will also report unused third-party dependencies (e.g., node modules). Removing these can be a huge win since their type declarations may be many thousands of lines.

In fact, it's likely that the majority of the types in your project come from third-party code. You can run tsc --listFiles to get a printout of all the sources that go into your TypeScript project:

```
$ tsc --listFiles
.../lib/node_modules/typescript/lib/lib.es5.d.ts
.../lib/node_modules/typescript/lib/lib.es2015.d.ts
.../lib/node_modules/typescript/lib/lib.es2016.d.ts
.../lib/node_modules/typescript/lib/lib.es2017.d.ts
...
```

The results may surprise you! Sometimes one dependency can pull in hundreds or thousands of others (Item 70 describes a way to avoid this). A good way to visualize this is with a treemap. Since `tsc` will spend more time on a large file than a small file, you'll want to visualize the number of bytes in each file being compiled.

Here's the magic incantation (the `stat` syntax may vary depending on your platform):

```
$ tsc --noEmit --listFiles | xargs stat -f "%z %N" | npx webtreemap-cli
```

For one of the author's projects, the results looked like Figure 9-8.

```
ts (109.7m)
node_modules (102.9m)
googleapis/build/src (80.5m)
apis (80.5m)
```

| compute (18.4m) | | | dialogflow (4.5m) | | dfareporting | | healthca | content | securit | retail | displ | visio |

| alpha.d.ts (6.1m) | beta.d.ts (5.4m) | v1.d.ts (4.9m) | v2.d.ts (1.4m) | v2beta1.d.t (1.4m) | v3.4.d.ts (1.2m) v3.5.d.ts (1.1m) | (1.5m) | (1.5m) | (1.2m) | (1.1m) | (997. | (915 |

v3beta1.d.t (873.8k) | v3 d.ts (870.9k) | v3.3.d.ts (1.1m)

| container (906.4k) | logging (863.2k) | dataproc (817.4k) | videointell (790.5k) | gkehub (753.9k) | dns (751.7k) | cloudres (715.6k) | drive (711.3k) | documer (693.3k) | cloudass (691.1k) | jobs (679.1k) | admin (673.4k) | containe (672.6k) | manage (670.6k) | tagman (639.4k) | dlp (630.5k) | datacati (616.6k) | deployn (612.7k) | youtube (595.0k) |

| cloudbuil (580.2k) | appengi (564.4k) | sqladmin (557.3k) | run (556.9k) | vmmigra (552.0k) | storage (535.3k) | monitor (501.6k) | private (499.2k) | analyti (485.7k) | dosconfi (464.9k) | cloudid (463.8k) | networ (436.1k) | artifac (416.4k) | games (415.8k) | recom (415.1k) | firesto (412.7k) | cloudti (411.5k) | domai (408.3k) | datap (395.1k) | adexc (394.9k) | metas (390.4k) | spann (388.2k) | cloud (367.8k) | analyt (381.4 |

| pubsut (379.0k) | androi (368.5k) | remote (364.1k) | bigqu (356.5k) | service (354.0k) | servic (351.5k) | adexc (350.2k) | datast (349.5k) | datafi (343.0k) | class (341.3k) | datam (332.1k) | androi (330.4k) | datala (325.1k) | netwo (322.7k) | iam (316.4k) | servic (314. | cloud (313 | prod. (308 | sasp (306.(| capi (304.(| ga (297.(| adse (295 | ml (294.(| gmail (285.(| cloud (284.(| bigqu (283.(| notet (281.(| trans (281.(| netw (280.(| shee |

| @types (5.0m) | | | @octokit (3.5m) | | @material-ui (3.4m) | | @emotion | @elastic | @google- (942.5k) | puppete (801.2k) | csstyp (700.9 | google gax |

| jquery (1.0m) | node (712.6k) | lodash (441.7k) | p5 (420.5 | openapi- types/types.d.t (1.5m) | core (1.2m) | plugii rest- endp(math | styles (1.5m) | system (1.5m) | serialize (1.5m) | elasticsea (1.2m) | cloud (1.0m) | | |

Figure 9-8. Treemap of the files that TypeScript considers, weighted by file size.

This is a lot of code: nearly 110 MB! And most of it is evidently Google APIs? Many of these were APIs (compute, dialogflow, dfareporting, healthcare) that my project did not use. As it turned out, Google bundled all 300+ of its APIs as a single package, weighing in at an impressive 80.5 MB. My project depended on only one or two APIs, but this design meant that it still pulled in all three hundred of them.

In this case, updating to a newer version of googleapis fixed the issue since they added support for depending on just one API. If a dependency is particularly large, you may want to look into alternatives. You may also notice that you're pulling in multiple versions of the same library. The solution is to update versions until your dependencies align (Item 66).

Regardless of the actions you take, the treemap visualization will make you more aware of what you're building and put you on the scent of potential issues. Before looking at my treemap, I hadn't thought much about my project's use of googleapis. Afterwards, I couldn't think of much else!

Incremental Builds and Project References

These only affect build (`tsc`) performance.

If you run `tsc` twice in a row, it will repeat all its work on the second invocation. But if you set the `incremental` option, it will do something smarter: on the first invocation, it will write a `.tsbuildinfo` file that saves some of the work it's done. On the second invocation, it will read that file and use it to check your types more quickly.

TypeScript lets you take this incremental approach a step further with "Project references." The idea here is that if your code base has distinct parts (say client/server or source/test), then changes to one should have a limited effect on the other. In particular, if you change the implementation of a function in your source (but not its type signature), then TypeScript shouldn't have to redo type checking for your tests. And no change to the tests should require TypeScript to redo type checking for your source.

To set up project references, you create a *tsconfig.json* file for each distinct part of your repo. These files say which other parts of your code they can reference. Your tests will reference your source, but not the other way around. You also typically have a top-level *tsconfig.json* for shared configuration. Here's what the setup might look like:

```
root
├── src
│   ├── fib.ts
│   └── tsconfig.json
├── test
│   ├── fib.test.ts
│   └── tsconfig.json
├── tsconfig-base.json
└── tsconfig.json
```

Here's what these files look like:

```
// tsconfig-base.json
{
  "compilerOptions": {
    // other settings
    "declaration": true,
    "composite": true
  }
}
// tsconfig.json
{
  "files": [],
  "references": [
    { "path": "./src" },
    { "path": "./test" }
```

```
    ]
  }
  // src/tsconfig.json
  {
    "extends": "../tsconfig-base.json",
    "compilerOptions": {
      "outDir": "../dist/src",
      "rootDir": "."
    }
  }
  // src/fib.ts
  export function fib(n: number): number {
    if (n < 2) {
      return n;
    }
    return fib(n - 1) + fib(n - 2);
  }

  // test/tsconfig.json
  {
    "extends": "../tsconfig-base.json",
    "compilerOptions": {
      "outDir": "../dist/test",
      "rootDir": "."
    },
    "references": [
      { "path": "../src" }
    ]
  }
  // test/fib.test.ts
  import {fib} from '../src/fib';

  describe('fib', () => {
    it('should handle base cases', () => {
      expect(fib(0)).toEqual(0);
      expect(fib(1)).toEqual(1);
    })

    it('should handle larger numbers', () => {
      expect(fib(2)).toEqual(1);
      expect(fib(3)).toEqual(2);
      expect(fib(4)).toEqual(3);
      expect(fib(5)).toEqual(5);
      expect(fib(16)).toEqual(987);
    });
  });
```

That's a lot of configuration! Here are the interesting bits:

- The src and test *tsconfig.json* inherit a shared base configuration that sets composite and declaration (to output *.d.ts* files).

- The top-level *tsconfig.json* consists only of a list of references to subprojects.

- The `test` *tsconfig.json* references `src` but not the other way around.

With this setup in place, you can run `tsc` with the `-b` / `--build` flag to make it act as a sort of build coordinator. After a first run, if you make a change to *src/fib.ts* that does not affect the API, you'll see something like this:

```
$ tsc -b -v
Project 'src/tsconfig.json' is out of date because output
  'dist/src/tsconfig.tsbuildinfo' is older than input 'src/fib.ts'
Building project 'src/tsconfig.json'...
Project 'test/tsconfig.json' is up to date with .d.ts files from its
  dependencies
```

The last line is the important one. Our change didn't affect the *.d.ts* files (it was an implementation change, not an API change), so the test project didn't need to be rebuilt.

There are a few caveats to be aware of with project references:

- In order for them to be useful, you must have `declaration` set, so that `tsc` outputs *.d.ts* files on disk. If you use `noEmit` or run `tsc` via `webpack`, `vite`, or some other tool, then project references won't help you.

- Project references are most useful in large monorepos. The general rule of thumb is that they're helpful primarily if you have more first-party code than third-party code (i.e., more lines of your own code than in node modules). This is rarely the case for small- to medium-sized projects, but it's often the case at large corporations.

- While creating a small number of projects can speed up your interactions with TypeScript, creating too many can do the opposite. Try to scope projects to large chunks of your code. Creating distinct projects for `src` and `test`, or `client` and `server`, will be a win on large apps. But creating a separate project for each of your thousand UI components will create organizational overhead and is unlikely to improve TypeScript performance.

Simplify Your Types

This affects both build and editor performance.

Suppose you want to create a type to represent a year. Item 29 encouraged you to craft types that can only represent valid states, so you craft a type that should hold up for the rest of the millennium:

```
type Digit = '0' | '1' | '2' | '3' | '4' | '5' | '6' | '7' | '8' | '9';
type Year = `2${Digit}${Digit}${Digit}`;
const validYear: Year = '2024';
```

```
const invalidYear: Year = '1999';
//    ~~~~~~~~~~ Type '"1999"' is not assignable to type
//                '"2000" | "2001" | "2002" | ... 996 more ... | "2999"'.
```

While it's interesting that we can represent this type using TypeScript's type system, it may not be wise. The error hints at why: the Year type is a union with a thousand elements! Every time TypeScript has to do something with this type, it will have to check all of these. This is likely to make tsc and tsserver sluggish. Better to use something simpler like a string or a number, or even a branded type (Item 64) if you want to model this distinctly.

This is an extreme example, but enormous unions do sometimes arise, and you should be aware that they can be a performance problem. Other ways to make your types more efficient include:

- Extend interfaces rather than intersecting type aliases. Item 13 goes into great detail about the similarities and differences between type and interface. Usually they are interchangeable. But for subtyping, TypeScript is able to operate more efficiently with extends.

- Annotating return types. Item 18 discusses the pros and cons of adding type annotations, but providing explicit annotations on the return type of functions can save TypeScript work in inferring the type.

You should be particularly careful if you're writing complex recursive types. Item 57 goes into more detail about how to keep these from blowing up.

Things to Remember

- There are two forms of TypeScript performance issues: build performance (tsc) and editor latency (tsserver). Recognize the symptoms of each and direct your optimizations accordingly.

- Keep type checking separate from your build process.

- Remove dead code and dependencies, and be on guard for code bloat in type dependencies. Use a treemap to visualize what TypeScript is compiling.

- Use incremental builds and project references to reduce the work tsc does between builds.

- Simplify your types: avoid large unions, use interface extension rather than intersection types, and consider annotating function return types.

CHAPTER 10

Modernization and Migration

You've heard that TypeScript is great. You also know from painful experience that maintaining your 15-year-old, 100,000-line JavaScript library isn't. If only it could become a TypeScript library!

This chapter offers some advice about migrating your JavaScript project to TypeScript without losing your sanity or abandoning the effort.

The less code you have, the easier it will be to migrate. So it's a good idea to remove deprecated features and do a round of dead code elimination before you start a Type-Script migration. You may want to hold off on other forms of modernization, however: converting a jQuery web app to React will actually be much easier once you've adopted TypeScript.

Only the smallest codebases can be migrated in one fell swoop. The key for larger projects is to migrate gradually. Item 81 discusses how to do this. For a long migration, it's essential to track your progress and make sure you don't backslide. This creates a sense of momentum and inevitability to the change. Item 82 discusses ways to do this.

Migrating a large project to TypeScript won't necessarily be easy, but it does offer a huge potential upside. A 2017 study found that 15% of bugs fixed in JavaScript projects on GitHub could have been prevented with TypeScript.[1] Even more impressive, a survey of 6 months' worth of postmortems at Airbnb found that 38% of them could have been prevented by TypeScript.[2] If you're advocating for TypeScript at your organization, stats like these will help! So will running some experiments and finding

---

1 Z. Gao, C. Bird, and E. T. Barr, "To Type or Not to Type: Quantifying Detectable Bugs in JavaScript" (*https://oreil.ly/4RFfl*), ICSE 2017.

2 Brie Bunge, "Adopting TypeScript at Scale" (*https://oreil.ly/i-L60*), JSConf Hawaii 2019.

---

early adopters. Item 80 discusses how to experiment with TypeScript before you begin migration.

Since this chapter is largely about JavaScript, many of the code samples are either pure JavaScript (and not expected to pass the type checker) or checked with looser settings (e.g., with `noImplicitAny` off). We'll make occasional reference to the author's dygraphs charting library in this chapter as an example of legacy code in need of modernization and migration. dygraphs is a venerable old JavaScript library that saw its most active period of development from 2009–2016.

Item 79: Write Modern JavaScript

In addition to checking your code for type safety, TypeScript compiles it to any version of JavaScript, all the way back to 2009 vintage ES5. Since TypeScript is a superset of the *latest* version of JavaScript, this means that you can use `tsc` as a "transpiler": something that takes new JavaScript and converts it to older, more widely supported JavaScript.

Taking a different perspective, this means that when you decide to convert an existing JavaScript codebase to TypeScript, there's no downside to adopting all the latest JavaScript features. In fact, there's quite a bit of upside: because TypeScript is designed to work with modern JavaScript, modernizing your JS is a great first step toward adopting TypeScript.

And because TypeScript is a superset of JavaScript, learning to write more modern and idiomatic JavaScript means you're learning to write better TypeScript, too.

This item presents some of the highlights of modern JavaScript, which I'm defining here as everything introduced in ES2015 (aka ES6) and after. This material is covered in much greater detail in other books and online. If any of the topics mentioned here are unfamiliar, you owe it to yourself to learn more about them. TypeScript can be tremendously helpful when you're learning a new language feature like `async`/`await`: it almost certainly understands the feature better than you do and can guide you toward correct usage.

These features are all worth understanding, but by far the most important for adopting TypeScript are ECMAScript modules and ES2015 classes. We'll look at those first and then quickly list some of the other highlights. If your project is already using these features, then count your blessings! Your migration will be much easier.

Use ECMAScript Modules

Before the 2015 version of ECMAScript (ES) there was no standard way to break your code into separate modules. There were many solutions, from multiple `<script>` tags, manual concatenation, and Makefiles, to Node.js-style `require` statements or AMD-style `define` callbacks. TypeScript even had its own module system (Item 72).

Today there is one standard: ECMAScript modules, aka `import` and `export`. If your JavaScript codebase is still a single file, if you use concatenation or one of the other module systems, it's time to switch to ES modules. This may require setting up a tool like webpack or ts-node. TypeScript works best with ES modules, and adopting them will facilitate your transition, not least because it will allow you to migrate modules one at a time (see Item 82).

The details will vary depending on your setup, but if you're using CommonJS like this:

```
// CommonJS
// a.js
const b = require('./b');
console.log(b.name);

// b.js
const name = 'Module B';
module.exports = {name};
```

then the ES module equivalent would look like:

```
// ECMAScript module
// a.ts
import * as b from './b';
console.log(b.name);

// b.ts
export const name = 'Module B';
```

You can adopt ES modules in your TypeScript without adopting them in the generated JavaScript, which may be a more difficult change. If you set the `module` option to `"commonjs"` in your *tsconfig.json*, for example, TypeScript would compile the second code sample to the first one.

Use Classes Instead of Prototypes

JavaScript has a flexible prototype-based object model. But by and large, JS developers have ignored this in favor of a more rigid class-based model. This was officially codified in the language with the introduction of the `class` keyword in ES2015.

If your code uses prototypes in a straightforward way, switch to using classes. That is, instead of:

```
function Person(first, last) {
  this.first = first;
  this.last = last;
}
```

```
Person.prototype.getName = function() {
  return this.first + ' ' + this.last;
}

const marie = new Person('Marie', 'Curie');
console.log(marie.getName());
```

write:

```
class Person {
  constructor(first, last) {
    this.first = first;
    this.last = last;
  }

  getName() {
    return this.first + ' ' + this.last;
  }
}

const marie = new Person('Marie', 'Curie');
console.log(marie.getName());
```

TypeScript struggles with the prototype version of `Person` but understands the class-based version with minimal annotations. If you're unfamiliar with the syntax, TypeScript will help you get it right.

For code that uses older-style classes, the TypeScript language service offers a "Convert function to an ES2015 class" quick fix that can speed this up (Figure 10-1).

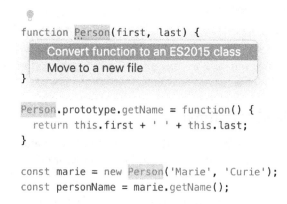

Figure 10-1. The TypeScript language service offers a quick fix to convert older-style classes to ES2015 classes.

Other Features

Adopting ES2015 modules and classes will have the greatest impact on facilitating your code's migration to TypeScript. But there are many other new features of Java-Script: a new version comes out every year! Having at least a passing familiarity with them will help you write more succinct and idiomatic JavaScript, and hence Type-Script. If any of the features in this list aren't familiar to you, do some Googling to learn more. Even just knowing the name of the feature can be helpful.

- Use `let` and `const` instead of `var` to declare variables. The reason is that `var` has some quirky scoping rules. If you're curious to learn more about them, read *Effective JavaScript*. But better to avoid `var` and not worry!

- Use `for-of` or array methods like `map` instead of C-style `for(;;)` loops. The three-part C-style `for` loop introduces an index variable that you may not otherwise need, is easier to get wrong, and doesn't adapt as well to iterators (as described in Item 17). See Item 60 for more on how to iterate over objects in TypeScript.

- Use `async` and `await` for asynchronous functions instead of callbacks or raw Promises. This is covered in detail in Item 27.

- Prefer arrow functions to function expressions because they're more concise and they preserve the `this` value from their surrounding context. Item 69 explains `this` binding.

- Use default parameter values. Traditionally you'd set default values on function parameters in the implementation, but in modern JavaScript you can put the default value directly in the declaration (`function foo(param=123) {}`). In TypeScript this has the added advantage that it allows the parameter's type to be inferred from the default value.

- Use compact object literals and destructuring assignment. Rather than writing `{x: x}`, you can just write `{x}`. This encourages consistent naming of variables. Conversely you can write `[x, y] = pair` to unpack values from an array (or object). This works particularly well with TypeScript tuple types.

- Use `Map` and `Set` instead of objects for associative arrays. If you've ever tried to read the string `"constructor"` or `"prototype"` off of an object, you'll know why. The ES2015 containers avoid the many problems that stem from JavaScript's conflation of objects and associative arrays.

- Use optional chaining to facilitate working with nullable values. Rather than writing x `&&` x.y, you can just write x?.y. You can also use this to conditionally call a function that could be `undefined`: `fn.?()`. But, as Items 33 and 37 explain, better still to avoid `null` values altogether.

- Use "nullish coalescing" (??) to fill in default values instead of ||. If x is 0, then x || 10 evaluates to 10, whereas x ?? 10 will be 0. Conflating truthiness and null-ishness is a common source of bugs. You generally want to check for null, and ?? helps you do that.

- Don't bother with "use strict". This enables "strict mode," an ES5 (2009) innovation that opts you into a less error-prone variant of the language. TypeScript is more strict than strict mode. It will even include "use strict" in its output JS when you're in module mode (i.e., import and export) to keep you in strict mode at runtime. In other words, putting "use strict" in your TypeScript source has no effect.

These are just a few of the many new JavaScript features that TypeScript lets you use. TC39, the body that governs JS standards, is very active, and new features are added year to year. The TypeScript team is currently committed to implementing any feature that reaches stage 3 (out of 4) in the standardization process, so you don't even have to wait for the ink to dry. Check out the TC39 GitHub repo (*https://oreil.ly/ OT8Uu*) for the latest. As of this writing, the Pipeline, Records, and Tuples proposals in particular have great potential to impact TypeScript.

Things to Remember

- TypeScript lets you write modern JavaScript whatever your runtime environment. Take advantage of this by using the language features it enables. In addition to improving your codebase, this will help TypeScript understand your code.

- Adopt ES modules (import/export) and classes to facilitate your migration to TypeScript.

- Use TypeScript to learn about language features like classes, destructuring, and async/await.

- Check the TC39 GitHub repo and TypeScript release notes to learn about all the latest language features.

Item 80: Use @ts-check and JSDoc to Experiment with TypeScript

Before you begin the process of converting your source files from JavaScript to Type-Script (Item 81), you may want to experiment with type checking to get an initial read on the sorts of issues that will come up. TypeScript's @ts-check directive lets you do exactly this. It directs the type checker to analyze a single file and report whatever issues it finds. You can think of it as an extremely loose version of type checking: looser even than TypeScript with noImplicitAny off.

Here's how it works:

```
// @ts-check
const person = {first: 'Grace', last: 'Hopper'};
2 * person.first
//  ~~~~~~~~~~~~ The right-hand side of an arithmetic operation must be of type
//              'any', 'number', 'bigint' or an enum type
```

TypeScript infers the type of `person.first` as `string`, so `2 * person.first` is a type error, no type annotations required.

While it may surface this sort of blatant type error, or functions called with too many arguments, in practice, `@ts-check` tends to turn up a few specific types of errors.

Undeclared Globals

If these are symbols that you're defining, then declare them with `let` or `const`. If they are "ambient" symbols that are defined elsewhere (in a `<script>` tag in an HTML file, for instance), then you can create a type declaration file to describe them. For example, if you have JavaScript like this:

```
// @ts-check
console.log(user.firstName);
//          ~~~~ Cannot find name 'user'
```

then you could create a file called *types.d.ts*:

```
interface UserData {
  firstName: string;
  lastName: string;
}
declare let user: UserData;
```

You may need to adjust your *tsconfig.json* file so that TypeScript is aware of this file. If it is, it will make the error disappear.

This *types.d.ts* file is a valuable artifact because it models the environment in which your code runs (Item 76). It will become the basis for your project's type declarations.

Unknown Libraries

If you're using a third-party library, TypeScript needs to know about it. For example, you might use jQuery to set the size of an HTML element. With `@ts-check`, TypeScript will flag an error:

```
// @ts-check
$('#graph').style({'width': '100px', 'height': '100px'});
// Error: Cannot find name '$'
```

The solution is to install the type declarations for jQuery:

```
$ npm install --save-dev @types/jquery
```

Now the error is specific to jQuery:

```
// @ts-check
$('#graph').style({'width': '100px', 'height': '100px'});
//           ~~~~ Property 'style' does not exist on type 'JQuery<HTMLElement>'
```

In fact, it should be .css, not .style.

@ts-check lets you take advantage of the TypeScript declarations for popular Java-Script libraries without migrating to TypeScript yourself. This is one of the best reasons to use it. Make sure you install the types for the version of the libraries that you're using. Item 66 explains how to do this and discusses what can go wrong if you have mismatched versions.

DOM Issues

Assuming you're writing code that runs in a web browser, TypeScript is likely to flag issues around your handling of DOM elements. For example:

```
// @ts-check
const ageEl = document.getElementById('age');
ageEl.value = '12';
//    ~~~~ Property 'value' does not exist on type 'HTMLElement'
```

Item 75 is all about how the DOM is typed and how to resolve these sorts of errors in TypeScript code. As a quick recap, the issue is that only HTMLInputElements have a value property, but document.getElementById returns the more generic HTMLElement.

If you know that the #age element really is an input element, then this is an appropriate time to use a type assertion. But this is still a JS file, so you can't write as HTMLInputElement. Instead, you can assert a type using JSDoc:

```
// @ts-check
const ageEl = /** @type {HTMLInputElement} */(document.getElementById('age'));
ageEl.value = '12';   // OK
```

If you mouse over ageEl in your editor, you'll see that TypeScript now considers it an HTMLInputElement. Take care as you type the JSDoc @type annotation: the parentheses after the comment are required.

This leads us to the next type of error that comes up with @ts-check: inaccurate JSDoc.

Inaccurate JSDoc

If your project already has JSDoc-style comments, TypeScript will begin checking them when you flip on @ts-check. If you previously used a tool like Google's Closure Compiler that used these comments for type checking, then this shouldn't cause major headaches. But you may be in for some surprises if your comments were more like "aspirational JSDoc":

```
// @ts-check
/**
 * Gets the size (in pixels) of an element.
 * @param {Node} el The element
 * @return {{w: number, h: number}} The size
 */
function getSize(el) {
  const bounds = el.getBoundingClientRect();
  //                 ~~~~~~~~~~~~~~~~~~~~
  //     Property 'getBoundingClientRect' does not exist on type 'Node'
  return {width: bounds.width, height: bounds.height};
  //      ~~~~~ Type '{ width: any; height: any; }' is not
  //            assignable to type '{ w: number; h: number; }'
}
```

The first issue is a misunderstanding of the DOM: getBoundingClientRect() is defined on Element, not Node. So the @param tag should be updated. The second is a mismatch between properties specified in the @return tag and the implementation. Presumably the rest of the project uses the width and height properties, so the @return tag should be updated. It could even be dropped since TypeScript will happily infer a return type.

You can use JSDoc to gradually add type annotations to your project. The TypeScript language service will offer to infer type annotations as a quick fix for code where it's clear from usage:

```
function double(val) {
  return 2 * val;
}
```

You should see a dotted underline under val in your editor. Clicking this should offer the Quick Fix, as shown in Figure 10-2.

```
// @ts-check

function double(val) {
    return 2 *  (parameter) val: any
}
            Parameter 'val' implicitly has an 'any' type, but a better type
            may be inferred from usage. ts(7044)
            Quick Fix...
                Infer parameter types from usage
```

Figure 10-2. The TypeScript Language Services offer a quick fix to infer parameter types from usage.

This results in a correct JSDoc annotation:

```
// @ts-check
/**
 * @param {number} val
 */
function double(val) {
  return 2 * val;
}
```

This can be helpful to encourage types to flow through your code with `@ts-check`. But it doesn't always work so well. For instance:

```
function loadData(data) {
  data.files.forEach(async file => {
    // ...
  });
}
```

If you use the quick fix to annotate `data`, you'll wind up with:

```
/**
 * @param {{
 *   files: { forEach: (arg0: (file: any) => Promise<void>) => void; };
 * }} data
 */
function loadData(data) {
  // ...
}
```

This is structural typing gone awry (Item 4). While the function would technically work on any sort of object with a `forEach` method with that signature, the intent was most likely for the parameter to be `{files: string[]}`.

You can get much of the TypeScript experience in a JavaScript project using JSDoc annotations and `@ts-check`. This is appealing because it requires no changes in your tooling. But it's best not to go too far in this direction. Comment boilerplate has real costs: it's easy for your logic to get lost in a sea of JSDoc. TypeScript works best with *.ts* files, not *.js* files. The goal is ultimately to convert your project to TypeScript, not to JavaScript with JSDoc annotations.

The true value of `@ts-check` is organizational: it can be a useful way to experiment with types, discover blockers, and get a sense for how difficult migration will be *before* you ask management to commit to a weeks- or months-long TypeScript transition.

Things to Remember

- Add "`// @ts-check`" to the top of a JavaScript file to enable type checking without converting to TypeScript.
- Recognize common errors. Know how to declare globals and add type declarations for third-party libraries.
- Use JSDoc annotations for type assertions and better type inference.
- Don't spend too much time getting your code perfectly typed with JSDoc. Remember that the goal is to convert to *.ts*!

Item 81: Use allowJs to Mix TypeScript and JavaScript

For a small project, you may be able to convert from JavaScript to TypeScript in one fell swoop. But for a larger project this "stop the world" approach won't work. You need to be able to transition gradually. That means you need a way for TypeScript and JavaScript to coexist.

The key to this is the `allowJs` compiler option. With `allowJs`, TypeScript files and JavaScript files may import one another. For JavaScript files this mode is extremely permissive. Unless you use `@ts-check` (Item 80), the only errors you'll see are syntax errors. This is "TypeScript is a superset of JavaScript" in the most trivial sense.

While it's unlikely to catch errors, `allowJs` does give you an opportunity to introduce TypeScript into your build chain before you start making code changes. This is a good idea because you'll want to be able to run your tests as you convert individual modules to TypeScript, as described in Item 82.

If your bundler includes TypeScript integration or has a plug-in available, that's usually the easiest path forward. With webpack, for instance, you install `ts-loader`:

```
$ npm install --save-dev ts-loader
```

and configure it in your *webpack.config.js*:

```
module.exports = {
  module: {
    rules: [
      {
        test: /\.tsx?$/,
        use: 'ts-loader',
        exclude: /node_modules/,
      },
    ],
  },
  // ...
};
```

Most unit testing tools have an option like this as well. With `jest`, for instance, you install `ts-jest` and pass TypeScript sources through it by specifying a *jest.config.js* like:

```
module.exports = {
  transform: {
    '^.+\\.tsx?$': 'ts-jest',
  },
};
```

If you run your code through Node.js, the easiest option is to set up `ts-node`. You can either use this as a drop-in replacement for the `node` command or register it with `node` so that it can understand TypeScript:

```
$ node -r ts-node/register main.ts
```

If your build chain is custom, your task will be more involved. But there's always a good fallback option: when you specify the `outDir` option, TypeScript will generate pure JavaScript sources in a directory that parallels your source tree. Usually, your existing build chain can be run over that. You may need to tweak TypeScript's JavaScript output so that it closely matches your original JavaScript source (e.g., by specifying the `target` and `module` options).

Adding TypeScript into your build and test process may not be the most enjoyable task, but it is an essential one that will let you begin to migrate your code with confidence, as we'll discuss in the next item.

Things to Remember

- Use the `allowJs` compiler option to support mixed JavaScript and TypeScript as you transition your project.
- Get your tests and build chain working with TypeScript before beginning large-scale migration.

Item 82: Convert Module by Module Up Your Dependency Graph

You've adopted modern JavaScript, converting your project to use ECMAScript modules and classes (Item 79). You've integrated TypeScript into your build chain and have all your tests passing (Item 81). Now for the fun part: converting your JavaScript to TypeScript. But where to begin?

When you add types to a module, it's likely to surface new type errors in all the other modules that import it. Ideally, you'd like to convert each module once and be done with it. This implies that you should convert modules going *up* the dependency graph: starting with the leaves (modules that import no others) and moving up to the root. (Only computer programmers think the roots of trees are at the top!)

The very first modules to migrate are your third-party dependencies since, by definition, you import them but they don't import you. Usually this means installing @types modules. If you use the lodash utility library, for example, you'd run:

```
npm install --save-dev @types/lodash
```

These type declarations will help types flow through your code and surface issues in your use of the libraries. Make sure to match package versions (see Item 66). If your third-party libraries bundle their types, you can skip this step. TypeScript will find them straightaway.

If your code calls external APIs, you may also want to add type declarations for these early on. Although these calls may happen anywhere in your code, this is still in the spirit of moving up the dependency graph since you depend on the APIs but they do not depend on you. Many types flow from API calls, and these are generally difficult to infer from context. For example, you might replace:

```
async function fetchTable() {
  const response = await fetch('/data');
  if (!response.ok) throw new Error('Failed to fetch!');
  return response.json();
}
```

with:

```
interface TabularData {
  columns: string[];
  rows: number[][];
}
async function fetchTable(): Promise<TabularData> {
  const response = await fetch('/data');
  if (!response.ok) throw new Error('Failed to fetch!');
  return response.json();
}
```

Now types will flow from all calls to fetchTable. As Item 42 explained, it's better not to write types from scratch if you can find an existing source of truth for them, such as a spec or database schema.

As you migrate your own modules, it's helpful to visualize the dependency graph. Figure 10-3 shows an example graph from dygraphs, a medium-sized JavaScript project, made using the excellent madge tool.

The bottom of this dependency graph is the circular dependency between *utils.js* and *tickers.js*. There are many modules that import these two, but they only import each other. This pattern is quite common: most projects will have some sort of utility module at the bottom of the dependency graph.

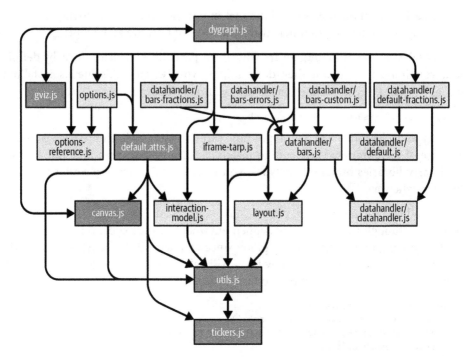

Figure 10-3. The dependency graph for a medium-sized JavaScript project. Arrows indicate imports. Darker-shaded boxes indicate that a module is involved in a circular import.

If you'd like to take any guesswork out of the ordering, you can run a topological sort on your dependency graph. Placed in a spreadsheet and perhaps coupled with the number of lines of code in each file, this can give you a good sense of how far you've come and how much work is left to do.

As you migrate your code, focus on adding types rather than refactoring. If this is an old project, you're likely to notice some strange things and want to fix them. Resist this urge! The immediate goal is to convert your project to TypeScript, not to improve its design. Embarking on unrelated refactors will slow you down, make code reviews harder, and increase the risk that you introduce bugs. Make a note of code smells as you find them and add them to a list of future refactors. File bugs now, fix them later. If this means using any or @ts-expect-error, that's fine.

There are a few common errors you'll run into as you convert to TypeScript. Some of these were covered in Item 80, but there are some new ones, too, notably undeclared class members and values with changing types. Let's look at each of these errors and how to address them.

Undeclared Class Members

Classes in JavaScript do not need to declare their members, but classes in TypeScript do. When you rename a class's *.js* file to *.ts*, it's likely to show errors for every single property you reference:

```
class Greeting {
  constructor(name) {
    this.greeting = 'Hello';
    //   ~~~~~~~~ Property 'greeting' does not exist on type 'Greeting'
    this.name = name;
    //   ~~~~ Property 'name' does not exist on type 'Greeting'
  }
  greet() {
    return `${this.greeting} ${this.name}`;
    //           ~~~~~~~~           ~~~~ Property ... does not exist
  }
}
```

There's a helpful quick fix (see Figure 10-4) for this that you should take advantage of.

Figure 10-4. The quick fix to add declarations for missing members is particularly helpful in converting a class to TypeScript.

This will add declarations for the missing members based on usage:

```
class Greeting {
  greeting: string;
  name: any;
  constructor(name) {
    this.greeting = 'Hello';
    this.name = name;
  }
  greet() {
    return `${this.greeting} ${this.name}`;
  }
}
```

TypeScript was able to get the type for `greeting` correct, but not the type for `name`. After applying this quick fix, you should look through the property list and fix the any types.

If this is the first time you've seen the full property list for your class, you may be in for a shock. When I converted the main class in *dygraph.js* (the root module in Figure 10-3), I discovered that it had no fewer than 45 member variables! Migrating to TypeScript has a way of surfacing bad designs like this that were previously implicit. It's harder to justify a bad design if you have to look at it. But again, resist the urge to refactor now. Note the oddity and think about how you'd fix it some other day.

Values with Changing Types

TypeScript will complain about code like this:

```
const state = {};
state.name = 'New York';
//    ~~~~ Property 'name' does not exist on type '{}'
state.capital = 'Albany';
//    ~~~~~~ Property 'capital' does not exist on type '{}'
```

This topic is covered in more depth in Item 21, so you may want to brush up on that item if you run into this error. If the fix is trivial, you can build the object all at once:

```
const state = {
  name: 'New York',
  capital: 'Albany',
}; // OK
```

If it is not, then this is an appropriate time to use a type assertion:

```
interface State {
  name: string;
  capital: string;
}
const state = {} as State;
state.name = 'New York';  // OK
state.capital = 'Albany';  // OK
```

Type assertions are problematic and best avoided (Item 9 explains why), so you should refactor this eventually. But for now, an assertion is expedient and will help you keep the migration going. Leave yourself a TODO comment or file a bug to clean this up later.

If you've been using JSDoc and `@ts-check` (Item 80), be aware that you can actually *lose* type safety by converting to TypeScript. For instance, TypeScript flags an error in this JavaScript:

```
// @ts-check
/**
 * @param {number} num
 */
function double(num) {
  return 2 * num;
}

double('trouble');
//     ~~~~~~~~~
// Argument of type 'string' is not assignable to parameter of type 'number'
```

When you convert to TypeScript, the @ts-check and JSDoc stop being enforced. This means the type of num is implicitly any, so there's no error:

```
/**
 * @param {number} num
 */
function double(num) {
  return 2 * num;
}

double('trouble');  // OK
```

Fortunately there's a quick fix to move JSDoc types to TypeScript types, as shown in Figure 10-5.

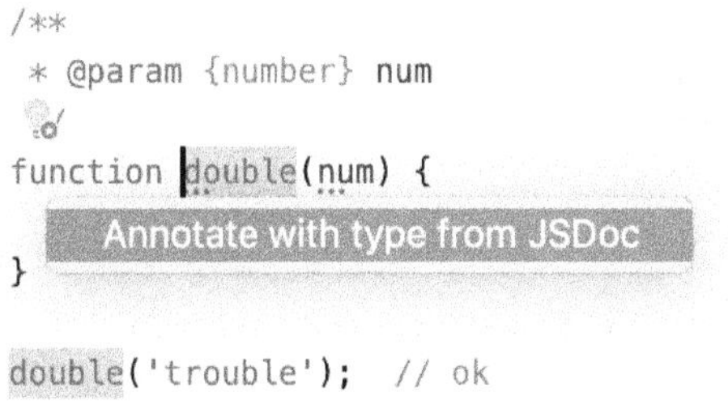

Figure 10-5. Quick fix to copy JSDoc annotations to TypeScript type annotations.

Use this quick fix if it's available! Once you've copied type annotations to TypeScript, make sure to remove them from the JSDoc to avoid redundancy (see Item 31):

```
function double(num: number) {
  return 2 * num;
}

double('trouble');
//     ~~~~~~~~~
// Argument of type 'string' is not assignable to parameter of type 'number'
```

This issue will also be caught when you turn on noImplicitAny, but you may as well add the types now.

Migrate your tests last. They should be at the top of your dependency graph (since your production code doesn't import them), and it's extremely reassuring to know that your tests continue to pass during the migration despite your not having changed them at all. TypeScript migration is a pure refactor. It should not change the runtime behavior of your code or your tests.

Things to Remember

- Start migration by adding `@types` for third-party modules and external API calls.
- Begin migrating your own modules from the bottom of the dependency graph upwards. The first module will usually be some sort of utility code. Consider visualizing the dependency graph to help you track progress.
- Resist the urge to refactor your code as you uncover odd designs. Keep a list of ideas for future refactors, but stay focused on TypeScript conversion.
- Be aware of common errors that come up during conversion. Move JSDoc types into TypeScript type annotations if necessary to avoid losing type safety as you convert.

Item 83: Don't Consider Migration Complete Until You Enable noImplicitAny

Converting your whole project to *.ts* is a big accomplishment. But your work isn't done quite yet. Your next goal is to turn on the `noImplicitAny` option. TypeScript code without `noImplicitAny` is best thought of as transitional because it can mask real errors you've made in your type declarations.

For example, perhaps you've used the "Add all missing members" quick fix to add property declarations to a class, as described in Item 82. You're left with an `any` type and would like to fix it:

```
class Chart {
  indices: any;

  // ...
}
```

`indices` sounds like it should be an array of numbers, so you plug in that type:

```
class Chart {
  indices: number[];

  // ...
}
```

No new errors result, so you then keep moving. Unfortunately, you've made a mistake: number[] is the wrong type. Here's some code from elsewhere in the class:

```
getRanges() {
  for (const r of this.indices) {
    const low = r[0];
    //    ^? const low: any
    const high = r[1];
    //    ^? const high: any
    // ...
  }
}
```

Clearly number[][] or [number, number][] would be a more accurate type. Does it surprise you that indexing into a number is allowed? Take this as an indication of just how loose TypeScript can be without noImplicitAny.

When you turn on noImplicitAny, this becomes an error:

```
getRanges() {
  for (const r of this.indices) {
    const low = r[0];
    //          ~~~~ Element implicitly has an 'any' type because
    //               type 'Number' has no index signature
    const high = r[1];
    //           ~~~~ Element implicitly has an 'any' type because
    //                type 'Number' has no index signature
    // ...
  }
}
```

A good strategy for enabling noImplicitAny is to set it in your local client and start fixing errors. The number of errors you get from the type checker gives you a good sense of your progress. Tracking your type coverage (Item 49) can also give you a sense of progress during this phase of migration.

Run your tests with every change and commit frequently because you may only discover that you've made a mistake later. You may find it helpful to fix noImplicitAny errors going "up the graph," as described in Item 82. You can commit the type corrections without committing the *tsconfig.json* change to your repo until you get the number of errors down to zero.

You might also choose to prioritize type safety in some parts of your codebase over others, perhaps by fixing noImplicitAny errors in your production code before your unit tests. If you use project references (described in Item 78) then you can even have distinct *tsconfig.json* files with different strictness settings for different parts of your project.

There are many other knobs you can turn to increase the strictness of type checking, culminating with `"strict": true`. But `noImplicitAny` is the most important one, and your project will get most of the benefits of TypeScript even if you don't adopt other settings like `strictNullChecks`. Give everyone on your team a chance to get used to TypeScript before you adopt stricter settings.

Things to Remember

- Don't consider your TypeScript migration done until you adopt `noImplicitAny`. Loose type checking can mask real mistakes in type declarations.
- Fix type errors gradually before enforcing `noImplicitAny`. Give your team a chance to get comfortable with TypeScript before adopting stricter checks.

Item Mapping Between First and Second Editions

All but one of the items from the first edition can be found in the second as well, though sometimes with significant changes. The lone retired item covered TypeScript's `private` field visibility modifiers. The same material now lives in Item 72, which advises you to use ECMAScript standard `#private` fields instead.

The second edition includes two new chapters as well as new items scattered throughout the book. This means that item numbers from the first edition generally won't match the second. If you see a reference to an *Effective TypeScript* item that seems to be talking about something else entirely, it may be from the first edition. This table will direct you to the right place.

Table A-1. First edition to second edition item mapping

1st ed.	2nd edition item number: title
1	1: Understand the Relationship Between TypeScript and JavaScript
2	2: Know Which TypeScript Options You're Using
3	3: Understand That Code Generation Is Independent of Types
4	4: Get Comfortable with Structural Typing
5	5: Limit Use of the any Type
6	6: Use Your Editor to Interrogate and Explore the Type System
7	7: Think of Types as Sets of Values
8	8: Know How to Tell Whether a Symbol Is in the Type Space or Value Space
9	9: Prefer Type Annotations to Type Assertions
10	10: Avoid Object Wrapper Types (String, Number, Boolean, Symbol, BigInt)
11	11: Distinguish Excess Property Checking from Type Checking

1st ed.	2nd edition item number: title
49	69: Provide a Type for this in Callbacks if it's part of their API
50	52: Prefer Conditional Types to Overload Signatures
51	70: Mirror Types to Sever Dependencies
52	55: Write Tests for Your Types
53	72: Prefer ECMAScript Features to TypeScript Features
54	60: Know How to Iterate Over Objects
55	75: Understand the DOM hierarchy
56	72: Prefer ECMAScript Features to TypeScript Features
57	73: Use Source Maps to Debug TypeScript
58	79: Write Modern JavaScript
59	80: Use @ts-check and JSDoc to Experiment with TypeScript
60	81: Use allowJs to Mix TypeScript and JavaScript
61	82: Convert Module by Module Up Your Dependency Graph
62	83: Don't Consider Migration Complete Until You Enable noImplicitAny

Index

N

named types, 95
namespaces, 309
naming
    function parameters, 218
    types, 177-180
narrow scope for any type, 185-188
narrowing types, 10, 106-111, 202
nested structures, 113
never type, 33, 233-234
    exhaustiveness checking, 261-267
    as optional, 276-279
Node (DOM hierarchy), 326
Node Package Manager (npm), 283
Node.js source maps, 317-318
noEmit, 341
noEmitOnError, 15
noImplicitAny, 8-9, 218, 360-362
noImplicitThis, 10
nominal typing, 279-282
non-null type assertions, 10, 48
noUncheckedIndexedAccess option, 10, 205
npm (Node Package Manager), 283
null checking, 106
null values
    avoiding in aliases, 148-149
    excluding, 108
    pushing to perimeter of types, 150-153
    strictNullChecks, 9-10
nullable values, 347
nullish coalescing operator, 110, 348
number-valued enums, 306, 308
numeric index signatures, avoiding, 85-88

O

object destructuring syntax, 113
object literals, type annotations with, 93
object spread syntax, 105-106
object wrapper types, 50-52
Object.entries, 269
Object.freeze, 102
Object/object types, 198
objects
    for any type precision, 189
    building, 104-106
    index signatures
        alternatives to, 81-85

avoiding numeric, 85-88
iterating over, 267-270
refactoring parameters as, 169
soundness traps, 205-206
type inference, 90-91, 101-103, 118
type narrowing, 109
type-safe approaches versus monkey patch-
    ing, 198-202
variance in, 208-209
omission, errors of, 261-267
open types, 20
OpenAPI, 320
optional chaining operator, 48, 347
optional never type, 276-279
optional properties, 165-168, 210-211
options (see configuration settings)
output, produced with type errors, 14-15
overload signatures versus conditional types,
    227-230
overloading functions, 17, 193, 302

P

parameter properties, 308-309
parameters (see function parameters)
peerDependencies, 284
performance
    effect of TypeScript types on, 17-18
    of TypeScript compiler (tsc), 336-342
PgTyped, 257-258
Pick, 75-78
Postel's Law, 142-146
precise types, 20
precision
    with any type, 188-190
    of types, 172-177
preserveConstEnums, 306
primitives, 50-52
private modifier, 311
problem domain vocabulary, 177-180
programming (see type-level programming)
project references, 339-341
Promises, 127-132
properties
    aliases and, 113-114
    assignability of optional, 210-211
    default values, 166
    excess property checking, 46
        disabling, 84

About the Author

Dan Vanderkam is an independent software developer based in upstate New York. He was previously a principal software engineer at Sidewalk Labs and a senior staff software engineer at Google. He also worked on open source genome visualizations at Mount Sinai's Icahn School of Medicine, as well as on Google search features used by billions of people (search for "sunset nyc" or "population of france"). He has a long history of building open source projects.

When he's not programming, Dan enjoys rock climbing at the nearby Shawangunk Ridge, hiking in the Catskills, and birdwatching all around the world. He writes at *effectivetypescript.com* and at *danvk.org*. He earned his bachelor's in Computer Science from Rice University in Houston, Texas, and lives in Wallkill, New York.

Colophon

The animal on the cover of *Effective TypeScript* is a red-billed oxpecker (*Buphagus erythrorhynchus*). These birds inhabit a fragmented range across eastern Africa, from Ethiopia and Somalia in the northeast to a few pockets in South Africa; however, these birds can be said to inhabit the range of the grazing animals on which they spend almost all their lives.

Red-billed oxpeckers are related to starlings and mynahs, although they are of a distinct and separate family. About eight inches long and weighing about two ounces, these birds have a bark-brown head, back, and tail, with paler coloring below. Their most striking physical features are their red beaks and red eyes set off by bright yellow eyerings.

Dominating the life of this bird is where and how it finds its food: red-billed oxpeckers feed on ticks and other animal parasites, and they perch on animals as they forage. Their host animals are most often antelope (such as kudu and impala) as well as large animals such as zebra, giraffe, buffalo, and rhinoceros (elephants do not tolerate them). Red-billed oxpeckers have evolved adaptations to assist them in their search for food, such as a flat beak to pierce thick animal hair, as well as sharp claws and a stiff tail to hang on to their host animals. These birds even conduct courtship while perched on a host animal, leaving only during nesting season. Parent birds raise three chicks in a nest hole (lined with hair pulled from their host) close to the animal herds so that they can feed themselves and their young.

The birds' relationship with their animal hosts was once seen as a clear-cut and classic example of mutualism (a mutually beneficial interaction between species). However, recent studies have shown that oxpeckers' feeding habits don't significantly affect hosts' parasite loads; additionally, oxpeckers actually work to keep animals' wounds open, so that they can feed on their blood.

Red-billed oxpeckers remain common across their range; although pesticide use is a threat, their adoption of domestic cattle herds as a food source helps their population remain stable. Many of the animals on O'Reilly covers are endangered; all of them are important to the world.

The cover illustration is by Jose Marzan, based on a black-and-white engraving from *Elements of Ornithology*. The series design is by Edie Freedman, Ellie Volckhausen, and Karen Montgomery. The cover fonts are Gilroy and Guardian Sans. The text font is Adobe Minion Pro; the heading font is Adobe Myriad Condensed; and the code font is Dalton Maag's Ubuntu Mono.

Printed in the USA
CPSIA information can be obtained
at www.ICGtesting.com
JSHW051805100624
64551JS00011B/515